A PERSIAN STRONGHOLD
OF ZOROASTRIANISM

A PERSIAN STRONGHOLD OF ZOROASTRIANISM

based on the Ratanbai
Katrak lectures, 1975

MARY BOYCE

OXFORD
AT THE CLARENDON PRESS
1977

Oxford University Press, Walton Street, Oxford OX2 6DP

OXFORD LONDON GLASGOW NEW YORK
TORONTO MELBOURNE WELLINGTON CAPE TOWN
IBADAN NAIROBI DAR ES SALAAM LUSAKA ADDIS ABABA
KUALA LUMPUR SINGAPORE JAKARTA HONG KONG TOKYO
DELHI BOMBAY CALCUTTA MADRAS KARACHI

© *Oxford University Press 1977*

British Library Cataloguing in Publication Data
Boyce, Mary
   A Persian Stronghold of Zoroastrianism
   – (Ratanbai Katrak Lectures; 1975)
   1. Religious life (Zoroastrianism)
   I. Title II. Series
   295′ .4′0955   BL1525

ISBN 0–19–826531–X

*Printed in Great Britain
at the University Press, Oxford
by Vivian Ridler
Printer to the University*

Dedicated to
Agha Rustam Noshiravan Belivani
and his wife
Khanom Tahmina Mundagar Abadian

PREFACE

THE present work is based on six lectures given in 1975 in the series of Ratanbai Katrak lectures founded at Oxford in memory of his wife by the late Dr. Nanabhai Navroji Katrak. I am indebted to the Electors for inviting me to give these lectures, and to the Oxford University Press for allowing me to expand them for publication. Even with this concession, much necessarily remains still unrecorded which I learnt from the Zoroastrians of Sharifabad-e Ardekan, a little village at the northern end of the Yazdi plain. While on leave from the School of Oriental and African Studies, University of London, I spent twelve months in Iran during 1963–4, and most of this time I was able to pass in Sharifabad, thanks to the great kindness and hospitality of Agha Rustam Noshiravan Belivani and his wife Tahmina Khanom. To them and to their children I owe the warmest debt of gratitude. I was shown much helpfulness too by their relatives and friends, and by the Zoroastrian villagers at large, who received an unexpected stranger in their midst with truly remarkable tolerance and kindness. Since what I learnt of the Sharifabadis was so striking and admirable, I trust that the following pages will constitute both a faithful record of what they taught me, and at the same time a tribute to them themselves.

My gratitude is due also to Khanom Ferangis Shahrokh, to whom I turned on arrival in Tehran. Apart from sacrificing her own time on my behalf there, she kindly gave me an introduction to Arbab Jamshid Sorushian of Kerman, who, with his wife Humayun Khanom, has shown so much hospitality to European visitors to Iran, patiently helping them to understand something of his own community. Through Humayun Khanom I was received into the home of her brother, Arbab Faridun Kayanian of Yazd, and I am grateful to him and his family for allowing me to impose upon their kindness for several weeks. At their house I met Shehriar Zohrabi of Mazraᶜ Kalantar, one of their tenant farmers, who at their prompting hospitably invited me to his village for the festival of Mihragan. From Mazraᶜ I visited neighbouring Sharifabad, and there I was privileged to remain.

My first hosts in the city of Yazd were a Moslem family, that of the late Agha Abbas Mohitpour, who not only sheltered me initially (there were no hotels then in Yazd), but showed me thereafter unstinting kindness and friendship, despite my entire preoccupation with Zoroastrian affairs. It is a cause of keen regret to me that it is impossible to write about the Zoroastrians of Yazd without casting the Moslems in the role of villains, just as it is impossible to write an account of Jews in Europe without showing Christians in a hateful light. Under the present Pahlavi dynasty the Zoroastrians of Iran have come to share the rights of citizenship equally with their Moslem fellow countrymen. The community has prospered, and individual Zoroastrians have attained high position; but in the old centres of Kerman and Yazd local prejudice, deep-rooted, dies hard, and in 1964 the Zoroastrians there still suffered local pressures and disadvantages. In the following decade there were many changes, with the Tehrani community growing steadily in numbers at the expense of the older ones. As the Zoroastrian population of Yazd and its villages dwindled, it became more vulnerable to the forces of change, and new developments brought shocks to young and old alike, as well as creating fresh perspectives and opportunities. Nevertheless, so strong is tradition in Sharifabad that in 1975 Agha Rustam was able to assure me that nothing described in this book had fundamentally changed.

Since my stay in the village I have published a number of articles containing matter derived from what I learnt there. These are cited in the footnotes simply by a shortened title, without author's name, and full references are given in the bibliography at the end of the book. A problem in the body of the work has been to attain consistency in proper names and technical terms between forms in standard Persian and in 'Dari' (the Zoroastrian dialect). In general the former have been preferred, as more widely familiar, but the Dari ones are often given also, either in the text or following the Persian ones in the index, and occasionally, for religious technical terms, they are the only ones available. It has proved impossible to avoid some inconsistencies, however. Thus, for example, the archaic form 'Ardvahišt' has been used for the name of the divinity, but the current 'Urdibehišt' for the month devoted to him. As is illustrated by these two words, the letter 'š' has been used as a convenient sign in both Persian and Dari words for the sound rendered by 'sh' in place-names (such as Shiraz) and in modern personal names; and 'č' is similarly employed for 'ch'. In general the Yazdis prefer the sound 'p' to 'f', and though they would write 'Faridun', 'Faramarz', they say 'Paridun', 'Palamarz'; and, having come to know individuals by these latter forms, I have used them here, together with 'Erdeshir' rather than 'Ardashir', and other small variants on standard written usage. For convenience the Greek letters 'γ' and 'δ' have been employed very occasionally to avoid the clumsiness of 'gh' and 'dh' in rendering a voiced guttural or a dental fricative in Dari or Avestan words. For simplicity's sake, the length of vowels in Persian or Dari words is marked only at their first occurrence, and in the index.

As to the writing of personal names, some use has been made here of the Persian *izafe*, a linking particle which is never written in the Arabic script. In spoken Persian this particle is used to join all proper names, whether given or family ones. Fixed surnames came into existence in Iran, by government decree, only this century, and were still not much used by the villagers among themselves, so that I did not always learn them. So by a convention, in the following pages a given name followed by a surname is written without the particle, e.g. Bahram Khademi, whereas one followed by the father's name (the old way of identification) is joined to it by the particle, e.g. Rustam-e Bahram. Nicknames were the commonest way of distinguishing people, and one middle-aged man was known as Rustam-e Tehrani, because as a boy in the 1930s he had lived briefly at the capital, being one of the first Sharifabadis to visit that then remote place. This nickname in itself showed the enormous changes that had taken place in three decades, for already by 1964 there was frequent coming and going between the village and Tehran, and the easy mobility of a motorized age was beginning to affect the lives of its inhabitants.

I am grateful to Dr. Michael Fischer of Harvard University (who himself worked as an anthropologist in Yazd in 1970 and 1971) for kindly sparing time to read a set of proofs, and to make helpful comments. I am also indebted to the Oxford University Press for their courtesy, thoroughness, and impressive skill.

CONTENTS

LIST OF PLATES

ABBREVIATIONS

Note: for abbreviated titles of books which follow an author's name see under that name in the bibliography.

AMI	*Archaeologische Mitteilungen aus Iran*
Bd.	Bundahišn
BSOAS	*Bulletin of the School of Oriental and African Studies*
D.	Dastur (general courtesy title for a Zoroastrian priest)
JAOS	*Journal of the American Oriental Society*
JRAS	*Journal of the Royal Asiatic Society*
Riv.	*Rivāyats* (see under Dhabhar, B. N., and Unvala, M. R. in the bibliography)
RSO	*Rivista degli Studi Orientali*
Šnš.	Šāyest nē-šāyest
Vd.	Vendidad
VDI	*Vestnik Drevnei Istorii*
Y.	Yasna
Yt.	Yašt

1

THE VILLAGE OF THE TWO 'CATHEDRAL' FIRES

IT is now generally agreed that the Arab conquest of Iran in the seventh century A.D. was not achieved by a few great battles, but took more than a generation to accomplish; and that, although Islam was established thereby as the state religion, it needed some three hundred years, or nine generations, for it to become the dominant faith throughout the land. During this time the Zoroastrians continued to look for leadership to their high priest, the Dastūr dastūrān, hereditary successor to the prelate who in the days of the Sasanian Empire had been head of the established church. For two or three centuries after the conquest the Dastur dasturan continued to be a person of dignity and influence; but late in the ninth century the tide began to ebb swiftly for the Zoroastrians, with Islam now enjoying the full support of temporal power everywhere. It was then that the founding fathers of the Parsi community left their homeland to seek religious freedom in exile in India;[1] and thereafter those who held by their ancient faith in Iran were steadily ground down into the position of a small, deprived, and harassed minority, lacking all privileges or consideration.

The only two places where Zoroastrians succeeded in maintaining themselves in any numbers were in and around Yazd and Kerman. These are oasis cities in the very centre of Iran, surrounded by mountain and desert, and far from frontiers or royal courts. The narrow, enclosed plain of Yazd (a little over thirty miles in length) 'lies on the skirts of the land of Pars',[2] that is, on the northern edge of the old kingdom of Persia proper, the homeland of the Sasanians; and it was there that the Dastur dasturan sought refuge when life grew too dangerous and oppressive in Pars itself. The region was hardly one to attract Arab settlers, for the climate is harsh, with

---

[1] After a sojourn in Div, these migrants appear to have landed at Sanjan in Gujarat in A.D. 936, see S. H. Hodivala, *Studies in Parsi History*, 67–73.

[2] *Riv.*, ed. Unvala, ii. 452, transl. Dhabhar, 614.

burning summers and searingly cold winters; and since the rainfall is scanty, the plain is partly desert—in some places glittering white with salt, in others covered by shifting, engulfing sands. Much of the rest is now rough shingle or parched earth, after years of drought; but in earlier times these areas probably bore thickets of wild pistachio, tamarisk, and other trees, which would have sheltered beasts of prey and have helped to isolate the oasis villages. These are scattered about the plain, set either by natural springs, or at the end of long underground channels (*qanāts*) which bring water to them from the surrounding hills. The ground slopes gently down from north-west to south-east; and in the south-eastern corner, which as the lowest point has the best supply of water, stands the city of Yazd. This, like the other cities of Iran, must have been early seized and garrisoned by the Arab conquerors; but probably the villages of the inhospitable plain were long left more or less to themselves— which is presumably why the Dastur dasturan sought shelter there.

The particular place which he made his abode was known by the fourteenth century (when it first appears in records) as Turkabad. It is in the north-western corner of the plain—as far as possible, that is, from Yazd itself, the centre of local government. It is, on the other hand, near a famous and probably ancient Zoroastrian mountain shrine.[3] Both these facts may well have had a part in determining the high priest's choice of this spot as refuge, together doubtless with the existence there of staunch and resolute Zoroastrians, who had the courage to receive him to live among them.

Just to the south of Turkabad is a village long known as Sharifabad; and it must have been when the Dastur dasturan came to Turkabad that two great sacred fires were brought to this neighbouring place, where they were housed humbly in small mud-brick buildings indistinguishable from ordinary rustic homes. Both fires were Ātaš Bahrāms, which are as it were the cathedral fires of Zoroastrianism; and one of them is known to the villagers as Āδor Kharā. This is a dialect form of Ādur Farnbāg, which was the name of one of the three chief sacred fires of ancient Iran. Before the downfall of the Sasanians Adur Farnbag was established on a hill in Pars.[4] It is recorded that after the conquest its priests made desperate

---

[3] i.e. the shrine of Bānū-Pārs, see below, pp. 248–55.

[4] For the literature on this fire and its site see K. Schippmann, *Die iranischen Feuerheiligtümer*, 86–94. In early Moslem times the ancient fire was called (by dialect variations) either Āδur Farrā or Āδur Khwarrā. The latter form would have developed naturally in due course into Kharā.

efforts to save it from extinction, even dividing its embers and keeping them as two fires in different places;[5] and it seems that in the
end one group followed the high priest to his chosen haven, bringing
their fire to burn in safe obscurity in Sharifabad.[6] This in itself must
have been a startling honour for so small a place; but the honour was
compounded, for yet another Ataš Bahram was established there,
which down the centuries the villagers held in even greater reverence
and esteem. This fire they knew simply as *the* Ataš Bahram; and
since there was only one such fire that could have meant more to
Persians than Adur Farnbag, it seems that this must be the ancient
sacred fire of Istakhr, which had been under the special care of the
Sasanian royal house, and doubtless after its downfall remained the
particular charge of the Dastur dasturan. Its former magnificent
temple is known to have been despoiled and in ruins by the ninth
century,[7] and its priests probably found various refuges for it before
bringing it also to this remote and undistinguished haven, close to
the abode of the high priest.

The priests who carried these two sacred fires to Sharifabad
evidently settled there to continue tending them; and the two small
villages of Turkabad and Sharifabad became thereafter the ecclesiastical centre of Irani Zoroastrianism. It was evidently of them that
the Frenchman Chardin had heard tell in the seventeenth century,
when he wrote of the Zoroastrians:[8] 'Their principal temple is near
Yazd . . . This is their great fire-temple . . . and also their oracle and
academy. It is there that they communicate their religion, their
maxims, and their hopes. Their high pontiff lives there always, and
without quitting it. He is called the Dastur dasturan. This pontiff

---

[5] See Mas'udi, *Prairies d'or*, §1402 (ed. Ch. Pellat, Paris, 1965, ii. 540–1);
Ibn al-Faqih, *Bibliotheca Geographorum Arabicorum*, v. 246, transl. P. Schwartz,
Iran im Mittelalter nach den arabischen Geographen, i. 91.

[6] This suggestion was earlier made by the present writer in the Burton
Memorial Lecture given at the Royal Asiatic Society in 1973.

[7] See Mas'udi, op. cit., §1403.

[8] See his *Voyages en Perse et autres lieux de l'Orient*, Amsterdam, 1735, ii.
183. Chardin further locates this 'principal temple' as being 'in a mountain 18
leagues' from Yazd. These 'leagues' would be French ones, $2\frac{1}{2}$ miles in length,
which makes a reckoning of 9–10 miles further than between Sharifabad and
Yazd by the present highway; but the old highway ran along the other side of the
plain, and allowing for a rough reckoning of farsakhs, then turned into leagues,
the discrepancy does not seem significant. Admittedly neither Turkabad nor
Sharifabad are 'in the mountains', but they are near mountain shrines. It is
quite possible, moreover, that Chardin's informants (in Isfahan) had no wish to
give him too precise a description of the temple's whereabouts.

has with him several priests and several students who form a kind
of seminary. The Mahometans allow it because it is inconspicuous,
and generous presents are made to them.' These last words show
that the Zoroastrian community must have loyally supported their
high priest, so that he had the means to secure safety through bribes;
and probably during those obscure centuries many of the old religion
made pilgrimages, on foot and donkeyback, to Sharifabad and
Turkabad, and gave offerings to maintain both the college of priests
and the great sacred fires.[9]

It seems probable that the Dastur dasturan took refuge in
Turkabad not later than the eleventh century, by which time conditions had become generally harsh for his community; but the
first evidence for his residence there comes in A.D. 1478. It was then
that the Parsis of India, seeking authority on certain matters of
observance, sent back the first of a series of messengers to the mother
country to make contact with their co-religionists there. These
messengers continued to come at irregular intervals from then until
towards the end of the seventeenth century, and they returned to
India with letters, treatises of instruction, and sometimes manuscripts.[10] Colophons of these manuscripts show that they were
written in Turkabad or Sharifabad;[11] and the signatures of the
accompanying letters (which are preserved by the Parsis) prove that
throughout these centuries the Dastur dasturan, the acknowledged
head of the Irani community,[12] had his residence in Turkabad.

[9] A French traveller who visited Yazd in the early nineteenth century, after
the Dastur dasturan had removed there (see below), wrote of the Zoroastrians:
'Pilgrimage to Yazd is a strict obligation, and none among them can dispense
with making it at least once in his life. They then bring presents to the high
priest' (Gaspard Drouville, *Voyage en Perse fait en 1812 et 1813*, 3rd edn.,
ii. 210).

[10] For a list of the treatises of instruction, called *rivāyats*, with their dates,
see B. B. Patel, 'A brief outline of some controversial questions that led to the
study of religious literature among the Parsis', *K. R. Cama Mem. Vol.* (ed. J. J.
Modi), Bombay, 1900, 173–4; and for a critical scrutiny of the dates see Hodivala,
Studies, 276–349.

[11] Among the priestly copyists from these two villages were the well-known
scribe Mihraban Noshiravan Rustam Shehriar, himself Dastur dasturan towards
the end of the seventeenth century, and his brother Khosrow, who identified
himself in a colophon as being 'of Turkabad in the province of Yazd'. On these
and the other scribes see further Boyce, *History*, vol. iii (in preparation). Three
'dynasties' of high priests, holding office from father to son, can be traced from
the end of the fifteenth to the end of the seventeenth century.

[12] Kerman had its own Dastur dasturan, and in the nineteenth century the
two prelates appear to have been on a footing of equality and independence.
Even in the earlier period some Parsi messengers went direct to Kerman, and

One letter has the signature of twenty-eight priests from Turkabad and Sharifabad.[13] Leading laymen also signed these letters[14]—descendants presumably of those small landowners and peasant farmers who had had the courage to receive the high priest and the sacred fires in the beginning. A letter of 1510 gives the number of Zoroastrians in the two villages as four hundred, a figure which seems to refer to the heads of households and leading men only.[15]

The last letter to bear the signature of a high priest living in Turkabad is dated to 1681[16]—about half a century after Chardin wrote his account. Some time during the next hundred years the Dastur dasturan removed from there to the city of Yazd, where the holder of this office was found residing by travellers in the late eighteenth century, and where he continued to live thereafter. There is no record of exactly when, still less why, the move was made; but given the deep tenacity of the Zoroastrians, and their reluctance to introduce change, the likelihood seems that the Moslem authorities decided that they wanted the leader of the Zoroastrian community more directly under surveillance. His priests went with him, and from then on it was Yazd which was the ecclesiastical centre for the Zoroastrians of the region, and a priests' quarter, the Mahalle-ye Dasturan, grew up there beside the older one inhabited by the laity.[17]

brought back letters signed only by Kermani priests; but every letter which went round the whole Irani community for signature was signed first by the Dastur dasturan of Yazd, and then by other priests of Turkabad and Sharifabad. The Dastur dasturan of Yazd was not only regularly accorded precedence, but was referred to as the 'Great Dastur' (dastur-e ʿazam).

[13] i.e. the letter accompanying the Rivayat of Kamdin Shapur (A.D. 1558), see Hodivala, Studies, 315–16.

[14] e.g. the Rivayat of A.D. 1511, see Hodivala, Studies, 294.

[15] This is how the figure was interpreted by E. W. West, Sir J. J. Madressa Jubilee Vol., Bombay, 1914, 445. [16] See Hodivala, Studies, 339–40.

[17] The letter of A.D. 1511 bears the signatures of twenty-one laymen from the city of Yazd, but not one of a priest, although the community there numbered then some 500 persons (i.e. heads of households). After the Dastur dasturan went to Yazd, almost all the priests of the area seem also to have established their permanent homes in the city, and thereafter it was from there that they went to the villages for limited periods in rotation (the various hušts or parishes being redistributed at intervals by lot). There were, however, exceptions. Thus one priestly family kept their fixed abode in Mobareke, having (according to their own tradition) come to this tiny village from Isfahan in the seventeenth century at the time when the Safavid Shah Husayn was persecuting the Zoroastrians; and there they continued to live, the priests for four generations going into Yazd (no great distance) for the gahambars and all other collegial priestly activities. D. Khodadad Neryosangi remembered the last of them, D. Kai Khosrow, well. [After writing the above I learnt in London in 1976 of a living

After this, Sharifabad and Turkabad were served, like any other villages, simply by 'hūšt-mōbeds' (that is, parish priests), appointed for a period by the Dastur dasturan in Yazd. Down to the beginning of the present century there were priests enough for several to work together in a village, each looking after the families in one particular lane or lanes.

The two great fires, the oldest in the whole Zoroastrian community, remained, however, probably for safety's sake, in their humble shrines in Sharifabad. To Moslems one fire is like another, and probably the authorities took no special cognizance of these.[18] Devotion to the fires continued to be deep and sustained in the village, although early in the twentieth century, because of the difficulties of maintaining both fittingly, they were united to burn as one in the temple of the greater Ataš Bahram. The name of Aδor Khara was not forgotten, but no tradition of the history of the fires survived, although it was remembered that Turkabad had been a famous 'dastūr-nišīn', that is, a dwelling-place of priests. Such gaps in tradition are less surprising than it may at first sight seem. Even in the days of their temporal power Zoroastrians tended not to dwell overmuch on mundane events, having their concern rather with eternal things; and in Islamic times, although their priests maintained a modicum of traditional learning, the laity, hard-pressed to earn a livelihood, were in general illiterate—as indeed were most of the Moslem population around them. Two or three hundred years is a long stretch of time when there are no written records to prompt the memory, and when poverty and persecution tend to concentrate thought on present struggles. The sojourn of the priests among them left the Sharifabadis an inheritance of a deeply in-grained and well-instructed orthodoxy, which was kept alive by constant observances; but the history of the fires which they so faithfully tended passed into oblivion.

tradition of the removal of the Dastur dasturan and his priests from Turkabad to Yazd. Mr. Shehriar Yadgar Bekhradnia, formerly of Jarfarabad, told me that he had heard of it as a small boy in the 1920s from his grandfather, Jamshid-e Bahram-e Shirmardan, then a centenarian. No date, naturally, attached to the tradition.]

[18] It appears that the present Ataš Bahram of Yazd was installed there in the 1790s with the help of a pious Parsi of Surat, Seth Nassarwanji Kohyari (see B. B. Patel, *Pārsī Prakāš*, vol. i, Bombay, 1960, 83 n., 876 n.; and further Dara M. Meherji-Rana, *Dastūrān-dastūr Meherjī-Rānā Yādgārī Granth*. Bombay, 1947, i. 457–60). (For knowledge of these Gujarati sources I am indebted to my friend Dastur Firoze M. Kotwal.)

Virtually nothing can be learnt of Sharifabad and Turkabad during the eighteenth and early nineteenth centuries; but in the mid nineteenth century disaster overtook Turkabad, in the shape of what was perhaps the last massed forcible conversion in Iran. It no longer seems possible to learn anything about the background of this event; but it happened, so it is said, one autumn day when dye-madder—then one of the chief local crops—was being lifted. All the able-bodied men were at work in teams in the fields when a body of Moslems swooped on the village and seized them. They were threatened, not only with death for themselves, but also with the horrors that would befall their women and children, who were being terrorized at the same time in their homes; and by the end of a day of violence most of the village had accepted Islam. To recant after a verbal acknowledgement of Allah and his prophet meant death in those days, and so Turkabad was lost to the old religion. Its fire-temple was razed to the ground, and only a rough, empty enclosure remained where once it had stood.

A similar fate must have overtaken many Iranian villages in the past, among those which did not willingly embrace Islam; and the question seems less why it happened to Turkabad than why it did not overwhelm all other Zoroastrian settlements. The evidence, scanty though it is, shows, however, that the harassment of the Zoroastrians of Yazd tended to be erratic and capricious, being at times less harsh, or bridled by strong governors; and in general the advance of Islam across the plain, though relentless, seems to have been more by slow erosion than by furious force. The process was still going on in the 1960s, and one could see, therefore, how it took effect. Either a few Moslems settled on the outskirts of a Zoroastrian village, or one or two Zoroastrian families adopted Islam. Once the dominant faith had made a breach, it pressed in remorselessly, like a rising tide. More Moslems came, and soon a small mosque was built, which attracted yet others. As long as the Zoroastrians remained in the majority, their lives were tolerable; but once the Moslems became the more numerous, a petty but pervasive harassment was apt to develop. This was partly verbal, with taunts about fire-worship, and comments on how few Zoroastrians there were in the world, and how many Moslems, who must therefore possess the truth; and also on how many material advantages lay with Islam. The harassment was often also physical; boys fought, and gangs of youths waylaid and bullied individual

Zoroastrians. They also diverted themselves by climbing into the local tower of silence and desecrating it, and they might even break into the fire-temple and seek to pollute or extinguish the sacred flame. Those with criminal leanings found too that a religious minority provided tempting opportunities for theft, pilfering from the open fields, and sometimes rape and arson. Those Zoroastrians who resisted all these pressures often preferred therefore in the end to sell out and move to some other place where their co-religionists were still relatively numerous, and they could live at peace; and so another village was lost to the old faith. Several of the leading families in Sharifabad had forebears who were driven away by intense Moslem pressure from Abshahi, once a very devout and orthodox village on the southern outskirts of Yazd; and a shorter migration had been made by the family of the centenarian 'Hajji' Khodabakhsh, who had himself been born in the 1850s and was still alert and vigorous in 1964. His family, who were very pious, had left their home in Ahmedabad (just to the north of Turkabad) when he was a small boy, and had come to settle in Sharifabad to escape persecution and the threats to their orthodox way of life. Other Zoroastrians held out there for a few decades longer, but by the end of the century Ahmedabad was wholly Moslem, as Abshahi became in 1961.[19] It was noticeable that the villages which were left to the Zoroastrians were in the main those with poor supplies of water, where farming conditions were hard.

Under the Pahlavi dynasty, which took power in 1925, the rule of law was fully extended to Zoroastrians, and the violence in Moslem pressures had almost disappeared by the 1960s; but other factors were then hastening the erosion of the Yazdi community, notably the attractions of Tehran, with its wide opportunities and relative freedom from religious strife and prejudice. The local Moslem population was swelling steadily in numbers (thanks largely to better medical care), and as Zoroastrians left for the capital there were always Moslem families eager to move into their old

[19] A little fire-altar of solid stone was rescued from Ahmedabad by a group of young Sharifabadis (under the leadership of Noshiravan, Agha Rustam's father), who rolled it laboriously across the desert to the safety of their own village, where it now stands in the fire-temple. The last Zoroastrian family left Abshahi in 1961, after the rape and subsequent suicide of one of their daughters. Hajji Khodabaksh's own mother was of an Abshahi family. After her death his father married again, this time an Ahmedabadi bride, and through this marriage Khodabakhsh had a half-brother, Bahram Surkhabi (known as Bahram Škundari or 'Beetroot Bahram') who was some fifty years younger than himself.

homes, and this meant a steady infiltration of the dominant faith into Zoroastrian strongholds. At the end of the nineteenth century there were still a number of villages in the Yazdi plain which were wholly or almost wholly Zoroastrian, and there were Zoroastrians too in villages over the mountains to the north, around Biyabanak. The last left there early this century,[20] and by the mid 1960s, of the thirty-one villages in the Yazdi plain which still had Zoroastrians in them, not one was entirely Zoroastrian. In addition to the losses caused by migration or conversion to Islam, there were others due to the fact that (much to the sorrow and perplexity of the community) relatively large numbers of Zoroastrians embraced Baha'ism, and many suffered accordingly in the terrible Baha'i massacres which took place in Yazd early this century. No Sharifabadis succumbed to the proselytizing of the new faith, but even among them the growth of the Moslem population was rapid after the Second World War. At the beginning of the century there were only two or three Moslem families in the village, but by 1964 there were reckoned to be about a thousand Moslems to only some seven hundred Zoroastrians.[21] Two Husayniyas had been built,[22] and the call of the mu'azzin sounded loudly over the Zoroastrian quarter, which itself was being steadily penetrated by Moslems as Zoroastrian families sold up and left for Tehran.

Naturally even in the Yazdi region, famed for its religious fervour, there were Moslems who were not particularly zealous, or burning to vex the unbeliever; and in some of the suburban villages the two communities lived tolerantly together. In the past too there had

[20] The last Zoroastrians in Biyabanak, four brothers and a sister, tenant-farmers, left there in about 1900 to save the sister from the attentions of a local Moslem. They sought the protection of their Zoroastrian *arbāb* (landowner) in Yazd; and he sent one of them, Isfandiyar, to act as his agent in developing the then tiny hamlet of Hasanabad-e Maybod (see further below). He was still living there, in his eighties, in 1964.

[21] In 1976 the figures were 455 Zoroastrians and 510 Moslems, the drop in the population representing movement to the cities (information from Agha Rustam).

[22] Such places of worship are found in most Moslem villages of the Yazdi region. The older one in Sharifabad was built at the end of the nineteenth century on ground between the village and the neighbouring town of Ardekan, which was the original area of Moslem settlement. The second one was built in the 1950s in the more recent settlement on the south side of the village, known to the Zoroastrians as the *Shahr-e Lukhthā* 'Town of the Naked', because of the numbers of impoverished Moslems who had crowded there. Zoroastrians had always to pass through one or other of these Moslem quarters to reach the highway to Yazd, or Ardekan with its shops and secondary schools.

clearly been variations in the attitudes of Moslems towards the 'gōr'—the contemptuous term, a form of 'gabr' or unbeliever, used generally for a Zoroastrian—though condescension, as far as one can judge, was general. This, however, was social as much as religious, for the poverty of the down-trodden Zoroastrians was proverbial.[23] Since the region is not one to attract strangers, many of its inhabitants must be of Zoroastrian ancestry, and some devout Moslems there admit to a Zoroastrian forebear, sometimes as far back as the seventh generation.[24] Some conversions, enforced like those of Turkabad, or entered into with little spiritual conviction, left the convert with affectionate and regretful thoughts towards his old faith, and the descendants of such a one were more likely to be mild, or at least just, in their dealings with Zoroastrians than those of converts who embraced their new religion with fervour, and felt a corresponding zeal to stamp out the old one, and to harry those who clung to it. Fair or tolerant Moslems the Zoroastrians called *najīb* 'noble', the others *nā-najīb* 'ignoble', and such broad distinctions sometimes characterized whole communities. Thus the Sharifabadis were separated only by the highway from the town of Ardekan, whose inhabitants they regarded as markedly *na-najib*; and so they preferred to have all their dealings, as far as possible, with the kindly Moslems of Maybod on the further side of the plain, even though this involved them in far more exertion. Apart from such local divergences, there were naturally all the factors of individual temperament, education, and social position to affect Moslem attitudes towards a religious minority. In the past Zoroastrians probably suffered most from gangs of roughs, the dreaded *lūtīs* (sometimes hired for the purpose by their betters), who were able to pillage, maltreat, or even murder non-Moslems with little fear of being brought to justice.

Whatever the particular frictions of local history which led to the forced conversion of Turkabad in the nineteenth century, its neighbour Sharifabad was able to survive as a stronghold of Zoroastrian orthodoxy. The historical reasons for this orthodoxy are plain, and there were a number of factors which favoured its sturdy

[23] 'When the Muslims wish to describe a man as very poor, they say he is as poor as a Gabr': Drouville, *Voyage en Perse*, ii. 209.

[24] Unless there were special circumstances (such as *sayyid* descent) the Moslems, like the Zoroastrians, seemed in general content to carry their ancestry back no further than seven generations—a fair span for a predominantly oral tradition.

survival. To begin with, the Yazdis as a group were markedly conservative in comparison with the Zoroastrians of Kerman and Tehran, for reasons that were partly historic, partly geographical. The Tehrani community was relatively new, created by migrants from Kerman and Yazd over the previous hundred years or so; and since the 1930s it had had close contact with reforming Parsis in Bombay, as well as experiencing the modernizing influences of its own large cosmopolitan city. The Kermani community was as old as the Yazdi one, but was decimated in wars of the eighteenth and nineteenth centuries, and being so reduced in numbers became less resistant to outside influences. Then geographically the whole Yazdi plain was until recently very isolated, except for the camel caravans which passed across it. It is difficult to realize, now that the progress of the 1970s has linked Yazd to Tehran by road, rail, and air, so that travel between the two places need be only a matter of hours, that up to the 1920s it could take as much as three dangerous, exhausting weeks to journey there from the capital.[25] Even to reach any of the nearest cities, Kerman, Shiraz, or Isfahan, was an eight-day journey, often fraught with peril;[26] and so Yazd remained 'insular beyond the insularity of islands',[27] with the world the other side of its mountains an unknown place for most of its inhabitants. Life there had changed little, in outlook, knowledge, or customs, since the Middle Ages, even for the Moslem majority, and within this remote, largely self-sufficient community the Zoroastrians were thrust into their own added isolation, especially in the further villages; and though even there they had to suffer the exactions of the tax-farmer, and erratic raids and tyrannies, for much of the time they were left alone in their poverty, and were able to follow a wholly traditional way of life. These circumstances, however hard for individuals, were ideal for preserving unchanged ancient beliefs and practices.

[25] Agha Sohrab Lohrasp, for many years headmaster of the Zoroastrian Marker School in Yazd, told me that this was the time the journey took by horse and carriage when he travelled from Tehran to Yazd to take up his appointment in the early 1920s. He shared the carriage with seven others, four of whom died on the journey or soon after, too exhausted to survive the illnesses which they contracted on the way.

[26] These local journeys could be dangerous to both health and wealth, thanks to brigands, and the sudden, fierce sandstorms of the region, which at their worst can damage sight or hearing irremediably.

[27] Napier Malcolm, *Five Years in a Persian Town*, 36. This book gives a vivid account of the isolation of Yazd at the beginning of the twentieth century.

The separation of the Zoroastrians from the rest of the community was enforced as thoroughly as possible by the Moslem authorities. Thus the 'gors' were forbidden to take up crafts or professions which might bring them into contact with Moslems, and were in the main restricted to farming and labouring work. They had, moreover, to wear distinctive clothing, so that they could be instantly recognized and shunned. Traditionally Iranian peasants dressed in blue,[28] but Zoroastrian men were forbidden to wear this or any other colour, and had to have garments of undyed cotton or wool, with roughly tied headgear to mark their lowly state. Their women wore a modest but richly coloured costume which was probably that worn by village women before the Arab conquest; but they were clearly distinguished from their Moslem sisters by their refusal to veil their faces—a refusal which, since many of them were comely, needed courage to maintain. There were many stories, written and told, of the rape and abduction of Zoroastrian girls, and the oldest village women recalled how sometimes the prettiest among them would have to blacken their teeth and disfigure their faces with dirt before leaving their houses. In general, however, the Zoroastrian women made no concessions, and their dignified and open carriage, at home and abroad, was all the more striking in contrast with the shrouded, self-effacing bearing of their Moslem sisters. As for the men's clothing, the restrictions on it lasted into the twentieth century; and one of the Sharifabadi villagers[29] told me how, as a boy, he travelled to India in 1913 with a group of Zoroastrians, who were asked in Shiraz (by a fine irony) if they were Arabs, because of their curious light-coloured clothes. When they explained that they were Zoroastrians they were surprised to evoke no scorn, but only a friendly interest, and a prophecy that when they returned from India they would be wearing European dress. This, however, they could not safely have done in Yazd itself before the rise of the Pahlavi dynasty. Many other restrictions on those of the old religion were long enforced there, some only mildly vexing, others well calculated to make life more wretched and miserable. Thus, for example, they were not allowed to build the wind-towers which in summer caught what breezes there were and brought cool air down into the houses. Nor were they permitted to ride horses, but must

---

[28] The continuity of usage in this respect as far as Moslem Iran is concerned has been pointed out by A. Tafazzoli, *AMI*, N.F. 7, 1974, 192–3.

[29] Erdeshir Qudusi.

go even long distances at the donkey's plodding pace, and even then they were required to dismount if they met a Moslem. But all such harassments—and there were many[30]—were petty compared with the fact that neither their lives nor property were ever wholly safe, since the rule of law extended to them only haphazardly.

The Zoroastrians for their part had no desire to fraternize with their oppressors; and they took a deliberate measure to secure for themselves a degree of protective isolation when they adopted a local dialect, incomprehensible to speakers of standard Persian, for their own use. This dialect the Sharifabadis called simply (when pressed to give it a name) *gap-e vehdīnān*, 'the tongue of those of the Good Religion'. It is also, artificially but conveniently, now called 'Darī', on the wrong assumption that it is an ancient 'court' or learned language.[31] 'Dari' was once spoken by all Zoroastrians, priests and laity, in Yazd and Kerman. It was seldom written, and with the scattered nature of the community local differences in pronunciation developed, so that the Yazdi Zoroastrians could tell a man's village by his speech. By the middle of the twentieth century 'Dari' had almost died out in Kerman, where it was by then known only to members of the older generation; but it was still flourishing in 1964 in the Yazdi area, where Zoroastrians spoke nothing else among themselves—unless a Kermani were present. In Sharifabad there were then still a few old women who understood and spoke no Persian, but only 'Dari', having had no schooling and little contact with the outer world; and they were naturally admirable guardians of old traditions.

The breaking-down of the isolation of the Irani Zoroastrians began in the mid nineteenth century, largely through the efforts of the Parsis, and of those Iranis who had managed to flee in secret to India (for the Zoroastrians were then forbidden to travel abroad). After a long and difficult campaign the annual poll-tax on Zoroastrians—the chief instrument of extortion and abuse—was abolished in 1882; and Zoroastrians were permitted, moreover, to enter trades and professions. What made it possible for the community to take advantage of this concession was that Parsi benefactors (and

[30] See Napier Malcolm, op. cit. 44 ff.

[31] It is unfortunate that the first Europeans to study this dialect adopted for it the insulting Moslem term of 'Gabrī'. On it see chiefly W. Ivanow, *RSO* xviii (1939), 1–58, and Jamshid S. Sorushian, *Farhang-e Behdinan*, who gives the pronunciation of both Kerman and the city of Yazd. The forms given in the present work are all in the dialect of Sharifabad.

Iranis who had settled in Bombay) gradually established, not only in Yazd and Kerman but in all the Zoroastrian villages, primary schools, where a basic Western-type education was given. And with schooling and new opportunities, the Iranis, a small, inbred, deprived community, defied genetic and social theory by breaking out with dazzling talents; and soon they were producing not only enormously wealthy and influential merchants but also (in proportion to their numbers) a host of able professional men—doctors, teachers, engineers. The parallelism with the history of the Parsis is striking; and how much is to be attributed to a sturdy heredity, how much to the religion which nurtured both communities, is a problem to ponder.

The period that followed, from the late nineteenth century down to the Second World War, was in many ways a golden age for the Yazdi Zoroastrians. New education and ideas had not yet begun seriously to challenge old orthodoxies, and new wealth and influence were put largely at the service of the faith. With relaxation of the restrictions which had prevented Zoroastrians erecting any but the humblest buildings, this period saw a great reconstruction of temples and shrines, as well as the endowment of religious charities. Yet though the new prosperity at first advanced the faith, the seeds of change were being sown. Many of the Zoroastrians who took up professions were the sons of priests, the traditional learned class; and as time went on, more and more joined the flight from an ancient, exacting calling that was wholly out of harmony with the contemporary world. In the 1930s there were still some two hundred priests in the city of Yazd;[32] by 1964 there were not ten. Moreover, those Yazdis who went out into the wider world and returned brought with them new knowledge and ideas, and so old beliefs and ways came to be challenged.

Sharifabad, in its remote corner of the plain, shared to some extent in these developments. It too received its school, and it too lost thereafter many of its ablest sons, first to Bombay and then to Tehran. Yet those who remained in the village were able to continue very much in the old manner, and in a measure their reluctance to have truck with the modern world (which was necessarily a non-Zoroastrian one) was deliberate. They preferred the ways of their forefathers. Even as late as 1964 the impact of the outer world on the village was slight. There was a noticeable absence of men in their

[32] Information from D. Khodadad Neryosangi.

twenties and thirties, most of whom were away in Tehran;[33] but the pattern of living in Sharifabad itself was as yet barely affected, and mental perspectives were little changed. External communications were few, with no newspapers and only one or two radios, little used. No one entered a cinema or encountered television, and books were little read. Daily life continued to be laborious and hard, with crops being skilfully coaxed from a difficult soil by means of limited supplies of brackish water.[34] In the main it was subsistence farming, the two chief crops being corn and cotton, which of necessity (because of the soil conditions) were still sown and harvested by hand. The wheel was virtually unused in the fields since it was difficult to get anything bigger than a bicycle over the irrigation ditches, and so pack-animals—donkey, cow, and occasionally camel—still did most of the carrying and hauling. These animals were all stabled, as in the dangerous old days, inside the small, fortress-like houses,[35] which were huddled together for protection—though the surrounding village-wall had long been demolished. Food was simple, basically wheaten bread with goat's milk cheese, mutton broth, and fruits and herbs in season (though this was luxurious compared with the basic diet of harsh rye bread and herbs which had sustained life for earlier generations). Plainness of diet was one, mundane, reason why religious festivals were eagerly looked forward to, since these meant a break in the monotony. In general religion dominated the villagers' lives, providing them not only with a purpose for living, and explanations for all phenomena, but also occupation (through innumerable observances) and diversions, with feast days and merrymaking. There were few aesthetic pleasures to be had, except from the beauties of nature, which were keenly and consciously enjoyed; and since these could be rejoiced in as the work of God, this delight itself could be brought within the framework of the faith.

In the 1970s, material life in Iran was modernized with a rush, and the old isolation of Sharifabad was broken into as the means of transport and communication were speeded up. Some of the dusty lanes through the village were tarred, and cars dashed up and down them. Telephones were installed, radios became common, and

[33] It was calculated that in 1964 fifty to sixty of those officially resident in the village were away, mostly working in Tehran, though a few still maintained older connections with Bombay.

[34] See in more detail 'Some aspects of farming', 121–40.

[35] See 'The Zoroastrian houses of Yazd', 125–47.

oil- and gas-stoves began to replace the ever-burning wood-fires which had been so carefully tended in every Zoroastrian home. This decade saw in fact a major onslaught (all the more devastating for being unplanned and unmotivated) on the rhythms and habits of village life, and so, indirectly, on the age-old orthodoxy which they had helped to sustain.

That the orthodoxy of Sharifabad truly represented that of ancient Zoroastrianism can be established from the scriptures of the faith (the Avesta); from its secondary literature in Pahlavi (dating in the final redactions largely from Sasanian and early Islamic times); and from sporadic notices by foreign writers in the past—Greek, Roman, Syrian, Armenian. Moreover, the beliefs and ways of the Yazdi Zoroastrians can be shown to be in the main identical with those of the Parsis before the latter came first under Western and then under modern Hindu influences.

The essential tenets of the old orthodoxy were these: there is one uncreated God, Ohrmazd, who is wholly good, and the Creator of all good things. All worship is directed ultimately to him, although it may be addressed immediately to one of a number of lesser divinities, brought into being by him to help in his great task of vanquishing evil. These divinities are called yazad or ized 'One to be worshipped', or amahraspand 'Bounteous Immortal'.[36] Ohrmazd is opposed by Ahriman, the Hostile Spirit, also uncreated but wholly evil, who in his turn has his helpers, the demons, to aid him in attacking the good. Man's task in life is to fight, together with his Creator Ohrmazd and the Amahraspands, against Ahriman, by thinking, speaking, and doing well, by performing prescribed acts of worship, and by keeping the purity laws. By so doing he will both gain his own salvation at death, in paradise above, and help to achieve the ultimate salvation of the whole world, which will some day come about through the utter defeat of evil.

These clear-cut and noble tenets can be readily grasped, and are imprinted on the mind of every Sharifabadi child, through precept and example. The complexity in Zoroastrian doctrine lies in the prophet's teachings about one group of the Amahraspands, six great beings who belong particularly to his own revelation. These six were apprehended by Zoroaster as the first divinities to be created by Ohrmazd; and their original concepts were subtle and profound.

[36] The literal meanings of these ancient Avestan words are naturally no longer understood.

Here we need concern ourselves only with the beliefs of the Sharif-abadis in modern times, which though simplified appear to embody still the core of the prophet's teachings. In brief, the six Amahra-spands are Vahman, the hypostasis of 'Good Purpose', of the will to achieve the good life; Ardvahišt, 'Best Righteousness'; Shahrevar, 'Desired Dominion', who embodies just authority; Spendārmad 'Bounteous Devotion'; Hordād 'Health'; and Amurdād, 'Long Life' or 'Immortality'. The meanings of the divinities' proper names were no longer understood; but it was firmly believed that if these six beings were duly reverenced, both in daily life and through acts of worship, they would sustain a man and endue him with virtue, while also, like the other lesser Amahraspands, protecting and helping him in the vicissitudes of life.

How these great beings were to be reverenced was inculcated in the orthodox from childhood; but in part the theological basis for observances is difficult at first for the outsider to grasp. To under-stand it one has to remember that Zoroaster lived a very long time ago, possibly about 1500 B.C. or even earlier; and that he was a learned man, a priest, familiar evidently with the scholastic specula-tions of his time and place, and deriving from them a basis for his own doctrines. These speculations incorporated, naturally, what is now an immensely archaic picture of the cosmos, one which belongs to the same stage of human development as, for instance, the Hebrew ideas about genesis. Thus the ancient Iranian philosophers thought that the world was divided into seven parts, which had been created successively. The first of these was the sky, which they held to be a hard shell or globe that passed beneath the earth as well as arching over it. This globe they apprehended as being of stone—a theory apparently generally held by the Indo-Europeans. The second creation, water, they thought filled the lower part of this globe; and earth, the third, lay upon the water like a great flat dish. Then were made in turn the living creations of plants, animals, and man; and finally fire was fashioned, the seventh creation, which as well as existing in its own right also permeated all the rest, giving them warmth or energy. In the old pagan religion this sevenfold creation was probably attributed to the agency of various gods; but Zoroaster saw it as the planned and purposeful handiwork of the supreme Lord, Ohrmazd, helped by the six great Amahraspands whom he had first called into being, and who, with his own Creative Spirit, made up a mighty heptad. Each of these seven, Zoroaster taught,[37] brought one of the seven creations into being, and remains its lord and protector. So Shahrevar, representing the kingdom of God, created the sky, closest to God's present kingdom of Paradise; Spendarmad, 'Devotion', fashioned the humble earth. Water belongs to Hordad, Health, plants to Amurdad, 'Immortality'. Vahman, 'Good Purpose', created beneficent animals and Ohrmazd himself, through his Spirit, made man, the chief of creations. Lastly Ardvahišt, hypostasis of the order and rightfulness which should pervade all things, fashioned fire, which runs through all the physical world.

This remarkable doctrine links the material with the immaterial, making the entire world in origin holy; and accordingly positive injunctions are laid on men to serve the seven great Amahraspands, both by pursuing the good life in ways which will be ethically pleasing to them, and also by cherishing the seven physical creations which they have made. Man, that is, must care both for his own moral and physical well-being, and also act as steward of the other six creations, which unlike him have not the power of conscious choice. Thus in one of the Pahlavi books Ohrmazd is represented as saying to his prophet Zoroaster:

In that material world of mine, I who am Ohrmazd [preside] over the just man, and Vahman over cattle, Ardvahišt over fire and Shahrevar over metals, Spendarmad over earth and virtuous women, Hordad over waters, and Amurdad over plants. Whoever teaches care for these seven [creations] does well and pleases [the Amahraspands]. Then his soul will never arrive at kinship with Ahriman and the devs. If he has cared for them, then he has cared for the seven Amahraspands, and this he must teach to all mankind.[38]

In this passage Shahrevar is said to preside over metals. This is a development of scholastic theory whereby the substance of the sky was identified as rock-crystal and so classified as a metal,[39] presumably because crystal was won from rock, like metallic ores. Shahrevar, lord of the sky, is therefore lord of metals also, and since, as it is said in another Zoroastrian treatise, 'no one can take hold of the sky, nor can anyone defile it',[40] it was only through caring

[37] That these doctrines were expounded by the prophet himself has gradually been established by the labours of successive scholars, for a survey of which see Boyce, *History*, vol. i, chs. 8 and 9.

[38] *The Supplementary Texts to the Šāyest nē-šāyest*, ed. and transl. by Firoze M. P. Kotwal, xv. 5–6.

[39] See H. W. Bailey, *Zoroastrian problems in the ninth-century books*, ch. iv.

[40] *Saddar Bundaheš*, 75.1 (ed. Dhabhar, 146, transl. Dhabhar, *Riv.* 556).

for metals here below that man could serve this Amahraspand materially. This service was interpreted, among other ways, as being to use money wisely and well, not squandering it, but giving it generously in charity to the deserving poor. As for the other five creations, water and fire are to be kept undefiled, and earth is to be made fertile through careful husbandry. Plants are to be tended, and it is a sin, for instance, wantonly to destroy a tree. Animals must be kindly treated, and no domestic creatures should ever be overworked, underfed, or abused. This linking of the physical and moral has proved wonderfully effective in sustaining the general observance of a highly disciplined ethical code among Zoroastrians down the ages, and in Yazd the Moslems bore reluctant witness to the moral stature of the otherwise despised 'gor'. Thus they were very ready to employ Zoroastrians in field and garden, not only because of their skill and industriousness, but also because of their honesty; and there was a proverb among them that one should eat at the house of a Jew (to be well fed), but sleep at that of a Zoroastrian (where one could trust one's hosts in all things).

In such respects there was no difference between the Zoroastrians of town or village, Iran or India. The moral code of 'good thoughts, words and deeds' was the same for all. Yet there is no doubt that the full range of Zoroastrian commandments with regard to the seven creations remained at its most significant for those who worked on the land, thus following a pattern of life not so far removed from Zoroaster's own; and though the principles of these commandments could be applied also in urban life (and indeed accord in part most admirably with contemporary ideas of conservation), it was certainly easier to maintain the old, coherent orthodoxy in a village like Sharifabad than in a complex modern city. Plainly if Zoroastrianism had survived as a state religion, with colleges of learned priests and an educated laity, the archaic doctrine of the seven creations would eventually have been reinterpreted, just as the Old Testament cosmogony has been reinterpreted by Jewish and Christian scholars, and would have come to provide a symbolic basis for belief and practice; but since the Zoroastrians were reduced by circumstances to an intellectually starved minority, which remained in ignorance of any scientific developments after the ninth century A.D., they were spared the need to struggle with new knowledge, or to re-examine the dogmas of their ancient faith. It was for this reason that the sudden impact of Western science proved such a shock to educated Parsis in the mid nineteenth century, causing many of them not to attempt to reassess their traditional doctrines but largely to abandon them.[41] The oppressed Iranis were able in their isolation to continue longer believing that this earth was the centre of the universe, and man the crown of creation, brought into being for a clear purpose which had been made known to him through a complete and final revelation. Such beliefs were satisfying ones to live by, and when one considers the intellectual difficulties which beset the modern 'liberal' Zoroastrian, it is hard not to envy the calm certainties which the otherwise harsh lot of the Sharifabadis had allowed them to maintain.

Though the world of traditional Zoroastrianism was thus re-assuringly comprehensible, man was called upon to live in it strenu-ously. Zoroaster's radical dualism means that this earth is seen as a battleground, in which the malignant forces of evil strive ceaselessly to corrupt every good thing; and so his followers are required to be like front-line soldiers, never slackening in either discipline or courage. Zoroastrianism is therefore an exacting faith, whose spiritual rewards are not to be lightly won. Its dualism is of a kind, however, which has been termed 'pro-cosmic',[42] for it lies not between spirit and matter, but between the good creation of Ohrmazd, which embraces both spirit and matter, and the negative, hostile one of Ahriman. There is no reason, therefore, why man should not enjoy to the full the creature pleasures of this material world, all pure joys and delights being in themselves part of the creation of Ohr-mazd, just as griefs and pains are assaults against them by his adversary. The Zoroastrian ideal is that of a joyful and upright spirit in a strong, vigorous body; and though excess of any kind is to be deplored, so is deficiency, so that, for instance, to fast is as bad as to over-indulge, since both alike weaken the body and diminish legitimate pleasure. Among the minor sensual enjoyments which Zoroastrians used to relish was the temperate drinking of wine, and in this matter the villagers of the Yazdi plain, who grew their own grapes, continued stoutly to defy the ordinances of Islam. The men regularly washed down their bitter rye-bread with cupfuls of wine, though the women contented themselves, except on feast-

---

[41] In this they were encouraged by the Christianized interpretations of their faith which were brought to them from nineteenth-century Europe, notably by Martin Haug in the 1860s.

[42] See U. Bianchi, *Zamān i Ōhrmazd*, ch. v.

days, with herbal concoctions. In this one respect, however, Reza Shah was unkind to Zoroastrians, for in his reign all wine-making was forbidden except under licence. This law coincided with an improvement in the Zoroastrians' standard of living, which enabled them to buy imported tea and sugar. So men and women alike became tea-drinkers with the rest of Iran, and turned most of their grape-juice, regretfully, into vinegar.

The fact that Zoroastrianism, like Judaism, is a religion which encourages the enjoyment of life, and has a robust practical approach to most matters, must be, one would think, one of the factors which has enabled it to survive in the most adverse circumstances. In the main its precepts and practices work with the grain of human nature, not against it; and once one has accepted its discipline—which is not so hard for those brought up to it—it is on the whole life-enhancing to be an adherent of the Good Religion (as Zoroastrians themselves term their faith). Even devout Moslems of Yazd acknowledged this in part, commenting on the gaiety of Zoroastrian festivals in contrast with the melancholy character of most of their own. For them, holy occasions called for weeping and mourning, but for the Zoroastrians to worship in sadness is to drive away the divine.

Yet though Zoroastrianism is essentially a sturdy and optimistic faith, the orthodox Sharifabadis were keenly conscious of the reality and power of evil. They lived in awareness of the presence of God and the Amahraspands, and in hope of heaven; but they had also a sharp sense of the active hostility of Ahriman and his forces, and fear of hell was a powerful moral deterrent. One of the village women possessed an illustrated copy of the *Ardā Vīrāz Nāmag*— the little Zoroastrian prose work which is held to be a forerunner of Dante's *Divine Comedy*—and she and others used sometimes to terrify themselves by looking at those pictures which showed, with crude vividness, the torments of the damned. Moreover, living as they did in a small, isolated community, with the mysterious desert around them, lapping against their unfenced fields, the Sharifabadis had a lively apprehension of the local workings of evil, and suffered the dread of devils and jinns, both in the great empty places and lurking about their homes. Some weaker souls succumbed, indeed, at times to practising a mild white magic in an attempt to control these unseen beings and to force them to remove sickness or blight or other misfortunes; but in true Zoroastrianism evil is to be defied, not subjugated or appeased, and the leaders of the Sharifabadi community were vigilant to discourage such practices (which were much indulged in by their Moslem neighbours). They were fully prepared, however, to acknowledge the efficacy of holy words, and Avestan verses were used in talismanic fashion on many occasions.

Since there were so few priests remaining in the Yazdi area, Sharifabad had come by the 1960s to form a single hušt or parish with two other villages. One of these, Mazra' Kalantar, was out in the middle of the plain, and was slowly dying of drought. This, like Sharifabad, was an old, orthodox village, whose dwindling population did its best to maintain the ways of their forefathers. The other, Hasanabad-e Maybod, was developed early in the twentieth century by enterprising Zoroastrian merchants, who used their wealth in a traditional manner to make fertile the desert. Springs of sweet water were found there, under the higher mountain ranges on the further side of the plain from Sharifabad, and Hasanabad had become a flourishing place, with fine orchards and abundant crops; but it had no fire-temple, and lacked the rooted traditionalism of the other two villages. Since one priest had to serve all three places, cycling miles in heat and cold across the desert, his time was fully spent in performing essential acts of worship, and the rites of marriage and death; and so moral and practical leadership devolved very largely upon leading laymen.

The Zoroastrian population of the three villages was estimated in 1964 to be just over 1,200 persons, with 140 in drought-stricken Mazra' Kalantar (where there were only some half a dozen impoverished Moslem families), and about 200 in prosperous Hasanabad (beside a sizeable population of Moslems and Baha'is).[43] There was a formally instituted Anjoman for the Zoroastrians of the three villages, that is, an elected council with responsibility for guiding and administering the community's affairs.[44] This met in Sharifabad about every fifteen days, and had a membership of fifteen persons, eleven from Sharifabad, and two each from Mazra' and Hasanabad. The Anjoman had charge of the communal funds

[43] Mazra' Kalantar, like Sharifabad, was proud of the fact that no one there went over to the new faith.

[44] The minutes of this Anjoman go back to 1947. The cities of Yazd and Kerman have Anjomans with older records, starting in the mid nineteenth century. This type of council, with a chairman and written records, was fostered by the Parsi agent Manekji Limji Hataria (for a sketch of whose life and activities see 'Manekji Limji Hataria in Iran'). Long before that, however, the Irani Zoroastrians had been under the governance of their elders, who were officially recognized by the Moslem authorities, see, e.g., Chardin, *Voyages*, ii. 180.

and various trust funds, from which they maintained the sacred
fires with their two buildings,[45] the small village shrines, and the
dakhma (funerary tower) with its ever-burning fire, which stood in
the desert to the south of Sharifabad, within sight from the edge of its
fields. The Anjoman also paid two men to act as corpse-bearers or
nasā-sālārs (usually referred to simply as the sālārs, in Dari thālārs),
and provided them with complete outfits of white garments for
their work; and they further employed a man and an elderly woman
as pākšūs ('those who wash clean') to lay out the dead. The Sharifabadis gave generously but unobtrusively to the communal funds
which the Anjoman dispensed, holding that such charitable acts
should ordinarily be known only to God and the giver.

In 1964 the head of the Anjoman, and mayor (kad-khodā) of
the village of Sharifabad (representing both Zoroastrians and
Moslems) was a remarkable man, Agha Rustam Noshiravan
Belivani, to whose wise and resolute leadership the local Zoroastrians
owed much. His forebears had played a leading part in the affairs of
Sharifabad for at least seven generations,[46] and his father, great-
uncle,[47] and great-grandfather had all been mayors before him
(further back in this respect tradition did not go). This meant that
they had been in a position of authority during the challenging
years when the laws of the land, promulgated in remote Tehran,
were granting Zoroastrians a freedom and equality which some of
the local Moslems were bitterly reluctant to concede in practice.
Naturally this long-established family had many blood-ties with
others in the village, and had been responsible for various benefactions there. The boys' primary school, for instance, was founded
by a cousin who had no sons of his own.[48] It was here that Agha
Rustam acquired a basic education, which he pursued so ably that

[45] The now empty building of Aδor Khara is still carefully maintained (see
further below, p. 81).

[46] Their names, in ascending order, are Noshiravan, Gushtasp, Khodarahm,
Gushtasp, Belivan, Jamshid, Pavarza. The unusual—perhaps indeed unique—
name of Belivan was adapted by Agha Rustam to form a surname when fixed
family names were introduced in Iran. There is a tradition that the family was
founded by a remote forebear who came from Khorasan to settle in the village.
Similar family traditions are not rare in Yazd and Kerman, for these two regions
were the last bastions of the old faith, to which, evidently, Zoroastrians withdrew
from other regions as conditions there grew intolerable.

[47] Namely Turk Jamshidi, the third son of Khodarahm, whose daughter Bibi
was married to Noshiravan. First-cousin marriages are favoured by Zoroastrians,
and in this the Moslems of Iran have held to the way of the old religion.

[48] Namely Jamshid, the eldest son of Khodarahm.

he went on to qualify as a lawyer; but instead of then departing
like so many others to Tehran, he remained in Sharifabad, practising,
as the only Zoroastrian lawyer in the region, in the thriving small
town of Ardekan nearby. Of his sisters one, Murvarid, married
Paridun Jehangir Rashidi,[49] a tenant farmer whom Agha Rustam
persuaded to take on the arduous task of acting as guardian of the
dakhma, and daily tending its ever-burning fire. Another sister,
Piruza, became the second wife of Dastur Khodadad Shehriar
Neryosangi, whose uncle had been hušt-mobed in Sharifabad for
many years, and who was himself thus persuaded to settle there.
(Some such special tie was needed, since Sharifabad was an un-
popular parish with the Yazdi priests, for not only was it far from
the city, but the Ardekani Moslems were notorious for seeking to
vex their Zoroastrian neighbours.) D. Khodadad was a priest pre-
eminently suited for Sharifabad, for he was steeped in orthopraxy.
As a young man, when he had been newly made priest, he was
appointed by the Dastur dasturan[50] to be one of the four 'atašbands'
or servers of the Ataš Bahram in Yazd, and this work he did for
four years (with fifteen days on, fifteen days off, for the service was
exacting, especially in a hot climate). The other atašbands were all
venerable men. One of them, D. Mihragan, then in his nineties,[51]
was deeply versed in the rites of tending the sacred fire, and was
entrusted also with the general training of young priests in liturgy
and ritual; another, D. Ardeshir Shehriar, specialized in administering the great purification of the barašnom-e nō-šwa. Together they
instructed the young Khodadad in these and many other things
during his years of service at the fire-temple. Both the knowledge
and the discipline of those days remained with him, so that he
was not only an authority on the traditional beliefs of the faith,
but scrupulously upheld its observances, guarding his own ritual
purity, moreover, as strictly as possible, a fact much valued by his
parishioners.[52]

[49] The Rashid from whom the family took its surname was Paridun's great-
grandfather, who had come to Sharifabad from Abshahi. The Rashidis had inter-
married a great deal with the Belivani family group.

[50] D. Namdar Shehriar, the last generally acknowledged incumbent of this
ancient office.

[51] He had been at one time atašband of the Dadgah fire at the Tehran house
of the great Zoroastrian merchant, Arbab Jamshid Bahman.

[52] In 1971 D. Khodadad left the hušt of Sharifabad to become priest-in-charge
of the relatively new fire-temple in Shiraz, but four years later he returned to
live and work there again.

Even with such a priest living among them, the laity in Sharifabad had to do many tasks which in the past would have been done by priests, notably tending the sacred fire and caring for the shrines. These tasks were undertaken mostly by elderly men and women of known probity. Minor religious services too were often solemnized by laymen, when D. Khodadad had been called away to one of the other villages of his parish; and in general in 1964 Sharifabad was striving, without help or encouragement from outside, to maintain as fully as possible the observances of its ancient faith, while at the same time keeping alive its ethical and spiritual dignity.[53]

The Sharifabadis were not alone in this endeavour, for there were of course devoutly orthodox Zoroastrians in the other Yazdi villages also, and in the cities of Iran; but the communal tradition was undoubtedly strongest among them. I had heard the village lauded in this respect before visiting it; and when I did so, I had the immense good fortune to be invited by Agha Rustam Belivani and his wife Tahmina Khanom to become their guest. For the next seven months I had the privilege of living as a member of their household, enjoying their friendship and that of their children; and in the following pages I hope to be able to describe something of what I learnt through their kindness and that of their relatives, and of the villagers at large, whose patience and courtesy seemed endless. Among them, two who were especially helpful were Khanom Sarvar Afshari from Aliabad, who had married an uncle of Agha Rustam's, and who, coming into the village from outside, was able to draw illuminating comparisons between the ways of Sharifabad and other places; and Agha Erdeshir Qudusi, a friend of Agha Rustam's, who had spent many years in India.

In general, because of the strength of their faith, the Sharifabadis were ready to expound their beliefs and observances unreservedly, and D. Khodadad likewise displayed a constant readiness to enlighten and teach. By a minor piece of good luck I had been able to acquire a woman's bicycle in Yazd, one imported two decades earlier for an English missionary, and I could thus accompany him on his journeys about his parish, and so learn something of the other two villages, as well as a little of the duties and responsibilities

---

[53] Indeed, outside influences from their co-religionists tended to be positively discouraging, with reforming Zoroastrians from Bombay or Tehran coming to the village to lecture against the maintenance of many ancient observances. Such lectures had had little or no effect by 1964, beyond rousing a deep, though courteously bridled, indignation.

of a Zoroastrian priest. The way to Mazraᶜ lay across the desert, and even on the road to Hasanabad we seldom met more than one or two people. The only direction in which D. Khodadad was unwilling to have my company was through Ardekan, for he felt it hard enough to have to traverse its unfriendly streets as a Zoroastrian priest, without the added provocation of being accompanied by an unveiled woman on a bicycle.

The Sharifabadis had constant communication with the other Zoroastrian villages, and since these will necessarily figure from time to time in the following pages, a brief account of them seems desirable. They differed greatly in character, some being old places like Sharifabad itself, with cramped houses and twisting, narrow lanes, and these all had their own fire-temples. Others, like Hasanabad, were relatively new settlements, developed during the previous hundred years or so by Zoroastrian merchants, and these had more spacious dwellings, with gardens, and wide, tree-lined streets. Many of these too had their own places of worship. In the 1960s the whole Yazdi region was suffering from drought, and some villages were severely affected, and were becoming slowly depopulated. Apart from their individual characteristics, the Zoroastrian villages formed four separate groups. The one comprising Sharifabad and its two neighbours was the furthest from the city of Yazd, and was administered from Ardekan. The group next to them, to the southeast, was formed by villages of the Rustāq or 'Rural District' of Yazd. There were six of these, strung out along or near the highway—that is, on the more arid side of the plain—namely (reckoning from north to south) Aliabad, Jaᶜfarabad, Husaynabad, Asrabad, Allahabad (pronounced Elabad by the Zoroastrians),[54] and Nusratabad. There were also a few Zoroastrians at Mehdiabad-e Rustaq and Izabad. All these villages carried their dead to the dakhma of Elabad, set superbly on the solitary, knife-edged hill of Zarch. None was very old—at the most, it was reckoned, three or four hundred years—and all were menaced, in varying degrees, by shifting, devouring sands, for drought had killed their protective bamboo-thickets and lines of trees.

Beyond the villages of the Rustaq came the suburban ones, in

[54] All the village names sounded a little different in Dari, but three, indicated here in brackets, were known to the Zoroastrians only in their contracted forms, which are used accordingly throughout this book. Some of the other colloquial pronunciations are given in the index after the standard form. Sharifabad itself, for instance, was always spoken of as Sharfabad.

a ring round Yazd. Their inhabitants called themselves *šahrī*, 'of the city', as distinct from *malatī*, the term they used for someone who lived in Yazd itself. To the east (reckoning again from north to south) were three old villages, Kanu, Narseabad, and Mariamabad (called Moriabad) and a relatively new one, Mehdiabad-e Yazd. To the west were other old villages, Kuče Buyuk, Khorramshah, Qasimabad, Rahmatabad, and Mohammadabad (Mandavad) on the Yazd–Kerman highway. This last-named village had had a sizeable Zoroastrian population up to the 1940s, but in 1964 there were only four Zoroastrian families left, and two of them were preparing to depart for Tehran. The other two suburban villages, Ahrestan and Khairabad, both old, were on the road from Yazd to Shiraz, a little further to the south-west, that is, than Kuče Buyuk and Khorramshah. They and all the other suburban villages carried their dead to the dakhma of Yazd itself, not far from Rahmatabad.

Finally there was the group formed by the pretty upland village of Taft, higher up the Shiraz road, and the villages near it. These (to name them from the direction of Yazd) were Mobareke, Cham and Zainabad, with two newish ones, Khalilabad and Husayni, where there were only a few Zoroastrian households remaining. These villages all bore their dead to the beautifully placed dakhma of Cham. Cham itself and Mobareke were suffering badly from drought, and their population was dwindling. Nevertheless the whole group, being (after Sharifabad) the remotest from urban influences, preserved the old ways and traditions very faithfully. Its villages had followed the example of the Sharifabadi group in forming a collective Anjoman, whose representatives met in Taft. The suburban villages, and those of the Rustaq, had no such organization. Some relied on the Anjoman of the city of Yazd, others had their separate Anjomans and managed their own affairs.

In 1964 the small band of Yazdi priests (some of them only part-time clergy) were stretched to minister at all adequately to this scattered Zoroastrian population. All the villages of the Rustaq had been made into a single hušt, and there a certain Gushtasp from Elabad (who had undergone *no-šwa*) was officially nominated dastur-e deh or 'village priest', and he officiated at all minor ceremonies, the hušt-mobed coming from Yazd only for the major ones, that is, those concerned with death, and the marriage-service. (Each priest kept a little book to record the date of every death among his parishioners, and he was expected to come for the related ceremonies without any reminder from the family.[55]) Taft and its villages formed another hušt, and the remaining priests divided Yazd and the suburban villages among them. The Sharifabadis themselves, with characteristic foresight and energy, took steps to send D. Khodadad's fifteen-year-old son Shehriar to Bombay in 1965 to be made priest, in the hope that he would return to minister to them; but he felt no vocation, and there were then no other new entrants to the priesthood in Yazd.

As well as the locally instituted, semi-official post of dastur-e deh, an older lay office existed, that of the dahmobed. The title probably means 'servant of the priest', and the position was a respected one, somewhat like that of a churchwarden in Anglican Christianity. There was a dahmobed in every village, and one in the city of Yazd, and the office clearly had nothing to do with any shortage of priests, since it is attested already in the Rivayats.[56] The dahmobed was appointed by the local elders, but the post tended to become hereditary, and in Ahrestan one family had passed it down from father to son for eight generations, with no more than a formal ratification at the death of each. The incumbent there in 1964, Erdeshir Dahmobed (he had taken the title as surname), wore white like a priest when engaged on his duties; and, himself an old man, he recalled how his father, living to well over a hundred years of age, had handed him the keys to the village fire-temple on his death-bed, as a hereditary trust. He, like other dahmobeds, knew a good deal of Avestan by heart, and could solemnize the 'outer' religious services when necessary. The duties of dahmobed and lay atašband complemented each other in ways that varied slightly from place to place (in Elabad indeed the two offices were held by the one person); and though Sharifabad had two dahmobeds in 1964, it nevertheless assigned more duties than other villages to its atašband. Yet there as elsewhere the existence of this old office demonstrated the close traditional involvement of the laity in acts of worship and religious affairs, and contributed to their being able to maintain observances faithfully even without the help of priests.

[55] This is the custom also among the Parsis.
[56] See, e.g., Dhabhar, Riv., intro., lxii.

2

THE WORSHIP OF OHRMAZD
AND THE CREATIONS

ZOROASTER is the only founder of a great revealed religion who was a priest; and as such he clearly knew the value of observance, and therefore provided his followers with firm guidance for their devotional lives. He himself, so the tradition says, was the author of the greatest of the Zoroastrian prayers, the Ahuna vairyō or Ahunvar, a brief utterance in honour of Ahura Mazda which is for the Zoroastrian what the Lord's Prayer is for the Christian. It is the first prayer that is taught to a child. It is uttered at every act of worship, public or private, and because of its sanctity it can be used in all vicissitudes, and (if repeated a prescribed number of times) may at need replace all other devotions. Thus some of the older Sharifabadi women could not read and knew little Avestan by heart; and for certain religious exercises they made themselves rosaries on which they could tell the number of Ahunvars as they recited them.

As for times of private prayer, it was ordained that the Zoroastrian should pray once during each of the five watches of the twenty-four-hour day—an invaluable religious exercise which Muhammad adopted from Zoroastrianism. Zoroastrians pray standing, and, as enjoined by their prophet, in the presence of fire—that is, either facing the sun, or before a hearth-fire or temple-fire, or a lighted lamp—so that this may help them to fix their thoughts on righteousness. Every time that a Zoroastrian prays, he unties and reties the sacred cord, the 'koštī', which he wears round his waist, so that the Iranis call this basic act of worship 'making new the sacred cord' (*koštī nō kartwun*).[1] The words spoken then are addressed to Ohrmazd the Lord, and include an execration of Ahriman.

The essential prayers for each watch take only some five minutes or so to say, once thoroughly learnt. Nevertheless, to say them

---

[1] The Pahlavi term *kwstyk* is pronounced as *koštī* in Dari, as *kustī* by the Parsis. The Parsis use the idiom *kustī bastan*, 'to tie the *kustī*', for this basic rite.

regularly five times a day is an exacting discipline, although it is not necessary for the laity to break the night's sleep to do so. The usual custom (followed also by Moslems) is to recite the prayers of the third watch just before sunset, make a pause as the sun goes down, and then say those of the fourth watch, which has then just begun. The devout get up before dawn to say the prayers of the fifth watch, and when the sun has risen they welcome the new day with the prayers of its first watch. The five obligatory prayers can thus be said in three groups, the third time of prayer being during the noontide watch. The custom of the twofold dawn and sunrise prayers conflicts, however, with another religious duty, for Zoroastrians hold that each new day should be welcomed, not only with godly thoughts and words, but also with cleanliness and order. So another custom, strictly observed in Sharifabad, was that the women got up at first light to sweep and dust and tidy; and they finished their work, as the sun came up, by carrying round the house a small panful of embers from the hearth-fire on which they scattered dried marjoram leaves to give out a pleasant fragrance. Finally, the pan was set outside the house-door, so that the lanes of the Zoroastrian quarter were full of sweet scents to greet the rising sun.[2] If all this was done, it was believed, the yazad Sroš would visit the house with his benign presence, and the day begin auspiciously.

Women could not do all this work between dawn and sunrise and also say two sets of prayers; but the priests of old declared that, although a man has the duty to pray, a woman's best act of devotion is the work of her hands, as she serves father, husband, or son. In the Belivani household in 1964 the boys were still too young to have put on the sacred cord, and so Agha Rustam prayed alone on behalf of the whole household each morning, his deep voice filling the small courtyard with sonorous Avestan as he stood facing east, where the sun came up over the mountains. In general, even in devout Sharifabad, the full number of five daily prayers was said only on holy days and during pilgrimages, and otherwise most men were content, on working days, to say either the morning or evening prayers; but in this duty I never knew Agha Rustam to fail, whether he slept under his own or another's roof.

The other regular act of devotion incumbent on Zoroastrians was keeping seven annual feasts of obligation. Tradition has it that these

---

[2] For similar observances carried out by Parsi women in Gujarat see Seervai and Patel, 'Gujarāt Pārsis', 209.

feasts were founded by the prophet himself, and they are therefore of the greatest holiness, so that to neglect them is a sin which 'goes to the Bridge'—which weighs, that is, among one's evil deeds at the day of judgement. Records (beginning from Sasanian times) show that these seven feasts have been kept devoutly and generally by rich and poor, in good times and in bad, down the centuries, and 1964 in Sharifabad saw no slackening in the ancient observances. Despite the tradition that these holy days were founded by Zoroaster, their Avestan names suggest a remote pagan origin: they appear to have begun, that is, as festivals to celebrate the seasons of mid spring, mid summer, and mid winter, harvest, and the return of cattle from summer pastures, the annual visitation of All Souls, and New Year's Day. But Zoroaster, it seems, drew together this diversity of feasts to form a uniform chain of six, which he refounded to celebrate the six creations, with the seventh, New Year's Day, held to honour the seventh creation of fire. The six were called collectively in Avestan the 'times of the year' (*yāirya ratavō*), and were known in Middle Persian as 'gāhāmbār', reduced in current speech to 'gahāmbār', 'ga'āmbār', or 'gāmbār'. The first of them, Mid-Spring (Maidhyōi.zarəma), celebrated the first creation, sky; and so on through the year, with homage paid to water, earth, plants, and cattle successively, until the sixth feast, that of Hamaspathmaēdaya, kept originally on the last day of the year, commemorated the creation of man. The correspondences in this way of the six gahambars and the six creations are set out in detail and with great clarity in the Pahlavi books. The seventh feast, Nō Rūz, which honours fire, celebrated the creation which brought life and energy to all the rest. The first five gahambars were kept with uniform observances, but the sixth one and No Ruz both had their special rites. At all gahambars the religious services are devoted to Ohrmazd himself, as the Supreme Creator.

Originally each of the gahambars, like No Ruz, lasted for a single day; but at the beginning of the Sasanian period a major calendar change, imposed, it seems, by the power of the Persian throne, brought confusion to the Zoroastrian community, which resulted in the keeping of what were thought to be the old *and* new feast days, four days apart.[3] After a generation or two had lived with this state of affairs, the difficulty was solved by linking each pair of days together, thus forming continuous six-day festivals. This practice

[3] See 'On the calendar of Zoroastrian feasts', 513–39.

lasted for several hundred years; but eventually, some time after the tenth century, a day was lopped off each (to bring them all into accord with the festival of the five intercalary days, instituted at the calendar change); and since then they have been kept in this way.

The six gahambars, it was enjoined, were to be times of worship and joy; and only necessary work should be done then. This injunction would obviously have been easier to keep when each feast lasted for only a day; and in a farming community a good deal of necessary work had to go on during the extended festivals, such as ploughing, sowing, and irrigating, hay-making and harvest, as well as caring for stock. To do work which was not essential was regarded, however, as a sin; and so boys enjoyed a happy break from such irksome tasks as weeding in the fields, and women and girls abandoned spindle and loom, which otherwise were seldom idle. The Zoroastrian calendar does not know the Semitic division into weeks, and provides no regularly recurrent rest-day. The five-day festivals thus provided welcome and well-earned breaks in routine. (It is a major factor in the weakening of traditional Zoroastrianism in the towns that there, as a minority, the Zoroastrians have to accept the Moslem pattern of a Friday holiday, and cannot, if they work for others, get time off to keep their own holy days.)

There are a number of other five-day festivals in the Zoroastrian year whose observance is meritorious, but not obligatory; but the gahambars were sharply distinguished from them, not only because of their greater sanctity, but also because, on account of this, they alone were regularly endowed. Since to keep them was of the greatest merit, it was held to benefit the soul if a man set aside a piece of property—a house, or a field, or rights over water—to found an annual celebration on one of the gahambar days; and so piously was this carried out that in an old and orthodox village like Sharifabad not a single one of the thirty gahambar days lacked its endowed observances. This custom of making pious foundations is undoubtedly ancient, and was probably practised already in Parthian times, if not earlier, although the first clear evidence of it comes from the Sasanian period. Zoroastrian usages of this kind, it is held, provided the model for the Islamic institution of *vaqf* or charitable bequests;[4] and the Zoroastrian practice itself continues with regard to gahambars down to the present day. It even received an added

---

[4] See Anahit Perikhanian, 'Private endowment-funds in ancient Iran' (in Russian), *VDI*, 1973, 3–25.

impetus in Moslem times because of a particularly harsh law, which provided that if one member of a Zoroastrian family embraced Islam, then he inherited everything and his brethren were left penniless. This was undoubtedly a powerful incentive to adopt Islam; but by one of the odd anomalies which characterized the dealings of the authorities with Zoroastrians, if a pious bequest by one of the old religion were duly set down and registered, then this was respected, and the endowment could not be alienated even in favour of a convert. Plainly where Zoroastrian communities dwindled and grew weak, such trusts were ignored and swallowed up; but where they remained in reasonable strength, as in the Yazdi area, it was possible to maintain these bequests. Piety and prudence united, therefore, to encourage their foundation. The local Moslems claim indeed that, on the scale in which it was done, the practice was unfair to the children, depriving them of their inheritance; but the way it worked was that a member of the family was nominated as trustee of the endowment, and he cultivated the fields or lived in the house, setting aside a portion of the crops or a certain sum of money, as if in rent, for the annual celebration of the gahambar. Admittedly his livelihood was thus diminished to a fixed extent, but at least it was assured. Endowments were distributed as far as possible among different branches of a family, in the interests of fairness; and since all the extended family joined together in preparing for and celebrating the gahambar itself, this was an excellent means of furthering solidarity among them. Hence it is said, in a Zoroastrian text; 'Everyone who has founded a gahambar has rejoiced the souls of his ancestors for seventy generations.'[5] The direct forebears of Agha Rustam Belivani, back to seven generations, all founded gahambars, whose trusts are distributed among seven branches of the extended family. Until recently members of all seven lived in Sharifabad, but three are no longer represented there (their members having all removed to Tehran).

There is no longer any need to found gahambars to secure inheritances; indeed, such efforts have been made under the present dynasty to treat Zoroastrians fairly that it is now possible, if the local Anjoman acts energetically, to maintain an endowment even if the heirs have become Moslems and wish to alienate it. Thus the Sharifabadi Anjoman administers one gahambar fund on behalf of a Moslem family in the village, the celebration itself being carried

[5] *Riv.*, Unvala, i. 435, col. b, line 1.

out, as a pious duty, in Agha Rustam's house. In this case the endowment was made three generations ago. The founder's son was a reluctant convert to Islam, and was glad to have the observances continued, but the grandson was a Moslem by upbringing and conviction, and would willingly have made an end of them, had the law permitted. Although the founding of gahambars thus no longer served a worldly purpose, piety ensured the continuance of the practice. A new one was inaugurated in Sharifabad in 1963 by Rashid Shirmardi, who worked in the Yazdi administration, and who endowed this gahambar for the souls of his father and mother, who had died in poverty some twenty and ten years earlier respectively; and in 1970 Agha Rustam himself endowed one jointly with his wife Tahmina, thus adding an eighth generation to the family chain.

At each gahambar ceremony the names of the founder and his forebears were remembered both at the religious services and at the social gatherings, and this again was a strong aid to family tradition. When a new foundation was instituted, the first religious service was solemnized at the fire-temple; but thereafter it was customary to hold the service at the founder's house, both during his life and after his death—for it was believed that his soul would return to share in the observance and enjoy the offerings together with the divine beings. Hence there was a great reluctance among the orthodox to sell a family house, especially to non-Zoroastrians, though economic pressure sometimes made this necessary; and about ten houses in Sharifabad stood empty in 1964, with the owners either themselves returning annually to celebrate the family festivals there, or entrusting relatives still living in the village to do so. Similarly D. Khodadad owned a fine house in the priest's quarter of Yazd, which was deserted except for the annual celebration there of a gahambar.

The purposes of a gahambar endowment are to provide both for religious services and for social gatherings, where people would come together in loving kindness and share the food which had been blessed at these services. The technical term for this food was *čašnī*, 'that which is tasted'; and to partake of it, it was believed, was to receive spiritual and physical strengthening. It is also called *yād-būd*, i.e. that which is eaten in remembrance (*yād*) of the departed. Some of this food was always sent to members of the family who could not be present at the service, and to the sick and bedridden in the village, but all who were able were expected to come to share with their fellows in the rites of the festival. If a gahambar were given by a man with whom one had quarrelled, it was one's religious duty to forget the bitterness and accept his hospitality. It was further said that every member of the community ought to found a gahambar; and if he had not the means to establish an annual observance, then he should endow one to be celebrated every second, fourth, or even eighth year. If he could not do even this much, then he should give his services to help at another's gahambar; and above all he must not fail in attendance, so that he could contribute his good-will and prayers. As it is said in the *Rivayats*: 'If one who is poor does not resort to the place where the gahambar is celebrated, this is so great a sin that it is not proper for those who tie the košti to associate with him, or to enter his house, or to bring him to their homes, or to aid him, or to accept his testimony.'[6] Agha Rustam said further that if work kept one unavoidably away (as at lambing time or when crops must be irrigated), then one should take pains to go past the gahambar house and put a stone on its roof, as a sign that one participated in spirit. It was characteristic of Sharifabad that still in 1964 the villagers not only accepted this duty of communal observance, but carried it out eagerly and joyously, whereas in other places an indifference was even then often shown to all but a family's own ceremonies.

Since Sasanian times, the chief religious ceremony proper to the gahambars has been the Yašt-e Visperad, this is, the 'Service of All the Masters', which is dedicated above all to Ohrmazd, the supreme Master. This is a long, intricate act of worship, which should be performed within a ritual precinct by at least two priests, between sunrise and noon. In 1964 it was still so celebrated six times a year at the chief fire-temple of Yazd, on the first day of each gahambar-festival, on behalf of the whole community;[7] but in Sharifabad itself, as in other villages, the only services which could then be performed were the short Yašt-e dron consecrated early in the morning by the priest, usually in his own house, and the Āfrīnagān-e Gahāmbār with associated short acts of praise and thanksgiving,[8]

---

[6] *Saddar-Bd.*, end of ch. 50.   [7] See 'Pious Foundations', 277 with n. 48.

[8] One recital of the Afrinagan-e Gahambar was followed by two of the Afrinagan-e Do Dahman, one *karda* of the Afrinagan-e Sroš, and finally the Afrin-e Gahambar. In the *Rivayat* of Kamdin Shapur it is said that the liturgy should consist of two Afrinagan-e Gahambar and one of Do Dahman, but the present Yazdi practice accords with that of the Shenshai Parsis, see Dhabhar, *Riv.*, intro. xlviii.

which was solemnized at the house of the founder of the observance—
for this is an 'outer' service, which may be performed in any clean
place, during any of the three daylight watches by a single priest.
All the lesser gahambar services are, like the Visperad, devoted to
Ohrmazd.

The custom of celebrating these services at the house of the founder
of the gahambar meant that on a day when there were several endowments the priest and congregation moved steadily around the
village. If there were only a moderate number of observances, the
priest began to solemnize them early in the afternoon, which allowed
the men to attend first to their field-work; but on some days there
were so many that he began at about ten o'clock in the morning,
and continued, with a midday break, until dusk. The most popular
gahambars were the fifth and sixth, both celebrated in high summer,
when the long days allowed time for this pause at noon. On shorter
winter days the celebrations, though fewer, followed one another
almost continuously. Seen from the roof of one of the village houses,
the procession which formed on these occasions was curiously
moving, partly from the sense which it gave of something age-old
and loyally maintained. First came the priest himself, dressed in
white, and with him the village elders, also often in white or light-
coloured garments, walking gravely. Then there was the inevitable
jostle and push of boys, penned in by the house-walls which flanked
the narrow lane. Then other men, mostly elderly, but with a sprinkling of younger ones, some returned for the occasion from Tehran;
and finally a group of matrons and little girls, gay in their bright
traditional clothes, predominantly red and green. Black was never
seen in any garment, among men or women, for this was the Moslem
colour; nor yellow, which was held to be unlucky. There were no
young women or older girls in the procession, for they by custom
attend only the celebration of gahambars in their family homes.[9]
According to the teachings of Zoroaster, men and women are equal
in the spiritual life, with an equal hope of attaining heaven, and
compared with their Moslem sisters of the Yazdi region, the Zoroastrian women enjoyed an enviable degree of dignity and freedom.
But girls were carefully restricted, for social reasons, and at all
gatherings men and women were seated separately, the women
having always the worse position.

[9] Among the Parsis separation went further, and no females attended any
gahambars until early in the present century.

For every act of worship, whether private observance, family rite, or one involving the whole community, Zoroastrians insist on complete physical and ritual cleanliness. For them, as a Parsi has remarked, cleanliness is not next to godliness, but a part of it; and among the things which are held to drive away the divine beings and prevent them receiving men's prayers are both moral failings, such as hatred, anger and spite, and the physical ones of dirt and disorder. To preserve cleanliness in an oasis village such as Sharifabad was not easy. Water was in short supply; and everything was kept inside the houses—animals, poultry, corn, hay. Moreover, at intervals sudden fierce winds would spring up across the plain, bringing stinging clouds of sand into the open courtyards of the houses, and thence into all the rooms. Nevertheless, even on ordinary days, by dint of hard work, the Zoroastrian houses were kept clean and neat, and for a festival they were swept and garnished with even greater zeal. It was also the custom on the morning of a gahambar to splash the mud-brick walls around the house-door with whitewash, or to set white marks around it, such as the imprints of an open hand, a good-luck sign. White is the colour of purity; and the fresh marks were partly a welcome to divine visitants, partly to show everyone that a gahambar was to be celebrated there to which they should come, for no invitations were ever issued for a gahambar service. This holy occasion was open to everyone. As well as preparing the house thoroughly, each individual washed from head to foot—usually by the simple means of sluicing with buckets of water in the cattle-byre—and put on fresh clothes. Thus physical cleanliness was achieved. Ritual cleanliness was also demanded, however, which meant that no one might take part in the observance, or in the preparations for it, who had been in contact with impurity and had not yet been ritually cleansed, or who was suffering from any uncleanness himself.

The heaviest part of the preparations was in providing the food to be consecrated, so that all who came might have their share. In general Sharifabad had maintained a traditional plainness in diet, and the villagers did not strive, as sometimes happened elsewhere, to outdo one another in the range and delicacy of festival foods. They preferred rather to keep these simple, so that they might provide amply. The endowment of individual gahambars naturally varied in value, and sometimes originally substantial bequests had dwindled in worth down the years; but depending on

the endowment, there were three essential foods which were consecrated and distributed to the gahambar congregation. Firstly,
there was *lurk*, a festival delicacy made up of seven kinds of fruits
and nuts, which perhaps originally belonged especially to the celebration of the seven obligatory feasts, but which is now distributed on
other holy days also. According to D. Khodadad, *lurk* should
consist of such things as the following: *senjed* (the fruit of the
oleaster), dates, raisins, walnuts, almonds, dried apricots, plums,
and mulberries. Of these *senjed*, he said, was the most important,
and indeed these rather dry and uninteresting fruits were always
present in *lurk*, no doubt for the practical reason that oleasters
grew along every irrigation ditch (adding greatly to the beauty of the
fields), and their fruits kept indefinitely. All the other ingredients
which he named could also readily be had locally, but often in 1964
a white sweetmeat was included, a modern luxury. The second food
distributed was bread, freshly baked in rounds like thick griddle-
cakes, called in Dari *luwok*. Up to the last century the *luwok* would
have been made of rye, but now the bread was always wheaten.
For the gahambars the Sharifabadis baked little rounds, the same
size as the ritual bread, called *drōn*, which was consecrated in
religious rites. (The custom of using unleavened dough for the
dron was no longer observed in the Yazdi region, so that the small
luwok and *dron* were indistinguishable.) Finally, when the endowment was sufficient, there was meat, provided by sacrificing a sheep or
goat. At a gahambar there might be a distribution of *lurk* only, or of
bread only; but at the best-endowed observances there was provision
of all three, *lurk*, bread, and meat.

Whenever bread was provided, there was much work to be done
the night before. All food to be blessed had to be prepared in ritual
purity (for it is a sin to consecrate anything unclean); and in the
houses of wealthy merchants in Yazd it was usual to have a second
kitchen which was kept solely for cooking food for religious purposes.
Every fire-temple too had a place with earthen oven and hearths for
preparing ceremonial foods. In a village home, however, all that
could be done was to dust and sweep and scour the one kitchen,
which though thus clean, invariably had its mud-brick walls
blackened by wood-smoke, which escaped only through a hole in
the roof.

The bread-baking for a gahambar was shared by family and
friends, and although hard work it was thoroughly enjoyed, as

a happy, convivial part of the festivities. The leaven was sought especially from a house where some dough had been kept from a recent baking for a religious observance; and there were so many family rites in Sharifabad (and also so many elderly women who lived alone and strictly kept the rules of purity) that there was never any difficulty about this. Mixing and kneading the dough, in great round pans, was men's work, and was done in the early evening. The men, who later did the baking also, were paid for their labours in corn, the usual village currency; but the women who came to help did so for nothing, as an act of piety—their personal contribution to the gahambar. At nightfall the boys of the family would go to relatives and friends to ask them in the name of the master of the house to give their aid; and later—sometimes, if it was to be a big baking, at ten o'clock, sometimes at two or three in the morning—they went round again to say that the oven-fire was lit, and that the helpers should come. The bakers swathed their heads and necks in cotton cloths, and wore heavy cotton gauntlets to protect their hands and arms from the heat of the fire. The women helpers broke bits off the dough and shaped them into little flat rounds, which the bakers put four at a time on a wooden platter and clapped against the hot earthen sides of the oven. As the baked loaves were taken out a few minutes later, other women gathered them up and put them in baskets to cool. The kitchen would grow very hot, even by night, and much tea was drunk. Girls enlivened the time with music, usually singing to a big tambourine, and small boys dozed in corners, and woke up to eat hot bread and enjoy the scene. When the baking was done, if there had been an animal sacrifice the carcass was put into the hot oven to roast; and then a clean cloth would be laid on the floor and all the helpers would sit down to share a convivial meal, with more tea to wash away the heat of the work.

The weary workers then separated, perhaps at four or five in the morning, to snatch a little sleep. (Often their number included women in their late seventies, who took their full share in the night's work.) The women of the house might well do without any sleep, however, so many were the tasks ahead of them. After the dawn sweeping and dusting, one of the household went to the priest with a bowlful of wheat or flour (which was his recompense for the ceremony that he was to perform), and *varderīn*, that is, fruits and herbs to be blessed by him as he solemnized the Yašt-e dron at his own house.[10] Afterwards these were fetched back to be eaten by the family as *čašni*. Meanwhile the house of the gahambar filled gradually with relatives from other villages, or from the city of Yazd, come by bicycle, donkey, or the morning bus to join in the celebration; and they had to be fed, and all made ready for the celebration of the gahambar itself.

The first gahambar which I was privileged to attend in Sharifabad was in the fourth festival, Ayāthrim, popularly called the 'Gāmbār-e Isfand', which then fell in February according to the traditional calendar. This celebration, on the first day of the festival, was held by Erdeshir Khodadadi, who lived in Tehran but had returned to an empty house to celebrate his grandfather's gahambar. After the night's convivial baking, first the men of the extended family, and then the women, were entertained to a morning meal. Then the courtyard and the surrounding rooms were sprinkled with water and swept once more, and at about noon the general company began to gather, until the courtyard was full of men and boys, with female relatives joining the women of the house in the kitchen. There was also a group of little girls of about five or six from some of the poorer village families, too young to be bothered by rules of propriety, who pushed their way sturdily through the throng in the yard and also disappeared into the dark kitchen.

This was in fact the first gahambar outside her own family circle which my young companion Piruza, then seventeen, Agha Rustam's second daughter, had ever attended, though her ten-year-old brother Gushtasp was a veteran of all such occasions. She and I retreated to the flat roof, from where we could also see the lane outside. A band of small boys were waiting at the house-door to go in with their school-teacher; and an old Moslem woman was there in her black veil, and a large patient dog, both hoping for doles of food. (Moslem beggars came regularly from Ardekan to seek charity from the Zoroastrians, but they made their way as unobtrusively as possible, to avoid the taunts of their co-religionists in Sharifabad.) A Moslem youth, instantly distinguishable by his blue shirt and black trousers, came down the lane driving a cow; and on seeing the Zoroastrian boys he picked up some large stones and flung them over the cow's

---

[10] *Varderīn* is evidently an abbreviation of Dari *myazd var drīn* (Persian *bar drōn*), the 'offering upon the *dron*'. The term was used as a synonym for *myazd* (see Sorushian, *Farhang*, 171, s.v.). The amount of recompense (*ašōdād*) offered to the priest varied with the size of the endowment.

head in their direction, but without hitting any of them. They stood their ground, and as he came level he hurled another stone directly at the dog, which yelped with pain and fled inside the house.

Inside the courtyard every man as he entered greeted the host, who was at the inner door to welcome his guests; and then each man, standing wherever there was room—knee-deep in boys if necessary—said the košti-prayers, facing the sun. When he had finished, he sat down on the cobble-stones of the courtyard, facing the *pesgam-e mas* or 'great portico'. The traditional Zoroastrian houses have two or four small porticoes opening on to the central courtyard, and one of these, called the 'great' one, regardless of its size, was kept especially for religious services, that is, although it might be used for most everyday purposes, efforts were made to keep it free from any ritual impurity.[11] For the act of worship a carpet was spread in this 'great' *pesgam*, and D. Khodadad took his seat on it, cross-legged, with the village elders at his side. For the recital of an Afrinagan service certain things were always set before him to be consecrated: fire in a metal vase and pure water in a bowl; sprays of evergreen (myrtle or cypress); milk and wine (or vinegar), bread and fruits, preferably pomegranate and quince. For this particular Afrinagan-e gahambar there was also a great mound of *lurk* on a striped cotton cloth, and big metal basins full of bread and meat, the latter shredded into small pieces. Other food was being cooked, and was brought to the carpet by the mistress of the house while the service was in progress, to provide what the Sharifabadis called *bōy-o-brang* 'odour and roasting';[12] for Zoroastrians, like the Hebrews of old, traditionally believe that the divine beings 'inhale the pleasant fragrance' of offerings, and are content. So the priest sliced in half the fruits which were set before him, to release their scent, and newly cooked foods were brought hot to the carpet. These might include any 'pure' foods such as were normally eaten. (There were a few things which were eaten but were regarded as ritually impure, and so never to be consecrated. These included the head, forelegs, and blood of the sacrificial animal.) There were, however, three essential dishes which were always prepared, and efforts were made to have these cooked if possible by a woman who

---

[11] See 'The Zoroastrian houses of Yazd', 128–9, with illustrations.

[12] Sorushian (*Farhang*, 19) gives the Yazdi and Kermani pronunciation of the last element as *bereng*, and translates the word by Persian *bū*, 'odour', taking the phrase as a hendiadys; but in Sharifabad it was pronounced and understood as above.

had undergone *nō-šwa*, that is, the great purification, and so was especially 'pure'. One of these dishes was *sīrōg*, which is a thin round of leavened dough, pierced with three holes, and fried with ritual purity either in the rendered fat of the sacrificial animal, or in specially prepared sesame-seed oil. Another was an egg, similarly cooked. This was held to be especially for the soul of the founder of the feast, for eggs were used in all observances connected with the dead, perhaps because of the symbolism of the round egg, new life and immortality. The third ceremonial food was a remarkable dish, *sīr-o-sedōw*, 'garlic and rue' which was also called the 'broth of Sroš'. For it garlic and rue were pounded together, then mixed with turmeric and cummin seeds, chopped coriander leaves, pepper, and salt. This mixture was fried until piping hot, when vinegar and water were added, and the resulting liquid was poured into a bowl containing chopped dried mint and some broken bits of 'clean' bread. *Sir-o-sedow* was primarily a ceremonial dish, prepared for its pleasant but pungent odour; and there is a story in old books of how it was invented to check the appetite of Ahriman. He had presented himself in the guise of a beggar at a gahambar feast given by Jamshid, and was devouring all that was put before him. In despair at not being able to satisfy a guest, Jamshid appealed to heaven, and was inspired to prepare *sir-o-sedow*; and after the first mouthful Ahriman declared himself sated and withdrew.[13] Nowadays the whole preparation is often used ritually. Nevertheless, so plain and unvarying was the daily village diet that towards the end of my stay I found myself joining the few who enjoyed *sir-o-sedow* eaten as a sop with bread, or sprinkled as a relish on other less highly seasoned dishes.

When D. Khodadad was ready to begin the service, the atašband of the fire-temple, standing at the side of the *pesgam-e mas*, raised his voice and addressed the congregation, using a fixed formula: 'Behdins [i.e. those of the Good Religion], know that today a gahambar is to be recited in the name of so-and-so, son of so-and-so. Ask that God should have mercy upon him, and upon those who have had a share in this pious work, and upon those who have entered here.' D. Khodadad then began the service, reciting steadily and with concentration, his eyes upon the fire and the objects to be blessed. The Avestan words were incomprehensible to all; but while the boys merely chattered and fidgeted unheedingly, the men con-

[13] See *Riv.*, Unvala, i. 428–9; Dhabhar, 322–3.

tinued softly reciting, either the liturgy of the service itself, if they knew it (but not in unison with the priest), or their own Avestan prayers, thus creating a murmurous undercurrent of sound to the priest's louder intoning. It was recognized in Sharifabad that every member of the congregation who wore the košti had a duty to join in the recital of Avestan, and only visitors from Tehran sat silent through the services, sometimes not even saying the košti prayers. There were, moreover, fixed points in every Afrinagan service where the congregation was required to make responses; and these points were signalled to them by the atašband as he stood watching the priest.[14] A moment is reached when the latter, as he utters the Avestan word *āfrīnāmi*, picks up one of the myrtle sprigs lying before him, and then the atašband turns to the congregation, right hand uplifted with the forefinger raised, and they repeat this word in full-throated response, also raising their right hands in the same way. Almost immediately, at the word *vīspō.khvāthrəm*, the priest takes up two sprigs of myrtle, the atašband raises his first and middle fingers, and the congregation follows him, repeating this word also. This ritual occurred four times in each gahambar service, and the explanation given for it was that one finger raised meant 'God is one', two fingers 'He is not two'. Whether or not this represents the original meaning of the ritual, it seems likely that such a deliberate affirmation of Zoroastrian monotheism developed under pressure from those Moslem polemicists who wilfully misinterpreted Zoroastrian dualism as meaning that Zoroastrians acknowledged two gods, rather than one beneficent and one malignant power. It is not easy to find a direct connection between the ritual and the text of the liturgy; but there is no doubt that the shared actions and responses united priest and congregation in a strong sense of corporate worship. For an observer the brief, sonorous responses were very impressive, and even the boys became momentarily alert. (It was in theory the duty of the atašband to act as *srōšāvarz* or discipliner, and he should, Agha Rustam said, carry a whip-chain with him, and brandish it over unruly boys; but the days of such firm measures seemed to be past, even in Sharifabad.)

At the end of the service was recited the brief Āfrīn-e Dahmān, also called the Hamāzōr-e Dahmān, because after it the worshippers make *hamazor*. This ritual, which seems to symbolize brotherly unity, was performed in the following way: the priest turned to the

[14] See Pl. Ia.

man seated next to him on the carpet, and each took the other's right hand between the palms of his own, while exchanging the greeting *hamāzōr bēm*, 'May we be of one strength'.[15] This salutation was passed down the line of those seated on the carpet. Meantime the atašband took up the metal fire-vessel and carried it around the congregation, withershins, calling out loudly as he did so *Hamazor bem*. There was a general response with these same words, and each man, as the fire was carried past him, stretched out his right hand and drew the smoke towards him, passing his hand down before his face from forehead to chin.

Then the master of the house prepared the *čom-e šwa* 'meal for the dog' (an essential rite which must be considered more fully later). The Sharifabadis also prepared a *čom-e māhī* 'meal for the fishes', by pouring some of the consecrated water into a glass, and adding broken bits of 'clean' bread and dried fruits. This was then poured, with recitation of Avesta, into a running stream—being evidently in origin a libation to the waters. The rest of the consecrated water was poured out on the ground, a libation to Spendarmad, earth; and the remains of the consecrated wine were sometimes dashed against the side of the courtyard, to release its fragrance as it touched the sun-warmed wall.

While such things were being prepared or done, the dahmobed and two helpers tied round their waists big striped cotton cloths, and filled these with the food to be shared among the congregation. (Since Erdeshir's gahambar was endowed for bread, meat, and *lurk*, three men were needed for this work.) The portion of bread was regularly two rounds for a man, and one for each woman and child, with meat and *lurk* in proportion. Especially large shares of everything, with larger rounds of bread, were given to the servants of the community, that is, the priest himself, the atašband, the dahmobeds, the guardians of the dakhma and the village shrines, the salars and the pakšus. Some of the food distributed was eaten sociably on the spot, and the rest was wrapped in clean napkins to be carried home, together with portions for the bedridden and those unavoidably absent. The host then stood again by the house-door, to bid his guests farewell, and they took their leave with a fixed formula: 'May *gāh* and *gahāmbār* protect thee!' Such leave-takings were

---

[15] The Parsis say instead *Hamāzōr bēd, hamō ašō bēd* (see Modi, *CC*, 209). The Irani usage was recorded by Khudayar Dastur Sheriyar in *Sir J. J. Madressa Jubilee Vol.*, ed. J. J. Modi, 305.

carried out with a grace and grave courtesy worthy of the courts of princes.

At the lane-door a little group of hopeful dogs had gathered by then, and they pleaded for a share of the food in the napkins, and got doles of bread, broken into three, the sacred number. Two Moslem beggars who were waiting by this time also received something from the master of the house, with a hearty *Khōš āmadīd* 'You are welcome!'; but food thus given in charity to unbelievers was never consecrated, but was taken to them direct from the kitchen. (Similarly at the gahambar celebrated on behalf of a family now turned Moslem, unconsecrated *lurk* was regularly sent to them.)

Since there were other gahambars to be celebrated on that day, the priest and elders, having left first, led the way, in the manner described above, to the next house, where the same observances were repeated. Sometimes there would be two endowed ceremonies at one house, solemnized in succession, and then every man present would 'make new the košti' again between the services, because this observance must precede every separate act of worship. The atašband carried the metal fire-vase with him from house to house, adding to the fire in it a few embers from each hearth-fire which had cooked food for a gahambar; and at the end of the day he took the vase to the fire-temple and set it in the presence of the sacred fire, for it was said that if a fire grew cold alone it went to the *divs*, but if it grew cold within sight of a sacred fire it went to the Amahraspands.

These were the basic rites of a gahambar, which might be shared in, without invitation, by any Zoroastrian who was in a state of purity, whether from the village or coming from outside. The other hospitalities of the five-day festivals were private matters, decided on by individual families, and for these invitations were given by word of mouth. These invitations, carried by boys, were again couched in set terms, as follows: 'So-and-so, son of so-and-so, sends his greetings and invitation to you, that you should come at noon and share the gahambar-salt with a mouthful of food.' These words were usually called out at the open house-door, and the formal answer of acceptance would come back from the depths of the house: 'We shall give you this trouble.' Such noonday gatherings were sometimes big affairs, and were conducted with a characteristic Sharifabadi mixture of simplicity and courtly good manners. A typical one, given by Turk Jamshidi, Agha Rustam's great-uncle, followed the celebration at his house of a gahambar with bread and meat. Long strips of cloth were laid on the ground in the *pesgam-e mas*, and the men and boys took their places at them. Turk himself being away in Tehran, his brother Jehangir did the honours for him, receiving the guests and waiting on them throughout the meal, while Turk's young son Rustam acted as water-pourer, filling and refilling glasses with courteous attentiveness. There was merry talk and laughter, with only two people following the ancient custom of eating with *bāj*—that is, in strict silence, between an initial and a concluding Avestan prayer.[16] (This custom was held to show respect to the Amahraspands Hordad and Amurdad, who protect the creations of water and plants.) One of the two was the priest, who sat flanked by loquacious laymen, but never then or on any other occasion when I was present broke his discipline of silence. I myself several times forgot, when sitting by him, that he ate and drank under this rule, and spoke to him during a meal; and he would then simply shake his head, and wait until he had finished and had 'left the *baj*' before answering. Even on the hottest summer days I never knew him to drink a sip of water without first 'taking the *baj*'.

The other persons who still ate 'with *baj*' were the salars, the corpse-bearers, who in their professional impurity followed almost as strict a rule of life as the priest in his purity. One of them, Khosrow, being a nephew of Turk's, was present by invitation at this gahambar feast. He had brought his own small square cloth, so as not to make contact (*paivand*) with others as he ate, and his own plate and glass. He spread the cloth in a corner of the *pesgam*, said the initial *baj*, and ate in silence. Jehangir waited on him with the same warm courtesy and attentiveness which he showed his other guests, serving him lavishly, while Khosrow indicated his wishes by signs of the hand.[17]

---

[16] See 'Zoroastrian bāj and drōn—II', 298-306.

[17] I also saw Khosrow sitting knee to knee among kinsmen in packed gahambar congregations; but a salar would go only to houses where he had once been invited, for there were families who regarded his presence as contaminating and dangerous, and who preferred merely to send the festival food to his home—always in generous double quantities, since his work was regarded as highly meritorious (*bā arj*). Others would never ask a salar to help them in the fields, lest he blight the earth and crops. It was one of the anomalies of Sharifabad in 1964 that while Khosrow himself pursued this ancient calling, with all its rules and restrictions, his younger brother was a veterinary surgeon with a thriving practice in Tehran. Khosrow had been a salar for about seven years. His younger partner, appointed in 1962, had succeeded to a man who had done the work for some twenty-odd years, and had been deeply respected for his self-discipline and

After the men and boys had eaten, the women and girls, who had been talking gaily in a side-room, rose in a colourful flock and came to take their places; and Jehangir waited on them as he had waited on the men, though a girl-cousin took over young Rustam's part. Lastly, when all their guests had been served, the family ate, while the others sat about the courtyard and entertained one another with talk and song.

There were still two or three houses in Sharifabad which offered a general hospitality, in princely style. At one, when the people had all gathered to hear the recital of the Afrinagan-e Gahambar, the master of the house had the outer door shut and barred, and kept the whole company captive to be his guests at the noonday meal. At two other houses the old custom was kept up of entertaining after dark. (This used to be the general practice, until a certain dahmobed persuaded most of the village to change to midday for their convivial gatherings, as more convenient.) At one of these houses, belonging to Rashid Rashidi, the whole Zoroastrian community of several hundred souls was invited to an evening meal. There was a big endowment here, with a gahambar of bread and meat at midday; and after dark there was noise and confusion in the narrow lanes as throngs of people came and went in merry family groups. With so many guests there were innumerable sittings, and as each finished they rose and made room for others. Their host was an old and sick man who could not move from his place, but his sons and a brother dispensed the usual gracious hospitality on his behalf; and despite the bustle and coming and going there was a sense of deep underlying piety, and of warm-heartedness towards one's fellow men. Another generous act of hospitality was performed by one Mihraban, who invited all the children from the two village schools, boys and girls (some sixty to seventy in all), to breakfast at his house before the recital there of the Afrinagan-e Gahambar. (The boys were fed, naturally, before the girls.)

The food on these festive occasions usually included meat-dishes (since in the hard times of the not so distant past holy days were often the only times in the year when the villagers tasted meat). A dish frequently offered to those who helped with the night-baking was *khīn-e jušunda*, 'boiled blood'. For this wheat-flour and salt

scrupulousness. (The salar had to live a semi-segregated life in his own home, avoiding *paivand* with his family while eating and drinking, and exerting, like the priest, a constant care.)

were added to the blood of the sacrifice, and when this mixture had hardened it was fried, water was added, and the whole brought to the boil, making a rich gravy which was sprinkled over other dishes— often over the fried liver. But since liver is ritually pure, while blood is not, the portion of liver for the dog had to be set aside before this was done. Another regular festival dish was *gīpā*. This consisted of a mixture of chopped meat with rice, herbs, fat, and seasoning, which was simmered in little bags made from the sheep's stomach. A tiny *gipa*, made from the end of the stomach, which formed a neat natural bag, was prepared especially for the dog, and was called a *bāybāyūk*. Other main dishes were *šurvā-ye beryānī*, a gravy-soup cooked in a pot at the bottom of the oven, under the roasting sheep; *šurvā-nakhōδ*, meat-soup with dried peas; meat fried with onions; other fries of marrow, onions, and eggs; and various thick pottages, with or without meat. In addition there was always freshly baked bread and usually white cheese, and in season garden-stuff such as lettuce, mint, or radishes.

In the intervals between the religious services and the family feasts, everyone spent the five festival days as he chose. Most went at some time to the fire-temple, to pray before the Ataš Bahram. For older people there was much visiting between houses, to meet relatives who had come from elsewhere, and plenty of talk went on; while young people met—girls and youths separately, of course—to sing and dance and amuse themselves. Often too they went in small groups round the village shrines, offering prayers and lighting candles at each; and the children played everywhere, and enjoyed the bustle of the preparations in different houses. Since the girls could not share with their young brothers the pleasure of going to a succession of gahambar celebrations, they made their own amusements, meeting at each other's homes to play games such as blind man's buff, tag, and skipping.

The first five gahambars were identical in observances, and were distinguished from one another only by the number of endowed ceremonies, and by the characteristics of the changing seasons. The sixth and last, at the year's end, had, however, some special usages, because it celebrated the achievement of all creation, except for pervading fire; and this was signalized by modelling all sorts of different things in diverse materials. Since these were to be consecrated, all the work was done with the greatest care for cleanliness and purity. The women and girls made a sweet dough, with

Ia (*above*). The moment of the first congregational response during an Afrinagan-e Gahambar (see p. 43). (D. Khodadad is in the corner, with Agha Rustam, in a straw hat, on his left. The man nearest the camera on the Dastur's right is Kay Khosrow-e Yadgar, with Hajji Khodabakhsh beside him, then Erdeshir Qudusi and Rustam Shehriari. Gushtasp, Agha Rustam's son, is sitting in front of Kay Khosrow, looking towards the atašband.)

Ib (*left*). Piruza, Agha Rustam's second daughter, giving the *čom-e šwa* (see p. 144).

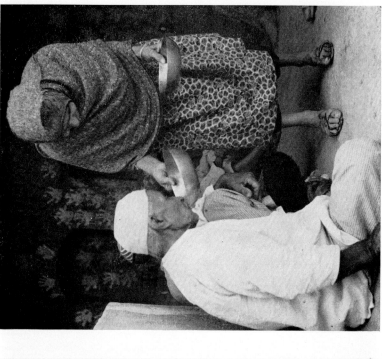

IIb. Piruza-e Dinyar giving Hajji Khodabakhsh a drink of water during *no-šwa* (see p. 122).

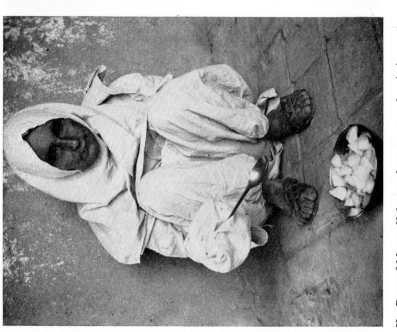

IIa. Banu of Mazra'-e Kalantar about to eat melon during *no-šwa* (see p. 123).

'pure' leaven, and shaped out of it stars and the moon, little figures of people, and familiar household objects such as a ladder, a hammer, or a shuttle of a loom. The boys, having washed face and hands, fetched fine clay from a bank just outside the village, mixed it with 'pure' water, and kneaded it into a smooth mass; and the next day, when this had begun to harden, the family joined in modelling it into free-standing figures. Among the favourites were domestic animals, cows, donkeys, sheep, and often a camel with panniers and a rider. A nightingale was often fashioned, and, oddly enough, another favourite was a peacock, its spread tail made with little clay-tipped sticks, which quivered if it was touched. Little sticks were also used for the legs of standing animals, and were then covered with clay. Household objects were modelled in clay too, such as a sugar-loaf, bowls, or a three-legged stool. When the clay was quite dry it was whitewashed, and the little pure white models were set in a group in the *pesgam-e mas*, to bear witness to the triumphant conclusion of all the works of creation. This custom was once general in Yazd itself and all the villages, but by 1964 it had been so long discontinued, except in Sharifabad and Mazraʿ, that only old people remembered it elsewhere.

The sixth gahambar merged partly with the feast of All Souls, Farvardīgān or Panjī, which had originally been kept on the last night of the old year, but which, as a result of the Sasanian calendar changes, was prolonged for ten additional days, the last five coinciding with the gahambar. Both festivals were accordingly followed directly by New Year's Day, No Ruz, the seventh feast of obligation. This was a very joyful holy day, which in ancient pagan times had presumably been simply a celebration of spring, held to welcome the resurgence of life in field and byre; but when Zoroaster refounded it, he made it more complex, a Janus-faced feast of great theological significance. On the one hand, as a spring feast it now not only celebrated the renewal of life here on earth, but served to remind his followers that one day, when evil had been overcome and the Last Judgement was at hand, men would break out of their graves, as leaf and blossom now break out of earth and branch, and would be raised up again in the flesh (for Zoroaster was the first to teach the conjoined doctrines of the resurrection of the body, the Last Judgement, and life everlasting). So, as a feast of hope and renewal, No Ruz was celebrated with symbols of newness and freshness, with a giving of gifts and a donning of new garments. Yet, on the other hand, it was the seventh feast of obligation, devoted to Ardvahišt and his creation of fire, and so it looked backward also to the old year, whose chain of festivals it triumphantly completed. Hence it was celebrated also with many and varied rites containing the number seven.

The dedication of this great holy day to Ardvahišt was marked chiefly in this way, that from midday of No Ruz the noontide watch, called 'Rapithwin', was restored, and all prayers said during its three hours contained an invocation of Ardvahišt.[18] Rapithwin, the spirit of noon, is a helper of Ardvahišt, as an embodiment of fiery heat. All through the summer, the beneficent season, his watch was kept, but with the onset of winter at Ayathrim, the fourth gahambar, Rapithwin was held to depart beneath the earth, there to keep the springs of water and roots of plants warm, and so prevent them dying from frost; and his watch was annexed to the first one, 'Hāvan', which was under the protection of Mihr, and he, therefore, was invoked then in all its prayers. But when No Ruz came to usher in spring and summer, then Rapithwin returned to earth, and the noontide prayers were addressed once more to Ardvahišt. His return offered not only an annual joy, but a yearly reminder of the doctrine that one day a perfect time, perennial summer, would be established again for ever upon earth. The observance of his watch, marking so vividly Ardvahišt's annual triumph over devilish winter, was plainly intended to bring this doctrine home, through recurrent devotional practice, to every worshipper;[19] and one could indeed hear the joy in the voices of village elders as they reminded their fellows in the early days of the new year that 'We have Rapithwin!'

Yet even in Sharifabad the doctrinal significance of what should have been the linked celebration of No Ruz and the six gahambars had been lost sight of; and the likelihood is that it had already been obscured for Zoroastrians before the coming of Islam through the confusions which followed the Sasanian calendar reform. These affected No Ruz more drastically than any other festival, and led in the end to its celebration being split between three days of the year, so that there came to be a secular No Ruz in the spring (which, being secular, survived under Islam), and two separate days for the

---

[18] On this and what follows see in detail 'Rapithwin . . .', 201–15.

[19] For the strong likelihood, therefore, that the watch of Rapithwin was instituted by Zoroaster himself see Boyce, *History*, i. 258–9.

religious No Ruz in Farvardin Mah (at whatever time of year that happened to be). So important were all three feasts that their celebration must be described in separate chapters hereafter. This multiplying of observances shattered the old, simple structure of the Zoroastrian devotional year, so that the fundamental link was lost between No Ruz and the gahambars. In consequence, the latter came to be celebrated as feasts simply in honour of Ohrmazd the Creator, rather than in honour of Ohrmazd and the six Amahraspands; and the little figures modelled at the sixth gahambar were thought of, not as celebrating the achievement of the six creations, but as being part of the rites of All Souls—as playthings, that is, for the souls of children. In this respect, therefore, what one must assume to have been one purpose of Zoroaster's foundation of the seven great feasts— to imprint his basic doctrines firmly in the minds of all his followers, simple as well as learned—was thwarted. What was presumably another purpose, namely to foster solidarity among them by bringing them together for worship, continued to be fulfilled; and there is no doubt that endowing and celebrating so many gahambars was one of the factors which helped to keep the Sharifabadis a close-knit community, united through the practice of their faith.

There was, moreover, another means by which their prophet's teaching about the seven Amahraspands and the seven creations was brought home almost daily even to the unlettered, and that was through the symbolism of the religious services. This symbolism was expounded to me in exactly the same terms by an old farmer in Mazraʿ Kalantar, by Agha Rustam, and by a Yazdi priest serving the Ataš Bahram in Tehran, D. Khosrow Jamshid Mobed. The seven Amahraspands, they each independently explained, were physically represented at every religious service through their own creations, in the following way: to Ohrmazd belonged the priest himself and the Avestan which he recited, to Vahman the milk, to Ardvahišt the fire, to Shahrevar the metal utensils, to Spendarmad the earth upon which the rite was enacted (the priest sitting always cross-legged upon the ground), to Hordad the water, and to Amurdad the bread, herbs, and fruits. This symbolism was generally under-stood by the Sharifabadis (for they and the villagers in Mazraʿ Kalantar were well instructed, from father to son, in the basic tenets of their faith); and so the link between the Amahraspands and their creations was continually presented to them in visual terms, as they took part in Afrinagans and other acts of worship.

Apprehending the doctrine, the villagers were conscious of serving the Amahraspands through their creations in their daily lives also, and this was yet another way in which their faith worked with the grain of human nature, adding an extra sense of purpose to the necessary tasks of every day. It was the religious element in their care of water and earth, plants and animals, which made Zoroastrians renowned even beyond the regions of Yazd and Kerman as good husbandmen, stockmen, and gardeners. Care for the creation of Shahrevar made them thrifty and yet charitable, and respect for that of man showed itself in honesty and uprightness. In the case of several of the creations their service also took special devotional forms. Thus there were mighty trees which were venerated individually as representatives of the creation of Amurdad; and in general evergreen trees—cypress, myrtle, and pine—were especially reverenced as symbols of immortality, as was the pomegranate, because of its many-seeded fruit. Such trees were regularly planted around fire-temples. The pomegranate was also cultivated in orchards, but even so to destroy a pomegranate with sweet fruits was regarded as a sin, and when in 1960 one died in the courtyard of Agha Rustam's house, he sent for a Moslem labourer to dig out the roots.

Water too was much reverenced, at springs and streams, and its cult was parallel in some respects to that of fire. These two were the most venerated of the creations, and so many and important were the rites connected with them that these must be considered separately in later chapters. A final point to be made in concluding this one is that the Zoroastrian veneration for the seven creations never stops at the physical world, or even with their own especial divine guardians, but has always for its final object the Creator of all things good, Ohrmazd himself.

3

SOME INDIVIDUAL RITES OF PIETY AND CHARITY

In one of the *Rivayats*[1] it is said that, if it were impossible, because of poverty, for anyone in a community to found a gahambar, then all the faithful there should join together to celebrate what the writer calls a 'gahāmbār-e tōjī', to which each should contribute what he could. The literal meaning of *tōjī* is obscure, but the learned translator of the *Rivayat* sought to connect the word with one surviving in Persian as *tōžī*, used for a 'schoolboys' picnic', and with the verb *tozīdan* in the sense of 'to gather, collect'. Communal celebrations of this kind among the Parsis were described by a European traveller in the eighteenth century; but in Iran by the twentieth century all celebrations during the six great seasonal festivals had come to be endowed, and the term 'gahambar-e toji' was then applied there to what for the laity was a very similar observance, that is, an Afrinagan service, with distribution of *lurk*, or *lurk* and bread, dedicated either to Ohrmazd or to one of the lesser yazads, and performed at some other time of year as an individual act of piety and charity. Such an observance, which (unlike the seasonal gahambar ceremonies) could be carried out, if wished, after sunset, and in any 'clean' place, might be performed only once, or become a regular institution. A gahambar-e toji was seldom endowed, however, and so a different verb was used in its respect: one 'gave' a gahambar-e toji, whereas one 'founded' a gahambār-e cakhra (in Dari gaambār-e čāra), that is, a true gahambar which belonged to the 'cycle' of the great six. Small ritual differences existed, moreover, in that the little rounds of bread for consecration belonged only to the major celebrations,[2] while for the humbler gahambar-e toji large rounds were baked as for everyday use, these being easier to make and distribute, and by custom in Sharifabad a blood sacrifice was never made for a gahambar-e toji.

The reasons for giving a gahambar-e toji were various. It might

---

[1] *Riv.*, Unvala, i. 439; Dhabhar, 325 and n. 1.   [2] See p. 38.

be done simply as an act of worship, or as one of thanksgiving, or of contrition, to atone for some offence which had perhaps been the cause of sickness or misfortune. It was because of celebrations of this third type that the word *toji* had come to be popularly linked with the Persian verb *tōzīdan* 'to expiate'. Celebrations of the second and third kind were often connected with a vow, taken to perform this ceremony in return for divine favour. A gahambar-e toji was also an essential part of the rite of 'exalting the fire'.[3] Because of the frequency of the celebration firstly of the gahambar-e čakhra (with numerous performances on each of thirty days in the year), and then of the misnamed gahambar-e toji, which was properly simply an Afrinagan or 'service of blessing', the term *gahambar* had come to oust in Sharifabadi (and indeed Yazdi) vocabulary that of *Afrinagan*, and was used generally to refer to any short 'outer' service, the standard liturgy being adapted, through different dedications, to a variety of occasions. D. Khodadad, however, often preferred the word *jašan* for such occasional services, using this in its basic sense of 'act of worship'.

The first gahambar-e toji which I myself attended was in Mazraᶜ Kalantar. It had been established by an old farmer, Rustam, and his niece Piruza as an act of worship and charity for the benefit of their souls, and it was celebrated annually in the village square on the first day of the Jašn-e Mihr Ized. This feast fell early in February, and so the celebration took place after sunset to let the men have all the short daylight hours in the fields. That year the night was dark and dank, with some drops of rain, and the carpet for the ceremony was spread under the arched entry of the village water-tank. D. Khodadad could not come from Sharifabad, so the service was conducted, with full ritual, by the dahmobed, with the village school-master and the miller sitting beside him on the carpet and also reciting the liturgy. Rustam was seated close by, his fine old face illumined by the fire- and lamp-light, and the other men and boys were packed around them, in the entry and on the steps leading down to the water-tank. The women and girls were out in the square, huddled in groups round small fires lit for warmth; and at one of these Piruza with some helpers did the ritual cooking for *boy-o-brang*, carrying the dishes as they were ready to place them before the dahmobed. At the end of the service the atašband, who had stood as usual to give the ritual signs to the congregation, exchanged a

[3] See below, p. 189.

hand-clasp, with the right hand, with each of the three men on the carpet, and then carried the fire-vessel round for the *hamazor*. When he reached the edge of the male assembly he handed the vessel over the heads of the last rank to one of the women, who bore it round those in the square. A brimming bowl of food was prepared for the *čom-e šwa*, and *lurk* was distributed, with a generous triple handful to each of the celebrants, and then the congregation drifted contentedly away into the rainy darkness.

In Sharifabad a similar gahambar-e toji, given purely as an act of worship, was, unusually, endowed, probably because it was linked with the celebration of a gahambar-e čakhra. The foundation had been made some seventy or eighty years earlier by the father of Erdeshir Dabestani, a village schoolmaster; and it was in honour of Shah Varahram Ized. The gahambar-e čakhra, which was generously endowed, with a blood sacrifice, was celebrated on Varahram Ruz of Tir Mah, the fifth day of the fifth gahambar; and on every other Varahram Ruz throughout the year, eleven times in all, a gahambar-e toji with *lurk* was celebrated at the fire-temple.

Another recurrent gahambar-e toji in the village was linked with the lesser rite of an 'āš-e khairāt' or 'charity pottage'. This observance had been instituted only two years earlier by the parents of a twelve-year-old boy, who had fallen backwards down a *qanat* well. Lines of these wells stretched along by some of the field-paths, and the smooth earth sloped straight down into the well-shaft, and in summer became as hard and slippery as ice. Mercifully the boy fell into deep water in the middle of the stream, missing the stones and clods which might have broken his back, and managed to crawl to one side, barely conscious, from where he was dragged up to safety by his companions. So every month thereafter, in thanksgiving for his escape, his parents distributed an aš-e khairat at the well-mouth, on the day of the accident, except in the 'beloved' months dedicated to fire and the guardian of fire, Azar and Urdibehišt, when instead they gave a gahambar-e toji at the empty Dastur's House (which was kept for religious observances).[4]

The gahambar-e toji could on occasion be a communal rite. Thus the Sharifabadis regularly held one whenever a group of them were together at the mountain shrine of Hrišt, each contributing to the *lurk* for this corporate act of worship (which thus seemed to merit the epithet of *toji*, properly understood). Similarly an aš-e

---

[4] See further below, p. 119.

khairat could be distributed as a communal act. Thus the Sharifa-badis all joined together for such an observance on the day after the Jašn-e Mihr Ized.[5] Every family then gave a contribution of corn, lentils, and the like, which they took to the fire-temple. There in the kitchen immense black cauldrons were set on two hearths, and the grain was simmered slowly together with the haunch-bones from the Mihr Ized sacrifices. The cooking began about ten o'clock in the morning. One of the dahmobeds was in charge, armed with a huge ladle lashed to the end of an ash-pole, and two other men with poles stirred the cauldrons. Others kept the wood fires burning brightly, so that it was hot work, even on a February day. People kept coming and going, to bless the work, and there was a constant murmur of Avestan from the hall of the fire-temple. The pottage was ready at about two o'clock, and a good, sustaining brew it was; and through-out the afternoon women from the poorer families came in ones and twos with bowls and basins to be filled. The dogs who had been patiently waiting kept the place tidy by licking up every splash of pottage that dropped from the dahmobed's ladle; and two Moslem beggar-women ate their dole on the spot, in small bowls which they had brought with them.

In the past, Zoroastrian theologians differed as to whether or not it was right to give alms to unbelievers, some holding that to do so was to strengthen Ahriman and the forces of evil, others main-taining that one weakened thereby the demons of poverty and hunger;[6] and practice differed also in the twentieth century. In Kerman I had seen food given by Zoroastrians to Moslem beggars, as in Sharifabad; but once I was privileged to attend a big anniversary-ceremony at the house of Arbab Shehriar of Nusratabad, where the day's ceremonies ended with the distribution of an aš-e khairat (again cooked in the fire-temple kitchen). Two men ladled it out, and I ventured to ask one of them what he would do if Moslem mendicants appeared, and he replied simply, with a fierce flash in his bright blue eyes, 'They would not dare!' He went on to say that the Nusratabadis never gave alms to Moslems, who (he opined) did nothing to deserve them. The village was a relatively new settle-ment, founded about 1880, and probably most of the Zoroastrians who came there did so to escape harsh pressures elsewhere. Even in their new home, however, they suffered much from city roughs

[5] Reckoned as the *seventh* day of the festival.
[6] For references see 'Toleranz und Intoleranz', 337–8.

descending on them from Yazd, so that a special fieriness of spirit may well have grown up among them. But indeed it was the charity of the other places which was the more remarkable, in the light of the Zoroastrians' prolonged sufferings everywhere at Moslem hands.[7]

The Nusratabadi pottage was made as a charity and *yād-būd*, in memory of the dead man and for his soul's sake; and it was distributed to every Zoroastrian house in the village, being carried by boys in basins which were the *vaqf* property of the fire-temple. These basins they put on pads on their heads, and for some of the smallest of them it was quite a feat balancing the steaming hot vessel, especially as it was a cold winter's day with a bitter wind blowing to numb their bare hands and feet; but they came and went briskly and cheerfully, for the comforting reward of a bowlful of the pottage when they had done.

A big aš-e khairat—on an even larger scale than this one—was distributed every year during the spring No Ruz holiday at the mountain shrine of Pir-e Hrišt, not far from Sharifabad. This was done in fulfilment of a vow by Mihraban Kerbasi of Yazd, who had long been childless. He had solemnly sworn at the shrine that if he were granted a son, he would perform this charitable act there every year; and thereafter, in 1952, his wife bore him a boy, their only child. So each year in the spring Mihraban went with his son to Hrišt to fulfil his vow, and people travelled from Yazd and all the villages to take part in the observance. In 1964 great cauldrons of rice-pottage were cooked and shared among all those present at the shrine, and some was sent for *čašni* to the Belivanis, and was eaten cold. It tasted good even so, though the wood-smoke flavour was then more pronounced than usual.

Much more commonly an aš-e khairat was a small affair, confined to the family and chosen friends and neighbours. If the pottage were distributed as far as three doors away, said D. Khodadad, then this was by definition a 'khairat'—an act of charity—which benefitted the giver's soul. The rite was therefore often performed simply to acquire merit, and especially during the 'beloved' months of Azar and Urdibehišt, for these were months of *yek-e dah* when (it was believed) the merit of each good work was multiplied by ten.

[7] The almost certainly ancient custom of distributing 'charity pottage' was kept up by the Moslems of Iran; but it would have been unthinkable that any adherent of the old faith should ever have asked for or received a share in a Moslem benefaction. Even the Nusratabadis, however, occasionally (when away from their own village) gave doles to Moslem beggars, see below, p. 265.

When the rite was on a small scale, the preparation and distribution alike of the pottage was left to women, the men's part being simply to eat a bowlful of it when they came home from their day's work.

Such small occasional aš-e khairat could be held almost anywhere —at the house itself, in the fields, at the door of a shrine, by a stream, or often *sar-e kītar* 'at the top of the lane'; and there were a variety of recipes to match the variety of places, although on such modest occasions meat was never an ingredient. The most popular pottage was *āš-e hmīr* 'dough pottage' (Persian *āš-e rište*), for which fine strips of dough (not unlike noodles) were added to a vegetable broth. Then there was wheaten pottage, *āš-e gannom*, and *āš-e kāšk*, made with barley, and *āš-e šūlī*, for which flour was sieved and roasted before being added to the broth. This was cooked especially during the winter months, as it was very satisfying.

On one auspicious day in late April the Belivanis gave a small aš-e khairat in the angle of the lane outside their home. It was a very quiet lane, with only the Rashidis' house beyond theirs, and Murvarid Khanom was of course among those invited, together with Piruza her sister (D. Khodadad's wife), three women friends, and their young children. As usual in Sharifabad, the preparations were shared by hostess and guests as a thoroughly enjoyable, sociable part of the proceedings. In mid afternoon a fire was lit in the lane and a big covered pot full of water was set on it. The dough, already mixed, was carried out there, and the first of the guests arrived, bearing sweetmeats and marjoram, which she distributed among us, and also half a bowl of sieved flour, which she emptied on a clean white cloth spread on the ground. The other guests did the same in their turn, and a merry group formed round the cloth and worked as a team, kneading the dough, rolling bits of it out flat with long slim rolling-pins, flouring the pieces with the guests' fine flour, and cutting them into thin strips. During this process the small boys begged for bits of dough, and, wrapping them round peeled sticks, cooked them at the fire to still the pangs of hunger as they waited, while Parizad, D. Khodadad's elder daughter, played the tambourine and there was singing. Meantime a big beetroot had been sliced into the simmering pot, to be followed by several pounds of beans and chickpeas, and a bowlful of fried onions seasoned with pepper, salt, and saffron. When these were all well cooked, the strips of dough were added, and in about five minutes the pottage was ready, and was eaten merrily round the fire just before the sun went down.

Bowlfuls of the pottage were given to the guests to take home for the men of their families, and when the pot had been emptied, a candle was lit on each side of the cooking-fire, and Parizad performed the curious little rite of 'Nakhod-e mošgel-gošāy', while the Rashidis' pretty little speckled hens, let out for the purpose, pecked up every bit of flour or spilt pottage around us. Then Piruza, Agha Rustam's daughter, collected in a brazier the embers of the cooking-fire (which by this rite had become *yešte*, consecrated) and took them to the fire-temple. There we found D. Khodadad and Rustam the atašband seated in the hall reciting the evening prayers, their tenor and baritone voices blending pleasantly. Piruza put her little brazier on the pillar-altar there, and Rustam rose in silence and with a *bara* (a metal implement consisting of a flat disc on a long handle) transferred part of the embers from it to a big vase, already nearly full of embers from other consecrated fires, which was standing on the altar. Then, the sun having set, D. Khodadad rose in his turn, took a single *bara*-ful of embers from this vessel, and carried it into the sanctuary, where he laid it on the ash at the rim of the sacred fire itself, before performing the evening *bōy* ceremony, with ringing of the sanctuary bell.[8] While we waited and watched, a youth and two young boys came in to say their evening prayers.

An aš-e khairat was frequently given in this simple fashion to invoke divine blessings for some special undertaking, as when some-one was setting out on a journey; and one was often held to celebrate a young child's birthday. Agha Rustam's little son Shahvahram, a sweet-tempered and delightful baby, as fair-skinned and blue-eyed as a northerner, had his first birthday in May of 1964, and an aš-e khairat was prepared in the house with the aid of a throng of affectionate relatives and friends, who as they arrived scattered their marjoram leaves over his small green bonnet. This time a barley-pottage was cooked, and since the cooking was done indoors there was dancing as well as singing by the girls. The final ritual was exactly the same, with candles lit each side of the hearth-fire, the recital of Nakhod-e mošgel-gošay, and the carrying of embers to the fire-temple, for these were fixed elements in offering a domestic aš-e khairat.

Just as the aš-e khairat could be a separate act (as on these occa-sions), or form part of a more elaborate observance, so too the ritual of Nakhod-e mošgel-gošay 'the difficulty-resolving peas', although

---

[8] For these matters see in more detail, below, pp. 72 ff.

essential to it, could also be performed separately, and very often was. This was purely a matter for women, and being very simple was a rite which even the poorest widow could afford to carry out. All that was needed for it was a handful of chickpeas, as they had been brought in from the fields, although the more affluent would make this a bowlful, and often mix raisins with the peas. The rite could, like an aš-e khairat, be performed anywhere; and the first time that I was aware of it in all its details was when it was done by Agha Rustam's elder sister Banu (who lived in Yazd) at the shrine of Hrišt. She climbed the hill to the shrine accompanied by her sisters Piruza and Murvarid, and her nieces Shahnaz and Piruza (Agha Rustam's daughters). She spread out a kerchief full of peas and raisins in the shrine's porch, and began, with Shahnaz's help, the tedious everyday task of picking out the chaff which was mixed with them. As she did so, she told a long, rambling tale about a poor wood-gatherer and his beautiful daughter. In the beginning, the story ran, these two were so sunk in poverty that the father despaired; but one night three beings clad in green appeared to him in a dream, and bade him buy chickpeas and tell his story and do good (that is, give away the peas in charity), and then they would make him rich. He did as they told him, grew wealthy, and went on pilgrimage, exhorting his daughter not to neglect the rite while he was away; but she, though meaning well, forgot. She met a princess, was befriended by her, but was subsequently suspected of stealing her jewels and was imprisoned. The father, returning, chided his daughter, performed the rite again, and then, with divine aid, established her innocence. She was pardoned by the king, who betrothed her in marriage to his only son; and she never thereafter forgot to perform the rite at frequent intervals.

All the time that Banu was telling this story (familiar to the others in every detail), her niece Piruza kept up a constant encouraging stream of *Bale, bale*, 'Yes, yes', as is required by the rite, while once Shahnaz reminded her of a sentence she had forgotten. When the story was finished, the elder Piruza took over with a soft murmur of Avestan, until the peas were judged to be perfectly clean. Then they were carried into the shrine, and a handful was scattered over the sacred rock. What remained was distributed in handfuls, with a murmured blessing, to each person present in the shrine or met on the way down the hill. In Sharifabad itself the initial rite was performed anywhere—at home or in the lanes—and then a handful of peas would be taken to one of the shrines and left on its pillar-altar, and the rest distributed to companions or people met along the way. Since the rite ended with Avestan (any Avestan prayer was acceptable), the peas were consecrated, *yešte*, and so to eat them conferred a blessing. Anyone might eat those which were left at a shrine. This humble little observance embodied admirably the Zoroastrian ethic that man must care for his fellow man, and that charity to others is needful before one can look for divine help oneself. Poverty in Iranian villages naturally did not await the coming of Islam, and the observance seems to be an old one, since a similar rite, with an identical story, was carried out by Parsi women in their traditional centres.[9]

Men, too, naturally sometimes felt the need to make some small special act of thanksgiving or intercession, and then they would usually go to the fire-temple or a shrine, light candles, offer incense, and pray. Thus Isfandiar of Mazraʿ Kalantar told me how one summer's day when he was cycling home from the fields with a load of cucumbers on his back he in his turn slipped on the edge of a *qanat* well and fell in, bicycle and all; but he was as lucky as the Sharifabadi boy, since he landed in the dry water-course with the cucumbers underneath him and the machine on top, so only the fruits were seriously hurt. There was a shrine close by, and as soon as he had recovered he made haste to light candles and make offerings there in thanksgiving for his escape. Men also on occasion offered the costly blood sacrifice, when the boon they sought seemed a great one, or they had much reason for thankfulness. The Sharifabadis usually made this offering at one of the mountain shrines, and the rite will be considered in detail in the chapter concerning them. One time when I was present at such an offering made as an individual act, independent of any major observance, was when D. Khodadad's son-in-law Kaus, who lived in Tehran, had injured his right wrist, so that he could not work. He offered a pure white goat (carefully chosen for its colour) at the shrine of Hrišt, with a prayer for healing. This too was a family observance, to which men and women alike were invited from three or four of the extended family group. Some of the meat was eaten at the shrine, and the rest was brought back to the village to be shared among other relatives and

---

[9] Information from Mrs. Khorshed Daruwala, formerly of Aden, where many traditional ways were preserved in isolation. She translated the Parsi version of the story for me from a Gujarati *Khorda Avesta*.

friends, and sent as additional 'khairat' to the community officials (the atašband and others). A gahambar-e toji with *lurk* was solemnized at the shrine itself.

Women seldom made an animal sacrifice, unless jointly with their husbands, but there were some elaborate minor observances carried out by women alone, at which hens were offered up. One of the main authorities in the village for the exact performance of such rites was Shirin-e Set Hakemi, who in 1964 was well over a hundred years old, and had outlived not only her husband and all her ten children, but her grandchildren as well. She moved bent double, like the conventional image of a witch, but with an effort could straighten herself briefly and regard one with great dark eyes, set in what had clearly once been a beautiful face. She spoke only Dari, and could neither read nor write, but her memory was capacious and clear, and she possessed a wealth of knowledge about old ways, and about these semi-secret observances performed by women for their own especial needs. Of her deep, sincere piety there was no doubt—a fact which one had to reconcile as best one could with the nature of some of these rites, which seemed purely magical in character. Several of them centred on setting out on a cloth or *sopra* (Persian *sofre*) a variety of objects and foodstuffs in honour of some supernatural being, the rite being called accordingly the Sopra of So-and-so. One of them, performed to get relief from illness or pain, was the Sopra-ye Sabzī, 'The Green One's Cloth'. The sufferer and the wise woman who helped her had to prepare this cloth together in unbroken silence, and no one must intrude on them, or 'the person below the earth' (*ādam-e šīw-zwīn*) would not accept their offerings. Further, no inscribed *vaqf* vessels might be used on the cloth, no iron or salt was to be placed there, no Avestan might be uttered, nor the name of God invoked. After the cloth was fully prepared, with the sacrifice of a black hen, the sick woman lay down beside it, and the helper covered her with a green covering, scattered marjoram leaves over her, and withdrew. She had to sleep there alone all night, and on rising must break her silence by invoking 'Shāh Parī and the daughter of Shāh Parī', and then taste a little of everything on the cloth.

The rite itself thus seemed thoroughly irreligious, with every care being taken to do nothing which might drive away the evil powers; for 'Shah Pari' was conceived as a heartless and capricious creature, able to help, but given also to such malicious pranks as stealing a baby that was left alone and leaving a miserable changeling in its place. Yet the intention of the rite itself was innocent, to obtain help for an illness which would not yield to medicine; and in each case described to me the trouble seemed psychosomatic, and was cured by the rite. The woman or girl, that is, had become unexpectedly 'unclean' in a holy place, and was so oppressed by the burden of her sin that she became really ill and needed something more than physicking to help her recover. There were priestly rites available,[10] but the old wives' ones sometimes seemed more efficacious to the troubled women. Moreover, care was taken to limit any malign effects of practising them. Thus when the Sopra-ye Sabzi was concluded, the priest was asked to come to the house to pray. Further, the seven silver coins that had been placed inside the roasted hen on the cloth must be used to buy oil for sanctuary-lamps, the eggs and white cheese from the corners of the cloth must be given to the poor, and the rest of the food must be shared hospitably with whoever came to the house.

Such pious conclusions to the rite did not mollify the elders of Sharifabad, who were strongly opposed to such dubious practices; but a problem which confronted them in any rituals devoted to 'Shah Pari' was the identity of this supernatural figure. On the one hand, there was Shah Pari the stealer of infants, who was clearly queen of the malicious *pairikās* of the Avesta, shameless servants of the Evil One, with whom one should have no dealings. On the other hand, 'Pari' was regarded as an abbreviation of the name of Paridon or Pariyon, the Avestan Thraētaona (Persian Faridun), who was endowed with powers of healing, and whom Zoroastrian priests regularly invoke, with a special Avestan prayer, for help in times of sickness. Between wise woman and priest the invocations of *pairika* and semi-divine physician appeared by the twentieth century to have become inextricably confused. D. Khodadad himself explained to me that Shah Pari was a benign being, a *fereŝte* (angel), not like the many wicked *pairikas*. Shirin too and the other village women were positive that Shah Pari was male, but said that he had two daughters, one clad in white, the other in green, thus linking him with the female *paris*. Because of such developments, the dubious cult of Shah Pari was difficult to check, and it had indeed received a great stimulus through apparently miraculous happenings in the twentieth century at the village of Kuče Buyuk, not far from Yazd.

[10] See pp. 208–10.

Here there lived a very kind, good, religious woman named Mihrbanu. As a fourteen-year-old orphan she had been married to a man of sixty, and her sorrows were increased when the first two sons she bore him died. The third child, also a boy, was only six months old, and ailing, when her husband too died. She was in despair when she dreamt that two women, the daughters of Shah Pari, came to her and offered to care for the child as Shah Pari's son, if when he grew up he would perform charitable acts and do good, which Mihrbanu gladly undertook on his behalf. Further, they said, she was to set apart a room in her house as belonging to them, and lay a Sopra-ye Shah Pari in it regularly. In the morning she found the baby actually sitting up sturdily, in perfect health. She duly swept and garnished a room for her visitants, and latched its door, but the door at once flew off the latch, and thereafter she never could fasten it herself. But other, invisible, hands opened or shut it, and sometimes a lamp was mysteriously lit there, and every month she set out in it a Sopra-ye Shah Pari.

The boy, generally known as Sohrab-e Shah Pari, throve, went to Bombay, and prospered there; and he sent back money to adorn the room. Mihrbanu had a pillar-altar built in it, and a water-tank beside the house, for the use of the whole village; and the monthly observance of the Sopra became famous, so that not only women seeking sons, or cures for illness, flocked there, but men too came, among them well-to-do and respected citizens of Yazd, who offered sheep and goats, so that the rites became more and more elaborate. (The men were not admitted to the inner rite, but met in the courtyard to make their offerings and vow their vows.) On one day in the year, that of the original miracle, the setting-out of the cloth was particularly lavish, and the throng of people grew to be so great that the Kuče Buyuk elders (not wholly approving) protested, and this special observance was abandoned, the cloth being set out thereafter in the same way each month.

The observance of a Sopra-ye Shah Pari, although it became prominent through Mihrbanu, did not originate with her, but seems to have been of some antiquity; and, unlike the Sopra-ye Sabzi, it was admitted within the orbit of the faith. Thus, as old Shirin affirmed, Avestan belonged to the rite, with the košti-prayers, and iron and salt might be put on the cloth. A woman would vow to set out the Sopra in the hope of divine help, and she must then do so monthly for the first year, and thereafter usually annually. Thus another Shirin from Cham, whom I met when she came to Sharif-abad for *no-šwa*, told me that her grandmother had begun a Sopra-ye Shah Pari in order to be blessed with children. She herself had learnt from her the story of Shah Pari (different, she said, from the one Mihrbanu told at her Sopra). She then offered a Sopra in her turn for the boon of a happy marriage, which was granted her; but when she went with her husband to Tehran she abandoned the rite, mainly because of practical difficulties (such as keeping a special room for it in the house). However, when two years previously she became very ill, she began it again, was cured, and thereafter maintained it annually, and also lit candles in the room on holy days.

The first Sopra-ye Shah Pari (as far as was known) ever to be prepared in orthodox Sharifabad had been instituted only a few years earlier by Khorshed Kausi, after she had borne seven daughters. She went to Kuče Buyuk, made an offering at Mihrbanu's Sopra, and vowed to prepare one herself for the boon of a son. The next year a son, Khodadad, 'Given by God', was duly born to her; and she in her turn dreamt that night that a sumptuously clad man— Shah Pari himself—appeared to her, and said that he would come each month as the guest of Khodadad, and that such-and-such a room should be set apart for him. In her dream he led her to this room; and the next morning she found that an unfinished piece of cloth on the loom outside was fully woven. So on that day, Zamyad Ruz, in each month throughout the first year, Khorshed prepared the Sopra, inviting friends to the rite; and at the end of the year she sacrificed a sheep, and there was great rejoicing. Thereafter she spread the Sopra annually, and declared that she would sacrifice another sheep when Khodadad (then a handsome five-year-old) was fully grown. (Khorshed's husband had died three months after Khodadad was born, and of her daughters six had married and left the village, one to live in Bombay, the other five in Tehran, so only Golchihr remained to help her mother in the home, and with the annual observance.)

Piruza Belivani had represented her mother Tahmina at the in-auguration of the Sopra, and in 1964 she went again, taking me with her at Khorshed's kind invitation. The night before, Khorshed had put steel into a bowl of water, with marjoram leaves; and that morning she had bathed and remained fasting. The floor of the little, windowless room devoted to Shah Pari was almost wholly covered with white plaster, and on this, having said the košti-prayers, she laid a snow-white cloth. There was a mirror at the back, two candles on whitewashed bricks, fresh greenery, and rose-water in a glass flagon. Three tall sugar-cones were covered by green silk handkerchiefs, and one bore an old-fashioned silver bridal ornament over the handkerchief, another a gilt chain. There was every other possible white thing on the cloth, from a little saucer full of gypsum to white cheese, sweetmeats, milk, cooked rice, peeled almonds, and salt. There were fruits, cut open, in abundance, and a pomegranate with a silver coin stuck in it. There was wine and vinegar, nuts, raisins, herbs, melon, and sunflower-seeds. Towards the front of the cloth was a big silvery tray, and each guest brought with her dried peas for Nakhod-e mošgel-gošay, and poured them on to it. All brought candles too, and lit them on the floor in front of the cloth, so that the room grew very bright; and each, having lit her candle, said the košti-prayers. Other gifts, as well as the peas, were brought to be put on the cloth, and some offered hens, which were duly sacrificed in the yard. The additional cooking for *boy-o-brang* was noodle-pottage, bread, and the essential *sirog* and eggs, and some of these things, as they were cooked, were brought to the cloth with the hens, roasted and stuffed with rice and seven kinds of spices. Many other cooked dishes were set out there already, carefully prepared the day before.

Meanwhile those in Shah Pari's room continued to recite Avestan till all had assembled, at about noon. Then the tray with its mound of chickpeas was lifted off the cloth and put on the floor, and everyone sat in a circle round it. A young girl poured pure water into a copper bowl, and sprinkled marjoram leaves on it; and throughout the recitation which followed she and two other little girls beat on this copper bowl with sticks. (One of the three was Paridun Rashidi's pretty little daughter Keshwar, a six-year-old.) Khorshed herself sat with the big mirror from the cloth in her hands, and gazing into it told three stories in succession, while the rest were at work cleaning the peas. The first story was that of Nakhod-e mošgel-gošay itself, the second that of Shah Pari, and the third an account of her own vow and its happy consequences. The story of Shah Pari was another rambling folk-tale, and neither in this Sharifabadi version nor in that told in Kuče Buyuk had it anything to do with Paridon/Thraetaona, or any marked ethical content, Shah Pari appearing in it as a strange, capricious being. After the three stories were told, Khorshed prayed softly in Avestan until the peas were finished.

Then she rose and, taking the copper bowl, carried it round the company, putting a spoonful of the water into the cupped hands of each person. Finally, she sprinkled some of the peas on the cloth, between the many dishes, and gave a handful to everyone present.

The little room had grown very hot, with the burning candles and so many of us packed into it; and the rite being finished, the company adjourned to the courtyard for singing and dancing, and some cheerful mime, with Parizad, the Dastur's daughter, dressed as a man, and another girl as a fashionable Tehrani woman, in short sleeveless dress, looking startlingly immodest in that village setting. Then the midday meal was eaten, and the company broke up with many expressions of gratitude and goodwill. Some went into Shah Pari's room to take their leave, much to the disapproval of an older woman, who pointed out to me that they were *dast-prangīn*, that is, they had not washed their hands after eating, and so were in no fit state to enter a holy place. The next day D. Khodadad was asked to the house to pray, and recited the *Ahunavad Gah* beside the Sopra; and this concluded the ceremony for that year.

Although the Sharifabadi elders looked askance even at the Sopra-ye Shah Pari, as an unnecessary rite outside the mainstream of orthodox observance, it is readily understandable why their womenfolk, suffering from two great pressures—the need to bear sons and to keep the purity laws—should have sought help in diverse ways when they failed under either. There were other small rites performed by men and women, even in Sharifabad, to avert evil or to obtain good, which belonged, like the Sopra-ye Sabzi, to folklore and magic rather than to religion; but in the main it was a matter for admiration how well the villagers upheld the basic principles of their faith, in worshipping only God the Creator and his ministers. While doing so they sought also to do good to their fellows, so that a spirit of kindliness and charity informed their minor as well as their major observances.

4

SACRED FIRES AND EMPTY SHRINES

DOWN the centuries Zoroastrians have been called by those of other faiths 'fire worshippers', a name which thinking members of the community indignantly reject, saying that they worship only God. Fire, they declare, was appointed by Zoroaster simply as an object in whose presence men should pray, in order to fix their thoughts on righteousness—for fire, he taught, was the creation of Ardvahišt, the hypostasis of all that is right and just. To pray before fire is thus, they argue, no more than to pray before a crucifix or icon; and, living as they do among Moslems, they sometimes call fire a *qibla*, the thing, that is, which helps them to turn their thoughts towards God, as the *qibla* in a mosque helps the worshippers there to turn towards Mecca.[1]

This, the standpoint of the intellectual Zoroastrian, has probably been that of individuals down the ages. The matter is not, however, as simple as it thus sounds. Long before Zoroaster preached, fire had been an object of cult for the Iranian peoples, who venerated the hearth fire as a god within the home—a god whom they worshipped with threefold ritual offerings, of wood, incense, and oblations of fat.[2] This cult, common to the Indians and Iranians, may well go back to Indo-European times. Among the pagan Iranians it had evidently become enriched, at least for the learned, by the philosophical concept of fire as the pervasive element—the seventh creation— which animates all the world; and there were also ethical ideas attaching to it as a symbol of justice, because of its use in judicial ordeals. All these elements of ritual and belief seem to have been gathered together by Zoroaster when, in the light of his own revelation, he placed fire under the protection of Ardvahišt, and enjoined

---

[1] The usage is supported by an interpolated verse in the Persian epic (see Firdausi, *Shahnama*, Tehran edn., 1935–6, i. 19, line 9), and presumably evolved in early debates between Zoroastrians and Moslems.

[2] See Boyce, *History*, i. 70, 153–5.

on his followers that they should pray in its presence, and should think, as they made their offerings to it, of all that it represents.[3]

The Zoroastrian cult of fire is thus complex, embracing immensely archaic and primitive elements as well as highly developed spiritual ones; and these occur together in the Avestan prayer to fire, the *Ataš Niyayeš*, which contains both morally elevated utterances from the *Gathas*, and others, clearly even more ancient in essence, which invoke fire as the god upon the hearth, one 'worthy of sacrifice, worthy of prayer, in the dwellings of men'.[4] Even if it had not been so—if Zoroaster in ordaining prayer in the presence of fire had been introducing something wholly new and symbolic—there can be no doubt that in the course of time fire would have grown to be more than merely an object for all but the most intellectual of his followers; for fire is not only a beautiful thing, but with its movement and changes of state seems to be alive, and can readily be apprehended as sentient and aware of the services of its worshippers, whose attention it constantly demands. Believers in other faiths have found no difficulty in induing immobile, undemanding statues with life, and it is not to be looked for that Zoroastrians should differ in this respect in their attitude to their icon, fire. Moreover, those who venerate images or pictures have tended to regard these as possessing an individual life, somehow distinct from the general concept of the divinity or saint whom they represent; and similarly most Zoroastrians regard a sacred fire, enthroned in its own consecrated house, both as representing the whole creation of fire and also as being an individual divine being, who dwells in that particular place and watches over his worshippers, accepting their offerings and hearkening to their prayers. So strong is this sense of the individual fire as a person that in old Parsi documents a sacred fire is regularly referred to as 'Srī Ātaš Sāheb'. In Sharifabad the villagers unquestionably regarded their fire as a divinity, powerful and protective; but veneration for it, although profound, was naturally subordinated to veneration for Ohrmazd, who was its Creator, as he is the Creator of all else that is good.

A further complexity—or enrichment—in the Zoroastrian cult of fire comes from the dedication of each temple-fire of the highest grade to Verethraghna, the ancient yazad of Victory, now known in

---

[3] For the literature on this subject, and the evidence that Zoroaster himself made the traditional offerings to fire, see Boyce, *History*, i. 214 ff.

[4] *Ataš Niyayeš*, 7.

Dari as Varahrām or Vahrām, in Persian as Bahrām. This dedication probably goes back to the time when temple fires were first installed as a development of the cult of the hearth fire—most likely, that is, to the fourth century B.C.[5] One can only guess at the reasons for it; but a paramount one was probably that these great fires were seen as warriors in the battle of Zoroastrianism against ignorance and alien faiths, and so were devoted, in a spirit of hope, to Victory. The cult of Verethraghna was evidently immensely popular in ancient Iran; and in time, because of the sense of his power, this yazad was called on by his worshippers not only to grant them success in war, but also to protect them in all the perils of daily life. Thus he came to be invoked, instead of the yazad Čisti, to guard wayfarers, becoming as it were the Zoroastrian St. Botolph or St. Christopher; and in the Seleucid period a shrine to him was carved at Bisutun, beside the great highway that passes under Darius's rock.[6] In Islamic times the Irani Zoroastrians raised other shrines to him as the Pīr-e rāh-gozār, the 'Traveller's Saint', while the Parsis in Gujarat named him Panth Yazad, the 'Divinity of the Way'. One of the little Irani shrines stood just to the north of Mazraᶜ Kalantar, by the old highway from Isfahan to Yazd,[7] so that travellers could pray there before setting out on the next stage of their journey, or light a candle in thank-offering as they approached the village. There was another such shrine at Ahrestan, a village just outside Yazd on the Shiraz road, where again travellers could pray either before setting out on a journey, or after completing it. The ancient hymn to Varahram (Yašt 14) was regularly recited, moreover, on behalf of those who went on journeys, to keep them under the yazad's protection.

Varahram was also invoked at other times of peril. Thus within recent memory there was an occasion when fierce storm-floods threatened to sweep away Zoroastrian houses in the hill-village of Taft; and the head of the local anjoman, Namir Mizanian, stood beside the waters with two of the village elders, chanting the hymn to Varahram, and their level dropped and the peril passed. D. Khodadad himself told me of another occasion when he was asked for help by a farmer in Hasanabad against a wolf which had learnt to swim down a *qanat* stream to get at his sheep. The Dastur stationed

---

[5] See 'On the Zoroastrian temple-cult of fire', 455 ff.
[6] See 'Iconoclasm', 100.
[7] The highway was moved to its present position in the reign of Reza Shah.

himself at a point by the stream and recited the *Varahram Yašt*, and when the wolf reached this point he was held in the grip of the water, and as he struggled the farmer was able to hurl a great stone down on his head and kill him. The hymn was also regularly recited at times of sickness and for the demon-afflicted. Varahram's power to protect and save from all such dangers, everywhere, was celebrated in a song composed in Persian, which was often sung at gatherings on holy days.

Varahram was not only venerated for his immediate power to help, but was longed for as an eschatological figure, whose visible coming would one day herald the restoration of the Good Religion, the overthrow of its persecutors, and the glorious end of time. In the *Rivayat* of Kamdin Shapur the text is given of a prayer, called the 'prayer to Bahram of miraculous power, king of the Mazda-worshipping religion', which used, it seems, to be recited at the end of every gahambar service.[8] In this, blessings were called down on all who had taken part in the gahambar, and the hope was expressed that the saviours who would restore the faith might come soon, namely Ušedar son of Zardušt, Pešotan son of Vištasp, and Varahram himself. The yazad was thus a focus for the hopes of oppressed Zoroastrians down the centuries; and he still sometimes appeared to his worshippers in dreams, a splendid figure on horseback, usually with two attendants clad either in white or green.

The sacred fire of Sharifabad is, as we have seen, an Ataš Bahram; and in the village ardent devotion to the yazad had become fused with veneration for the fire which was named for him, and which was said accordingly to be the most powerful of the village Pirs. 'Pīr', meaning 'old', 'venerable', is a word used by Irani Moslems for a saint whose tomb is made into a shrine (in the manner of the ancient Zoroastrian shrines to yazads), and then, by extension, the word is applied to the tomb itself; and in due course the Zoroastrians adopted it for their own shrines, probably partly to gain protection for them, since Moslems sometimes hesitated to outrage the sanctuary of even an alien Pir, for fear of supernatural vengeance.[9] The Sharif-abadis thus identified their sacred fire as a yazad by calling it a Pir; and moreover they named it, not the 'Fire of Varahram', Ataš-e Varahram, but Shah Varahram Ized-e Pak (which may be roughly rendered as 'King Varahram, the holy Divine One'), as if the fire

---

[8] See *Riv.*, Unvala, i. 405–8; Dhabhar, 318.
[9] See, e.g., below, p. 258.

were actually the divinity. They thus added a further elaboration to the already highly complex and significant cult of fire; but this particular development was plainly more due to feeling, born of deep popular devotion to both fire and yazad, than based on theological reasoning.

With so many elements contributing to its veneration, it is not surprising that their ancient Ataš Varahram should have been at the centre of the villagers' affections and of their religious lives. Not only the priest, but a number of his parishioners prayed daily in its temple, and almost all did so on special occasions. Many religious services were solemnized there throughout the year, and every domestic ritual and act of worship was linked to the sacred fire through the observance whereby embers from any other fire which had been consecrated by the recital of Avesta were carried to the temple to grow cold near it. This was the general custom throughout the Yazdi region, and used to be observed also in Kerman;[10] and it follows injunctions laid down in the Persian *Rivayats*. In these old texts it is said that embers from household fires should be taken to what is in effect the parish church, the Ataš-e Adaran; and that once a year embers from the various Ataš-e Adarans, which were regarded as servitors of the 'cathedral' fires, should be carried, with gifts, to the nearest Ataš-e Varahram;[11] but in Sharifabad the household embers were taken perforce direct to the Ataš-e Varahram itself.

Although this custom is enjoined in the *Rivayats*, nothing is said there of how the embers should be disposed of at the fire-temple, and various practices prevailed in the Yazdi area, which were observed in different villages without any discernible geographic pattern. Thus in a number of fire-temples there was a small slanting hole made through the thickness of an outer wall (which might be as much as two or three feet). This was called the *lok-e taš*, 'hole for the fire', and into it the laity placed the embers.[12] In the majority

[10] See 'Fire-temples of Kerman', 63–4.

[11] See *Riv.*, Unvala, i. 67, 68, 72; Dhabhar, 56, 57, 60, 61. Here it is stated that embers from a household fire should be carried to the fire-temple after the cooking of three successive meals, or every three days, and in one *Rivayat* it is even said that this should be done for every fire that has been used to bake bread; but perhaps such injunctions represent an excess of priestly zeal, and were quietly ignored by the laity. In the 1960s the practice was carried out only with consecrated fires.

[12] These *lok-e taš* varied in detail. That at Ahrestan was triangular in shape, with a framework of three stones and a little mud-brick hood above it; and the round one at Mobareke was covered by a wooden shutter, to be pulled up by

of such cases (at Mazra⁽ Kalantar, Ja⁽farabad, Kanu, Ahrestan, Mobareke, Zainabad, and Taft), this hole passed directly into the fire-sanctuary (the *ganza-taš*), where the embers fell into a specially made recess; and at Mazra⁽ Kalantar and Taft—two villages as far apart as possible—a metal rod passed between this recess and the pillar bearing the sacred fire, making a ritual connection or *paivand* between them. This was formerly the case also at the old Bar-e Mihr-e mas or 'Great Fire-Temple' in Yazd. In one village, Khorramshah, the *lok-e taš* let the embers fall into a tiny room beside the fire-sanctuary. In the other group of villages (which included Sharifabad itself, with Elabad, Aliabad, Qasimabad, Kuče Buyuk, Moriabad, and Khairabad), there was no *lok-e taš*, and the embers were variously disposed of. In Moriabad and Khairabad a big metal vessel, set on a stone, was kept for this purpose in one of the outer rooms. At Qasimabad a sort of trough to receive them, about eight inches wide and several deep, was let into the wall opposite the door of the fire-sanctuary; and at Sharifabad itself the embers were put either into a metal vessel, if this stood ready, or into a corner of the outer porch. In all these places at least once a day the atašband of the temple took up some of the ashes (which had fused their entity by lying together) and carried them into the fire-sanctuary, where he placed them on the rim of the pillar-altar, to make *paivand* with the ash at the edge of the sacred fire.[13] Only one village, as far as I could learn, in a measure combined these different observances. This was Elabad, where embers from fires consecrated at major ceremonies (such as gahambars, and the funerary rites of *čārom*, *sīrōza* and the first *sāl*) were put on a mud-brick shelf near the fire-sanctuary, and the ash was later carried in to the sacred fire in this way; but embers from fires sanctified at lesser rituals (such as subsequent *sals*, and minor domestic rites) were put in a recess in a wall at the back of the temple kitchen. This wall was common to it and to the fire-sanctuary, so that there was a *paivand* between these embers and the place of the sacred fire, as was the case with those put through the *lok-e taš* at Khorramshah. The only perplexing

a chain. At Ja⁽farabad the plain round hole was about 8 feet above the level of the lane, with two steps for mounting up to it (though on the other side of the wall the embers dropped to the same ground level again); whereas at Kanu the triangular, stone-edged hole (shaped like that at Ahrestan) was set only about 4 feet from the ground, Most, however, were placed at a comfortable level for the average adult to use, and were uncovered, the thickness of the wall being sufficient protection. [13] Cf. above, p. 59.

thing about such minor divergences is that they should have come into being in a relatively small area served by a closely knit community of priests. Under the system of assigning *hušts* by lot these priests, moreover, regularly exchanged their parishes, and so had to adapt themselves to the different local usages, it being the laity who, in this and similar small matters, maintained the tradition and continuity.

It was this sense of tradition which had preserved Sharifabad's sacred fire as an Ataš Bahram; for the villagers had known and loved it for too long for it to occur to them that its entity and character could change. Elsewhere it has been held that when an Ataš Bahram can no longer be served with the rites proper to a fire of this rank (which demand the attendance of at least two priests), then it must perforce be reduced to being a fire of the second rank, an Ataš-e Adaran. This was done early this century with the old Ataš Bahram in Kerman.[14] Sharifabad continued, however, to reverence its ancient fire as an Ataš Bahram, while serving it as best it could. In 1964 the one priest, D. Khodadad, was the official 'servitor of the fire', the atašband; but since his many parish duties often called him away, an elderly layman, Rustam-e Rashid, was appointed his deputy. Only these two ever entered the fire-chamber, although Rustam's wife Piruza cared for the rest of the temple. An Ataš Bahram should, it is held, be kept always burning brightly, as befits the king of fires; and the ceremony of *bōy dādan*, that is, of offering it dry wood and incense, should be performed with elaborate ceremony at the beginning of each of the five watches of the day.[15] This makes great demands in both fuel and time, and the Sharifabadi fire was tended perforce with the simpler rites of a village fire, that is, a fire of the third rank, an Ātaš-e Dādgāh, which may be cared for by a layman, provided that he is a man of upright character and keeps the laws of purity. The *bōy* ceremony took place only once in the twenty-four hours, in the evening. All that was usually apparent of the fire, therefore, was a mound of soft grey wood-ash.[16] Each

[14] This happened after the death in 1901 of the last Kermani Dastur Dasturan, D. Rustam-e Jehangir.

[15] See Modi, *CC*, 218–26. The third traditional offering, the *ātaš-zōhr* or oblation of fat, had been abandoned for decades by even the most conservative Iranis, although ritual traces of it remained. (See, e.g., 'Mihragān', 113, and below, p. 157.)

[16] Cf. the descriptions of sacred fires given by Strabo, xv. 3. 14, and Pausanias, v. 27. 5–6.

day, to sustain it, the fire received a small thick billet of dry wood, with the bark carefully removed so that there might be no impurity clinging to it. Pomegranate was held to be the best for this purpose, because it is close-grained and slow-burning; next, wood from the apricot or pistachio tree. All wood for the sacred fire was cut and stacked in summer, so that it could dry out thoroughly before use. The atašband, while reciting the appropriate Avestan prayers (which always included the *Ataš Niyayeš*), stood before the fire facing south, with the metal *bara* in his hand. With this he gently pushed aside the ash from the glowing embers of the previous day's billet, and set the new one directly upon these. He then drew the warm ash back around it, so that it was almost embedded, and scattered on top of it a handful of *kūzēr* (the hard sheath of the cornstalk, chopped small), which quickly caught light and blazed up. He then sprinkled on the flames a little frankincense, and the sweet smell filled the small chamber, thus completing the twofold offering. Only at high festivals did D. Khodadad make the full ceremonial offering to the fire of a 'throne', that is, six thinnish pieces of wood placed criss-cross, four below and two above, which soon caught fire and burnt brightly above the heap of ash.[17]

There was no window in the fire-chamber, and the walls were black with fragrant wood smoke, making it very dark; but a lamp, filled with 'pure' oil, was kept always burning there, within a span's length of the fire.[18] Until recently the sacred fire in this dark sanctuary, with its attendant lamp, was an unseen presence for most of its worshippers, beloved, reverenced, but never beheld. This was the case with all the sacred fires of Iran, and the reason for it is plain: as the persecution of Zoroastrians grew more intense, it became too dangerous to enthrone a fire in the sight of the congregation, for this meant that if Moslems broke into the building it was immediately visible, and could all too easily be desecrated or extinguished. Accordingly it became the custom, with fires of whatever grade, to

---

[17] For the 'throne' of wood, see Modi, *CC*, 221. Once when I was in Cham with D. Khodadad he was called on to show the hušt-mobed there (who had not his own thorough training) how to offer the 'throne'. In some of the other Yazdi villages the sacred fire was still tended several times a day in 1964. Thus in Khairabad the *bōy* ceremony was performed morning and evening, and at Mobareke and Moriabad at noon as well—that is, in all three daylight watches. For these 'extra' observances only thin twigs or *kuzer* were used, with incense. At Jaʿfarabad the atašband said that he put a new billet of wood on the fire only when this was necessary, which was sometimes every other day.

[18] On the preparation of the oil for this lamp see below, p. 98.

make the sanctuary very small and to hide it away in the furthest recesses of the building, with access only by a tiny inconspicuous door, no bigger than a cupboard's, through which the atašband had to creep on hands and knees.[19] Since only priests might enter the fire-chamber, the congregation at large gave up the joy of seeing their sacred fire for the better hope of preserving it unharmed. This development must have taken place after the migration of the Parsis, for they have kept the antique custom of setting the sacred fire in an open sanctuary, so that all who enter its temple can see it.[20]

It was presumably to compensate for this shutting away of the ever-burning fire that the Iranis developed the custom (unknown to the Parsis) of setting in the hall of a fire-temple a pillar or 'altar' which was a replica of the one which bore the sacred fire, and was called by the same name, that is, *āδokhš* or *kalak*.[21] These pillars were made of mud-brick, faced with such fine, hard plaster that it looked like stone. On the ones in the outer hall a fire could be set for communal or individual acts of worship, in whose presence the laity could pray and make their offerings. Such a fire was probably most often created from embers brought out by the atašband from the sacred fire itself; and when the prayers had been said, or the ritual completed, these embers would be carried back again to grow cold in the fire-sanctuary, leaving only an empty pillar in the outer hall to baffle an intruder. This remained the custom, established through centuries of observance, in Sharifabad and all the villages of the Yazdi area. In the hall of the Sharifabadi Ataš Varahram, as well as a tall, eight-sided pillar, there was a smaller, round one of solid stone, blackish in colour. This unusual *aδokhš* had been rescued from the

---

[19] Despite the extensive rebuilding of the old fire-temples, a number of such tiny doors could still be seen in 1964. Thus, for example, in the dignified and charming fire-temple of Mobareke the old fire sanctuary had been retained, and was entered by a small door of solid metal, about 4 by $2\frac{1}{2}$ feet square, and set, like a cupboard door, about 1 foot above the ground. There was a similar door into the sanctuary at Jaʿfarabad, and an even tinier wooden one, no more than 3 feet high, looking just like a cupboard door, into the *ganza-taš* at Kanu. Elabad too had a little wooden door.

[20] The evidence to establish this as the ancient custom is slight, but archaeologists have identified a number of temple ruins from Sasanian times with an ambulatory around a *gumbad* or domed sanctuary, and texts show that the walls of this sanctuary had openings in them. See in detail Schippmann, *Die iranischen Feuerheiligtümer*, under the Sasanian period (Tafel III and index); and further 'On the Zoroastrian temple-cult of fire', 463–4.

[21] On the names for the 'fire-altar' see W. Eilers, 'Herd und Feuerstätte in Iran', *Innsbrucker Beiträge zur Sprachwissenschaft*, 12, 1974, 307–38.

fire-temple of the neighbouring village of Ahmedabad, before this was abandoned;[22] and as well as a round depression in its top to contain fire, it had four small saucer-like hollows round the rim to serve as oil-lamps, with an incision leading to the edge of the stone for the wick, and between these, four little holes as sockets for candles.

The bigger, octagonal pillar was handsome and imposing, and stood in the very middle of a square hall which had a big central dome and four *pesgams* opening out of it, where a large congregation could gather. Down to the end of the last century the Ataš Varahram of Sharifabad still burnt in a lowly mud-brick building, looking outwardly like any other village house; but one of the villagers, Khodamurad-e Noshiravan, took a vow to build it a worthier temple.[23] The circumstances were these: he was a poor farmer who one snowy winter night fell down a *qanat* well at the edge of the village fields. There was no way to get out, and it seemed certain that he would freeze to death. In this moment of peril he prayed to Shah Varahram Ized, and vowed that if he were rescued he would rebuild the house of his sacred fire. It happened that two bulls kept as pack-animals at a mill nearby fell to fighting, and the weaker one broke out and ran away across the fields. The miller, in chasing it, passed close to the well, and Khodamurad called out to him. At first the startled man thought his was the voice of a jinn, coming from under the earth, but once reassured he hurried for ropes and hauled him out. Khodamurad was then faced in his poverty with the obligation of his vow; and so he left the village and went to Bombay, where he engaged in trade, sending back to Sharifabad every anna that he could save. It took him years to earn enough money for his purpose, and when at last he had remitted a sufficient sum, he returned to Sharifabad and spent the rest of his life there in contented poverty. The new temple was finished in 1903, which was a time when, although a number of decrees had been passed to improve the lot of Irani Zoroastrians, their lives were still full of danger. Accordingly, although the new temple of Shah Varahram is a dignified and pleasing building, whose dome rises proudly above the roofs of the surrounding houses,[24] nevertheless it has double entry-

---

[22] See above, p. 8 n. 19.

[23] For the following story, and all the information about the older building that was replaced by Khodamurad's, I am indebted to Agha Rustam, who had learnt these things from his father.

[24] The distinguished French archaeologist M. Siroux was so impressed by the

doors for protection, and the fire-sanctuary is still a small inconspicuous room hidden at the back of the main hall.[25] Moreover, this
had originally a little door of solid wood, which was exactly like
that of another small room (the *yazišn-gāh*) at the opposite corner of
the building, so that there was nothing to identify it to an intruder.

About half a century after Khodamurad's building was completed,
the Sharifabadi Anjoman repaired it and introduced some modifications. By then a number of the villagers had been in Bombay and had
become familiar there with the Parsi practice of setting a sacred
fire, not on a stone altar, as is the ancient custom of Iran, but in a
big silvery metal vase, like a huge goblet—a larger version of the vase,
called an *āfrīnagān*, in which fire is kept burning at religious ceremonies.[26] This innovation was probably made by the Parsis late in the
fifteenth century, after they had been forced to move their one sacred
fire from place to place for safety over a number of years, and had
presumably become accustomed to keeping it in a portable container; and so great was the prestige enjoyed by the Indian community with their co-religionists since the mid nineteenth century that
gradually this practice was adopted in the larger Irani fire-temples
also, notably in those of Tehran, Yazd, and Kerman. (It was undoubtedly thought that it represented the ancient custom, and that
such handsome and costly vases were one of the objects which had
been plundered from Irani temples during the years of oppression;
but in fact excavations of ancient sites, and antique rock carvings,

new temple that he made a detailed study of it, attributing it in part to Safavid
times: see his article 'Le temple zoroastrien de Sharīfābād', *Āthār-é Īrān*, III. i.
1938, 83–7. It is evident from his remarks on p. 85 that he mistook the villagers'
statements about the antiquity of the fire itself—and possibly of the previous
fire-temple—as referring to the present building. Similar mistakes have been
made by G. Gropp in his articles on Zoroastrian sacred buildings. In fact no
impressive Zoroastrian building erected in Islamic times in Iran belongs to a
date earlier than the latter part of the nineteenth century. The architect of Khodamurad's building must necessarily have been a Moslem, since Zoroastrians had no
experience then of building in anything but mud-brick; and he evidently adapted
traditional architectural forms to the Zoroastrians' special requirements, as
was the case with other Yazdi fire-temples. Modifications (such as the placing of
the altar in the fire-sanctuary, or the making of a *lok-e taš*) could be introduced
after the Moslem workers had finished. Some of the rebuilt temples were influenced by Parsi prototypes, which in their turn are all relatively modern
structures.   [25] See Siroux's plan, art. cit., p. 84.

[26] It seems in fact to derive its name from the most frequently celebrated of the
'outer' services, namely the ceremony of praise, the Afrinagan. The Parsis
pronounce the name as *afargāniun* (see Modi, *CC*, index, s.v.); the Iranis (when
speaking Dari) as *aprīgun* (see Sorushian, *Farhang*, I).

show that it is the pillar-altar which represents the genuine old tradition.) So in the 1950s the Sharifabadis in their turn imported a large German-silver vase from Bombay, with which they replaced the old solid pillar in the fire-sanctuary. This vase stands on a square stone base, about two inches high, and has a big cowl above it, to draw up the smoke. At the same time a brass bell, also acquired from India, was hung just inside the sanctuary door, to be rung by the atašband at the *bōy* ceremony. This again is Parsi custom,[27] unknown to the Iranis. There is no reference to it in the old liturgical books of the faith, but there are many gaps in these, and so it seems impossible to determine whether this is another Parsi innovation, now adopted in the Ataš Bahrams of Iran, or an old usage abandoned in Iran during the times of persecution, when worship had to be as inconspicuous as possible. Subsequently a Parsi priest, visiting Sharifabad, persuaded the village elders that it was proper that the sacred fire should be visible to all the congregation, and so, when a new and larger door was made for the sanctuary, all of metal, it was fitted with a small grille at eye-level; but since the fire-vase was set where the old pillar-altar had stood, a little away from the door, the fire could be seen only by standing close to this grille and looking sideways through it. The villagers themselves did not seem to value the concession, perhaps feeling that to gaze thus on the sacred fire itself had an element of sacrilege; and they continued in the main to say their prayers and pay their devotions to fire set on the big pillar in the outer hall.[28] Nowadays, when matches make it easy to light a fire, this is often kindled afresh rather than being made from embers from the sacred fire. This pillar itself was subsequently faced with grey tiles, with which the fire-chamber was lined, and the whole building paved—a further embellishment to their beloved shrine carried out by the villagers in 1961. The intention behind this was mainly to make it easier to keep the temple ritually pure, glazed

[27] See Modi, *CC*, 225.
[28] The Sharifabadis were not alone in this. Thus several of the village fire-temples (for example, at Khairabad, Qasimabad, Aliabad, Narseabad, and Cham) had been rebuilt with Parsi-type open grilles in the walls of their sanctuaries; but in each case these grilles were covered, in 1964, either with wooden shutters or with thick curtains, which, it was said, were never moved. An exception was in the striking and unusual fire-temple of Kuče Buyuk (rebuilt in 1890). Here the sanctuary was an octagonal brick room, about 14 feet high, set in the middle of a well-like space and looking itself not unlike a huge pillar-altar. This had a door and three big shuttered grilles, each about 7 feet high, which were sometimes opened to give a full view of the fire.

tiles being as impervious and washable as stone. (Previously only
the fire-chamber itself had been paved, with small pebble-stones,
this being all that was possible during the years of oppression.)
The tiles had every advantage in summer, but during the short,
sharp winters they struck bitterly cold underfoot—for Zoroastrians
observe the widespread custom of removing their shoes when
entering a holy place, while keeping their heads covered.

As we have seen, the villagers knew their sacred fire as Shah
Varahram Ized. Why it is that throughout the Irani community the
yazad should receive the title 'King' is a matter of some uncertainty.
It has been suggested that this came about through a contamination
in popular legend between the divinity and Shah Vahram Čobin,
the celebrated Parthian pretender of the sixth century A.D.;[29] but it
is perhaps rather that the warrior-yazad, who will one day appear
leading his armies, came to be thought of in terms of a mortal
king, who in ancient days was expected to lead his forces into
battle. Whatever the true explanation, it is a fact that Varahram is
regularly accorded this title; and it seems probable that it originated
with him among the yazads, and that its use was then extended as an
honorific, so that by now the title 'Shah' may be set before the
name of any divine person, regardless of congruity. So the other
great sacred fire of the village was known there as Shah Aδor Khara
Ized, literally 'King Fire-Khara, the Divine One'. Its shrine was
called the Bar-e Mihr-e kučīk, the 'Little fire-temple'; and this
continued to be a humble mud-brick building until the 1940s, when
the village Anjoman erected a more stately shrine, which raises a
slightly smaller but still dignified dome close beside that of Shah
Varahram.[30]

It may at first sight seem strange that it was an empty sanctuary
which was thus rebuilt in honour of Shah Aδor Khara. It was, it
seems, not long after the completion of the new temple of Shah
Varahram[31] that it became apparent that the cost of maintaining

---

[29] See K. Czeglédy, 'Bahrām Čobīn and the Persian apocalyptic literature',
Acta Orient. Hung., viii/1, 1958, 21–43.

[30] This rebuilding had not taken place when M. Siroux visited the village
(see p. 77 n. 24). He was evidently told of the existence of Zoroastrian sanctuaries
other than the Ataš Bahram, but received a confused impression that these were
all fire-temples, which had been seized by Moslems. See further p. 82 n. 34,
below.

[31] I was unable to learn a precise date for this event, but was told, in 1964,
that only those aged sixty or more could remember Shah Aδor Khara burning in
his own shrine.

IIIa. D. Khodadad making the libation to water in a garden at Hasanabad (see p. 191).

IIIb. Part of the company at the evening meal eaten by the dakhma at the Dadgah-e Tirmah (see p. 207).

IVa (*above*). A group of Panji figurines on the Belivani roof, with wind-towers in the background (see pp. 49, 224).

IVb (*left*). Tahmina Khanom preparing a spice-jar for Havzoru (see p. 217).

two sacred fires, even with simplified rites, was growing to be too great; for wood was becoming ever more scarce and expensive in the Yazdi area, and frankincense had to be imported at ever-increasing cost for the daily *boy* ceremony. So after grave deliberations the villagers decided to unite their two great fires to burn as one. This the Parsis most strictly maintain must never be done, since every sacred fire has its own individual life; but all that one can say is that the orthodox Sharifabadis, trapped by circumstances, did it, in a spirit of reverence and devotion. Both fires were, after all, of the same grade, Ataš Bahrams; and although the villagers now venerated the one conjoined fire as Shah Varahram, they did not forget Shah Aδor Khara. Not only was his shrine rebuilt, but it was lovingly maintained. It too had the central hall tiled, and an atašband was regularly appointed to care for the building;[32] and apart from individual devotions, every year certain other communal rites were solemnized there and attended by a large congregation.

Loyalty such as this was characteristic of the Sharifabadis, and indeed of the Irani Zoroastrians as a whole, for without this quality they would not have been ready to suffer so much for their faith. Moreover, the maintenance of the temple of Shah Aδor Khara becomes less remarkable when one realizes that the Sharifabadis, in common with all their Irani co-religionists, were accustomed to worshipping in empty shrines as well as in fire-temples. Such shrines were ordinarily dedicated to individual yazads, and at a remote period—that is, in late Achaemenian and Parthian times—they would have contained a statue to the divinity. Then an iconoclastic movement swept all images away.[33] Sometimes the statue was replaced by a sacred fire, but sometimes (presumably when there was difficulty in bearing the cost of this) the shrine, it seems, was left empty, with a fire being kindled there only on holy days and at special observances, as today in the outer halls of fire-temples. Possibly it is this historical background, possibly simply a tendency in an unwritten language to blur the nice distinctions between words, which leads the Sharifabadis to use the same terms interchangeably in speaking of their fire-temples or their empty shrines; that is to say, they may call the shrine a Bar-e Mihr, or the fire-temple a Pir, or refer to any or all of them by the Arabo-Persian

---

[32] In 1964 this was Khosrow-e Tirandaz, whose wife, Gulbanu-e Kai Khosrow, did most of the caretaking.

[33] See 'Iconoclasm among the Zoroastrians'.

word ma'bad, 'place of worship' (which probably replaced a deriva-
tive of Old Persian *āyadana*).[34] The guardian of a shrine, although
officially termed its khādem or 'servitor', was also commonly spoken
of as its atašband. This loss of verbal distinctions must have made it
all the easier to come to regard the temple of the Ataš Varahrām as
a shrine to Varahrām Ized, on the pattern of the empty sanctuaries.
This step could the more readily be taken because there existed a
famous Pir-e Shah Varahrām Ized—that is, an empty shrine dedicated to the yazad—in Kerman.[35] (In recent times shrines with this
dedication, which have become greatly beloved, have been founded
also in the Yazdi village of Khorramshah,[36] and in Tehran.[37])

Not every Zoroastrian village had empty shrines, and some
which had possessed only what they called 'little Pirs', often no more
than niches for candles, set beside water or a tree. Thus Mazra'
Kalantar, for instance, had three 'little Pirs' devoted to water. One
was a tiny shrine-room near its lower pool, with just space round the
pillar-altar for three or four people. The other two, the Pir-e Irsakh,

[34] On the former terms for fire-temples and image-shrines see ibid. 98–9,
and 'On the Zoroastrian temple-cult of fire', 456, 463. It was probably these
generalized usages of modern times which prevented M. Siroux obtaining a
clearer picture of the nature of the Sharifabadi sanctuaries (see p. 80 n. 30).

[35] On this shrine see Sorushian, *Farhang*, 210; G. Gropp, 'Die rezenten
Feuertempel der Zarathustrier (II)', *AMI*, N.F. 4, 1971, 272–3.

[36] No exact date is known for the creation of this shrine, but it is a matter of
recent tradition that formerly a great plane stood there, in the village square.
A man tried to fell this tree, but the sap seemed to him to flow like blood beneath
his axe (cf. p. 256, below), and he desisted and told his fellows, and they built the
shrine. This became sanctified by other small miracles, and grew to be greatly
venerated. In 1964 it had been recently repaired, and was then a biggish barrel-
vaulted room, tiled and with whitewashed ceiling. An octagonal pillar-altar
stood at the further end, and against one of its sides was a shorter pillar, with a
knife kept on it, for offering fruits. In the wall behind was a niche for candles.
For details of the building itself see Gropp, art. cit. 278–9.

[37] This shrine, in the old quarter of Amiriye, had been built (it was said) in the
1830s, at a time when there were only five or six Zoroastrian families in Tehran.
The original small room, square and windowless, is incorporated in the modern
brick building, which is provided with salons, a kitchen, and tables and chairs
in the carpeted main room. In the shrine-room the old pillar-altar has been
replaced by a round metal tray on a stand, and there is a slab-table along one
wall. Both are usually bright with candles, for the shrine is much loved. I was
once privileged to visit it as the guest of Mobed Rustam Shahzadi, who was
fulfilling a vow made with regard to his son's becoming a student. A 'gahambar-e
toji' was celebrated, the ritual and observances being essentially just as they
would have been in Sharifabad. A difference, in the big city, was that the shrine
was also full of the murmured prayers of other worshippers, who performed
their own individual devotions and paid no heed to the gahambar, whereas in
Sharifabad this would have been a communal act involving everyone present.

'Shrine of the (Upper) Pool', and Pir-e Sar-e Čašmak, 'Shrine at the Spring', were only candle-niches. A candle was set in these every night by a family which lived nearby, various people giving the candles as votive offerings throughout the year. Qasimabad had a Pir-e Senjed, a candle-niche set in a lane where a stream flowed under an oleaster (*senjed*) tree, and there were many other similar small wayside shrines.

Sharifabad had no 'little Pirs' of this kind, but it possessed two 'great Pirs', namely ancient and beloved shrines to Shah Mihr Ized and Shah Teštar Ized, the Avestan Mithra and Tištrya. Tištrya became linked, probably in early Achaemenian times, with a Western Iranian divinity, Tīri, and appropriated his feast-day, Tīragān. Mihragan and Tiragan, with No Ruz, were the only Zoroastrian feasts to win mention in the Talmud, which is an indication of their popularity; and, apart from the gahambars, they seem to have been the most widely celebrated of all the festivals of ancient Iran. There was a major shrine to Shah Mihr Ized at Kerman, which had a number of 'great Pirs'.[38] Yazd, however, had none;[39] and the existence of two at Sharifabad (with that to Teštar being apparently unique) seems yet another feature of its religious life which the village owed to the long residence there of the priests, and the coming of many pilgrims to venerate its sacred fires.

The greatness of the 'great Pirs' lay in their ancientness and extreme sanctity, and not in the material splendour of their shrines— for naturally during the centuries of oppression these, like the fire-temples, had to be as inconspicuous as possible, with nothing either within or without to tempt the spoliator. The two 'great Pirs' of Sharifabad were far apart, for Teštar, the yazad who brings rain, had his shrine outside the village, among fields, whereas Mihr, who is intimately linked with the cult, had his close to the two fire-temples.

[38] See Sorushian, *Farhang*, 209. There were several small shrines (some of recent date) to Mihr Ized in the Yazdi villages.

[39] On the Pir-e Vamiro there see below, p. 89. There was also the Pir-e Eliath, a large complex on the outskirts of the old town, near the Mahalle-ye Dasturan. This was set in what had once been a beautiful garden, drought-stricken in 1964. There was a well in the shrine room which was an object of veneration. Although the dedication was to a Moslem *rajal al-ghaib* (see 'Bibi Shahrbanu . . .', 30–1), the well-instructed said that this was simply a protective usage, and that the shrine was really to the yazad Sroš. This had been forgotten by most; but it was generally believed that Eliath came at dawn to houses which had already been swept and where water had been sprinkled in the courtyard and there was fragrance, which is orthodox belief about Sroš (see above, p. 30). Yazd also had a 'little Pir', the Pir-e Kušk-e kučīk, in the old behdin quarter.

Both shrines were rebuilt at about the same time as the temple of
Aδor Khara, that is, in the 1940s; and many of the villagers could
remember the former mud-brick buildings, tiny and dilapidated,
and each with so small a door that worshippers had to creep in on
hands and knees. Since the Pir-e Mihr Ized was hemmed in by
houses, there was not much scope for enlarging it at the rebuilding;
and it remained a simple room, domed and square, at the centre
of which was one of the eight-sided pillar-altars characteristic of
Sharifabad. Ordinarily this altar stood empty; but, at the expense of
the Anjoman, a supply of brushwood was kept at this and other
shrines, so that any one who wished could light a fire on the altar,
and pray and offer incense. Worshippers themselves brought more
wood, and also gifts of pure oil for the sanctuary lamp, candles and
such fragrant offerings as might be in season—sweet-smelling
flowers or herbs, or sun-warmed fruits, which were laid on the rim
of the altar. No one ever went empty-handed to a holy place,
although the gift which he brought might be of the humblest.
There was no rigidly prescribed pattern of behaviour for approaching
the divinity, but many touched the door-sill before entering in a
graceful gesture of obeisance, and uttered an invocation such as
'Yā Shah Mihr Ized!'

The occasions which took a villager to a Pir were as various as
those which take a Roman Catholic (for example) to the shrine of his
patron saint. He might go, that is, to ask a boon of the yazad, or to
render thanks for one already granted, or to make an act of contrition for some offence; or his visit might simply be to offer veneration, and this was especially the case on festival days, such as during
the six gahambars, when some of the pious went to all the village
shrines in turn. Each sanctuary, moreover, was thronged on its own
particular days, that is, the name-days of the yazad himself, which for
Mihr are the sixteenth of every month, with the sixteenth of the seventh
month being the holiest of all, since this is Ruz Mihr of Mah Mihr,
the first day of the Jašn-e Mihr Ized,[40] when all who could visited

[40] His feast was known throughout the Yazdi area by this name, but Shirin-e
Set Hakimi (see above, p. 62) said that she could remember it being called
'Mīragun' in Sharifabad, and this old name had been revived by the Tehrani
Anjoman. The celebration of the feast in Sharifabad differed in some small
respects from that in Mazraʿ Kalantar (for which see 'Mihragan'). Thus the blood
sacrifice was offered in each household, as in Mazraʿ, but the tongue was taken
at once to the priest. The carcass was roasted with the same ritual, but when it was
brought out of the oven the priest came to the house and recited the Dron-e
Mihr Ized over it (for details of the ritual see art. cit. 112–13). The carcass, thus

his shrine to pray and make offerings. Because of the sanctity of this feast, its ancient communal rites were celebrated at the Ataš Varahram; and the greatest observance which took place at Mihr's own shrine was the lighting outside it of a huge fire just after sunset on the feast of Sada, Mihr Ized being lord of both fire and sun.[41]

Teštar too was a much-loved yazad, but latterly circumstances had combined to dim the lustre both of his festival and his shrine. The oldest villagers could tell of charming customs, connected with rain-bringing, which belonged to the five-day Jašn-e Tir-o-Teštar,[42] but almost all that survived of these by the 1960s was merry-making by young people and children, who had a happy licence, on Ruz Tir of Mah Tir, to splash and duck one another in the village streams. As for the shrine of Shah Teštar Ized, this was among fields on the Ardekani side of the village, a position which gave scope at the rebuilding; and the new sanctuary was unusually light and airy, a domed hall, some fourteen feet square, with doors on all four sides, and in the middle an octagonal pillar-altar. When I was taken to visit it, there was a clay *afrinagan* beside this altar, that is, a simple clay pan to hold fire, with a hollow handle to give a draught. Such humble *afrinagans* (rather than the silvery vases now in general use) were, it seems, characteristic of the times of oppression, when both poverty and prudence dictated that nothing of the smallest material value should be used to provoke greed and the desecration of shrines; and in 1964 such clay vessels were still kept at the lonelier sanctuaries, which could not even then be effectively guarded. There was also a small, doll-like figure of a boy—a *pesarog*—hanging in the sanctuary. This had been put there in thanksgiving either for the birth of a boy, or for a son's survival of some sickness or danger; for although the communal cult of Teštar Ized had declined, the yazad was still beloved by individuals, and on his yearly feast-day his shrine was well frequented.

blessed, was then cut in two, lengthwise, and one half was carried ceremonially to the temple of Shah Varahram Ized, and the other half to that of Shah Aδor Khara, so that there should be no invidiousness. Fruits or *lurk* were sent with both, and one haunch was removed at the greater fire-temple. The communal gathering on the fifth day also took place there. In Sharifabad five Afrinagan services were solemnized on that occasion, first one alone, and then two by two— that is, two were recited simultaneously, one by the priest, the other by a lay elder. The congregation therefore said three sets of košti-prayers, one before the first service, the others before the two double ones. Thereafter there was a distribution of meat and *lurk* (but no bread), which was eaten communally in the temple. [41] See below, p. 181. [42] See further below, p. 206.

When this shrine was rebuilt in the 1940s, the opportunity was taken to create a beautiful walled garden around it. There was already a big old elm growing there; and the villagers planted other elms and aspens to give shade, together with oleasters, sweet pomegranates, and thickets of roses, with scented jonquils beneath them to flower in early spring. For more than a decade it was a place of delight, but then two misfortunes overtook it. The spring which watered the garden began to dry up, and the trees and plants to wither; and Moslem houses were built around it, where once there had been fields. Moslem hooligans ring-barked the great elm and killed it, and despite the high garden-wall the shrine was exposed to theft and desecration.

This shrine and that of Mihr Ized were the only two of ancient origin in Sharifabad. All that the villagers could say of either was that it was very, very old; and the likelihood is that both were established not long after the sacred fires were brought there, probably nearly a thousand years ago. Since the mid nineteenth century, however, individuals, free from the restraints which the presence of the priests must have imposed, have founded three other lesser sanctuaries, whose history is well known. The oldest of these is in a corner of the garden of Shah Teštar Ized, and the story which is told of its origin is as follows: over a hundred years earlier, before the abolition of the annual poll-tax on Zoroastrians, there lived a certain Bunyad, who was very poor and in debt. He did not dare to reap his few fields openly, fearing that his creditors would seize the scanty harvest and leave him with no means of paying the tax. He would then be faced with one of two choices—to become a Moslem or be beaten and tortured, perhaps to death. In the end he reaped his small crop by night, managed to thresh it unobserved, and again under cover of darkness took a single sack of grain to Ardekan to sell. As he was passing near the shrine of Teštar Ized a white-robed dervish appeared out of the night and begged for a handful of corn. As one poor man to another Bunyad gave it him. The dervish begged for a second, and again Bunyad let him have it. Then the stranger grew remorseful, and saying that he could not take them, since Bunyad was himself in want, he thrust both back into the sack and disappeared. Bunyad went on his way, but the sack seemed strangely heavy, and he wondered if the dervish had tricked him and put back stones; but when dawn came and he could look into the sack he found in it a double handful of jewels. He realized then that the white-robed stranger must have been Sroš, the yazad who, under Ohrmazd, has especial care for men. Bunyad sold the jewels, paid both the poll-tax and his creditors, and bought a large estate. Since the miracle had happened on Ruz Aštad of Mah Azar, he built a shrine to Aštad at the place where it had befallen; and this shrine was later enclosed in the garden of Teštar Ized. And whatever the truth of the story (Agha Rustam, who told it to me, said), not only was the shrine still standing, but the Anjoman still administered what remained of the generous bequests made in charity by Bunyad from his estate.

Aštad is much beloved, the hypostasis of justice (and closely linked therefore with Mihr). She is a female yazad, nevertheless her shrine was known according to standard usage as that of Shah Aštō Ized.[43] It was relatively large and dignified for the time when it was built, and had not been altered since. It consisted of a single low barrel-vaulted room, about twelve feet long. The door at one end was big for those dangerous days—a good five feet—but still one had to stoop to enter. At the further end there was a bench-altar running across the width of the room, with a hollow in it to hold fire; and above this, and over the door, small holes were pierced through the roof to let the smoke escape; but when the door was closed the little shrine was quite dark, except for the light from fire or candle. It was looked after by the khadem of Shah Teštar Ized, and was especially visited on the morning of the feast of Sada, that is, on Ruz Aštad of Mah Azar, the day of the miracle.

Another little shrine of Sharifabad slowly acquired sanctity, instead of being built as a holy place. This used to be known as the Pir-e Čōr Drakht, 'Shrine of the Four Trees', although there had been no trees growing close to it within living memory. It too was a shrine in the fields, and used to be just a humble flat-roofed room built to give shelter to those working there; but gradually a mysterious reputation grew up around it, and miracles were said to have happened, and no one dared sleep there at night, for dread of a divine presence.[44] Then Noshiravan-e Gushtasp, Agha Rustam's father, initiated the custom of celebrating a gahambar-e toji there

[43] There was a shrine in Kerman also to Shah Aštad Ized, see Sorushian, *Farhang*, 209.

[44] On such buildings in the fields, put up to give shelter on summer days and winter nights, see 'Some Aspects of Farming', 126 with Pl. X 2. In other Yazdi villages too these lonely little places sometimes acquired a supernatural aura, and had been made within living memory into shrines.

in the late afternoon of the first day of the festival of Mihr Ized, and the little room came to be regarded as a shrine and was known as Shah Mihr Ized-e Sahrā'ī, or 'Mihr Ized in the Fields'. In the 1940s Agha Rustam rebuilt it at his own expense, and made of it a charming small shrine, completely circular (about fifteen feet in diameter), with a domed roof, and a little entry-passage for added security, with an inner and outer door. There was a recess for festive-day cooking in this passage, though on communal occasions hearths were made too in the field-lane outside.

So matters remained until the late 1950s, when a miracle befell old Shirin-i Set Hakemi, who was the guardian of the shrine. She told how one dawn, as she was lying awake in her bed, a noble-looking man appeared to her, long-moustached and with a mirror under his arm. He declared himself to be Shah Paridun, and said that he was going to his own home, and that she should follow him. She rose up and did so, and he walked before her to the shrine and went inside. She entered after him, and found the place empty but full of the sweetest fragrance. She made the miracle known, and the village as a whole accepted it (though some were sceptical). The shrine was rededicated accordingly, so that thereafter on entering it most worshippers uttered the invocation 'Ya Shah Paridun!'. Nevertheless, the gahambar-e toji on the first day of Mihragan still took place at this sanctuary, after which the whole congregation went from there to the old shrine of Mihr Ized within the village.

It is doubtful if in the days of the priests a shrine could have been made in Sharifabad to Shah Paridun, for he is not a yazad, and only his spirit or fravaši can give help to men; and his cult, although an ancient one, tends, as we have seen, to be confused with magical practices concerned with the *paris*.[45] The last-created of the Sharifabadi shrines had also acquired a dedication that would probably not have been approved by the priests of old. The shrine itself was built some thirty years previously, in response to a dream by Mundagar-e Rustam Abadian, Agha Rustam's father-in-law; and for some time it was known simply as the Pir-e Mundagar, or Pir-e Mund,[46] a name which became corrupted into Pir-e Murād, the 'Shrine of Hope'. It was the smallest of the village sanctuaries, a little domed room which one entered directly from the lane in which it stood, not far

---

[45] See above, p. 63.

[46] It was not uncommon for a 'little Pir' to be named in this way for the man who had founded it, nearly always (it seemed) as the result of a dream.

from the shrine of Mihr Ized. It had a little low octagonal pillar-altar at the further end, and this, unusually, was flat-topped, instead of having a hollow for fire. As the years went by the villagers, with their instinct for worship, sanctified the little room with their prayers; and at last someone asked why it was that, although they as Zoroastrians venerated Ohrmazd above all other beings, yet they had no shrine consecrated especially to him. The orthodox answer is presumably that the Creator has the whole of his creation for a shrine, and is worshipped everywhere in every religious rite, and so needs no particular man-made sanctuary. But the Sharifabadis, although such traditionalists, seemed tolerant of most genuine devotional impulses, and so this smallest and last of the village shrines came to be dedicated to Ohrmazd himself, and was commonly called the *Pir-e Dāδvar Ōrmezd*, the 'Shrine of Ohrmazd the Creator', though some rejected this dedication and still referred to it as the Pir-e Murad. Sharifabad had accordingly in the end five shrines within the village, as well as the two fire-temples, which brought its holy places to the auspicious number of seven.

In general it seems that the six great Amahraspands were felt, like the Creator himself, to need no artificial sanctuaries, each being worshipped through his own creation. The one exception was Vahman, lord of cattle. In Mazraᶜ Kalantar, which in most respects was as orthodox as Sharifabad, there was a shrine set in the fields which was named for him as 'Vōmanrū', and Yazd had one similarly dedicated to 'Vāmirō';[47] that is, both these sanctuaries were devoted

---

[47] This shrine was in the same lane as the old Bar-e Mihr-e Račune'i (or Bar-e Mihr-e Mas). It used to be simply an old *čor-pesgami* house, with the sanctuary on the east side of the *pesgam-e mas*—the usual small, dark, windowless room, with a slab-altar at the east end. The shrine was much resorted to by childless women, and above the altar and along the south wall, in 1964, there were votive offerings of beautifully made rag dolls, two placed in elaborate cradles. People with other wishes too came to the shrine, which had an especial three-day festival each year when it was thronged, largely by villagers. This took place on the days Hormazd, Vahman, and Urdibehišt of Mah Hordad. On the first day offerings were brought for sacrifice, occasionally a sheep or goat, but more often hens. These were sacrificed on Ruz Hormazd, since Ruz Vahman itself is a *nā-būr* ('non-killing') day, on which no creature of Vahman may be slain, and no meat eaten. On that day meat from the sacrifice was prepared and some of it was taken 'round the lanes' to the old and sick; and on the third day there was feasting and rejoicing at the shrine itself. So popular had the cult become that a decade or two previously the three lesser *pesgams* were demolished and a large courtyard was made in their stead, to accommodate the throng of worshippers that gathered on this occasion. There were lesser assemblies on Ruz Vahman of each month, and then, as at the major occasion, a *sopra* was set out in the sanctuary, and the

to the 'Day Vahman' (the second of every month), their names
being contractions of 'Vahman Rūz'. Kerman too had a shrine to
Vahman, but this was more orthodoxly named the Pir-e Shah
Vahman Amšāspand.[48] The names of the other two shrines were
linked, however, with a significant fact: the Iranis have six 'beloved'
(azīz) days in each month, on which it is especially meritorious to
do religious acts. These are, in order through the month, Vahman,
Ādar, (Teštar)-Tīr, Mihr, Varahrām, and Aštād. The reasons why
these six days were especially favoured are not easy to determine in
each case, but there seems, naturally enough, to be a link between
them and the founding of sanctuaries. Thus Sharifabad had in the
end shrines to four of the six yazads concerned (if the fire-temple is
accounted a sanctuary of Varahram), and Kerman had shrines to
five (lacking only one to Teštar), for there was actually an empty
shrine there to Shah Adar Ized, the yazad of fire.[49] It is, moreover,
striking that Bunyad chose to dedicate his shrine in Sharifabad
not to Sroš, who performed the miracle which befell him, but to
Aštad, on whose day it happened. The fact of there being 'beloved
days' may therefore have come first, and have encouraged the making
of shrines to Vahman and Adar, who by older usage would scarcely
have been honoured in this way (though naturally the immediate
prompting to do so came for both the Yazdi and the Mazraᶜ shrines
in the usual form of a dream). That to create shrines for the six
Amahraspands generally was not orthodox usage is suggested by the
fact that none is recorded to Spendarmad, the special yazad of
farmers and of women, whose five-day festival was almost as popular,
even in Islamic times, as those of Mihr and Teštar-Tir.[50] There is,
however, a piece of debated evidence which, according to one inter-
pretation, suggests that the custom of founding sanctuaries for
Vahman may be relatively old, and that is Strabo's statement that in
one of the Persian shrines in Asia Minor in his day there was a
wooden statue to 'Omanus';[51] but whether this name is really to
be identified as that of Vahman is not certain.

Although the shrines of Sharifabad itself were very different in
age and character, each received its share of devotion, which was

guardian of the shrine, an old woman, told a folktale in ritual fashion (as
described above, pp. 66–7). This tale had no connection with the Amahraspand
Vahman, but once more had to do with the daughters of 'Shah Pari'.

[48] See Sorushian, *Farhang*, 210.   [49] See ibid. 209.
[50] See 'On the calendar of Zoroastrian feasts', 535–6.
[51] XV. 3. 15.

paid with a blend of high seriousness and gaiety; for when young people had said their prayers and made their offerings, one of them would often strike up on a tambourine and the others begin to sing or dance. The joyful noise could be considerable, with the throbbing instruments and a clapping of hands, in which older people too would join; but though it stopped if a grave elder appeared who wished to pray in peace, there was no feeling that the gaiety was in itself irreverent, or unwelcome to the divinity of the place. Indeed, I was once at one of the mountain shrines when young men were singing and dancing in the outer room, and a girl, for propriety's sake, held a shawl across the doorway to the inner sanctuary while one of her companions danced gracefully in the narrow space beside the sacred rock itself.[52] Those coming from another background could not always see this joyful activity as a part of worship, and some Parsi visitors tried to persuade the guardians of the shrines that it should not be allowed. So these conscientious men tried at times to check it; but Sharifabad was accustomed to worshipping in gladness, and these half-hearted efforts to create a uniformly solemn atmosphere at their holy places met with small success.

[52] The dancer on this occasion was Piruza, Agha Rustam's second daughter. Soon afterwards Agha Rustam himself came up to the shrine to pray, and all the young people at once fell silent and melted respectfully away.

5

THE LAWS AND RITES OF PURITY

WHETHER one is concerned with acts of worship, or holy places, or simply patterns of daily living, one is bound to become involved with one or other of the laws of purity, for these affect all areas of Zoroastrian life. The purity code of this ancient faith is a complex one, and some of its elements plainly go back to distant, pre-Zoroastrian times. These elements were developed and refined upon in the light of the prophet's dualistic teachings, and new ones were added. The resulting code was of immense importance to the orthodox, for they held that there was a threefold path to God, through acts of worship, observance of the purity laws, and ethical behaviour.

One of the evidently ancient elements in this code is belief in the ritual and actual cleanliness of the cow and its products. This belief, shared by the Hindus, must have evolved during the millennia spent by the ancestors of the Indians and Iranians as nomads herding cattle on the Asian steppes. During this great stretch of time they must have depended on their cattle for almost everything—for meat, drink, clothing, and also for the cleansing agent provided by their urine, with its ammonia content. The Indo-Iranians were naturally not alone among the peoples of the world in using urine for hygienic purposes; but it is a part of the immense conservatism of their descendants that both Hindus and Zoroastrians continued to employ it down to the twentieth century. So in orthodox Sharifabad cattle urine was still regarded as 'clean' even without consecration, a fact that was brought home to me by a trivial incident early in my stay there. I was standing with some of the Belivani children watching the cow turning Faridun Rashidi's oil-press, when she stopped to stale. I stepped back to avoid the splash, and Gushtasp looked at me with surprise and said: 'There's no need. It's clean.'

Gushtasp's attitude was natural, since for him the urine was the proper means for cleansing away pollutions and disinfecting all that was unclean, within and without. For external use it was taken directly from any bull, cow, or calf, and was called in Dari *pājōw* (from older *pādyāb*), a circumlocution for the factual term *gōmēz*.

For internal use, it had to be taken with special care from particular animals, in order to be pure enough to be consecrated. There was a long religious service for this purpose, the Yašt-e Nīrang-dīn, which was a Vendidad with especial rites, solemnized accordingly at night; and by transference the consecrated urine itself came to be referred to as *nīrang-dīn*, and then, more simply, as *nīrang*. In this case, D. Khodadad said, the urine should be taken from bull-calves, preferably white in colour, though in practice golden-brown ones had generally to be used. The chosen calves, or young bulls, were brought into two stalls in the old 'Gahāmbār Khāna' in Yazd, and were kept there for seven days, during which time they were given pure water to drink, and were fed on ritually clean food, offered them with recital of Avestan. The urine, taken on the seventh day, must not be taken during Rapatven Gah (that is, the noontide watch), but only during the morning and afternoon ones. A vessel was meticulously washed and dried for the purpose, and thereafter the liquid was strained through muslin into glass vessels. The initial service of consecration was carried out by seven priests, and thereafter a Vendidad should be solemnized over the *nirang* on the next six nights, to make a sevenfold consecration. Then the *nirang*, placed in stoppered glass jars, was set under the earth for forty days (either in a cellar or in a hole in the ground), before being taken into use. All agreed that the longer it could be kept the better, and an ideal time was thought to be seven years, five beneath the ground and two above. D. Mihraban-e Syavakhsh of Yazd told me that his father, an old priest, had indeed a small quantity by him that had been consecrated forty years (i.e. a very long time) previously. As it aged, the liquid became odourless and colourless. The last time that the elaborate service of consecration had been performed at the Gahambar Khana in Yazd was in 1961, when D. Khodadad went from Sharifabad to join six other priests who were versed in the Vendidad. After the sevenfold rites, each priest took a share of the *nirang* for use in his own parish. What D. Khodadad brought back to Sharifabad would be exhausted, he said, by 1965, and there was no hope of consecrating any more with due observances, since there were no longer the priests able to perform the ceremony.[1]

[1] *Nirang* being used in so many fundamental rites of purification, its due consecration was regarded as immensely important, and there are detailed descriptions of the service in the *Rivayats* (see Unvala, i. 576–85; Dhabhar, 347–57). It is still performed nine or ten times a year among the Parsis, and the detailed description of it given me by Dr. Firoze M. Kotwal (who had solemnized it

To understand the uses of *nirang* and *pajow* in combating pollution
one has to comprehend what constitutes uncleanness for the orthodox Zoroastrian. The essential doctrine of the faith in this respect is
that Ohrmazd created this world both perfect and static. The first
man, animal, and plant all existed in a state of physical maturity and
perfection, at the centre of a motionless world, with the sun ever
at noon; and the process of change, involving imperfection and
decay, is the work of Ahriman, who attacked the perfect creation of
Ohrmazd and corrupted it, bringing on it sickness, blight, old age,
and death, as well as all the range of moral and physical defects.[2]
The striving of Ohrmazd and all his creation in the present time is
directed towards overcoming these evils and restoring the world to
its pristine, unchanging perfection; and the purity laws are essentially
a series of battle orders, whereby the individual receives his instructions for combating the Adversary and his works during the course of
his own daily life, and so helping in this great cosmic endeavour.

Some of the ways in which this battle is to be fought are straight-
forward and can be generally appreciated (according, indeed, with
modern ideas of hygiene and conservation). Others are particular
to Zoroastrianism. Thus, since dirt, stench, and disorder belong
to Ahriman, the housewife is beginning the day's campaign when
she sweeps her home before sunrise, and fumigates it with sweet-
smelling herbs. In Sharifabad it was usual, when doing this, first
to sprinkle water over the courtyard in order to lay the dust;

himself in Navsari) tallied exactly with the prescriptions set out in the *Rivayats*.
Nothing is said there about the need for seven priests, or seven performances of
the Vendidad, and these would appear therefore to be subsequent elaborations.
Of the animals to be used it is merely stated that bulls are best, and failing them
oxen. In India the Parsis evolved the custom of consecrating a white bull and
keeping him both to provide hairs for the *varas* or metal ring used in all major
acts of worship (hence his name, the *varasya*), and urine for *nirang*; but they
too used ordinary bulls as well to provide enough urine for the service of consecration, contenting themselves with bringing these into a sacred precinct a day
beforehand (to the bellowed wrath of the *varasya*). In Navsari the extra bulls
were tethered in the courtyard and a hall of the Wadi Dar-e Mihr. For a sketch-
plan and description of the Yazdi 'Gahambar Khane' see G. Gropp, 'Die rezenten
Feuertempel der Zarathustrier (II)', *AMI*, N.F. 4, 1971, 275, 276. This remarkably
spacious and impressive structure is (*pace* Dr. Gropp) modern in its present
form, like all other Zoroastrian ones of any size, having been rebuilt within
recent memory. The use of *nirang* was abandoned early in the present century by
reformist Parsis, who substituted wine instead; and most Irani Zoroastrians
have likewise adopted wine or fruit juice now for this purpose.

[2] On these doctrines and their consequences see in more detail Boyce, *History*,
vol. i, ch. 6.

and this was permissible, since there is nothing essentially impure in dust. (In the Yazdi plain it consists indeed mostly of desert sand and grit blown into the wrong place.) It is held, however, in orthodoxy, that a human being is unclean on rising, being contaminated by the impurities of the hours of sleep; and so the old custom (now observed only by priests) was that a person should wash first with *pajow*, to remove these impurities, then say the košti-prayers, and only finally, being clean once more in body and soul, make an ablution with water. For water is one of the seven creations of Ohrmazd, and as such its purity must be guarded no less than that of the other six. So if some actual impurity is known or suspected, then this should first be removed by something which will make a barrier between it and the pure element of water. Similarly, there is an absolute prohibition against using the pure creation of fire to burn up waste matter. Nothing whatever may be put on fire except clean fuel, and the other offerings proper to it; and though meals may be cooked by fire, this should be done with precaution. Thus a Zoroastrian housewife was careful never to fill a pot too full, lest there should be spills or splashes; and if during the baking of bread a round of dough fell into the oven-fire, this was an offence which demanded an expiation, such as the recital of a certain number of *Ataš Niyayeš* (the prayer to fire). It was firmly believed in Sharifabad that, if left unatoned for, such offences would be punished. Thus on one occasion while I was in the village Shehriar, D. Khodadad's son, had a painful sty in one eye, and this he attributed to his having carelessly flicked a pellet of earth into their hearth-fire. So (though not neglecting to have treatment from the Ardekani doctor), he showed his contrition by reciting several *Ataš Niyayeš*.

This respect for fire and water sets the Zoroastrian apart from the adherents of all other faiths; and since it is only Zoroastrians who have purity laws with regard to these and the other five creations, to the orthodox all non-Zoroastrians are necessarily both unclean themselves and a threat to the cleanness of the world. Orthodox Shiʻi Moslems keep no less strictly a differently based purity code, and so in the Yazdi region the two communities confronted one another with mutual reserve. To the Zoroastrian the Moslem was a *bāmerd-e nā-pāk* 'an unclean so-and-so',[3] to the Moslem the

---

[3] The Sharifabadis could offer no explanation of the word *bāmerd*; possibly it is from **nāmerd* 'Unmensch'. They also called their Moslem neighbours 'Arabs', and regularly spoke of Ardekan as *Arabestān*, 'the place of the Arabs'.

Zoroastrian was a *gōr-e nājes* 'an impure unbeliever'; and the two parties sought accordingly to keep physical contact with one another to a minimum. This was strikingly illustrated at Elabad, where a Zoroastrian benefactor built a covered water-tank to provide drinking-water for the whole village, Moslem as well as Zoroastrian. The water-supply was in common; but two sets of steps led down to the tank, side by side, separated by a rail, and at the bottom of each was a tap, so that no Moslem hand need touch the Zoroastrian one, and vice versa. A similar arrangement was to be found in a number of other villages with mixed populations, provided always by a Zoroastrian (no Moslem ever allowed Zoroastrians to share in his benefaction). In Sharifabad itself each community had its own tank; but in the heat of summer it was customary for an official to ride about among the workers in the fields on a donkey laden with two big pitchers of water and with two drinking-mugs, one on one side for Zoroastrians, and one on the other for Moslems. It is true that the official himself had to belong to one or other faith, and to handle both mugs; but at least he was a man, and so not liable to the great uncleanness of women, which was the source of the liveliest apprehension for the Zoroastrians. Even so, those Zoroastrians who were maintaining strict ritual purity would not accept water from this source, but preferred to remain thirsty under the blazing sun. Moslem feeling in such matters could be just as strong, as I experienced once when alone with a group of Sharifabadi children in the main street of Yazd. It was a burning summer's day, and we were on our way to the mountain shrine of Nareke, on the further side of the city. One of the smallest children, thirsty after the journey from the village, begged for a drink of water. Her elder sister, not knowing the ways of Yazd, approached a street fountain, and at once we were surrounded by an angry group of Moslems, and the old hostile cry of *gor-e najes* went up around us. Fortunately at that moment the adults of the Zoroastrian party returned, and we were hastily bundled into a car and driven away. Even without this timely rescue we should probably have suffered nothing worse than jostling and insults, for police protection of Zoroastrians was vigorous in 1964; but in earlier times physical violence would certainly have followed, unless indeed some more liberal-minded Moslems had themselves intervened.[4]

---

[4] For a nineteenth-century instance of intervention by a Moslem on behalf of a Zoroastrian in the streets of Yazd see E. G. Browne, *A Year amongst the Persians*,

In Sharifabad itself children quickly learnt the conventions that separated the two communities. The Zoroastrians were still a good deal dependent on Moslem craftsmen and traders, and so Moslems came fairly frequently to their houses. There they were received with Persian courtesy, which naturally entailed offering food and drink; but this an orthodox Moslem would politely refuse, as was expected of him. I saw this myself in a striking way in the Belivani household, when a Moslem woman, a professional quilt-maker, came to the house several days in succession to help make up padded cotton quilts for winter bedding. All was friendliness, gossip was exchanged, and there was even much laughter, for quilt-making involves at a certain point pulling on the quilt to stretch it, and this developed into a joyous tug-of-war between fifteen-year-old Pourandukht and the quilt-maker. Nevertheless, during all the hot summer hours that the Moslem woman was at the house she never once accepted so much as a drink of water, producing various polite excuses for not doing so, which were equally politely accepted by Tahmina Khanom, although both were well aware of the real reason, the rigid barrier which the purity laws set between them in such respects.

Sometimes, however, where individuals were concerned, human kindness and courtesy made breaches in strict observance. Thus once at one of the mountain shrines a friendly Moslem driver, of casual orthodoxy, insisted on cooking food for his Zoroastrian passengers from another village; and Agha Rustam and his daughter Piruza, rather than create disharmony, accepted a pressing invitation to join them; but on their return to Sharifabad they went to the priest's house and drank *nirang* (ritually administered, with utterance of Avestan), in order to cleanse away the impurity which would otherwise have destroyed the purity conferred by their pilgrimage. Avoidance of food prepared by unbelievers was formerly common to the Irani and Indian communities, and down to the early nineteenth century even a Parsi layman could be made 'out caste' or excommunicated for eating such food.

As to uncooked foodstuffs, down to the early twentieth century the Yazdi Zoroastrians had only limited occasion to procure these from Moslems, being forced by poverty to live largely from their own

415–16. Once when I was with Tahmina Khanom in Yazd a small boy called her *Gōrōg*, 'Little *gōr*' to her face in the street. Had she been on home-ground in Ardekan, she said, she would have cuffed him soundly, but in unfamiliar Yazd she let it pass. The Sharifabadis had immense spirit, and despite their small numbers resisted local Moslem pressures sturdily.

produce; but some things they were obliged to buy, for instance cooking oil, since Zoroastrians were not allowed to own presses. They then boiled and strained the bought oil to purify it for their own use. For holy occasions, however, they preferred to use the rendered fat of a sacrificial animal, which would keep a year or two in a cool cellar. The first Zoroastrian in Sharifabad to defy the age-long ban and have his own press was Agha Rustam's father, Nosh-iravan, who set up a small one, turned by a cow, in a yard behind his house. With this he pressed seeds of the castor plant to yield pure oil to burn in sanctuary lamps. (Tahmina Khanom vividly recalled helping him in the early days of her marriage.) Later Paridun Rashidi set up a press in his turn to express the more costly sesame-seed oil for ritual cooking. The demand for this at festival times was great, and in summer the work was arduous because of the heat (the seeds having to be roasted first); but it was accounted highly meritorious, because it contributed to the celebration of the gahambars and other holy feasts. Formerly it was only on holy days that the villagers tasted meat, from the sacrifices, but by the 1960s they had accustomed themselves to buying small quantities for ordinary use from a little shop in the Moslem quarter (holding that the sin of slaying an animal without the proper rites was on the butcher's head). This meat, and any fruit or herbs which they bought from Moslems, they washed with great care on getting it home. Vegetable fat in tins was held to be clean enough for everyday purposes (being, it was thought, untouched by hand), but it was never used on holy days for ritual cooking.

Impurity by no means came wholly from the unbeliever, but, demon-created, could penetrate everywhere. Hence there was need for an embracing purity code, which is set out in all its final scholastic elaboration in the late Pahlavi books and the *Rivayats*.[5] Its workings can be traced in almost full force among orthodox Parsis down to the nineteenth century; but in the Yazdi area some of the ancient rules evidently came to be relaxed during the harsh oppressions of late Safavid and early Qajar times, when the community as a whole was reduced to dire poverty, and had evidently neither the energy nor means to maintain all the old prescriptions. A number continued to be strictly observed, however, although by 1964 even in orthodox Sharifabad it was noticeable that the older people tended to keep them both more conscientiously and with a greater awareness of their doctrinal basis than did the younger generation.

[5] For references see Boyce, *History*, ch. 12.

Within the general concept of all things being impure which had been brought into existence by Ahriman, there were certain categories of things which traditionally the Zoroastrians regarded as polluting. Thus all that leaves the human body is impure to a greater or lesser extent, including even the breath (which is why a Zoroastrian priest wears a veil over nose and mouth when he consecrates ritual objects, or is in the presence of what has been consecrated). Probably here ancient taboos have been brought together and elaborated in the light of the Zoroastrian doctrine that the original perfect creation was static, neither absorbing anything nor giving anything out. Coughing and sneezing are therefore deprecated, and since saliva is impure, no Zoroastrian should ever eat from the same plate as another, or drink from a glass which another has used—a rule most strictly observed by the Parsis. But this is one of the ancient restrictions which had come to be disregarded during the years of poverty and oppression, and was only strictly kept by priests, or at times when absolute ritual purity was sought for. Otherwise mother and children, or a pair of friends, often ate from the same plate; and at festival times it was usual for one wine glass to circulate for the drinking of toasts. Even in the houses of the wealthy in Yazd it was not uncommon to have only two or three glasses set on the table for the use of any who chose out of a numerous company. With this breakdown in the old purity laws—which in this case were at one with modern ideas of hygiene—went also the old prescription of eating in silence, a rule imposed, so the Pahlavi books say, out of respect for Hordad and Amurdad, the Amahraspands of water and plants.

In these respects D. Khodadad maintained rules abandoned by the laity;[6] and he did his utmost to avoid touching any food which was *prangīn* 'unclean', that is, tasted already by another, or in any other way not ritually pure. Ideally he would have liked to follow the old rule that a priest should eat food prepared only by himself, or by the women of a priestly house, who would know and strictly keep the rules of purity in every detail; but ministering as he did to three villages, he often had to accept hospitality from his lay parishioners. He would, naturally, never eat food prepared by an unbeliever.

Even more unclean than what leaves a healthy body naturally is any flow of blood, for primitive dread in this respect is reinforced by the doctrine that afflictions of every sort are Ahrimanic, attacks

[6] Cf. above, p. 46.

by the evil powers on the ideal state of physical wholeness. So bleeding from a cut or a pulled tooth makes a person unclean, and menstruation, being regarded as a recurrent sickness, is held to be almost the worst of all pollutions, and down the millennia the priests elaborated restrictions to lessen its evil effects. According to them 'the fiend that sits in a menstruous woman is the worst of all fiends in the world; for there is no fiend whose look alone can make a thing unclean, save only the fiend in a menstruous woman. . . . She afflicts and injures, knowingly or unknowingly, all the good creatures and creations of Ohrmazd'.[7] Such a one, it is held, cannot properly address the divine beings, and so she takes off the kušti during these days and does not pray.[8] This gives rise to a polite circumlocution for a woman in this state, who is said to be *bī-namāz* 'without prayer'; and since the mere glance of the *bi-namaz* was held to be contaminating, the harsh old usage was for her to withdraw and shut herself away from the rest of the household in a place where she could not see sky or water, earth, plants or animals, men or fire. This custom led to the Dari colloquial expression to describe a woman's withdrawal at this time, as *lok sda*, 'going to the hole'. This had no literal meaning for the younger generation, for memory of the old rigours was fading fast, and its full significance first came home to me when I visited a house in Yazd owned by D. Khodadad. This had belonged to his father, a very orthodox priest, but had been untenanted and therefore unaltered for thirty-six years.[9] Part of the building was thought to be at least a hundred years old, and here my guide, D. Khodadad's young married daughter Parizad, led me into a small yard, in which there was a tiny windowless mud-brick building, some five feet high by four feet across, thick-walled, and with a doorway only four feet by two feet. This, Parizad thought, must have been a hen-house; but her mother Piruza, joining us, explained that it was in fact the old *ganza-e punidun*, the place for a menstruous woman, the 'hole' of the idiom. The

---

[7] The oldest scriptural treatment of this subject is in Vd. 16. This is elaborated in greater detail in the Pahlavi Vd., Šnš. iii, and the *Rivayats* (see Unvala, i. 205 ff.; Dhabhar, 211 ff.). On observances among the Parsis in the early twentieth century see Modi, *CC*, 165–6.

[8] The history of this usage is, however, puzzling. It is common to the Iranis and Parsis, which would ordinarily suggest that it could be traced back to at least the ninth century; but that women should continue to pray during their periods is not only indicated in Šnš. (ed. Tavadia) iii. 32, but is positively enjoined in the *Rivayats* (see Unvala, i. 208.9, 216.15–16; Dhabhar 214, 221).

[9] See 'Zoroastrian houses', 138–42.

narrow doorway would have been covered by a curtain when the place was in use, making it very dark. Inside the tiny cell it was impossible to stand upright or to stretch out at full length; and it must have become stiflingly hot there in summer, for mud-brick absorbs and holds the heat, and there was no way of creating a cooling current of air. Here a woman who was *bi-namaz* sat by day and slept by night, safely shut away from all the creations and so made powerless to injure them. This harsh usage arose logically from the doctrine of the pollution lurking in a woman's gaze during this time. It was first recorded by a European traveller in the seventeenth century,[10] but the likelihood is that Zoroastrian women had suffered under it for countless generations previously.

Parizad was as much startled as I was by this glimpse into the past, for the observance had been much relaxed in the present century. This relaxation started among the wealthier families in Yazd, and spread thence to the villages.[11] In 1964 Sharifabadi women in their seventies could well remember how in youth they had spent all the days of their *bī-namāzī* in the dark *ganza-e punidun*; but these places had by then been destroyed, and the existing customs, though harsh enough, were less exacting. Segregation, that is, was still enforced, but not for so long or so completely. There were, however, still many onerous rules to be observed. Special clothes were kept for this time, which, though scrupulously washed and clean, were ritually impure, being reserved for this purpose. If, therefore, ordinary clothes become accidentally polluted (as by contact with a corpse), they are set aside, after cleansing, for use during *bi-namazi*. More usually the clothes were simply old ones, faded and shabby with use; and all ornaments, such as bracelets and rings, were laid aside, since nothing put on during these days might be worn at any other time. The *bi-namaz* also put on old shoes, either the local cotton *gīve*, or plastic sandals, either of which could be washed. In the ordinary way the villagers often went barefoot in summer, which was both economical and pleasant; but during menses a woman must never put an unshod foot to the ground, for this would pollute the earth, and grievously offend its guardian, Spendarmad. Having put on these old garments, the *bi-namaz* withdrew to the end of a passage or the corner of a room or courtyard, and there she

---

[10] See J. B. Tavernier, *Six voyages en Turquie, en Perse et aux Indes*, Eng. transl., London, 1684, iv. 166.

[11] For some details see 'Zoroastrian houses', 142.

remained for the next three days. She might sleep there too at night, or perhaps in summer take her bedding to a corner of the roof. This bedding, like her clothes, must be kept solely for this time, and consisted usually of thin worn quilts which could be easily washed. In priestly theory the *bi-namaz* should simply sit or sleep during these three days, doing nothing whatsoever; but even women of priestly family (in Iran and India) assured me that they never accepted this, and the village women roundly declared that, if the rich ladies of the city could afford to be idle, they could not. So they kept for this time dull sewing jobs, such as mending old clothes or patching the heavy cloths used in the fields. No embroidery or attractive needle-work was done then, and anything which was handled had to be purified afterwards by being steeped in *pajow* and left to dry in the sun.

The women in general loved bright colours and pretty things, and it was sad to see one of them thus eclipsed, sitting in the shadows in faded garments, bent over some plain and laborious handiwork. She was no longer, however, cut off from the life of the family. According to the priests of old, a righteous man became impure even by exchanging words with a woman at such a time; but I never saw the slightest reluctance on the part of anyone to speak to a *bi-namaz*, and a wife could therefore offer counsel and direct her household as a woman might from a sick-bed. Nevertheless, for the first three days she was forced to be a helpless burden upon others. She could not prepare food, or fetch it for herself when it was prepared. It must be set before her on a special dish, preferably of plated copper or glass (earthenware or tin were regarded as porous and therefore unsuitable). Her drinking-cup too was kept separate and had to be filled for her. If she stirred her tea, it should be with a silver spoon, for a tin one could not be made 'clean' again; failing this, it was best she should use a twig, that could be thrown away. The *Rivayats* required that the *bi-namaz* should be given less food than usual, and with the change from an active to a suddenly sedentary life this happens to be sensible. Such food as there was must be plain, and this rule was carefully observed by the villagers, who ate mostly bread at these times (without such relishes as cheese or herbs), and avoided all pungent or strong-smelling foods. This discipline, like all the rest, was self-imposed. I once saw, for instance, a small boy bring some roasted melon seeds and put them down before his mother, and she had almost taken some before she remembered her condition, and hastily drew back. After the third day, the *bi-namaz* had more freedom to move about, and some took considerable advantage of this; but even the laxest refrained during the whole of her period from baking bread, or setting foot on the *pesgam-e mas*, or tending the household fire. If she left the house, she walked carefully along the lanes, avoiding contact with anyone else, and trying not to go near running water. She would not sniff even at a distance the wind-blown scent of flowers, lest her enjoyment should wither them, nor would she pass beyond the lanes into the open fields, for fear of polluting the fertile earth and blighting the crops.

The harsh climate of Yazd sometimes made the regulations of *bi-namazi* physically hard to endure. Thus a series of ablutions had come to be prescribed for this time, to be made in winter as well as summer. In the *Rivayats* (which in this respect reinforce the teachings of older works), it is strictly enjoined that a *bi-namaz*, being 'unclean', should not wash at all with water, but use only *pajow*;[12] and this prohibition was obeyed into the twentieth century by Parsi women. There were, however, a number of observances common to menstruation and to the 'purification of the nine nights' (the *barašnom-e nō-šwa*), both being concerned with uncleanness; and it appears that because of this common element, in Persia after the seventeenth century some usages proper only to the latter came to be adopted also for the former. Thus the practice of three ablutions, which should be peculiar to *no-šwa*, came to be enjoined also for the time of *bi-namazi*, although doctrinally this was unjustifiable. Each ablution was performed in the open air, in a sheltered corner of the house-yard. The *bi-namaz* stood on a slab of stone, or failing this on bare earth, and a woman or girl who was 'clean' poured warm water over her from head to foot. In Yazd in this century the ablution was often made in a screened corner of the roof, but this was not approved in Sharifabad, since, although the living earth 'can shake itself free from impurity', a man-made roof cannot. The threefold ablutions took place usually on the first, third, and seventh day of the period (though there was some variation over the second ablution, which might also be performed on the fourth or fifth day). No ablution was ever performed at night. Although the practice might be tolerable, indeed pleasant in summer, it was an ordeal during the searing cold of winter days. Even when there was

---

[12] See e.g., Pahl. Vd. 7; Šnš. 3.16, 21b; *Riv.*, Dhabhar, 214, 218, 569.

snow on the ground, the older Sharifabadi women made their ablution in the open, but the younger generation was less hardy, and in
really bitter weather girls sought the shelter of a byre, at least for
the second and third ablutions, when the impurity was felt to be
less. (In large town-houses there was a stone-floored room set aside
for these occasions.) For the first ablution an urgent message often
had to be sent to a neighbour for her help; and it was after this that
the *bi-namaz* put on the old, shabby clothes proper to the occasion.
According to the *Rivayats* she should also put on a special sedra
and košti (the sacred shirt and girdle), and should re-tie the košti
seven times a day,[13] but in Persia women became accustomed to
laying both aside, shirt and girdle, since it was held that they ought
not to pray at this time. This usage may have arisen in part from the
fact that, since the custom developed of making three ablutions, a
woman had need of two complete sets of old clothes, the second to
be put on after the second ablution; and she would therefore have
needed two extra shirts and girdles, an additional elaboration and
expense. The clothes laid aside after the second ablution were washed
for the *bi-namaz* by a 'clean' woman or girl. They were never washed
in running water, but in a bowl; and the water in which they had
been washed was poured away carefully in a corner where the sun's
rays could reach and swiftly cleanse the suffering earth. (It caused
Zoroastrians much distress when Moslem women washed such
clothes in the running water of the village stream.) If in winter the
bi-namaz wore a thick garment (such as a cloth jacket or sheepskin
coat) which was difficult to wash each month, this would be sprinkled
with *pajow* and put in the sun to be purified.

Another physical hardship of *bi-namazi* arose from the fact that
the village houses were unheated during the bitterly cold winter.
By day the villagers ordinarily kept warm by working, and at night
families slept huddled snugly together; but the *bi-namaz* must sit
still all day and sleep alone at night, banished from the company
of husband or sisters. (Only a nursing infant might stay with its
mother, sharing perforce her uncleanness.) I saw what hardships
this could cause when I spent a week in early February at the house
of Shehriar Zohrabi in Mazraʿ Kalantar, when his wife Shirin was
bi-namaz. The cold was piercing, and the small brazier in the living
room was lit only when tea was made, and then gave out a fugitive
warmth. Shirin sat in a corner huddled in a sheepskin cloak kept

¹³ See p. 100 n. 8, above.

specially for this purpose, in which she also slept at night, but even so she shivered. Her smallest child, a girl, was only a toddler, and it needed constant coaxing and commands by the mother to keep the infant away from her, with some help from her only slightly older brothers.

In this instance the family was lucky in that there was a young girl, a neighbour's daughter, living with them, who was able to take over the cooking and cleaning and care of the children; but there was often real hardship incurred in keeping the restrictions of *bi-namazi*. Neighbours tried to help out, but sometimes the man had to add all the household tasks to his own burden of field-work. The restrictions could also press heavily on a girl living alone with elderly grand-parents, who were incapable of taking over her tasks (as was the case for Shahnaz, Agha Rustam's eldest daughter). In such difficult circumstances each did the best she could to keep the prescriptions. Even in a big household matters were not always easy, and Agha Rustam's daughter Pourandukht recalled, with a mixture of pride and laughter, a heroic occasion when she was only twelve years old, and her mother and two elder sisters became *bi-namaz* together, and she had to wait on all three of them, look after her father, care for three younger children, tend the stock, and cook and clean (all of which, her mother testified, she had accomplished remarkably well). The affliction was often sadly ill-timed, coming upon several at once, as on this occasion, or at the most vexatious moments. I saw a young wife compelled by it to remain shabby and aloof when her husband had just returned after many months' absence, and she longed to make herself pretty and to welcome him home. At another time Sarvar and her step-daughter Parichihr were *bi-namaz* together on a day when there was a big gahambar at their house, and both had to abandon their home abruptly in the midst of the preparations, leaving friends and neighbours to cook the food and receive the guests in their stead.

One of the liveliest dreads of the Zoroastrian woman was to be taken untimely by her menses in a holy place; and often a woman would refrain from going on pilgrimage through fear of this happening. In Sharifabad a girl had been afflicted in this way at the mountain shrine of Pir-e Hrišt about two years before I was there. She left the shrine at once, but was so shocked by the sin which she had involuntarily committed that despite hospital treatment she remained prostrate and in pain for nearly a year, until the strict performance of certain expiatory rites helped her to recover.[14]

Although to become *bi-namaz* for the first time was trouble and grief for a girl, yet it marked her entry into womanhood, and formerly sherbet and sweetmeats were distributed by her parents when it happened, although this custom had fallen into disuse. If the girl were already betrothed, her fiancé's family should send her presents, called *bar-lokī* 'for the door of the hole'—a new košti upon a tray, with some raw cotton, a piece of woven cloth, a mirror, comb, and stockings. After this, only pregnancy and old age gave a woman respite from the monthly ritual impurity. When menstruation ceased, the priests recommended of old that a woman should pay for the performance of a Davāzdah Hamast, that is, the celebration of twelve Vendidads, a ceremony described in the *Rivayats* as being like 'a great wind' which blows away all the 'sin of menstruation' (*dāstān-wunāh*).[15] Perhaps because there were too few priests left to perform this long ceremony, perhaps because it had always been too costly for the villagers, I never heard it even spoken of; but it was not uncommon for an old woman to undergo *no-šwa*, sometimes repeatedly, and to guard her ritual purity thereafter with the utmost strictness, rejoicing in being, for the first time since childhood, wholly and prolongedly 'clean'. Such women were sometimes then appointed the guardians of lesser shrines and played an active part in the religious life of the community.

The men accepted their women's ritual uncleanness as a trouble to all concerned, but an unavoidable evil of this life, to be stoically endured. Only a callow boy would sink to uttering taunts about it, although I once heard this done ('Yah! *you* can't go! *you're* unclean!'—a provocation which his exasperated sister, already grieved at having to forgo a longed-for pilgrimage, could not even answer in her condition with a well-merited clout). Even with the general acceptance by the community of the evils of this state, it remains a matter for admiration that the Zoroastrian women were not warped

---

[14] The Sopra-ye Sabzi (see above, p. 62) was sometimes offered for such cases, but this girl was cured instead by a threefold performance of the *Čerāy-e nō*, another rite carried out without priest or Avestan.

[15] *Riv.*, Unvala, i. 219.15–17; Dhabhar, 221. Authorities vary slightly as to the dedications of the twelve services, but in general these are to be devoted to the Amahraspands of the seven creations, and the yazads of such other natural phenomena as the sun and moon, stars, wind, and rain. See *Riv.*, Unvala, i. 211, 212, 219, 220; Dhabhar, 219–20.

by a sense of physical degradation, but retained their dignity and
self-respect. There were, of course, other aspects of the case. The
enforced rest, especially when it was no longer spent in the *ganza-e
punidun*, might be beneficial to health, as the priests maintained; and
if each woman suffered a monthly eclipse, she also had each month a
joyful re-emergence, freshly bathed and adorned, and with a conscious delight in the freedoms once more restored to her. There was,
moreover, a pride in keeping the rules prescribed, for which responsibility rested with the women themselves. The priests might speak of
the 'sin' of menstruation, but the women knew that they were no
more guilty of this than Eve's daughters of eating the apple. Rather,
they were the hapless victims. But by observing the prescribed
restrictions, they were not merely suffering passively, but were
helping positively to restrict the infection of evil and to limit contagion from the powers of darkness. They were thus combatants,
with the dignity given by battle-service; more polluted, necessarily,
than men, but also more greatly enduring.

The uncleannesses which we have so far considered come from
the living body. All dead matter is also in varying degrees polluting,
because death belongs to Ahriman, who brought it into the world.
To start with the relatively trivial, what is shed or severed from the
living body, that is, hair-trimmings and nail-parings, becomes at that
instant dead, and therefore contaminating. Apart from specific
Zoroastrian doctrine in this respect, there are also, evidently,
some very ancient beliefs involved here, especially with regard to
nail-parings, beliefs such as have been found among peoples the
world over. Thus I was told by more than one person in Sharifabad
and Mazra⁶ Kalantar that, if nail-parings were allowed to fall on
the ground, they would be seized by demons and made into swords
to slash their owner with in the hereafter. This ancient belief,
which is recorded in the Pahlavi books, reinforces the doctrine that
these parings are unclean and so must not be allowed to touch the
good earth. The Sharifabadis looked with abhorrence at their
Moslem neighbours when they shaved their beards or pared their
nails casually in the lanes outside their houses; and they would not
buy from a Moslem a cow or donkey with a halter on, for there was
a firm conviction that such halters, made apparently from horse-
hair, were in fact plaited from the long hair of Moslem women, and
so were utterly impure.

The Zoroastrians themselves gathered up and disposed of hair-trimmings and nail-parings with much care.[16] The method used in the Belivani household was to put them into a scrap of white cotton, laid on the ground at the centre of four *kaš*, or ritual furrows, drawn round it to pen in the contamination. The appropriate Avestan words were recited (Vd. 17. 9), and then this cloth was sewn up, and dropped on to a little bit of coloured cloth, which was tied round it. Then one of the household (usually a woman or girl) would roll up the sleeve on her left arm tightly above the elbow, and holding the tiny bundle in her left hand, well away from her body, would carry it to the *lard* or *nākhondān* ('place for nails'), and drop it in. This was a small square mud-brick building, on the outskirts of the village, with a chimney-like hole in the flat roof, and steps leading up to this, but no door.[17] One simply went on to the roof and dropped one's bundle in; and for the very old, for whom the steps were impossible, there was a little hole in a side wall. Periodically acid was dropped down the central hole to destroy what was inside, which till then had lain there without contaminating any of the creations (for the building was roughly paved). As for the bearer of the bundle, the Belivani custom, which seemed general in Sharifabad, was that she went straight home and made ablution, that is, had water poured over her from head to foot by a 'clean' person. In Mazraʿ practice was in some respects simpler, in others more complicated. Thus nail-parings and hair-trimmings were there put into a metal basin. No *kaš* were drawn, and the bowl was simply covered with a scrap of cloth, carried to the *lard* and emptied into it. Thereafter, however, the bearer made a threefold cleansing; that is, she set three stones on the ground, within *kaš*. Standing on the first she rubbed herself with *pajow*, on the second with sand, so that the pollution had been

---

[16] This is the practice also among Shiʿi Moslems in some other parts of Iran (for instance, among conservative families in Isfahan and Shiraz), who also observed some of the ancient restrictions with regard to menstruation; but in the Yazdi area, presumably because of the continued confrontation of the two communities, there seemed to have been a deliberate rejection of such Zoroastrian rules. Thus I once, for example, saw a well-to-do Yazdi Moslem paring his nails beside a cloth spread with food.

[17] This building had been erected on his own land as a charitable act by one Jehangir-e Khosrow. Within living memory Sharifabad had had three *lards*, but this was because the land on which the two previous ones had stood had been bought by Moslems, and not because the little buildings were full. The largely self-sufficient village had earlier known nothing of packaging or novelty goods, and had produced extraordinarily little waste, and none which could not be destroyed by acid, although by the 1960s tinned foods and plastic wrappings had begun to make their way there.

twice removed before she made ablution with water on the third stone. The metal bowl was likewise cleansed with *pajow*, then scoured with sand, and finally washed with water.

Already in 1964 it was only the elderly and the most strictly orthodox in the two villages who carried out all these observances, and younger women increasingly took the easier course of simply carrying the parings and trimmings out into the desert (which in Mazra' lay all about the village). Since it was dry dead matter, it was not so noxious as fluid impurity, and if laid on barren ground would do no harm. Dry dead matter might in general be disposed of in this way, even when it was Ahrimanic in origin. Thus, for instance, during the great house-cleaning which precedes the festival of Panji, Piruza Belivani came across a glazed jar that proved to be full of desiccated black beetles. In her disgust she dropped it, and their bodies rolled out over the floor. Her thirteen-year-old sister, Bibi Gol, at once fetched the kitchen tongs and a piece of paper, put the beetles one by one on to the paper with the tongs, and then carried the little package out to a piece of waste ground. On her return she asked her youngest sister, Mandana, to turn on the tap of the water-jar for her, so that she should not touch it herself, and very carefully washed her hands and the tongs. Pourandukht, watching, recalled a time when as a very small girl she had picked up a dead puppy by the tail to carry it out of the house, and her indignant mother had pounced on her, given her a scolding and made her make ablution at once. The proper procedure would have been to wrap a bit of cloth round her hand first, so as to avoid direct contact with the dead body.

In such cases the change from life to death was the vital factor—for a dog while alive was held to be the cleanest of all creatures, after a righteous human being, and small living insects were regarded with indifference. Otherwise life in a Persian village would be impossible. Flies settled thickly in summer even on consecrated food, and nothing could be done to prevent them, since this was set out in open *pesgams*. If, however, a *dead* fly should drop on food, this polluted it. This fact was brought home to me when I attended a ceremony at the dakhma, out in the desert. A bowl of milk had been carefully carried there for consecration, and just before the service began a fly was seen in it. The insect was hastily extracted with a metal spoon, and anxious looks were bent on it to see if it were still alive. Fortunately it was, for otherwise the milk would have become impure, and could not have been blessed.

Larger insects, such as big-bodied beetles, tarantulas, or the huge local wasps, were regarded as unclean in themselves, and it was a virtue to kill them, using Ahriman's own weapon of death to reduce his legions. Since they were impure when alive, they were only slightly more polluting dead. By the logical working out of this doctrine, the most polluting dead object in the whole world is the corpse of a righteous man, for he of all things belongs to Ohrmazd, and so, in order to overwhelm him with devil-created death, the powers of evil have to gather in force, and they remain about the body after the soul has left it, emanating an infective corruption. Zoroastrians treat the body of a co-religionist, therefore, with the same sort of care and precaution which others might take in handling the corpse of one who had died from a deadly contagion.

In Sharifabad most people died at home rather than in a hospital, and both family and neighbours were often necessarily involved. So with this and the many lesser causes of pollution in the world, means were needed to cleanse away the impurities which none could wholly avoid. The simplest of these means we have already encountered, namely outward cleansing through ablution, and inward cleansing through drinking *nirang*. There was also the more elaborate form of outward cleansing when a polluted person used first *pajow* and then sand before washing with water, and this threefold cleansing was elaborated in the two major purification rites, both of which should be administered to the unclean person by a priest.

One of these rites was *sī-šūy* or the 'thirty washings' (in Dari *sī-šūz*).[18] In this the priest first gave *nirang* to the person to be cleansed, and made him recite the appropriate Avesta. Then he gave him *pajow* to rub over his body nine times, sand nine times, and water nine times, making twenty-seven cleansings in all, before a final triple ablution with water concluded the thirty washings. During the twenty-seven cleansings the candidate moved, naked and in a squatting position, from one set of stones to another, from north (the direction of Hell) to south, his impurity diminishing steadily as he went. The stones themselves were enclosed by ritually drawn lines or *kaš*, which penned the contamination in. The priest in his purity stood outside these lines, and passed the unclean person the *pajow*, sand, and water in a ladle fixed on the end of a bamboo cane with nine knots in it; and even so he was careful not to touch him with the ladle, but poured its contents into his cupped hands from above.

---

[18] On this rite see further Boyce, *History*, i. 312–13, with nn.

The rite of *si-šuy* was still often carried out in the 1960s, and I once watched D. Khodadad draw the lines for it, and set out the stones, on a roof-top in Mazraᶜ Kalantar.[19] The purification itself, which was undergone fasting, took about half an hour. It was mostly administered to women (after an early miscarriage or other cause of impurity), and in that case another woman who had undergone *no-šwa* handed the candidate the *pajow*, sand and water, while the priest recited the Avestan close by. I met women in Yazd and the villages who said that they had undergone the rite more often than they could remember. Among men it was chiefly the salars who made use of this purification. They were supposed to go through it as often as possible (in the intervals of taking *no-šwa*), in order to keep down the level of contamination in their bodies. In their case a layman handed them the cleansing materials in place of the priest, who could not in his purity come so closely into contact (even when ritually protected) with ones thus impure. Occasionally other men asked for *si-šuy* also. I met one in Mazraᶜ who had undergone it in 1963, in order, he said, to rid himself of a long run of misfortune. In his case the purpose of the rite was thus semi-magical; but this was not doctrinally improper, since for orthodox Zoroastrians ill luck, like uncleanness, has a diabolical origin, and there is no logical reason why both should not be got rid of by a single process of driving off the evil powers.

The greatest of the purification rituals, which was much more widely undergone, was the *barašnom-e no-šwa*, or 'ablution of the nine nights', referred to simply as *no-šwa* or 'nine nights', for what distinguished this radically from *si-šuy* was that the initial, relatively short, purification 'on the stones' was followed by nine nights in retreat, during which the process of purification was continued under a strict religious discipline.[20] In India this rite had by the late nineteenth century become one almost solely for priests,[21] but in the

---

[19] For the proper layout of these furrows see *Riv.*, Unvala, i. 600. The furrows were still drawn in this way in Kerman in the 1960s, where it was rare to find anyone but the priests and very old women who had undergone *no-šwa*. In Yazd, however, where *no-šwa* was still regularly administered, a confusion had arisen, and the priests drew for the *si-šuy* the more elaborate furrows proper to the major purification, see below, p. 129.

[20] For the extensive literature on this rite see Boyce, *History*, i. 313 n. 112.

[21] See J. J. Modi, *The Persian Farziāt-Nāmeh . . . of Dastur Dārāb Pāhlan*, p. 16 n. 2: '. . . up to about 50 years ago it was not rare to see persons, both male and female, themselves going through the ceremony . . . But, now-a-days . . . the priests are paid to take Bareshnūms on behalf of other persons.' The move to exclude the laity from the rite seems to have begun among the priests of Bombay in the eighteenth century.

Irani community until the beginning of the twentieth century it seems to have been undergone at least once in a lifetime by almost everyone who could afford it, either personally or by proxy, for the doctrine had been evolved that every human being is polluted from the womb, and so must cleanse himself by *barašnom*. The common expression for this obligatory observance was to undergo the rite 'in order to cleanse one's bones'. According to one Zoroastrian work,[22] if a man has not been thus purified during his lifetime, the divine beings cannot bring themselves to approach his departed spirit, and he must wait to go to the Judgement Seat until his son or heir (*pol-guzār*) undergoes the cleansing for him, or pays a priest to do so.

The priests recognized four categories of candidates for *no-šwa*: firstly, children, from the age of ten, who were *sar-e šīr*, that is, innocent except from the impurities of birth and their mother's milk (which according to ancient physiology comes from her blood); secondly, the adult and ordinarily sinful or contaminated; thirdly, the heavily polluted (*rīmanī*), notably the salars or corpse-bearers, who should undergo *no-šwa* as often as possible, and at least every second year. They 'went on the stones' separately, and passed their retreat in a place apart. Fourthly, there were those suffering from a single severe contamination, who underwent *nō-šwa-e pajowī*, in which all ablutions, even those ordinarily performed with water, were made with *pajow*. This was a costly and arduous form of the rite, for the ammonia in the *pajow*, remaining on the skin for nine days, stung and caused irritation. In Sharifabad it was undergone in recent years by a woman for her dead daughter, who had been burned to death while *bi-namaz*—a most unhappy fate, for in thus losing her life she doubly contaminated the fire (not only with a dead body, but with one that was unclean even before death), and so burdened her soul with great sin.

Up to the 1950s, *no-šwa* was administered to all Zoroastrians of the region in the city of Yazd itself, which had a place in the Mahalle-ye Dasturan built for this purpose, called the *barašnom-gāh*.[23] This was set within a precinct enclosed by a high blank wall. A door in this wall opened from the lane into a small yard. On the other side of the yard there was a little doorway into a crooked passage, which led to the secluded *barašnom-gah* itself. This was a flat

[22] *Saddar Bundehesh* (ed. Dhabhar), ch. 72.
[23] On this see Jackson, *Persia past and present*, 383.

enclosure which, like a dakhma, was perfectly round, and for the same reason, namely that there should be no corners to hold pollution. There were recesses in the encircling wall in which candidates could put their clothes, but when the rite was not being administered there was nothing to see in the *barašnom-gah* but dusty trodden earth and scattered stones. There were two smaller enclosures within the precinct where the grossly impure (usually salars and women who had miscarried), 'went on the stones'. *Barašnom* was not administered during winter, for falling rain or snow would vitiate the rite, and most candidates chose to come during high summer. An especially popular time was just before the great festival of All Souls, celebrated currently in late July, for not only was the weather then warm, but there was an abundance of ritually pure food. This was helpful, since each *no-šwe* (as the candidate who completed the purification was called) was required to increase his merit by maintaining the ritual purity which he had attained for a minimum of forty days.

The prolonged rite of *no-šwa* is naturally a relatively costly one, and probably in the past few villagers could afford it for their children. Generally it was something to be planned and saved for, and, unless a particular reason arose, it was not undergone until adult life, when it was an event to rejoice in and commemorate. So some of the small brass bowls (*jām*) which were used for festive occasions bore inscriptions such as the following: 'The owner (is) Jehangir-e Khodabakhsh-e Isfandiyar of Mazraʿ Kalantar. We became *no-šwe* in Anno Yazdegirdi 1295' ('sāheb Jehāngīr-e Khodābakhsh-e Isfandiyār-e Mazraʿ Kalāntarī. 1295 Yazdegirdī nō-šwe budīm'). Leading villagers, however, like the merchants of Yazd, would sometimes send their children to become *no-šwe* soon after they had been invested with the sacred cord; and Agha Rustam himself underwent the purification at the age of twelve, riding into Yazd on donkey-back with a group of older people in the summer of 1932. When they reached the city (a twelve-hour journey) they found that with the others who had gathered there to undergo the rite they were a company of forty persons; and since forty is an auspicious number in Persia, they rejoiced at this.

There was a portico within the precincts of the *barašnom-gah* where the priests of the city would gather (those who were not themselves administering the rite), together with relatives and friends of the candidates. Here after undergoing the *barašnom* the candidates would come one by one, in their ritual cleanliness, and their kinsfolk would felicitate them and give them sprays of myrtle and cypress (laying these on the ground at their feet, since the *no-šwe* must have no direct physical contact with others once the rite has begun). When all the candidates had assembled, they went in a body to the house of the priest who was to be in charge of the retreat. Sometimes night had already fallen, and they could go without precaution through the empty lanes. If it were still day, someone would be sent ahead to see that there were no Moslems about in the Mahalle-ye Dasturan, for an encounter with an unbeliever would nullify the purification. The priests' houses in those prosperous years were often fine buildings, well able to accommodate large groups of candidates; and usually members of the priest's own family would act as 'parestārs' of the candidates, that is, they would prepare their food and attend upon them generally. Only the salars, in their professional impurity, made their retreat in some house not ordinarily occupied, where they would have lay parestars. The parestars must always themselves be *no-šwe*, however, and in a state of ritual cleanliness.

The rules for the nine nights' retreat were rigorous. The basic purpose was to continue the process of purification begun 'on the stones', and strict cleanliness, ritual and actual, was sought for throughout this time. Each candidate must bring with him two sets of spotlessly clean garments. One, which he put on after the *barašnom*, was of ordinary character, to be worn for sleeping and through the day. The other set was to be worn only for the nearly sacramental act of eating. These clothes must be white, and consisted, for men and women alike, of a headkerchief, sedra, outer shirt, trousers, and shoes of heavy woven cotton. They were all made of *kerbas*, the coarse undyed cloth woven at home; and when old people went through the ritual they often wore what they intended to be their death clothes (for a corpse is clad in just such garments, which must be used, not new).[24]

For eating, the hands must be covered, for additional purity, and this was usually done by drawing over them white cotton bags, tied at the wrist.[25] Till some forty years ago all Yazdis, rich and poor,

[24] See Pl. IIa.

[25] This is a practice which the Irani dasturs required also of women who were *bi-namaz* (see *Riv.*, Unvala, i. 212.8–10; Dhabhar, 222); but this appears to be one of the observances transferred to *bi-namazi* from *no-šwa*, for it was not practised among the Parsis. Unlike that of the triple ablution, it failed to establish itself among the Iranis themselves, and was not observed in the twentieth century.

Moslem and Zoroastrian, ate customarily with hands; but the ritual of *no-šwa* required an implement to be used. This was usually a deep-bowled copper spoon, often an heirloom, with its first owner's name engraved along the handle. Each candidate must also bring a copper bowl to eat from, and these too were often inscribed. If the candidate left the bowl on the floor while eating, then only the right hand that held the spoon need be gloved; but if he took the bowl up in his left hand, he needed two gloves. Before he ate, he had to say an Avestan prayer, and he must eat in silence, not letting the spoon touch his lips, but dropping the food into his mouth. Should the spoon touch his lips or teeth, he must throw it aside, and sign to the parestar to fetch him another. In no circumstances might he speak until he had recited the Avesta for after eating. Similarly, when he drank he should not let the bowl touch his lips. If he needed to drink between meals, when ordinarily clad, the parestar must hold the bowl for him, pouring the water into his mouth. The reasons for these various regulations were twofold: on the one hand, a desire to show all possible respect for the creations of water and plants, as represented in food; on the other, a wish to prevent the clean outer body becoming unclean through contact with the impure saliva.

The food given to the candidates must be plain and simple, and less in quantity than ordinary diet—a bare sufficiency for each person according to his needs. Meat must not be eaten for the first three days, and candidates sometimes chose to forgo it for the whole time. Nor might anything be eaten which had been prepared by non-Zoroastrians. Bread (baked by the parestars from home-grown wheat), fruit, herbs, and vegetable-broths were the staples of diet. Loaf-sugar was forbidden, and formerly only such things as dried mulberries or raisins could be used for sweetening; but later beet-sugar was allowed, since this could be refined by the Zoroastrians themselves. Tea too was formerly forbidden, and Mobed Rashid Rustami of Kerman told me that during the twenty-seven days of a threefold *no-šwa* (obligatory on Kermanis before they were admitted to the priesthood), he drank only water and milk taken from the cow by his own parestar. The prohibition against tea had since been relaxed, but the water with which it was made, and all drinking water, had to be especially pure. Smoking (which is never approved of) and snuff-taking were both forbidden during the retreat.

The candidates must not leave the house of the retreat (the

nō-šwa-khāna), or engage in any sort of work within it. They must not set an unshod foot to ground, or touch another person, or even let their clothes come in contact with another. By day each sat upon his own *čādor* or sheet of cotton cloth (which must be spread upon stones or bare earth or a mud floor, never upon porous brick). By night he slept upon this same thin cloth, with another drawn over him, but no quilt or pillow. Nor should he sleep much, for this is an indulgence. Men especially were urged to curtail sleep, and particularly during the first three nights; for a night ejaculation then annulled the *no-šwa*, and the candidate must depart. If the first three nights had passed, however, he might 'go on the stones' again, and start the nine nights once more from the beginning. Similarly, should a woman begin her menses during the first three days, her *no-šwa* became invalid; but if during the latter six days, she too might repeat the ritual, but after 'going on the stones' again she must sit in a place apart, so that her gaze did not fall upon others. That a woman should be allowed to complete the ritual in this condition is a puzzling concession, for she should be 'without prayer', and the recitation of Avesta is an important part of *no-šwa*; but possibly this concession reflects the usages of more ancient times, before restrictions on women during their periods grew to be so harsh and rigid.[26]

During the nine days the basic obligatory prayers were to be recited by all: the košti-prayers repeatedly, with those for the five watches of the day, and the prayers for before and after eating and answering a call of nature. It was good to recite a great deal of other Avesta also, and to read prayers in Persian, and especially, daily, to say a *patēt* or confession of sins. Some of the older women could not read, and knew little Avesta by heart, and they observed the times of prayer by long repetitive recitations of the two most holy prayers, the Ahunvar and Ašəm vohu. For this purpose they used rosaries, called 'band-e Ahunvar', either of thirty-three beads (the number of the divine beings) or a hundred and one (the number of the names of God). It was the duty of the parestar to instruct the ignorant about times of prayer, and to tell them the number of Ahunvars and Ašəm vohus to recite when the priest led the group in their devotions.

---

[26] See above, p. 100 and n. 8. It is possible that it was through this usage, which meant that ablutions were administered to a woman in the later stages of menstruation, that the practice developed requiring ablutions to be made throughout *bi-namazi*.

The ritual of *no-šwa* included, besides the initial purification, three additional ablutions, two (on the fourth and seventh days) to be made at the same time of day as the *barašnom* itself, and the third just after sunrise on the morning of the tenth day. There were also four drinkings of *nirang*, one at sunrise on the second day (which followed the *barašnom*), the next two at sunrise on the fifth and eighth days, and the last one immediately after the final ablution. There was thus thorough inner and outer cleansing. The ablutions were performed with sweet water, in which a little consecrated water had been poured.[27] After the second and third ablutions the candidate's clothes and the cotton cloth he sat and slept on were all washed, either by a woman who had undergone the purification herself, or by a young girl who had not yet become *bi-namaz*. New clothes for daily wear were brought by relatives, to be put on after the ablutions, and the white ones dried quickly in the summer sun. After answering a call of nature, a candidate had to wash his hands thrice with *pajow*, and rub them dry thrice with fine clean soil. Water should not be used for washing during *no-šwa*, except for the three prescribed ablutions.

Although the discipline of *no-šwa* was severe, the atmosphere maintained was quietly and serenely cheerful. In the intervals of the day there was talk and pleasant companionship; visitors were allowed and once the three first rigorous days were past, these visitors might produce diversions with singing and music. In these and other ways the *no-šwa* house had some resemblance to a hospital, with its strict routine designed to serve a single aim—in its case the cure of infective impurity—but with permitted relaxations also. Among the Parsis the discipline of the rite is as strict, but there is less austerity. The candidate is permitted a comfortable mattress to sleep on, and the food supplied to him is often varied and delicious. The additional hardships of the Irani practice seem un-Zoroastrian, since those of the Good Religion should not seek mortification; but they may well have arisen through circumstances, since poverty made a plain diet necessary, and cotton sheets were easy to provide and keep spotlessly clean. The unavoidable austerities were given a special significance, however, and gladly embraced; for it came to be believed that the nine nights' retreat had been instituted in remembrance of Zoroaster's imprisonment (after he had been slandered to the

---

[27] In general Sharifabad did not waste its scanty supply of sweet water on washing, but used brackish water for this.

still unconverted Kay Vištasp). So when the villagers slept uneasily and pillowless on the hard ground, they thought of their prophet lying without bedding on the floor of his cell, and the plain food was a reminder to them of his prison diet. There is no reference to such analogies in the *Rivayats*, nor any knowledge of them among the Parsis, so that the concept appears to be a recent one, shaped during the years of harsh endurance under Safavid and Qajar rule. Agha Rustam himself insisted that the parallelism was secondary, and should not be allowed to obscure the function of *no-swa* as a rite of purification.

The priests who administered *no-šwa* were naturally required to be themselves in the highest state of purity. Formerly there were several groups of them in Yazd, and in latter years there was a celebrated parestar, Parangis, daughter of D. Erdeshir Khodavendan, who was famed for her piety and knowledge of Avesta, and for being deeply conversant with the ritual. She had herself undergone the purification thrice, and she was much respected by the village women for her care in instructing them, as well as loved for her kindliness and cheerfulness of heart. Her death in 1962 dealt a blow to the administering of the rite in the city. The old *barašnom-gah* had not been used after 1960, but the rite had continued elsewhere on a smaller scale. In 1964 it was administered once more towards the end of August at Parangis's own old home, and among the five candidates was the blind Palamarz Rashidi of Sharifabad, who then became *no-šwe* for the twenty-eighth time, for the benefit of the soul of a departed citizen of Yazd.[28]

Some three weeks earlier Palamarz had undergone the purification with a larger group in Sharifabad itself. The administration of the rite there dated back to about nine or ten years previously, when D. Khodadad yielded to the entreaty of some old people who had never become *no-šwe* and who were daunted by the journey into Yazd. He told me that he had had many heart-searchings, because he

[28] Palamarz or Plamarz was the oldest brother of Paridun, and had lost his sight through an attack of measles when he was eight or nine. He had been carefully taught Avesta by D. Erdeshir-e Rustam (who was hušt-mobed of Sharifabad between D. Khodadad and his uncle, D. Bahram), and he knew by heart almost all the Khorda Avesta, together with the liturgies of the gahambar-services, the many other Afrinagans with their dedications, and the whole of the Gatha Ahunavaiti, used at funerals and on other occasions. Because of his lay ancestry and his blindness he could not become a priest, but he dressed regularly in white, kept strict rules of purity, and fulfilled many minor priestly functions, being held in high esteem because of his piety and self-discipline.

felt himself inadequate, since with the multifarious duties of his scattered parish he could not keep himself in a state of the highest purity (being obliged, for instance, often to eat in the houses of laymen). Moreover, administering *no-šwa* is very exacting, for the priest should recite the long office of the Vendidad by night to help drive away the forces of evil, as well as being with the candidates by day. Formerly the administering priest had assistants to help him. Now D. Khodadad was asked to give the purification single-handed, while carrying on his ordinary parish work. However, after much reflection he decided 'better bread of barley than no bread', and so began to administer it on a small scale, with his wife Piruza, Agha Rustam's sister, acting as parestar. At first only people from his own parish came, and he used his own house (in the traditional way) for the retreat. Then his aunt-by-marriage died, widow of the former hušt-mobed, D. Bahram, and she left their old *do-pesgami* house to the village. This, called 'the Dastur's House', was kept solely for religious purposes, and served thereafter, among other uses, for the nine nights' retreat.[29] It had a little high-walled yard, with its longer side running north to south, where the candidates 'went on the stones'. Another small yard at the further end of the building had steps leading down to a *qanat* stream, so that the place was well adapted for ritual requirements. By 1964 people were coming from outside the parish, and D. Khodadad administered the purification to three groups of candidates before Panji, and was being entreated to give the rite again in the autumn. Among those who came some had become *no-šwe* before in the city of Yazd, and they assured me that (as one would expect with a priest so scrupulous as D. Khodadad) it was administered in exactly the same way in Sharifabad as there. Through the great kindness of D. Khodadad, and of those undergoing the purification, I was able to be with two groups of candidates in the Dastur's House, and having their permission I propose to describe fairly fully what I saw and learnt among them.

D. Khodadad began administering the rite early in July to three women (who did not wish to be in a crush of candidates) from Cham, Mobareke, and Tehran. They finished their retreat during the time of the annual pilgrimage to the shrine of Banu-Pars, and, returning from there, we met them when they had just concluded the rite and were about themselves to make a pilgrimage, in their

---

[29] For a detailed description see 'Zoroastrian houses', 132.

state of purity, to Pir-e Hrišt. The day before, a group of fourteen men and women from Mazraᶜ, and one Sharifabadi, had joined them in the Dastur's House, having arranged their no-šwa to finish during Panji-kasog, leaving them time thereafter to make preparation for the Greater All Souls' Feast, Panji-mas. We ourselves were ritually clean from our pilgrimage, and Piruza Belivani and I went at once to the Dastur's House. Piruza herself, although only seventeen, had already become no-šwe twice, both times at her uncle's house in Sharifabad. The first occasion, when she was twelve, was for the sake of an aunt who had died by her own hand, without ever undergoing barašnom. Piruza had then had to recite all the Avestan prayers twice over, once for herself to 'cleanse her bones', and once for the soul of the dead woman. She was chosen to do this, rather than her elder sister, because of a placidity in her nature, a contentment in sitting still, which made the restrictions of the retreat less irksome to her than to some. Two or three years later she had had to undergo the purification a second time to rid herself of pollution incurred through helping at a still-birth; and being thus twice no-šwe, she was often asked to do ritual cooking, when everything must be very pure.

We arrived at the Dastur's House about an hour before sunset, and found the candidates a little weary towards the close of a long, quiet day, but ready to greet us with all the courtesy of the Yazdi villager. This being their second day, they had mastered the impulse to shake hands, and once the verbal salutations were over we all sat down again, carefully apart, to talk until it was time for the evening meal. The candidates were divided between the two *pesgams*. One of these had a small wind-tower (a late addition to the old house), and since this was therefore cooler and pleasanter, it was assigned to the men. There were five of them, three elderly—the atašband of the Mazraᶜ fire-temple, the guardian of the mountain shrine of Pir-e Sabz, whose name was Sam Khademi, and a farmer, Rustam-e Bahram, big, dignified, and taciturn. Of the other two, one, Rashid-e Khosrow, owned a small mill in Mazraᶜ. He was well versed in the basic Avestan texts, and often officiated there, with the dahmobed or the village schoolmaster, in 'outer' rituals.[30] One of his kinsmen had died a month before, and since only one of the salars could come, he had helped to carry the bier into the dakhma, and had therefore to undergo no-šwa in order to cleanse himself. The fifth of the group, Bahram-e Khodabakhsh Sami, was

---

[30] Cf. above, p. 54.

a vigorous man in his early thirties, who worked on a drilling-rig for a Tehrani firm of well-sinkers. At festival times he came home to Mazraʿ, and had begun to help in the ritual killing of sacrificial sheep. He had therefore been persuaded by Agha Rustam to become *no-šwe* to qualify himself properly for this. (The older sacrificer there, Jamshid Sami, had undergone the purification thrice to fit himself for the work.) Used to an energetic life, Bahram had faced with considerable reluctance the ordeal of nine days' enforced inactivity, and to strengthen his resolve his mother and other female relatives had joined him. The doyenne of the women candidates was, however, without doubt Piruza Sami, small, stout, serene, and gaily talkative, who was going through her sixth *no-šwa*, having kept the purity of her fifth unbroken from the previous summer. Her husband and daughter were dead, her sons thriving in Tehran; but rather than join them there, she continued to live alone in the spacious family house at Mazraʿ, observing the religious festivals and maintaining strict purity. Her hope was to become *no-šwe* seven times, and then to keep her purity thereafter to the end of her life.

Soon after we arrived, the candidates withdrew into side rooms to change into white for the evening meal. Their white clothes varied in a way which they would not have done in former times. Bahram-e Khodabakhsh, for instance, and two of the women who, like him, lived in Tehran, had clothes of fine factory-woven cotton and modern in style; and though the villagers were dressed in homespun cotton, Banu from Mazraʿ was the only one to be clad wholly in the traditional way, with long trousers to the ankle, the sleeves of her upper garment reaching to the wrist, and her headkerchief covering every strand of hair; and even she wore plastic sandals, instead of cotton *give*, on her feet.[31] The other women, like the men, had shorter trousers for coolness, and less enveloping clothes in general. But they all had dignity as, white in the shadows of the *pesgams*, they took their places again, each on his or her separate folded cloth.

Their chief parestar was Piruza, D. Khodadad's wife, who had two helpers. One was Piruza-e Dinyar, wife of the atašband of Shah Varahram Ized, the other Jehangir Jamshidi, both of whom had themselves undergone the rite, Piruza twice, Jehangir three times. Both had been busy in the kitchen, and now Jehangir went round the *pesgams* distributing from a newly woven basket copper bowls, all shining softly from a burnishing with wood-ash. He put one before

[31] See Pl. IIa.

each candidate, with a shining copper spoon in it. Then he carried round a big copper basin full of newly baked bread, broken into small bits, with which he filled the bottom of each bowl; and then a great saucepan, black outside with wood-smoke, from which Piruza ladled out a thick broth, made of onions browned in sesame seed oil, with home-ground flour and vegetables. When the bowls were filled, Piruza the Dastur's wife stood in front of the men, tall and straight as a grenadier in her red dress, and clearly and carefully recited the Avestan grace to be said before eating,[32] the men repeating it word by word after her. Then she crossed to the women's *pesgam* and recited it with them. The candidates then ate in silence, with slow and careful movements, made clumsy by the cotton bags drawn over their hands, and the need not to let the big spoons touch their lips or teeth. The parestars went round a second time with bread and broth, the candidates showing by signs if they wanted more. Then Jehangir gathered up the empty bowls to be washed in the stream that ran under the house, and the candidates withdrew to change from their white clothes. Water was given before sunset to any who were thirsty, but since they were then in ordinary clothes they could not touch the bowl themselves, and Piruza-e Dinyar held one to the lips of whoever wished to drink.[33]

As darkness fell, at about eight o'clock, the lamps were lit. There was a bright acetylene one in the women's *pesgam*, and the men came across to face it while they recited the prayers of the first night-watch, untying and retying the košti. The women mostly remained seated, reciting Avestan to their beads. Soon afterwards they withdrew to sleep in comparative coolness on the roof (where they might not go by day, for fear of seeing, or being seen by, Moslems). As it was only the third night, the men were discouraged from much sleeping, and they remained below, talking to one another to keep awake. Piruza the Dastur's wife went round, moreover, during the small hours with cane in hand, rousing those who slept too heavily. Even for a Yazdi villager, however, used at times to sleeping rough, the *no-šwa* house was not a place conducive to slumber. On the roof it was fairly cool, and the surface of plastered mud was more or less smooth under a cotton cloth; but there were mosquitoes, and towards morning the temperature dropped sharply, striking cold through the one thin covering which was allowed.

[32] That is, the *iθā āat yazamaidē* (see 'Zoroastrian *bāj* and *drōn*—II', 303).
[33] See Pl. IIb.

Down in the courtyard it was hot, and the small cobble-stones which paved the *pesgam* were uncomfortable in the extreme to lie on. The day's inactivity produced a weariness that did not lead to sleep; and during the small hours D. Khodadad recited part of the long office of the Vendidad in the little holy room off the men's *pesgam*, and from time to time there came a sharp ringing sound as he struck metal pestle against mortar. All in all the candidate did best to resign himself largely to wakefulness, finding what solace he could in meditation, and the glorious stars of a Persian night.

The next day, following the ordinary routine, they all rose before dawn while the sky was still dark, and the women came down from the roof. Led by the Dastur, the men recited the prayers of the second night-watch, and the women told their beads. Then there was a pause, during which each said what Avestan he chose, or was silent, until the stars paled and the sun rose behind the mountains. As its rays touched the roof they faced east, and recited the prayers of the first daylight watch, and some continued with the hymn for the day, which, since this was Bahram Roz, was the much-loved *Bahram Yašt*.

After this, they put on white clothes again and broke their fast with tea, made very sweet and spiced with pepper to counteract the 'cold' effect of the melons eaten in quantity at that time of year. Soon afterwards, bread and water-melon were served in small pieces in the shining copper bowls, and by eight o'clock they had changed back into their ordinary clothes, and the long quiet morning stretched ahead. Some talked, some dozed a little, some read Avesta, and Rustam-e Bahram seated himself in the sunny yard and read aloud a long confessional text in archaic Persian, while two of the women sat in front of him, listening intently.

The parestars meantime were very busy, for this was the fourth day, and the candidates had to make ablution in the early afternoon. Moreover, exactly ten days remained to Panji-mas, and so a whole group of Sharifabadis were beginning their *no-šwa* that evening. Water for twenty-five ablutions (including the parestars' own) had therefore to be carried up the steep steps from the stream, and stood to warm in the sunshine (for the *qanat* water, even in midsummer, was cold enough to pierce the marrow, after its long underground journey from the mountains). Ordinarily melon would have been served to the candidates half an hour before the midday meal, this being Yazdi custom; but because melon is a 'cold' food, this was omitted before the ablutions, and the meal was eaten early instead—a hot broth of rice and vegetables. Two women had arrived early from Aliabad to join the new group of candidates, and they, being not yet bound by the *no-šwa* restrictions, shared a bowl together. As soon as the candidates themselves had eaten and changed out of their white clothes, these were snatched away to be washed at the stream and dried in the midday sun. Two of D. Khodadad's young nieces, who were not yet subject to *bi-namazi*, did the washing, and his elder daughter Parizad spread the clothes out on the roof, snowy white against the blue of the sky. (The clothes in which each candidate had first 'gone on the stones' had already been washed, and were tied up in neat bundles ready to put on.)

The candidates then made their ablutions, in the second Havan Gah (for although it was late summer we were, according to the traditional calendar, in the twelfth month, Isfand, which is a 'winter' month without the noontide watch, Rapithwin). The ablutions took place in the same yard as the *barašnom*, where two sets of big stones, one for men and the other for women, had been placed at the southern end of the yard. Each candidate was first given one spoonful of *pajow* to rub over himself as he stood on the stones (for the second ablution there would be two, for the third, three). The water for the ablutions was brought in big glass stoppered jars, made at the village of Tejeng, near Nareke. These jars were charmingly irregular in shape and colour, and as they stood in the main yard, warming in the sun, they made a lovely gleaming row, dark green and pale green, cloudy blue and white. Once there had been fifteen of them, but breakages had reduced them to six, and they could not be replaced, for glass-making at Tejeng was ended, ousted by mass-production.

For the men's ablutions, Piruza-e Dinyar carried the heavy jars to the door of the *barašnom* yard, and Jehangir took them from her and administered the rite; for the women's they reversed these roles. As each man went to the yard, his košti, cap, and shoes were taken from him to be washed at the stream; and the Dastur's younger daughter, six-year-old Ab-Nahir, ran busily to and fro carrying them. The shoes were brought back to him to step into as he left the stones, and the cap for him to put on (a little cool dampness is no hardship in a Yazdi summer), and the košti were hung over the door of the main courtyard. Each man as he emerged, clad in clean but crumpled clothes, took his cord and, facing the sun, tied it on again with the appropriate prayers. It was the same for the women, except that each of them had among her clean clothes a fresh head-veil to put on, and they tied the kosti before returning to the main yard. One of them, Banu, after reappearing, sat down and said Ahunvars to her whole rosary of a hundred and one beads, as the equivalent of a confessional. When all the candidates were back, their clean white clothes, tied up in the cotton cloths which they sat and slept on (which had also been washed), were tossed down to them from the roof, and by early afternoon their own exertions were over, and they were sitting peacefully in their cleanliness. The men were still unshaven, though, and irked by a three days' growth of beard; for shaving was forbidden during no-šwa, since hair cut from the body is polluting. (Until the present generation almost all Persian men wore beards.)

The labours of the day were by no means ended, however, for the Dastur and parestars, for in ones and twos the new candidates were arriving. Like the group from Mazraʿ, they varied considerably in age and motive. One of the earliest to appear was Rustam-e Turk-e Khodarahm, a seventeen-year-old who was studying at the grammar school at Ardekan, and had made up his mind independently to perform this religious duty during the summer holidays. For all his youth, he was unfailingly dignified and self-controlled, and bore the trials of the retreat without any outward fretting. He arrived, though, with some natural shyness in this unfamiliar place, whereas almost on his heels, in perfect contrast, came the centenarian Hajji Khodabakhsh, veteran of six previous no-šwas, who settled in with swift efficiency. He had a neat bundle with him tied in a cotton cloth. Glancing neither to right nor left, he undid the cloth, and took out a bowl and two spoons of gleaming copper, which he put in the recess behind him. Then he sat down cross-legged upon the cloth, undid a second bundle containing his white clothes, and took out a little Avesta carefully wrapped in a purple kerchief. He retied the white clothes in their bundle, set them with his shoes beside him, and began to read aloud to himself from the Avesta. Young Rustam, seated next to him along the wall, looked reassured, I thought, by the little old man's calm procedures.

In addition to bringing his own few possessions, each candidate arrived with a contribution of flour for the bread-making, neatly tied in a white cloth. They all joined in buying firewood, and their families brought fruit and herbs during the nine days' retreat. This was in addition to the charge for the rite of eighty tumans—a hundred in the city of Yazd (as against ten for the brief *si-šuy*). If a candidate were undergoing the purification on behalf of another person, the family would pay all expenses, and give him in addition thirty tumans for his pains.

Another veteran among the Sharifabad contingent was blind Palamarz Rashidi, who like the Hajji was becoming *no-šwe* vicariously. The fourth man was a novice, like young Rustam, but with vastly more experience in living. This was Kay Khosrow-e Yadgar ('Kayōk-e Yādōk') who had left Sharifabad as a boy of thirteen, half a century before, to travel with a caravan from Yazd to Bandar Abbas, and thence by ship to India. Since then he had divided his life between that country and his Persian home, working turn and turn about with his brother, one tending their fields in Sharifabad while the other ran a chain of bakeries in India. He had travelled widely, and was alert, intelligent, and able. His busy life had kept him from the longer religious observances, but being in Persia during the relatively leisured days of high summer, he had chosen at last to become *no-šwe* in preference to making the pilgrimage to Banu-Pars.

The only Sharifabadi woman was Gulabi, stepmother of the khadem of Banu-Pars. She too had come to do *no-šwa* for another, and had a second client waiting for whom she hoped to repeat the rite in the autumn. She arrived looking worn and tired and shabby, after hard days of serving at the shrine during the pilgrimage, and she alone availed herself of the privilege which permits one who has already become *no-šwe* not to put on white clothes for eating, but simply to draw white cloths over the hands. Of the two Aliabadi women, both of whom were novices, one told me that she had suffered much illness and was in constant pain, and hoped that *no-šwa* would be beneficial. At the last moment Shehriar, D. Khodadad's fifteen-year-old son, added himself to the candidates, having resolved to become *no-šwe* before leaving for Bombay to attend a school for priests. This made the second group eight in number, so that there were twenty-three all told in the cramped old house, as well as the Dastur and parestars. From the crowded courtyard and *pesgams* no leaf or blade of green was to be seen, nor any prospect but the bare earth of the yard and the dusty earth of the walls, framing the blue sky. Such had probably been the setting for thousands of *no-šwas* administered in Sharifabad in the past, before the priests moved away to Yazd.

There was thus a fine variety among the full assembly of candidates. Most of them, young and old, were undergoing the purification for the first time, to 'cleanse their bones'; but Piruza Sami was performing an act of supererogation, in passing through it yet again on her own behalf, while Rashid Minuchihri was cleansing himself of a specific pollution. Finally a small group were taking the places of the vanishing priesthood, in that Bahram was seeking an especial purity in order to qualify himself for the priestly duty of sacrificing, and three others—Gulabi, Palamarz, and Hajji Khodabakhsh—were undergoing the rite vicariously for the souls of the departed, a task which would formerly have been assigned to priests, as the 'cleanest' members of the community. (In this regard it was an interesting fact that Hajji Khodabakhsh had worked for years as salar at the dakhma of Yazd; but he had long since cleansed his professional impurity through the *barašnom*, and, keeping the laws of purity strictly, was regarded by then as wholly fit to undergo the rite for another.)

The Sharifabadi group 'went on the stones' at about half-past five in the afternoon. Shehriar having not yet arrived, Rustam was accorded the privilege of going first (this was regular practice, the young being regarded, naturally, as less polluted). The stones had been standing some time in the sun, while the ritual lines were drawn round them, and, being as a schoolboy used to going shod, he said that he had nearly had the soles burnt off his feet. The little yard with its high walls held the heat, and after administering the *barašnom* to all five male candidates, D. Khodadad appeared hot and tired for a moment in the airier main yard, looking for all the world like a harassed surgeon, for he had stripped down to sedra and trousers, and wore the mouth-veil (like a surgeon's mask) up over his white cap.

After the briefest of pauses (for the day was nearing its close) he returned to re-draw the lines, reciting Avestan as he did so.[34] The multiple lines were shallowly drawn, as little furrows, in the earth of the courtyard by means of a metal pin at the end of a long bamboo cane. They went, in complex patterns, round nine sets of five stones, interspersed with nine sets of three stones. The sets of five represented

[34] If the candidates were all of one category, one drawing of the lines was valid for five persons, if all underwent the rite on the same day. The coming of night ended the efficacy of the lines. For the Avesta to be recited see Modi, *CC*, 121–2. (The Irani and Parsi administration of *barašnom* differs, however, in a number of small points of ritual.)

the nine holes in which in ancient times the candidate squatted to be cleansed, and those of three were there simply to prevent him having to place foot on the clean earth. D. Khodadad, explaining this, nevertheless attached a symbolism to the two sets of stones. The groups of five, he said, represented five evil things—lying, greed, lust, envy, and strife—and those of three, more generally, bad thoughts, words, and deeds; and all these faults the candidate should tread mentally underfoot as he moved from one set of stones to the next.

The three women then went on the stones one after the other, and Gulabi, who was last, with great kindness let me be present in a corner of the little yard while she did so. Jacky the dog was already there, tethered by a chain which had been passed through a small millstone that held him firmly at about the middle of the east wall of the yard—that is, on the candidate's left. The rest of the chain, which was fastened at the other end to a pair of scissors, was long enough for the candidate to hold it as she passed over the stones, so that she had *paivand* with the dog throughout.[35] The first set of stones consisted of three big ones, for firmness, and two little ones, making up the prescribed number of five. Gulabi squatted naked on these (her sandals being snatched away as she stepped out of them, to be washed), her right hand on her head, her left holding the scissors against her left foot. Through the open yard-door came the sound of the Dastur's voice as he recited the *Sroš Baj* up to the words *nəmascā yā ārmaitiš izāčā*, at which he paused. Gulabi repeated these last four words after him, and Piruza-e Dinyar then poured the first spoonful of *pajow* into her right hand, from a spoon tied to a nine-knotted bamboo cane, standing herself outside the ritual lines. (The *pajow* had a little *nirang* in it, and also a pinch of ash from the sacred fire.) Gulabi rubbed the liquid rapidly over her body in the way laid down in the Vendidad,[36] always the right side first, then the left, starting with the hair of her head, but not touching the soles of her feet, but instead rubbing one foot over the other (for it was held that the pollution was driven downwards and out through the soles of the feet, these becoming therefore too impure to touch). Parizad, as her father's deputy within the yard, then signed to her to move forward, and, still in a crouched position, she put her right foot on the next group of three stones, her left foot on

---

[35] In this respect Parsi usage differs: see Modi, *CC*, 128 ff.
[36] Vd. 9.15–26; see Modi, *CC*, 126–7.

the second group of five stones, and then brought her right foot up to the left, holding the scissors on their chain all the time against her left foot. (Even for the villagers, with their suppleness of body, it was not easy to do this and maintain balance.) While she was on the second set of five stones, D. Khodadad recited the same Avestan, but this time twice, and Gulabi repeated the last words (*nəmasča . . .*) twice, before receiving two spoonfuls of *pajow* (each fetched by Piruza from the Dastur in the passage-way). Then she moved in the same way to the third set of five stones, with a threefold recitation of the Avestan, and three spoonfuls of *pajow*. This brought her to the end of the first inner enclosure of ritual furrows (the outer ones went round all the stones).[37] She then moved forward across the dividing furrows on to the fourth set of five stones, and the same ritual as in the first enclosure was repeated exactly in the second one, on the fourth, fifth, and sixth sets of five stones. After this double ritual of cleansing thrice with *pajow* and prayer, she moved on to the seventh set of five stones. This took her into the third enclosure, which (since the contamination was now greatly reduced) was more lightly enclosed, with fewer furrows. Here the same Avestan was repeated once, by priest and candidate, and then Piruza gave Gulabi twenty-one spoonfuls of fine dry sand, scooped from a little heap at the side of the yard,[38] pouring some into her right hand, and some directly over her shoulders, so that she could dry herself thoroughly. She remained on this set of stones (Parizad having to sign imperiously to her to prevent her moving forward), and the Avestan was repeated, and she received from Piruza a spoonful of sweet water, from a vessel with a little consecrated water diffused in it. Then she moved forward, and the ritual was repeated as with the *pajow*, that is, with twofold Avestan and two spoonfuls of water on the eighth set of five stones, and threefold with three spoonfuls on the ninth set. Then she stepped on to the tenth set of five stones, put the scissors beneath her left foot, and stood up at last, turning back towards the left to face the dog.

On this tenth stone there was a final threefold ablution with water, that is, first the Avestan words were repeated with one and then with a second spoonful of water, and then Piruza brought a big

[37] For plans of the ritual furrows see *Riv.*, Unvala, i. 587 (where the stones within them are shown, however, in sets of 3–5–3, etc., instead of 5–3–5, etc.).

[38] This sand, and the fine dry earth kept for use instead of water by the privy, had been fetched by young Gushtasp Belivani and the family cow.

glass flagon and poured its contents over Gulabi from head to foot in a generous stream. She then handed her her sedra, which Gulabi put on, right arm first, then left, over her wet body (the little yard was still warm enough to make this acceptable). She wrapped a white cotton cloth round her waist, put her head-veil, folded, on her head, and her košti over her right shoulder. Then, covering her right hand with a fold of the sedra, she grasped the ends of her košti and also the spoon on its nine-knotted cane, forming *paivand* thus with Piruza; and keeping her eyes on the dog (with whom too she had *paivand* through the chain), she recited after D. Khodadad the concluding words of the *Sroš Baj*, which thus framed the whole rite with its protective power. Then she said after him, thrice, the following words in Persian (with Avestan forms): *Herbad pāk, sag ašō, pāk tan ašōi ravāne. tan-e fulān be-rasānād* 'Pure the priest, righteous the dog, pure the body for the righteous soul. May it [i.e. the benefit of the rite] reach the person of so-and-so.' (Had Gulabi undergone the purification for herself, she would have said, instead of *tan-e fulān, tan-e khwēšam*, 'my own person'.) Then she said thrice *Hamazōr hama ašō bēm*, with a bow each time towards the dog, thus completing the whole ceremony. Piruza withdrew the knotted cane, and Gulabi stepped off the stones into her newly washed sandals, completed her dressing with newly washed garments, and left the yard. Since she was the last candidate, Piruza then stripped off her own clothes, and Parizad poured water over her in her turn, to cleanse her from any possible contamination.

When all was over, the dog Jacky was released from his chain and left to roam the empty yard for a while in the moonlight to help a final purification. The discarded clothes of the candidates were also left in a corner of the yard to be purified by moon and sun before being washed for use after the first ablution of the *no-šwa*. The yard was regarded as dangerous for at least the next day, and anyone obliged to enter it kept as near the door as possible. (I myself sought unthinkingly to cross it to check a detail of the layout of the stones, and Piruza Belivani snatched me anxiously back.) On the second or third day the stones were raked together with a long-handled metal implement, and were sprinkled with *pajow* and sand before being left to the further action of sun and moon and wind.

It was nearly sunset by the time Gulabi had finished, and a supper of bread and water-melon was served at once. The Sharifabadi women did not have to change into white clothes for this, since they had neither slept nor answered a call of nature since making their ablution and putting on fresh garments. The next morning both groups had to drink *nirang*, and they all therefore put on their white clothes after reciting the prayers before dawn. Sunrise found them scattered about the yard and the *pesgams*, reading Avesta or reciting by heart, while the Dastur made his preparations. He very carefully washed, with sweet water, a small silver bowl and also two silver spoons (the smaller one being about the size of a dessert-spoon); and having filled the bowl with wood-ash, he placed it ready with the spoons and a small glass bottle of *nirang*. Had the candidates been fewer, they would have made a line facing east. As it was, the Dastur allowed them to stay where they were, to avoid the danger of brushing against one another, and as the sun rose over the mountains he began to administer the *nirang*, starting with the men. Before he did so his wife Piruza led them in the recital of the usual grace said before eating, and adjured them to keep silence. Each candidate remained sitting, and as the Dastur came to him, tilted back his head to receive the *nirang*. The Dastur poured the liquid carefully into the big spoon, and then from it, without spilling a drop, into the smaller one, from which he poured it into the candidate's mouth without touching his lips. Nevertheless, even though there had been no physical contact, between each administration he cleaned the bowl of the smaller spoon meticulously three times with the wood-ash. He took about half an hour to administer the rite to all the candidates and to the parestars, after which he washed the bowl and spoons again scrupulously before putting them away.

After a pause Jehangir distributed the copper eating-bowls and put fresh broken bread in them, and everyone was instructed to eat some, this being the necessary procedure after drinking *nirang*, so that the dry bread, almost a holy food in itself, should act as a barrier between it and other food. Since the evening meal had been a light one the night before (as it must be after *barašnom*), all meals were advanced that day. Water-melon was eaten at eight in the morning, and the main meal at half-past ten—an excellent fried dish of rice and pumpkins. The open spaces were so crowded that Piruza Belivani and I ate in the kitchen with the parestars, sweat pouring down our faces. Baking bread and cooking over an open fire in these tiny windowless rooms, with their heat-retaining mud-brick walls, was very exhausting in summer, and the work of the parestars was in every way heavy. From an hour before dawn to two or three hours after sunset they were busy, fetching water, kneading dough, baking bread, tending the oven and hearth fires, cooking meals, distributing food and water, washing up. (They were spared the drying of dishes, since in the clear desert air moisture evaporated almost instantly.) This was all in addition to carrying water and administering ablutions. It was, moreover, only for washing that the water of the stream under the Dastur's House was accounted 'clean', for there was another opening to it some fifty yards higher up, used by Moslems as well as Zoroastrians. All drinking-water had, therefore, to be fetched before dawn from a stream at the edge of the village fields. Jehangir used a gentle black bull as beast of burden for this, and they would arrive together daily at the door of the Dastur's House just as the stars were fading, the bull's panniers filled with big copper cans and smaller clay pitchers.

The candidates meantime, faced with two uneventful days, were reacting in their various ways. Among those from Mazraᶜ, Piruza Sami was as ever cheerful, and declared contentedly that they were in *tanbal-khāna* 'the house of laziness', with nothing to do but sleep and eat, and recite a little Avestan. Another woman agreed happily that they were like a stallful of well-tended sheep, eating what was put in their mangers without choice or care. But Bahram-e Khoda-bakhsh, rubbing the black stubble on his chin, was frankly pining for an end to his captivity, and the fifteen-year-old Shehriar, on his first day, was restless and bored, saying that it was all right for 'old people' (who for him included Bahram), but intolerable for the young. The schoolboy Rustam remained quiet and stoical, however, and gradually the rhythm of the calm days had its effect on Shehriar also. It was generally agreed that for the young the first days were the worst. By contrast, the weary Gulabi was perfectly content to be still and rest.

On the evening of the second day four school-friends came to visit Rustam. Visitors were always welcome, if they observed the strict rules; but when the boys asked hopefully for a tambourine, the Dastur's wife was firm. A tambourine was for the ninth night only, for with it came singing and dancing, and a danger of people brushing against one another. There was no objection to gaiety as such, however; and often in the long morning hours one of the women would be coaxed to sing. Once too the spirit moved Hajji Khoda-bakhsh, who had many of the instincts of a dervish,[39] and for half

[39] His title of 'Hajji' was indeed earned by his having made the pilgrimage to

an hour he paced to and fro in the courtyard, chanting verses from the *Shahname* very movingly in his harsh old voice. Another day Palamarz and Rashid-e Khosrow sang odes of Hafez, alternating with one another in two sweet tenors. There was also reading aloud from a great collection of the *Rivayats* which Agha Rustam had lent for the occasion,[40] and sometimes one of the men would read prayers in Persian, or one of the long confessional texts. Sometimes too there was just talk and teasing and laughter. No one might touch another, but it was permitted to roll a *dastambul* at a sleeper to wake him. These were pretty little sweet-smelling gourds, striped red and yellow, which fitted neatly into the hand like a medieval pomander, and were grown solely for their fragrance. They ripened at that time of year, and a number were scattered about the wall recesses of the Dastur's House, so that their scent could be enjoyed.

The following day was again a strenuous one, for the Mazraᶜ group made their second ablution, and the Sharifabadis their first, so once more the parestars had much water to carry, and the house-roof was covered with washed garments. With this day over, the Sharifabadis had in their turn completed the vital three initial days, and there was a slight relaxation in the air. That evening brought a cheerful throng of visitors for them, who sat about amiably without anything particular to say, very much like visitors to a hospital; and in the same way they had presents of fruit and herbs for the candidates, which were handed over to the parestars. Of fruits, only figs were rejected, because it was thought that their pitted skins made it impossible to wash them thoroughly enough. The Sharifabadis had discussed whether (as was permitted) they should club together to have a sheep killed for the fourth day, but like those from Mazraᶜ they decided against it. (If a sheep was killed during *no-šwa*, the head, feet, and pancreas had to be set aside, since these were ritually unclean. The rest of the carcass was seethed and the flesh eaten in small pieces. If meat were eaten, a little wine had to be drunk by all on the sixth day.)

The next day two visitors came in the morning from Hasanabad,

---

Mecca, in Moslem guise; and it was one of the baffling features of the local Moslem–Zoroastrian relationships that the Ardekani Moslems, instead of killing him for this sacrilege, accorded him the title, with a kind of perverse pride in such local enterprise. (On the strength of Yazdi local feeling against the world, triumphing sometimes over communal antagonisms, see Napier Malcolm, *A Persian Town*, 53 ff.)

[40] That is, the Bombay edition of Manockji Rustamji Unvala.

one with a big basketful of fresh mint from his fields, which was eaten as a relish with bread. This was ninth day for the Mazraᶜ group, and they would be leaving early the next morning (the secondary tradition has it that Zoroaster was released from his captivity soon after dawn); so in the late afternoon someone came from Mazraᶜ bringing the fresh clothes that they would put on after their final ablution. Ordinarily there would have been some merry-making that evening, but because of the death in Mazraᶜ within the month (which had obliged Rashid-e Khosrow to undergo the purification), this was muted. But Agha Rustam visited the Dastur's House with some others, and there was a telling of stories and a sense of quiet happiness and achievement. Even Bahram-e Khoda-bakhsh had succumbed in the last two days to the disciplined rhythm of the rite, and he told Agha Rustam that he was glad he had persuaded him to come. Jehangir was meanwhile busy by lamplight in the dark kitchen, kneading dough for a big batch of bread; for bread had to be baked that night not only for the candidates to eat as usual, but also for all the Mazraᶜ group to take some home with them, so that they would have 'clean' food to eat in the interval before they could bake their own.

Their last day was the first of Panji-kasog, the 'lesser Panji'. They made their final ablution as soon as the sun had risen, and drank *nirang*, after which they were free to return to the world. All had fresh clothes on, and some new ones, and the women looked lovely in their prettiest, gayest garments. Even the men had bright new caps and shoes, and their beards by this time had grown impressively, so that they made a handsome group. As soon as their old clothes had been taken off for the ablution they were washed, for it would not do for them, cleanest of the clean as they were, to return home with anything sullied. Then a handful of green herbs from a Sharifabadi garden was handed to each, and they set off for the fire-temple where they prayed, and laid their herbs on the pillar-altar in the outer hall, and were given sprays of the green myrtle which grew in the courtyard there.

From there they returned to the Dastur's House, receiving the congratulations of those they met in the lanes. (Several of the women stopped along the way at the house of Paridun Rashidi, to buy 'clean' sesame-seed oil from him for cooking in the days ahead.) At the Dastur's House they had a substantial meal of rice pottage, and bread with herbs. They ate in silence, with covered heads, but were able now to break their own bread and put it in their mouths with their hands instead of using a spoon. Each candidate then collected his belongings (with a great deal of talk), and was given two big rounds of freshly baked bread to take home, clapped between which was a little bit of 'clean' dough with which to leaven their own next baking. (The bread was wrapped in the cloth in which each had originally brought his contribution of flour.) By nine o'clock all were ready and sitting on their bundles in expectation of a jeep that was to take them back over the desert to Mazraᶜ. In the old days there would have been donkeys, slower but more reliable; for the jeep developed a mechanical fault, which was not repaired until half-past ten; and as the driver was unwilling to risk his tyres on burning sand at that hour, they had to wait until the cool of the evening, which they did with true Persian patience. By chance it was the day when a big bus-load of Moslem pilgrims were setting off for Mashhad, and from the Dastur's House we could hear the long-drawn cry through the lanes that summoned them to assemble at the village Hasaniya. Finally the jeep came, and the *no-šwe* poured eagerly out with their bundles, and new earthenware pitchers for fetching 'clean' water in, and glass bottles of 'clean' oil. The bundles went on the roof and somehow fourteen people and the driver went inside. As they were packing themselves in, a fine old Moslem, white-bearded and dignified, passed leading a donkey laden with the bundles of Mashhadi pilgrims, and courteous greetings were exchanged. The parestars waved the jeep away, swaying and bumping down the rough lane, and went back into the Dastur's House, quiet and comparatively empty now. The Sharifabadis were sitting peacefully about, having performed their second ablution that afternoon, and two lovely blue jays flew overhead in the light of the evening sun.

The next morning *nirang* was drunk according to the strict ritual, with all in a line across the courtyard, facing the rising sun; and after this the remaining days went quietly by, in an atmosphere of sober and cheerful seriousness. On the last day, as the work was so much less, Jehangir withdrew to see to his fields, and the Dastur himself brought 'clean' water from the distant stream. (Fortunately his other parish duties had been light during July, though he had had to recite the Avesta for several death-ceremonies, and on the Sharifabadis' last night celebrated a gahambar-e toji at the fire-temple.) There were again visitors on this ninth night, but the rejoicing was kept quiet, for fear that the sound of too much music would bring Moslem neighbours on to their roofs. (It was only that year that the dwellings next to the Dastur's House had passed into Moslem hands.)

On the tenth day (which was the last but one of Panji-kasog) there was again the butterfly transformation of the candidates, especially of Gulabi. She had come work-worn, in workaday clothes; but now, after the nine days' retreat, relaxed and rested, she looked radiant in lovely new clothes provided by the family of the dead woman for whom she had undergone the rite. Hajji Khodabakhsh too was in new clothes from head to foot, and during the whole of Panji-mas the bright stripes of his red and white cap shone out in the gahambar assembles. Only Palamarz looked unchanged, clad as ever in priestly white, ascetic and withdrawn.

When the early morning ablutions were over, the Dastur performed the *sedra-pušun* of two of his nieces (Pouran Belivani and Parvin Rashidi), and they and the candidates then went together to the fire-temple in the early morning sunshine, carrying their bunches of greenery, and after praying there dispersed to their own homes, each with his spray of myrtle. There kinsfolk and friends came to congratulate them, bringing green-wrapped sugar-loaves, and the *no-šwe* dispensed sherbet, and there was a festive meal for the family, with singing and rejoicing.

There then followed the exacting duty, for the *no-šwe*, of maintaining his or her ritual purity without the help of parestar and priest. This should be done for a minimum of forty days; it was desirable to do it for four months and ten days, and it was a great merit to do it, like Piruza Sami, perpetually. The basic rules for maintaining purity were that only 'clean' food might be eaten (nothing, that is, that came from a non-Zoroastrian source, and none of the 'unclean' parts of an animal), and only 'clean' water might be drunk, which meant that each day the *no-šwe* had to fetch his water at dawn from a distant stream. He must wash his hands scrupulously, up to the elbow, before eating, and must keep his own plate and drinking-vessel separate, and never touch anything *prangin*—that is, already tasted by someone else, or in any other way made less than perfectly pure. He must eat with covered head and in silence, having said an Avestan prayer, and must pray again after eating. He should not speak with Moslems, and especially not with Moslem women, who might be *bi-namaz*.

It was especially difficult for any woman who was herself subject to *bi-namazi* to keep her *no-šwa*, for during her menses she must be fed with a spoon, and given water to drink, by someone else who was keeping her *no-šwa*. (Piruza Belivani had in fact done this for a friend who became *bi-namaz* for the first time four days after they had been through *no-šwa* together.) Many women—the majority, perhaps—therefore regarded *no-šwa* as a rite for old age, a final purification only, and Sarvar went so far as to hold it wrong for a woman in her prime to undergo it, being an unclean vessel; but this was not orthodox.

Keeping *no-šwa* must always have been rigorous, but in the old days of isolated, largely self-sufficient Zoroastrian communities the difficulties were plainly less. Even in 1964 Piruza Sami said that she found it no trouble in lonely Mazraʿ, except for fetching water. She, however, lived by herself. In a crowded household there were many added complications. In a village like Sharifabad, which was near the 'Arab' town of Ardekan, and had itself several small Moslem shops, these were increased. No shop-bought oil or fat might be used in cooking, no baker's bread, no butcher's meat; and once one had become used to such conveniences, it was a greater hardship to do without them. In Tehran the problems were immense, although there was one convenience there, in that tap-water had been declared 'clean' by the priests. Smoking (never approved of) was absolutely disallowed throughout this time. If one should break any of these rules, by drinking *nirang* as soon as possible one could prevent the *no-šwa* becoming invalid.

The difficulties being so great, most of the villagers contented themselves with maintaining their *no-šwa* for the minimal forty days, and then formally abandoned it. The ritual for this was to 'tie it to a tree'. The tree must be a sweet pomegranate; and the *no-šwe*, while reciting the Ahunvar, tied about its trunk a green or white thread, fastening it with seven knots. He had thus 'given' his *no-šwa* to the tree; and he himself should then eat a dish of the ritually unclean *kalle-pače* (broth made from a sheep's head and feet) as a symbol of his own return to ordinary living. In this final act there seemed to be the intention of conferring the benefit of one's purity on the tree itself, felt to be one of the worthiest objects of the physical creation. That this was understood to be its purpose was shown by the act of D. Khodadad's son Shehriar, who, too impatient to maintain his purity for more than a few days, excused himself for abandoning it prematurely by explaining that he had given it to a pomegranate which had a sickly look, to help it thrive again. The rite thus demonstrates the power which orthodox Zoroastrians attribute to the state of purity.

By a parallel observance, similarly designed to allow time for a purification to permeate one's being, it was required that after drinking *nirang* for the first time one should consume only 'clean' food and drink for at least three days. On subsequent occasions, it was necessary only to avoid *prangin* food for this period. Piruza Belivani had already drunk *nirang* twenty-eight times by her eighteenth year, but her sister Pouran did so for the first time before her *sedra-pušun* at the Dastur's House. So during the following days, in addition to all her usual hard work, she prepared her own food separately with great care. She had fetched 'clean' dough from the parestars at the Dastur's House, and with this she baked herself tiny batches of 'clean' bread. At dawn each day she fetched 'clean' water in a little new earthenware pitcher, and when the family was eating meat-stew, or dishes fried with bought vegetable fat, she kept to eggs, fruits, and herbs with her fresh bread. After two days, it was Panji-mas, with abundant 'clean' food at every gahambar-meal, and so she was able without difficulty to maintain the purity of her first *nirang* for a full seven days.

6

DEATH AND THE MYSTERIES
OF THE DOG

WHEN death comes, Zoroastrians have two pressing duties: to
dispose of the polluting corpse with care and celerity, according
to strict rules, and to do everything possible to help the disembodied
soul to reach heaven and be blessed. The first duty should be fulfilled
within a day, the second should last at least thirty years—a contrast
which marks the difference in value between dead body and living
soul, the one belonging to Ahriman, the other to Ohrmazd. Both
sets of rites, of the one day and the many years, include immensely
ancient elements representing different historic layers of belief.
Some of the beliefs themselves were discarded millennia ago, but
the observances have long outlasted them.

Some of the most singular of the traditional rites of death, with
regard to both body and soul, required the presence of a dog; and
these one cannot hope to understand, even imperfectly, without
considering in historical terms the part played by the dog in Zoroastrian life. In distant days the remote forebears of the Iranians
must have had a close working partnership with dogs when they
lived as nomads on the Asian steppes; for the custom of riding
horses was then unknown, and they must have herded their cattle
on foot, and so have depended greatly on dogs to drive and guard
them. These two animals, the cow and dog, were presumably the
chief ones with whom the proto-Iranians had sustained contact;
and they both came, not only to share their ordinary lives, but also
to have part in their religious beliefs and practices—beliefs and
practices which in due course became part of the heritage of Zoroastrianism.

In recent times the Zoroastrians of the Yazdi plain have had
only a limited need for dogs, since they could not hunt or become
herdsmen,[1] and cattle in the oasis villages were kept in stalls. So the

---

[1] It was customary in the villages of the plain for most of the sheep, stalled
through the winter, to be put in charge of a shepherd in May and sent in a flock

practical use for a dog was chiefly as a guard against thieves and brigands, and to drive off wolves, hyenas, and jackals. The brigands have now gone, together with the wolves and hyenas, and even the thieves and jackals are less plentiful. Nevertheless, in 1964 there was still in every Zoroastrian village an abundance of dogs. Each oasis village had its own predominant type of animal, and Sharifabad and its two neighbours were therefore distinct from one another in this respect. Prosperous Hasanabad had huge, tawny, mastiff-like beasts, descended presumably from guard-dogs brought there for protection by the first Zoroastrian settlers at the beginning of this century, when the village was repeatedly plundered by robbers coming up from Fars. Most of these impressive creatures had owners, and were well fed and on acquaintance overwhelmingly friendly.[2] The dogs of Mazraʿ Kalantar were smaller and mostly sandy-yellow, but there was a striking group of long-haired white ones which were very handsome when cared for. Shehriar Zohrabi, in whose house I stayed, owned a beautiful animal of this strain, called Lali, to whom his children were devoted; but most of the Mazraʿ dogs were masterless, with the lanes for their only home. This was the case also in Sharifabad, for these two villages lacked the big gardens of Hasanabad, and the old houses were too cramped for it to be easy to keep dogs in them. The Sharifabadi dogs were mostly black and rather plain, though there was a strain of golden-brown, retriever-like animals. A few of the black dogs had the markings which are held to represent the 'four eyes' of the dogs of the Vendidad, that is, they had a light-brown fleck over each eye; but the villagers in no way singled these out or held them in especial respect.[3] White dogs were unknown in Sharifabad; but D. Khodadad himself owned a snow-white animal which he used for preference in rites and ceremonies, since white is the Zoroastrian colour. By a touch of irony

to the hills to graze the spring herbage there; but the shepherd was always a Moslem, and Zoroastrians were often reluctant to entrust their animals to him, saying that it was remarkable how often when an animal died 'accidentally' (for the benefit, they thought, of the shepherd's stomach), it chanced to be one of theirs.

[2] D. Khodadad, who though wiry was slight of build, used to approach at least one of his parishioners' houses there warily, so boisterous was the welcome given him by the friendly young dog.

[3] For such 'four-eyed' dogs (described otherwise as being yellowish, with yellowish ears) see Vd. 8.16, 17, 18. When I visited the smaller fire-temple in Karachi in 1963 the priests there kindly showed me the dogs which they kept for ritual purposes. One of these was 'four-eyed' (i.e. had the two flecks over the eyes), but again it was not for this reason esteemed above the other animal.

this dog, probably one of the last of the many thousands that have been kept by the Zoroastrian priests of Iran, was a pure-bred terrier imported from Europe and answering to the name of Jacky. He had been owned by an English family in Yazd, who gave him to the Dastur when they left, because he had admired him. He was much smaller than any of the lane-dogs, which even in Sharifabad and Mazra* were all large animals from working strains.

Most of the lane-dogs, however formidable they might look, were of touchingly meek and affable dispositions, and if not too frightened to let one approach would respond eagerly to a caress. Many, however, had learnt a desperate wariness, because of the increase in the Moslem population. In Sharifabad the dogs distinguished clearly between Moslem and Zoroastrian, and were prepared to go, with a diffident politeness but full of hope, into a crowded Zoroastrian assembly, or to fall asleep trustfully in a Zoroastrian lane, but would flee as before Satan from a group of Moslem boys. Moslems are not, of course, invariably unkind to dogs. Some themselves own herd- or watch-dogs, and apart from this there are naturally many Moslems who would not deliberately harm any creature. But undeniably there are others who are savagely and wantonly cruel to dogs, on the pretext that Muhammad called them unclean; but there seems no factual basis for this, and the evidence points rather to Moslem hostility to these animals having been deliberately fostered in the first place in Iran, as a point of opposition to the old faith there. Certainly in the Yazdi area *nanajib* Moslems found a double satisfaction in tormenting dogs, since they were thereby both afflicting an unclean creature and causing distress to the infidel who cherished him. There are grim old stories from the time when the annual poll-tax was exacted, of the tax-gatherer tying a Zoroastrian and a dog together, and flogging both alternately until the money was somehow forthcoming, or death released them. I myself was spared any worse sight than that of a young Moslem girl in Mazra* Kalantar standing over a litter of two-week-old puppies, and suddenly kicking one as hard as she could with her shod foot. The puppy screamed with pain, but at my angry intervention she merely said, blankly, 'But it's unclean'. In Sharifabad I was told by distressed Zoroastrian children of worse things—a litter of puppies cut to pieces with a spade-edge, and a dog's head laid open with the same implement; and occasionally the air was made hideous with the cries of some tormented animal.[4] Such wanton cruelties on the Moslems' part added not a little to the tension between the two communities.

Zoroastrian children for their part would cuff and pull dogs about, and men would kick the lane-dogs casually out of the way, but not hard enough to hurt; and in all their dealings with dogs there was an essential kindness and sense of responsibility. It is doctrine that in the good creation the dog ranks next below man; and if there is a ritual act to be performed that requires two persons, and only one is available, he may make *paivand* or 'connection' with a dog, by holding the animal on a cord, and so do what is needful. The dog fits so well into a moral scheme of things, with his virtues of faithfulness and courage and obedience, that he is felt to be able thus to partner man himself, even in the rites of religion.

It accordingly behoves man, as the stronger of the two, to look after this faithful friend, a duty which is enjoined on him in the Avesta.[5] In Sharifabad the lane-dogs were fed regularly, and the scriptural injunction was obeyed, that a bitch in whelp has a special claim to be cared for. Wherever a masterless bitch has her puppies, it is the duty of the owner of the land to feed her and them, and according to the Avesta, he should do so until the puppies are grown.[6] When I was in Sharifabad there was a gentle brown bitch in whelp who showed considerable intelligence in presenting herself wherever there was food, either on ceremonial occasions or in the fields, where she would let the children pet her and maul her about while she waited. She was very near her time at the Jašn-e Tir-Mah, when there is a communal observance at the dakhma; and she patiently plodded her way there, heavy as she was, over the desert track. She was exhausted by the heat when she arrived, and flopped weakly down in the shade of the adjacent buildings, lying on her side as if dead. Murvarid Belivani, Paridun's wife, filled the bottom of a broken pitcher with water and held it by her nose. At the smell of water the poor animal managed to struggle over on to her front and lapped the whole bowlful as she lay. By the time a second bowlful was brought she was able to get on her legs to drink it; and soon after she was moving about among the gathering in her usual gentle way, swinging her tail and receiving generous doles of food. She

---

[4] The young dog shown in Pl. Ib receiving the *čom-e šwa* was pitiably nervous, and had to be coaxed out of hiding by repeated calls, because he had been caught and savagely beaten earlier in the week by a gang of Moslem boys.

[5] Notably in Vd. 13.   [6] See Vd. 15.20 ff.

whelped at the dakhma that night, and its guardian, Paridun, took her food when he went there daily to tend the fire.

Such conduct seems understandable, if unusually kind—the working out, according to scriptural injunctions, of the ancient tradition of a people who had once lived by their herds, and had never forgotten their debt to the herd-dog and watch-dog. Yet when one looks into the matter more closely, very unusual features appear in the relationship between Zoroastrians and dogs. Thus it is required, in strict orthodoxy, not merely that one should feed a hungry dog, but that every household should give food to a dog at least once a day. Moreover, the dog should be fed before the family themselves begin to eat. This rule was still observed, in 1964, by D. Khodadad, who had the advantage of owning a house-dog, and was followed, more or less strictly, by most of the villagers. The standard portion for a dog was bread broken into three pieces; and whenever a group of Zoroastrians ate in the fields—as at harvest time, or the end of the cotton-sowing—a dog would join them, and receive this dole before they themselves ate. Moreover, many families fed one of the lane-dogs regularly once a day, before the evening meal; and at least one woman whom I knew set aside for this purpose a little of everything which she had cooked during the day.[7]

The most remarkable feature of this custom is that precedence was yielded to the dog. It was not at all a matter of giving a dog scraps and left-overs. It was to be fed *first*, with clean food untouched by anyone. For a poor rural community thus handsomely to support unproductive animals is remarkable; and the practice at religious ceremonies was even more striking, for then a complete 'meal for the dog' (*čom-e šwa*) was prepared from the consecrated food, either by the priest or by one of the family concerned; and this had to be given to a dog before the worshippers received their share of food and partook together of the communion meal.[8] The manner of preparing the *čom-e šwa* was as follows: three pieces of consecrated bread were dipped into the consecrated water, and laid at the bottom of a ritually pure metal bowl. Then a bit of every kind of food that had been blessed during the service was put into this bowl, together with other bits of bread which had been dipped into the liquid offerings

---

[7] Namely Shirin, the wife of Erdeshir Qudusi.

[8] It was always set aside first for the dog, though sometimes in practice it was not taken out to it immediately; but even though some delay was permissible, the *čom-e šwa* had always to be given before the sun set.

(the wine, milk, and *sir-o-sedow*). A roasted egg, shell and all, was added, and the bowl was topped off with more bread. One of the family, being in a state of ritual purity, and shod, then took the bowl to a dog. If the service had been attended by a large congregation, this had usually alerted at least one of the lane-dogs, who would be waiting hopefully at the house-door; but sometimes, especially at high festivals, when there were observances in many families, one had to go in search of a dog. There was a standard village call, *Gudū, gudū, biyū, biyū* 'Doggy, doggy, come, come!', which nearly always resulted in some hungry animal bounding eagerly up.[9] The food was then placed on the ground before him, and while he ate, its bearer prayed in Avestan, uttering one Ahunvar and one Ašəm vohu. The village dogs were not in the least fussy over food, and happily crunched down the egg-shell, and swallowed the highly seasoned *sir-o-sedow*, with anything else which might be offered them.

The villagers were sometimes at a loss to explain a traditional observance, but in this case there was no doubt in anyone's mind. All were clear that the food thus offered to a dog was for the benefit of a soul—the soul of the founder or beneficiary of the religious ceremony. And this was why the *čom-e šwa* was set aside before the congregation received its share of the consecrated food, the dead being thus given due precedence over the living. This was also the explanation of why food should always be given to a dog before one ate anything oneself, for this act was for the general benefit of the dead of one's own family—though sometimes it too was linked with care for a particular soul. Thus Piruza Sami of Mazra' Kalantar gave six pieces of bread to a dog each evening before sunset: three pieces, she explained to me, were on behalf of her dead husband, and three on behalf of her dead daughter. She and others who gave a daily dole to a dog did so at sunset because it is the time just after the sun has gone down which belongs particularly to the fravašis—the souls of the dead.[10]

Thus in traditional Zoroastrianism a dog was regarded as being able to act somehow as intermediary between the living and the

---

[9] It was only late in the ten-day festival of Panji that the dogs sometimes reached satiety.

[10] The Sharifabadis accordingly took care to avoid engaging in certain activities at this time of day, such as eating food themselves, or handling money. Thus I was once with Agha Rustam when he bought some eggs in a hill-village at dusk, and he postponed payment till the following morning.

Va (*above*). D. Khodadad solemnizing the Visperad at Havzoru in the Dastur's house (see p. 23).

Vb (*right*). Paridun Rashidi with the *varderin* to be consecrated during the Visperad (see p. 232).

VIa. Zari Rashidi (Paridun's aunt) receiving the *parahom* from Parizad, D. Khodadad's elder daughter (see p. 233).

VIb. Sarvar from Aliabad, wife of Turk Jamshidi weaving a *košti* (see p. 237).

dead. That this belief was once generally held throughout the community is shown by the fact that exactly the same usages prevailed—and in a measure still prevail—among the Parsis.[11] Plainly such a belief, originating presumably in the remotest past, is not susceptible of any easy explanation; and in seeking to understand it one has to take account also of the doctrine that a dog can by his gaze drive off demons and put pollution to flight. (We have already met a dog being used for this purpose in the *barašnom* purification.) How this doctrine itself arose must be a matter for surmise; but the ancient Iranians tended to group together the evils that afflicted them, seeing them all as created by Ahriman for their vexation, and since the dog, man's faithful ally, could defend him against visible dangers, such as wild beasts, it may have been thought, on analogy, that he could also help him by warding off the invisible attacks of hostile spirits. A factor in encouraging this belief may well have been a dog's habit of gazing unwaveringly at times into what seems empty space, as if seeing things invisible to his human companions; and indeed the Moslem villagers of Iran, however hostile to the dog, still say that this creature can see little *shaitāns* lurking in the corners of rooms.[12]

Further, there are Indo-Iranian—possibly even Indo-European—myths which connect spirit-dogs with death. The Vedas know two hounds, the messengers of Yama, who hunt out those who are to die, and accompany their spirits into the hereafter; and according to the Avesta two dogs await the spirits of the dead at the Činvat Bridge, which all must try to cross.[13] Here, Zoroastrians believe, both good and evil powers gather, each hoping to gain the soul; and whatever the original myth may have been, they naturally regard the spirit-dogs as beneficent, there to protect the soul, before judgement, from the prowling powers of darkness. This may well have been another factor in fostering the belief that a mortal dog could in the same

[11] Among them the *čom-e šwa* came to be known by the Gujarati expression *kutrā-no būk* 'share for the dog' (see Modi, *CC*, 404, 350). Even in Bombay the Parsis regularly fed the street-dogs as a religious duty down to the nineteenth century; and when in 1832 the British tried to round up the dogs there to destroy them as potential carriers of disease, it was the Parsis who led the resulting 'dog-riot' (see H. G. Briggs, *The Pārsīs or Modern Zerdusthians*, 39). In the early 1960s the Iranian authorities dealt in this way with the street-dogs of Yazd, so that in 1963 it was not always easy for the Zoroastrians to find a recipient there for the *čom-e šwa*.

[12] See Bess A. Donaldson, *The Wild Rue*, 45.

[13] Vd. 19.30, 13.9.

way protect the soul from evil forces while it still dwelt on earth.[14]

There is thus an ancient link between dogs and death. There is also the fact that the Indo-Iranians regularly made food-offerings to the dead, a practice maintained by both Zoroastrians and Brahmans to this day. This usage is clearly connected with the age-old belief, probably once common to all the Indo-European peoples, that the general fate in the hereafter was to pass to a kingdom of the dead beneath the earth, where the departed lived as shades, experiencing neither grief nor joy, and dependent on the bounty of their descendants for what little comfort they could know.[15] Food-offerings for the dead were laid on the ground, as the gateway to their abode. The spirits were duly summoned to receive them; and in Indian ritual texts it is said that, as these spirits perceive and enjoy the odours of the hot food, they absorb its essence, so that it gradually grows cold.[16] Thereafter it would be perilous for men to eat this food, the leavings of the potentially dangerous dead, and so the sacrificer is bidden to cast it away. In living Brahman usage it is thrown to the crows;[17] but evidently in Iran the custom developed of giving it to dogs to eat, for they, with their power over demons and the dead, could come to no harm thereby. This usage may well be purely Zoroastrian, for not only is there no parallel to it among the Brahmans, but it has a practical aspect which accords well with the admonitions of the Good Religion against waste, for herd-dogs and watch-dogs must be fed, and so piety and thrift could be conjoined. What thus developed presumably as one safe and sensible means of disposing of the hazardous offerings to the dead came in time to be regarded as the only permissible way of doing so.

Already, however, in Indo-Iranian times a hope, it seems, had been born that the strong and powerful in the community, that is,

[14] The dual aspects of the dog's protective role, physical and spiritual, are brought together in the seemingly late legend of Zarrīngōš, 'Yellow Ears', a dog who was brought into being by the word of Ohrmazd to guard the physical body of Adam/Gayōmard from Ahriman, but who also has his place near the Činvat Bridge. There he barks to frighten the *dēvs* away from the righteous. He moreover helps Mihr to check the demons who wish to inflict more than their due punishment on the damned, and he prevents anyone crossing the Činvat Bridge who has been cruel to dogs on earth. See *Riv.*, ed. Unvala, i. 256–7; Dhabhar, 259–60.

[15] For the evidence for this belief among the ancient Iranians see Boyce, *History*, i. 108 ff.

[16] See J. Gonda, *Die Religionen Indiens*, vol. i, 135–6.

[17] See e.g., J. A. Dubois, *Hindu Manners, Customs and Ceremonies*, 489 ff.

the warriors and priests, could attain to a different place in the hereafter, namely to paradise on high, which was not only bright with sunshine but full of all imaginable delights; and Zoroaster taught that this Paradise was within the reach of all—even of women and the poor[18]—if only they had lived the good life. In his revelation the dark underworld was transformed partly into a limbo for those who had been neither greatly good nor greatly bad, partly into a hell of torments, ruled over by Ahriman. Zoroastrians naturally always hope that the dear departed will attain to paradise, where they will taste bliss and have no need of any comfort that the living can bestow. Nevertheless, the immemorial custom prevails, with them as with the Brahmans, of providing food for the dead as if all had still gone down to the drear kingdom of shades beneath the earth, there to experience only nothingness.[19]

Although men shrank from touching food that had been enjoyed by the dead, they were accustomed to sharing devoutly in offerings consecrated to the gods, feeling themselves to be thus in communion with their divine guests. But it is the practice in Zoroastrianism (a practice which is at least as old as the oldest liturgical texts) to summon the fravašis of the dead to be present with the yazads at all religious ceremonies. Hence it came about that on every sacred occasion some of the consecrated food had to be set aside as the portion of the dead, to be given therefore to a dog. This portion always contained such dishes as were specially prepared for the fravašis, notably the symbolic egg; and these dishes must be freshly cooked, so that the spirits could enjoy their savour while the service was in progress. So it was that whenever Zoroastrians solemnized religious rites according to ancient orthodoxy, a dog had to be near at hand. These observances were not in the least mechanical or meaningless for the Yazdi Zoroastrians, who were vividly conscious of the unseen presence at their ceremonies of both divinities and the departed.

[18] See Y. 46.10.

[19] Lest such tenacity in 'chthonic ministrations' should seem to set the Zoroastrians and Brahmans apart among the followers of higher religions, one should perhaps remind oneself that food-offerings for the dead are also regularly made by, for example, Shiʿi Moslems and Christians of the Greek Orthodox Church, while it is a widely practised custom among Christian communities to place flowers as offerings on graves in autumn and spring, the seasons for ancient festivals of the dead. Modi was struck by the similarity in this respect between observances among French Roman Catholics and the Parsis (see CC, 431 n. 2).

The custom of giving food for the dead to a dog is thus likely to have been in origin practical, but with an element in it of the uncanny also, because of the beliefs in spirit-dogs, and in the mortal dog's powers over the unseen; and given this uncanny element, and the nature of the usage, it is hardly surprising that the dog should have come in time to be regarded as capable, not merely of consuming these offerings safely, but also of mysteriously representing the invisible dead—hence the Zoroastrian insistence on 'respect for the dog'. This aspect of the dog's role, though ever-present, appears most clearly in the rites which take place immediately at death and during the first year thereafter. These are in general well known,[20] and here it is proposed to touch only on their salient points, mainly in order to describe the beliefs concerning the departed spirit, and to indicate the part played in connection with them by the dog.

If a person was seen to be at the point of death, then the priest was sent for, and he recited a *patet* or formal confession on behalf of the dying man, and gave him *nirang* in three ritual administrations.[21] If death came suddenly, the *patet* was said thereafter; and the *nirang* was then poured on to bits of bread in a bowl and given to a dog, in the hope that the benefit would reach the departed spirit. When breath was extinct, relatives lifted the body and placed it on a stone slab somewhere within the house, with sand strewn around it, so that the good earth was thoroughly protected; and after this the corpse-demon, in Dari the *drōj-nesā*, was held to settle on it with all her pollution, and no one touched it again except those professionally appointed to do such work.

Meantime one of the family had gone to the priest with the message 'The soul of so-and-so is taking the road' (*vrūn pārsang ā gōrən*). He carried with him an egg, the symbol of immortality, and the priest roasted this in the embers of a fire while he consecrated a short *dron*

---

[20] The Parsi and Irani rites are essentially the same. On the former see Modi, *CC*, 48 ff.; on the latter Jackson, *Persia past and present*, 387–96. For a particular account of the observances as carried out in Sharifabad itself see Ardeshir Khodadadian, 'Die Bestattungssitten und Bestattungsriten bei den heutigen Parsen', Ph.D. thesis of the Freie Universität, Berlin, 1975 (in which the term 'Parsi' is used generally for 'Zoroastrian').

[21] Among the Parsis a few drops from the second *yasna*-preparation of *parahōm* (i.e. the infusion of consecrated *hōm*-juice, pomegranate, and milk) were given instead to the dying as a viaticum (see Modi, *CC*, 307 n. 1). This practice seems doctrinally soundly based (see Modi, *CC*, 52, Boyce, 'Haoma', 64), and probably the giving of *nirang* was a substitute, made by the Iranis in the light of the general pursuit of purity under the menace of death.

service in the name of Sroš, to invoke this yazad's protection for the departed soul. Thereafter the egg, blessed by this service, was given to a dog to eat.

In the old days, when there were many priests, a priest would then come to the house of death, leading a dog; but in the 1960s, of necessity, it was a layman who came, one of known probity, who had done no-šwa; and in Sharifabad the family then quit the house, abandoning the area of pollution to those better equipped to deal with it. The priest's proxy administered nirang once more to the newly lifeless body, as a last purification, and performed sagdīd, the act whereby the corpse was ritually 'seen by the dog', so that the pollution became less for those who must handle it. The Irani custom was that three pieces of bread, the basic and traditional portion for the dog, were placed on the breast of the corpse, and by this means the animal was induced to go right up to the body and so exercise its beneficent power against the droj-nesa.[22] The dog was then kept close to where the body lay, so that it could continue to act as guardian and protector of the soul, which was held to linger by the corpse's head. For added protection a fire was kept burning within three paces of the body (nearer would be a pollution for the fire); and on it was burnt the root of a plant called būδ-e nākōš, whose pungent smell was thought to have special properties against the evil powers, being (so D. Khodadad said) like a bullet fired against demon-foes.[23]

In Sharifabad one of the salars joined the pakšu, if the deceased were a male, to lay out the body, and while they were at work they made paivand, that is, they were joined by a košti tied round their right wrists, so that the contact might strengthen them against evil. As the woman pakšu had to work alone, she usually made paivand with the dog. (If a woman relative helped in this way, she had to undergo no-šwa thereafter.) The corpse was washed three times with pajow,[24] and then clothed from head to foot in white cotton garments, which must be clean but used—it is forbidden, as sinful

---

[22] This was the custom in both Yazd and Kerman. According to Briggs, The Pārsīs, 39, curds were used for the same purpose by the Parsis in Bombay in the early nineteenth century.

[23] This plant, which I failed to identify, grew in the desert and hills, and was dug up and dried for this special use. D. Khodadad used to obtain his own supplies from around the shrine of Banu-Pars. Its Dari name appears to derive from the odour it produces when burnt.

[24] Whoever did the actual washing drew a woollen glove over his right hand, with which he applied the pajow.

waste, to put anything new on the dead. These garments, which had sometimes been worn during no-šwa,[25] consisted of the sacred shirt, cotton trousers reaching to just below the knee, rough foot-wrappings, and a folded head-cloth tied under the chin. The hands were crossed over the breast, the legs were crossed in tailor-fashion, and the body was laid in a cotton sheet for a shroud.[26] This sheet should have been washed previously by the priest himself, in running water, and was to be sewn up with thread which had been woven by a young girl, and had also been washed by the priest. Only the face was left exposed, and this was covered by a small piece of white cloth which could be lifted for the second and third sagdids. Thus the wrappings of the polluting corpse were made as clean—indeed as pure—as humanly possible. Finally, a pair of open scissors was thrust into the shroud, on the corpse's breast, the points towards the feet. The metal blades had a part to play in warding off evil, but their other purpose was for slitting open the shroud in the dakhma. When all this had been done, and everything was ready for the funeral, the dog performed sagdid for the second time, the pieces of bread being laid upon the winding sheet.

Unless death had occurred late in the day, or at night, the funeral followed in a few hours. Any adult who wished might attend, man or woman; and with the mourners there gathered at the house those who were to carry the bier. Traditional Zoroastrian funerals are conducted on foot, and since the dakhma was out in the desert, teams of men (four, six, twelve, or even eighteen) were needed for this task. These bearers were drawn from among friends and neighbours, and it was thought meritorious to help in this way. Like the salars, they dressed wholly in white, with white cloths over their hands; but since they did not touch the shrouded corpse, but only the bier, they did not become seriously unclean, and a simple ablution after the funeral sufficed to purify them again. The white clothes, provided by the Anjoman, were washed after every time of use. (This was done at the Zād-o-Marg Khāna, 'House of Birth and Death', where too the iron biers were kept, and the salars made their regular ablutions.)

[25] Cf. above, p. 114.

[26] Because of the crossing of the legs, the shrouded corpse presented a tri-angular shape. This way of laying out the dead is enjoined in the Rivayats (see Unvala, i. 141.8; Dhabhar, 158, with discussion, n. 3). The Parsis tradition-ally lay out the corpse with straight legs, and great controversy arose when the Irani custom was introduced among them in the eighteenth century.

In Sharifabad the priest recited the funeral service at the house. This consisted, essentially, of the longest group of Zoroaster's own hymns, the Ahunavad Gah, recited in two parts, with a pause after Y. 31.4. When this pause was made, the salars lifted the shrouded body from the stone slab on to an iron bier, to which they tied it with a košti. At the end of the service all who intended to follow the bier said the Avestan prayer to Sroš, and then formed pairs, linked protectively with one another by a košti or a piece of cloth. The bearers too made *paivand* by a košti. The procession then set off, led by the priest with the dog, the bier being carried several paces behind these two. It was followed by the relief bearers, and then, at a respectful distance, by the double line of mourners. When the bearers changed over, they shifted the bier from shoulder to shoulder without setting it down on the good earth; and they must never glance behind them, but must keep their eyes steadily on the way ahead. They and the mourners walked in complete silence, for they had said the Avestan prayer to Sroš, and to speak would break its power.

The procession made its way slowly along the field-paths and over the desert track which led to the dakhma. Once there, the bearers set the bier down and withdrew thirty paces. The salars placed the body on a stone slab, and the priest recited yet again a confession on behalf of the soul, and said some other prayers. The salars then transferred the body to a lighter iron bier, which was kept inside the tower. The dog performed the third and last *sagdid*, and the priest recited the ancient formula of authorization for committing the body to the dakhma. The mourners uttered a last prayer together (which being in Avestan did not break the power of the *Sroš Baj*), and then the salars carried the body through the high, small door into the tower, and those outside saw no more.

Within the tower the salars laid the body down on the stones, and used the scissors set in the shroud to slit the cloth open a little way;[27] and they said words to comfort the soul,[28] which was believed

---

[27] Parsi usage is that the corpse-bearers strip the body, casting the torn clothes into the central pit of the tower (see Modi, *CC*, 66). To expose the dead naked is undoubtedly the ancient custom, which was presumably abandoned in Iran some time after the ninth century, because of the impossibility of preventing Moslems breaking into the places of exposure. (Jackson, *Persia past and present*, 392–3, writes of the removal of the clothes; but his informant, who had been in Bombay, was undoubtedly in this respect describing Parsi usage.)

[28] See Jackson, op. cit. 393.

during the three days after death to linger near both where the body lies and where it has lain—that is, at the dakhma and at its old home: 'Fear not and tremble not, O such an one' (they said) 'it is the place of your ancestors, and of [our] fathers and mothers and of the pure and good, for a thousand years.' And they committed it to the special care of the divinities who would judge it at the end of the three days: 'O Mihr Ized, Sroš Ized, Rašn Ized, the pure and just! We have withdrawn our hands from him, do you take him by the hand . . .'. These utterances were said in archaic Persian; and after some brief Avestan prayers the salars then withdrew respectfully backwards from the presence of the unseen spirit, and closed the dakhma door upon it.

When the funeral was over, the family returned again to the house which they had left; and for the next three days, while the soul was thought to linger on earth, they did everything which they could to comfort and help it. A little oil-lamp was kept burning continuously near the place where the corpse's head had rested. This was sheltered in a tiny open-sided 'house' made of four mud-bricks; and just in front of it a pair of open scissors was thrust, points downward, into the earthen floor, and something made of iron or steel was put on the stone slab (a metal chain or the long-handled metal *bara*). The villagers said that this was done so that 'the soul might not be lonely'; but the practice presumably represents the age-old belief in the power of iron and steel to ward off evil. Human vigil was also kept continually at the place, by a man for a man, a woman for a woman, and the watcher maintained a quiet murmur of Avestan prayers. Religious services were solemnized elsewhere each day by the priest, and he came to the house each afternoon to celebrate an Afrinagan and to say a confession for the soul's sake. The family moreover said a prayer—the Sroš Yašt sar-e šab—each evening at the beginning of the fourth watch, just as the stars began to show, since this time belongs especially to the spirits of the dead, who may help to protect the lonely, newly departed soul. This and all other prayers uttered during the first year after death ended with the words *az jāde-ye ašō ravān . . . be-rasād* 'May it reach the path of the blessed soul.' Further, each night during the fifth watch, from midnight until dawn, the priest solemnized the long night-office of the Vendidad, to help drive away the powers of evil, this being, D. Khodadad said, a strong aid to the soul, like clothes to a naked man.[29]

[29] It was impossible for D. Khodadad, placed as he was, to solemnize the

As well as praying, and procuring prayers to be said, the family also offered the departed soul all the material comfort that they could. Thus during this period ordinary food, such as the dead person enjoyed, was prepared with ritual cleanliness three times a day, and given, with Avestan prayers, to a dog. *Any* dog would do; but one of the lane-dogs was often brought in and chained in the yard for the three days, an alteration in its life which an old dog accepted gratefully, an inexperienced youngster with a touch of anxiety.[30] It was desirable that whoever gave the food to the dog should be closely connected with the deceased, by blood or marriage, and he or she must be in a state of ritual purity, and must always be shod, for the old religious rules (usually ignored through the habit of poverty) forbade Zoroastrians to set bare foot upon the ground. If it was a baby that had died, then bread soaked in warm milk was given. In no case did the dog receive meat during this time, for none was eaten during the three days of mourning. (Such particular abstinence is the nearest that Zoroastrians come to fasting, which they disapprove of as an activity that weakens the good body created by Ohrmazd, and saps the power and will to contend with evil.) Meanwhile, out at the dakhma the dakhmaban would be keeping the fire there blazing brightly all through the three nights, and would put *buδ-e nakoš* on it, to comfort and aid the soul.

On the third day after death, preparations began for receiving the divinities who would be concerned with the soul's fate as it left the earth. House and lane were swept with the greatest care, and incense was carried through the rooms; and in the late afternoon priest and mourners gathered at the house to solemnize the Yašt-e sevvom or 'Service of the third day'.[31] At this the priest led the company in

Vendidad service in its entirety, but he read portions of the book in the course of an abbreviated Yasna ceremony, celebrated necessarily without the help of a serving priest.

[30] Similarly in Navsari it was still the custom in the 1970s to tie up a dog (brought for the purpose by one of the nasa-salars) on the house-veranda during the three days after death, to receive this food (information from Dr. Firoze M. Kotwal).

[31] The Parsis call the *sevvom* service *uthamna*, the 'last' ceremony, i.e. of the daylight ceremonies of the three days. They also, however, use the same term for the service held at dawn of the fourth day, which the Iranis call *čārom*. Traditionally for the Parsis it is the *uthamna* of the third day which is of the greater importance, and in Kerman similarly more weight is laid on *sevvom* than on *čarom*, whereas in the Yazdi region it is the other way about. This may be one of the several ways in which the Parsis and Kermanis preserve an eastern (Khorasani?) tradition against the western one of Pars.

praying for the soul. The prayers said were, essentially, those proper to the afternoon watch, but each one was spoken twice, once on the mourner's own behalf, and once for the departed soul; and they were followed by a confessional. The last prayer was said as the sun was setting, and the dahmobed then distributed to all those present consecrated food, consisting of small flat rounds of bread (*luwok*) with chopped-up eggs and herbs, which were eaten in communion. As the mourners left they expressed their grief and sympathy with the family; but as far as possible the bereaved held tears in check— even a young mother or widow—for since sorrow belongs to the devil, Zoroastrians try to bridle it as much as possible.

During the last watch of the third day, usually at about one or two o'clock in the morning, another service was celebrated at the house, namely the Yašt-e šavgīre or 'Service of the night-watch'. During this a length of cloth, called in Sharifabad the 'sedra',[32] was blessed to provide a spirit-garment for the soul in the hereafter. The provision of clothes, like that of food, for the departed is a custom which evidently goes back to the remotest past, being similarly linked with the belief in a deprived and comfortless hereafter.[33] The cloth was of undyed cotton, spun and woven at home, and an old woman would often weave enough for her own and her husband's sedra, and keep the roll by her ready for use.[34] The cloth was sent to the priest to be washed by him before the ceremony in running water.[35]

[32] Elsewhere in Iran it was called *šavgīre* (by transference from the name of the service), and the Parsis know it as *shiav* (see Modi, *CC*, 81). The Sharifabadis in daily life usually referred to the sacred shirt as *šīv-kōštī* (i.e. '[the garment worn] under the sacred girdle').

[33] There is a reference to it in Yt. 13.50, in a passage which stems evidently from pre-Zoroastrian times.

[34] Thus in the house of Tahmina Khanom's parents the cloth for their sedra, woven by her mother Sultan, hung over a beam in the room behind the *pesgam-e mas*. The amount of cloth required was 18½ *zār* for a man, 16½ for a woman, and 3½ for a child (the *zar* being a rough measure from nose to outstretched fingertips). The custom in the 1960s was for the cloth to be shared between the priest and family. The priest should make a sedra for himself from his share, and part of the merit of the prayers which he said while wearing it then accrued to the departed soul. Or he might give the cloth to the poor, the soul then benefitting from this act of charity. The family used their share for some devout purpose, such as for a cloth (sopra) for setting out food on holy days, or for sedras for themselves.

[35] In Tehran tap water was adjudged sufficiently clean for this purpose (although this was one of the things, like eating bought bread, which made the strictly orthodox of the villages uneasy about going to live there). Once when I visited the Ataš Bahram in Tehran cloth for a sedra, newly washed by the priests, was drying across chairs in the main hall.

It was then blessed during the service together with a newly woven košti, and a piece of silver, either a coin or ring. This last item is known only in the Zoroastrian usage of Iran, not of India; and it seems possible that it derives (perhaps since the Seleucid period) from the Greek custom of burying the dead with a coin for Charon.[36] The family also provided for the service not the one egg usually blessed for a departing soul, but thirty-three, said to be for the ancestors, up to thirty-three generations back, who would come that night to support their descendant before his hour of trial.[37]

The service itself, which lasts about an hour, consisted of four short Yašt-e dron, solemnized one after the other, and dedicated first to Sroš, who cares for the spirit during the three days on earth; then to Rašn, who will hold the scales of justice at its trial, together with Aštad, the hypostasis of justice itself; then to the great company of the righteous dead, the fravašis; and finally to the yazad of the wind and spaces of the sky, Vāy, through whose realm the spirit must mount up at the next dawn.

Just before the sun rose on the fourth day the mourners assembled again at the house for the Yašt-e čārom, 'Service of the fourth day'. They each said the košti-prayers twice, once for themselves and once for the departing soul, and were led in other prayers by the priest. The atašband then asked each person present to declare how many prayers he was prepared to say privately for the soul's sake during the next ten days, and the grand total of these was announced to the gathering.[38] It was at this moment too that, if the dead man

---

[36] For silver coins found with bones in interments of the Sasanian period see S. Yeivin, *Second Preliminary Report upon the Excavations at Tel-hunar, Iran*, ed. Leroy Westerman, Ann Arbor, University of Michigan Press, 1933, 41; Aurel Stein, 'An archaeological tour in ancient Persis', *Geographical Journal*, lxxxvi/6, 1935, 494; J. Hansman and D. Stronach, 'Excavations at Shahr-i Qūmis, 1967', *JRAS*, 1970, 39; A. D. H. Bivar, 'A Sasanian repository at Shahr-e Qūmis', ibid. 156–8.

[37] An alternative explanation proferred was that they were for the thirty-three major *yazads* (who are in fact thirty in number, since four of the thirty days of the month are dedicated to Ohrmazd, but which are accounted as thirty-three, as if these four days were devoted to four distinct divinities). Formerly eggs from the little local hens were plentiful, even in poor houses, but if enough eggs could not be had, the number might be made up with walnuts. As with the cloth, the eggs were divided after the service between the priest and family, and the family used theirs for the food that was distributed among the mourners.

[38] This is another task which elsewhere in the Yazdi region would be performed rather by the dahmobed (see above, p. 28). As well as the prayers, charitable acts were sometimes announced to be undertaken for the soul's sake; and in India, as the Parsis grew wealthy, immense benefactions were at times promised

had left no son and heir, one was formally appointed, so that he might perform all the soul-ceremonies for him in the months and years to come. This appointed heir was called the *pol-gozār*, the 'bringer over the Bridge', for the ceremonies which he was to perform were thought to help the soul to cross the Bridge to heaven. It was held that to name the *pol-gozar* before sunrise on the fourth day was to satisfy the soul on this vital matter just before it quitted the earth.[39]

None of these activities can be logically reconciled with Zoroaster's fundamental teaching that each man must achieve his own salvation, and that the only way to do so is through good thoughts, words, and acts. However, among good acts the prophet clearly included the rites of worship; and it was natural human weakness which led his followers to extend this to acts of worship performed after death—that is to say, they reverted in this to age-old pious practices, while holding firmly to the essential doctrines of their new faith. Parallel developments can be traced in the history of all the higher religions. Attempts were made in due course by theologians to reconcile doctrine with practice, in that they said that rites performed after death only helped the soul if they had been wanted and intended by the departed while he lived, so that they represented, as it were, a working-out of his own good thought;[40] but naturally, regardless of this, the ceremonies were performed for all alike, in

by the family at the *uthamna*. For a more detailed account of the Irani ceremony see Khodayar D. Sheriar, 'The funeral ceremonies of the Zoroastrians in Persia', *Sir J. J. Madressa Jubilee Vol.*, ed. Modi, 312–14.

[39] Among the Irani Zoroastrians the *pol-gozar*, following ancient custom, inherits all the dead man's property, with the obligation to provide from it for his widow, if she survives him. He also takes his name in place of that of his natural father. Thus, for example, D. Khodadad's father Shehriar was the second son of D. Hamavand, a poor, hard-working priest. A well-to-do but childless priest, D. Namdar, died suddenly in an accident, leaving no kin, and so the Dastur dasturan appointed Shehriar to be his *pol-gozar*, and henceforth he was known as Shehriar-e Namdar, and inherited all the property. D. Khodadad in his turn made his own second son, Shehriar, the *pol-gozar* of his eldest son Rashid, when the latter died at the age of twenty, so that thereafter he was called Shehriar-e Rashid. The Parsis have similar customs, but they abandoned some time ago the right of the *pol-gozar* (or *pālak*, as they call him in Gujarati) to inherit the property, and among them he is now simply responsible for the ceremonies. The old custom could be very irksome for a spirited and capable woman who survived her husband; and after the death, in 1960, of Rustam Khodayar Boland of Yazd, his widow, Khorshed-Banu Kayanian, named as *pol-gozar* a myrtle tree at his family home, which thereafter was tended with special care. It was suggested to me by others that this unusual step might have been made on analogy with planting a tree as *vaqf* or *yād-būd* (a memorial).

[40] See *Dādestān ī dīnīg* (ed. Dhabhar), *Pursišn* 7.

a spirit of hope and piety—even, that is, for acknowledged sinners, such as suicides (although in their case there was a sorrowful feeling that the benefit of the rites was unlikely to reach them). The elaborate observances for the dead were yet another way in which Zoroastrianism was deeply satisfying to normal human instincts, in that they provided abundant means for the bereaved to be active and to feel that they were helping their dead, instead of being wholly cut off from them.

The belief was that it was while the mourners were praying to-gether before the dawn of the fourth day that the soul began its ascent; and it was held to reach the Bridge, which is also the place of judgement, just as the sun's rays touched the earth. There was a solemn, silent pause therefore at this moment, as the mourners accompanied it in their thoughts to the tribunal of Mihr Ized, the Judge over all. Then as the light increased they turned back to the everyday world, conscious of having given the departed all the aid in their power. The period of ritualized mourning was then over, and this fact was marked by the eating of meat for the first time since the hour of death. One of the undoubtedly ancient rites performed for the dead in traditional Zoroastrianism was the offering of blood-sacrifice. Since Zoroastrians do everything which they can in threes, three such sacrifices were made for every adult who died, a practice which in 1964 was still strictly observed in the Yazdi area. The first sacrifice was made on the morning of the third day after death, and the flesh was roasted during the night. The former custom in Sharifabad was that fat from the sacrificial beast, together with a paring from its horn and a scrap of the wool, was pounded up with garlic, rue and *buδ-e nakoš*, and offered by the priest at dawn to the sacred fire as an oblation on the soul's behalf; but Parsi influence was exerted to stop such practices,[41] and what was then done instead was that a candle was made from the rendered fat, with a wick of pure, homespun cotton, and this was set to burn before the Ataš Varahram just before dawn on the fourth day. The meat of the sacrifice was consecrated by the Yašt-e čārom, and was shared between the family and other mourners, the priest, his helpers, and the poor of the village. Formerly the Yašt-e čārom was held at the

---

[41] Yet the first at least of the three sacrifices was made still by Parsis down to the early nineteenth century; and instructions from Navsari to Bombay in 1823 were that the fat from it was to be offered at dawn on the fourth day to a temple-fire, together with frankincense or aloe-wood (see 'Haoma', 77–8).

dakhma itself, and after sunrise the gathering there became a convivial one, the food being washed down by an abundance of full-bodied wine—a custom whose passing D. Khodadad recorded with understandable regret. The dog naturally received his ritually appointed share of the sacrificial meat. This included some of the *andom*, which must also be partaken of by the priest. The *andom* consisted of pieces of seven inward parts of the animal, representing what in Avestan is called *iža*, in Sanskrit *iḍā*, that is, the essence of the sacrifice.[42] The dog was also given a hind-foot, but never one of the fore-feet, which are regarded as ritually unclean (as are the head and the blood).

These things were given to the dog on behalf of the soul, in the usual way; but there was a complication in that he also received that portion of every blood-sacrifice which is set aside for the yazad Hōm, the Vedic Soma, who was regarded in the common Indo-Iranian tradition as priest of the gods, and who was therefore assigned a share of every sacrifice, like a mortal priest. In recent usage his share was only the tongue of the animal, and this the priest roasted while consecrating a Yašt-e dron in honour of Hom Ized, and then gave to a dog.[43] In ancient pagan usage the yazad's share was perhaps burnt in the fire, which the Brahmans called the 'mouth of the gods'; but the Zoroastrians' reverence for fire prevented them putting anything on it except what was offered to it itself—fuel, incense, and the *zohr* of fat. So, it seems, the dog's role was extended, and from representing the invisible dead it came in this single instance to act as proxy also for one of the divine beings themselves.

The dawn of the fourth day saw the end of the regular feeding of a dog three times a day as the dead man's immediate representative; but this usage was continued in modified form for forty days—a favoured length of time for extended observances. During this period three pieces of newly baked bread (or at least unbroken 'clean' bread), together with a roasted egg, salted, were given to a dog each day at the hour of death. One of the lane-dogs quickly learnt what hour this was, and presented itself regularly at the house-door. For a dead child warm milk was substituted for the egg. Agha Rustam had himself lost a son in infancy, and for forty days his wife Tahmina continued thus giving bread soaked in warm milk to a dog.

[42] See in more detail, 'Ātaš-zōhr and Āb-zōhr', 107–8; Boyce, *History*, i. 163–4. The *andom* was prepared from the death-sacrifices and at Mihragan, but not at the gahambars, though even then bits from all the seven parts were included in the *čom-e šwa*.

[43] See in more detail, 'Haoma', 70–5.

If a child were born dead, the Sharifabadi custom was that if it was premature, the mother would herself wash the infant's body in *pajow* and stitch it into a clean white cloth steeped in the same liquid, for a shroud, leaving a loop of cotton. An iron rod was passed through this loop, and two young boys, if the infant were a boy, or two young girls for a girl, would carry the tiny body to the roof of the *lard*, and leave it there for the crows. If the child were still-born at the due nine months, then they had to carry the body all the way to the Kuh-e Surkh, the 'Red Hill', near the mountain shrine of Hrišt, three farsakhs from the village. Paridun Rashidi told me how his third son had been still-born in midwinter, and he had had to force his eldest son Rashid and another reluctant boy, both about ten years old, to struggle with the body through snow to the mountain. The youngsters, chilled and unhappy, were exhausted by the time they reached its foot, and in the end Paridun had himself to carry their small burden up the hillside. This custom seemed exceptionally harsh, since it forced children and grieving relatives to add to their natural distress. Yet though the bodies of the still-born were thus disposed of apart, religious rites were performed for them as for other children, in order (D. Khodadad said) to give strength to the unfledged soul. Naturally there were three sets of rites, with consecration of a sedra, but no blood sacrifice. The first set, with the priest reciting the Dron-e Barsom, the Dron-e Sroš, the Yašt-e Sroš, and such other Avesta as seemed to him appropriate, were solemnized nine months after conception, and the other two as rapidly as possible thereafter, to give the soul their benefit as soon as might be. It was believed that, lacking these rites, the infant's soul must go to hell, whereas, if they were performed, Sroš would care for it. (One can compare the similar Christian beliefs with regard to baptism.) Simplified rites, the concern only of the immediate family, were performed for all who died before reaching maturity, reckoned in traditional manner as fifteen years of age; but for children who had lived, these included the basic observances of the three days, with *čarom*, *siroza*, and *sal*. No Vendidad would be solemnized, however, there was no blood-sacrifice, and the consecrated food was shared among other children—it was held to be wrong to give any to an adult. The ritual portion was always, naturally, prepared for the dog.

The prolongations and elaborations of observances for the dead are evidently ancient, and they had their origins presumably in natural emotions of grief and caring, though one may suspect that they were fostered also by priests not wholly lacking in self-interest. In general an elaborate cult of the dead has been prominent in Zoroastrianism since very early times, and as the Zoroastrian community dwindled in numbers in Iran, the survivors seem to have grown ever more conscious of the great army of their dead, who alone cared for them amid a hostile world. Living as they did where their forefathers had dwelt, the Yazdis were constantly aware of the invisible presence of their ancestors, and were eager to cherish them as much as possible. Since they were Zoroastrians, this was no gloomy matter; rather they tried to create occasions of joy which they and the dead could share, an activity which they called *šād-ravānī*, 'gladdening the soul'. This endeavour extended to feasts held on funerary occasions, so that a stranger, plunged into a village gathering, would have been hard put to it to distinguish between a festival and a funerary feast.[44] Indeed one of the merriest assemblies which I was privileged to take part in was held on an occasion of double mourning in the hill-village of Taft. This combined the *sal* or first anniversary of the death of the head of a household (who had died comparatively young, leaving a youthful second wife with growing children), and the *siroza* or thirtieth day after the sudden death of one of his sons by his first marriage (who had been only six months wed himself, and who left a girl-widow expecting his child). The grief of the family was deep, and because of the sorrow of the double blow relatives and friends from all over the Yazdi plain exerted themselves to be present and give comfort.[45] So a great company gathered and condolences were offered by all to both widows during the day-time ceremonies; but an assembly held in the evening was as gay as possible, with singing, dancing, jesting, story-telling, and the drinking of toasts.[46] This may at first sight seem heartless; but in fact this part of the proceedings was felt to be

[44] There is no expression corresponding to *šad-ravani* in use among the Parsis, who tend to look askance at the robustness of the traditional Irani funerary feasts.

[45] I myself attended in company with Shehriar Zohrabi of Mazraʿ Kalantar and his friend Isfandiar, our host being Agha Dinyar Arghavani, to whom I remain indebted for his kindness in extending warm and gracious hospitality to a stranger on this sad occasion. It was in his house, and thanks to the kindness also of the hušt-mobed, D. Sorush, and his fellow priest, D. Mihraban Rashid Khorsandi, that I was able to be present at a Yašt-e šavgīre, and also to see for the first time the preparation of the *andom*.

[46] So large was the company that there were three sittings. Naturally the dignitaries—the two priests, the village school-teacher, and leading elders—were at the first, and most of them then withdrew, leaving it to the rest of the company to make merry when the meal was over.

for the souls of the dead themselves, who would (it was thought) be distressed to see those whom they had left behind indulging in grief for them, but would be gladdened to see them happy.[47] Neither of the widows was obliged to share in the actual merry-making, since both had much to occupy them in caring for their guests.

It was in general considered meritorious, and a sign of respect for the dead, to attend funerary feasts, and especially these particular ones of *siroza* and *sal*. On these important occasions the two further blood-sacrifices were made, and the religious services of the third night were performed again, with the consecration once more of clothing for the dead. More modest observances, called *rōza*, were maintained at the end of each of the ten months between the *siroza* and *sal*. The essential rite on these occasions was the recital, at the house of the deceased, of the Farvardin Yašt, the hymn to All Souls. This, which took from half an hour to a full hour, according to tempo, might be done at any time between sunrise and sunset. By reciting the Avestan text the priest consecrated whatever food had been prepared, which might be quite simple, or consist of all such dishes as the dead person had particularly enjoyed.[48] It must always, however, include those items which were essential to the 'meal for the dog', namely *sirog*, *sir-o-sedow*, and an egg.

After the first year, it was thought, the soul was no longer lonely and in need of so many special rites to help and comfort it; but an anniversary ceremony should be held in its honour for thirty years, roughly the length of a generation, or the time that son or grandson might be expected to live to maintain this observance. By then, it was believed, the soul had become fully one of the fravašis, the great company of the righteous dead; and so it was sufficient thereafter to observe the rites of Farvardigan, the feast of All

[47] Quarrelling or disorder of any kind were also held to distress the departed; and Murvarid, Agha Rustam's sister, told me how once Namir Mizanian of Taft (not at the time of the incident a particularly devout man) had been riding home from Yazd when he met two white-clad figures. They declared themselves to be two souls (*vrun*), driven away from their respective *sals* (anniversary ceremonies) by the quarrelling and undue smoke which filled the houses. So they had 'flown up on to the roof' and away. (*Vrun*, Murvarid interpolated, are winged, like the fravašis.) The two turned down the track leading to the dakhma of Yazd, and after three paces vanished. A little further along the road Namir met men returning from the *sals*, who listened to his strange story and agreed that there had been much smoke and wrangling there. (On the subtleties of distinction between 'fravaši' and 'ravān/vrun' see Boyce, *History*, i. 117–29.)

[48] Unless the deceased had been unusually distinguished, or beloved, the observances naturally tended to become simpler with the passing of the years.

Souls, to set aside the 'meal for the dog' after all religious services, and to give clean food daily to a dog.

This daily giving of unconsecrated food to a dog on behalf of the dead is plainly an extension of the original observance, and it is not hard to see how it would have come about. Once the practice was established of giving the consecrated food-offerings for the dead to a dog, then this act, being very frequently performed, must gradually have merged with the ordinary daily feeding of herd- and house-dog, and so have led to this being itself regarded as a rite which served the departed. The development was probably a slow one, but may well be very old. It must certainly have been firmly established before the downfall of the Sasanians, in order for it to be maintained by both branches of the Zoroastrian community down into modern times. Apart from the unique contribution of the dog, the Zoroastrian funerary observances are paralleled with startling closeness by those of ancient India,[49] and so must be supposed to have their origin in the remote past of the Indo-Iranians. The two peoples, it is thought, began to drift apart in the third millennium B.C.; and so these rites, inherited by Zoroastrians from the pagan past, must have a history of at least five thousand years, and probably immeasurably longer.

One factor which helped to fit the dog for its unusual part in the rituals of the Zoroastrian faith was that, as we have seen, it was regarded as a moral creature, as standing exceptionally high in the scale of creation. In death, therefore, its body, like that of a righteous man, was regarded as highly polluting, and even to see a dead dog damaged ritual purity, and obliged the orthodox to bathe at once. (Hence it was an easy form of harassment by na-najib Moslems to toss the bodies of dead dogs into Zoroastrian lanes.) Ordinarily when a masterless lane-dog died, its death went unnoticed, but this was not so with a house-dog. He, having spent his days in company with the family, was known to be very 'clean', in addition to his other virtues; and so his death, like that of a person, repre-sented a special triumph for the powers of evil, and due rites were necessary in this case also, both to limit the contagion and to help the spirit of the dog itself. The traditional Zoroastrian doctrine was that all creatures which were brought into being by Ohrmazd have a spirit or soul, which endures after death, hence the importance of taking the life of a creature of the good creation only ritually (that is,

---

[49] See Boyce, *History*, i. 120–1.

in sacrifice), whereby the consecrated spirit was not harmed; but it was only for the faithful house-dog that further efforts were made to help his spirit to reach heaven. When he died, it was as when a human dies: one of the family went to the priest carrying an egg, with the traditional message 'The soul is taking the road', and the priest solemnized the Dron-e Šroš as for a human soul, but with only three twigs of *barsom* in his hand, instead of the five required for a layman and seven for a priest.[50] The body was carried away to a barren place, with an old sedra or sacred shirt for shroud, tied with a košti; and brief rituals were performed thereafter on the fourth day at dawn, and on the thirtieth day and the first anniversary. The Zoroastrian thus rewarded his dog's faithfulness with an equal loyalty, even after death. Loyalty is one of the greatest virtues for Zoroastrians, and it is partly because the dog is *haqq-šenās*, acknowledging obligations towards those who feed him, that they esteemed him so highly (contrasting him in this with the cat, which they regarded as a typically Moslem animal, treacherous and selfish, now all blandishments and now suddenly scratching and biting the hand that caressed it).[51] So we return to the fact that the Zoroastrian regard for the dog is in part rational, being in fact shared by large sections of humanity. But this rational regard is blended with a large element also of the mysterious, connected with immensely ancient beliefs about the nature of evil and the fate of the soul in the hereafter.

[50] There was firm agreement on these observances both among the priests of Yazd (all of whom had kept dogs in their time), and among the older generation of laymen in both Sharifabad and Mazraᶜ Kalantar.

[51] The two animals, dog and cat, having been championed by the two communities, it was natural that the Zoroastrians should contrast the dog's virtues with the cat's failings. They firmly declared, moreover, that it was the cat, a creature of darkness, which was unclean. If one of a cat's whiskers touched food, D. Khodadad stated, anyone who ate that food would waste away; and a bowl from which a cat had eaten remained unclean after seven washings. Especial care was taken not to let a cat into the room where a dead person lay, for its glance would, in contrast to the *sagdid*, allow demons to enter the body. No Zoroastrians kept cats in Sharifabad, but 'Moslem' cats sometimes slipped into Zoroastrian houses after dark in search of food, and if they were seen something would be flung at them. This was the only active unkindness shown to them. There was never any question of seeking them out to torment them. Orthodox Parsis share the Irani dislike of cats, and have as a rule no dealings with them. Yet such traditions are sometimes broken, and just as a Moslem family will sometimes keep a pet dog, so, accompanying the servants of Arbab Faridun Kayanian when they took *yad-bud* to the poor in Yazd, I met an old, bedridden Zoroastrian who lived alone, and had for his constant companion a magnificent long-haired cat, which sat sedately on the floor by his pillow.

7

THE SPRING NEW YEAR AND THE HUNDREDTH-DAY FEAST

THE ancient Iranian calendar, observed, it seems, by Zoroastrians till the downfall of the Parthians, had twelve months of thirty days each, and accordingly slipped back steadily against the natural year, being the shorter by over five days. It was kept in accord with it, however, by the frequent insertion—about once every six years—of a thirteenth month. This calendar was reformed under the first Sasanian king by the addition (on the model of the Egyptian calendar) of five days set at the end of the year.[1] These five days were piously named by the reformers the Gāthā (Gāh) days after the five groups of Zoroaster's hymns. The 365-day year was too close to the natural one to make the traditional intercalation of a month any longer a practical measure, since it now took 120 years to amass thirty days from the quarter-days disregarded annually.[2] Accordingly, the new calendar was left to recede slowly against the solar year, and the Zoroastrian holy days, which with their symbolism are closely linked with the seasons, became gradually divorced from them. Two attempts were made to correct this state of affairs, one during the late Sasanian period and one again in about A.D. 1006; but both had only a temporary effect. By 1964 the religious New Year, No Ruz, had again receded so far that it was being celebrated in high summer, with 1 Farvardin coinciding with 31 July in the Gregorian calendar.

To complicate matters, the Parsis (who had once intercalated a month after settling in India, in an attempt to keep 1 Farvardin as a spring feast)[3] observed a calendar which lagged one month behind the Irani one. This they called (by a Gujarati term) the

---

[1] On these matters see 'On the calendar of Zoroastrian feasts'.

[2] At least one group of Sasanian scholars evidently held that it was desirable to make such an intercalation every 120 years, and they even wrote as if this system were in operation, thus confusing subsequent studies of the matter.

[3] The evidence points to this being the only intercalation of the kind ever to be made. It was probably carried out between A.D. 1125 and 1250.

'Shenshāī' calendar, to distinguish it from the Irani one, which they named simply *qadīmī* 'old'. Late in the nineteenth century a group of reforming Parsis attempted to resolve all confusion by adopting what was virtually the Gregorian calendar, with a leap-day every four years, set after the 'Gatha' days, and No Ruz always in the spring. This calendar they called *faṣlī* 'seasonal'; and they truly believed that in using it they were reverting to what must have been the original calendar of their faith, since clearly this had once been in harmony with the seasons. These Parsis, although only a small group, exerted influence in time on some reforming spirits among the Zoroastrians of Iran, who decided to accept this fixed calendar in their turn, and to introduce it if possible throughout their own community. In this endeavour they were helped by the fact that Reza Shah Pahlavi had adopted a similar fixed calendar as the national one of Iran; and moreover (influenced, it is said, by Arbab Kay Khosrow Shahrokh, the first Zoroastrian member of the Iranian parliament), he chose to use the old Zoroastrian names for its months, in preference to ones of Arabic origin, to give it a traditional character.

Thereafter Arbab Kay Khosrow, working together with Arbab Sorush Sorushian of Kerman, and Arbab Sohrab Kayanian of Yazd, carried on a long campaign among his co-religionists, reasoning, exhorting, and cajoling, to persuade them all to adopt the fixed calendar. The reformers strengthened their case by naming this calendar, not by the colourless term *faṣlī*, but by the emotive one *bāstānī* 'ancient', labelling the 365-day one firmly *nā-dorost* 'incorrect'. The conservative members of the community continued to call the latter *qadīmī* 'old', as the Parsis had done, and damned the fixed one by terming it *jadīd* 'new'. (In the following pages, to avoid confusion, they will be referred to as the traditional and reformed calendars respectively.) The priests and a number of the laity were perfectly familiar with the workings of a fixed calendar, but they regarded this as a secular way of reckoning, tainted with un-Zoroastrian influences, and no fit way to calculate holy days and religious observances. Nevertheless, by prodigious exertions, the reformers brought it about that in 1939 their calendar was adopted by Zoroastrians throughout Iran. The Yazdis were deeply perturbed, however, by the measure, and a few years later, led by their priests, most of them reverted to the traditional one. Since then, both calendars have been in use in their region, according to individual choice, for though the priests themselves abandoned the reformed one in a body, nevertheless they were prepared, when asked, to celebrate family observances according to it.[4]

In Sharifabad Agha Rustam's father Noshiravan, having carefully studied the arguments of the reformers, was convinced by them, and with the help of a dahmobed, who was similarly persuaded, did his utmost to bring the villagers to adopt and keep the fixed calendar. As his son said, it was a remarkable intellectual achievement that he, a small farmer of limited education, living in this most conservative of Zoroastrian communities, should not only have grasped the complex arguments involved, but have decided to act on them and make this major break with tradition. The weight of village opinion was against him, however, and when most of Yazd reverted to the traditional calendar, Sharifabad followed suit. Noshiravan held to the reformed calendar for a time in his own family, but in isolation this proved impractical, and by 1964 the traditional one had generally prevailed.[5]

Reversion to the traditional calendar did not mean, however, that the Sharifabadis and other Yazdi Zoroastrians failed to celebrate No Ruz annually at the spring equinox, together with all the rest of their fellow countrymen. Spring in Iran is an enchanting season, and it marks the end of a harsh winter, which is endured with few defences because it is so short. Moreover, spring itself, so sweet and fresh, quickly ends in burning summer. So the age-old custom of taking a prolonged holiday in order to enjoy this loveliest time of year was too pleasant ever to give up; and accordingly, after their calendar-reform, the Sasanians evolved the practice, maintained by traditionalist Irani Zoroastrians to this day, of celebrating No

---

[4] Both calendars were sometimes observed within the same family. Thus out of piety the Kayanian family kept the anniversary day of Arbab Sohrab according to the reformed calendar, but otherwise used the traditional one. I was much indebted to Khanom Simindukht, Arbab Sohrab's widow, who most kindly collated for me the reformed calendar for 1963/4, printed in Tehran, with the traditional one, maintained through unwritten custom and usage.

[5] Influence was nevertheless constantly being exerted from Tehran in favour of the reformed calendar, and the resulting perplexities for the Yazdi villagers were such that once, when I was present at a discussion of such matters in Moriabad, an elderly man turned to me and asked grimly if I did not think that the whole problem had been invented by Moslems to plague those of the old religion. The Zoroastrian reformed calendar coincided with the national one only for the first thirty days of the year, for the national Farvardin Mah has thirty-one days, whereas all the months of every Zoroastrian calendar are uniformly of thirty days, with the five 'Gatha' days gathered together at the end of the year (becoming six in number every fourth year in the reformed calendar).

Ruz twice over, once as a religious observance on 1 Farvardin, as this moved through the seasons with the 365-day year, and once as a fixed secular feast at the spring equinox. This secularization of the spring No Ruz made it possible for Moslem Iran to retain this one feast while rejecting all the holy days of Zoroastrianism, and it is accordingly the only festival which Zoroastrians share with their Moslem compatriots.[6]

In the interests, moreover, of harmony—there being no religious principle at stake—the Zoroastrians had adopted in recent times the national practice of beginning the festival formally at whatever time was officially proclaimed for it each year, rather than always at dawn on 21 March, which would be their own traditional usage. By the twentieth day of the month (which in 1964 corresponded to Ruz Dai-be-Din of Aban Mah in the traditional calendar) the great spring-cleaning of houses had taken place, and on that day everyone bathed and put on fresh clothes, which included at least one new garment. In the Belivani family young Gushtasp had a pair of new striped trousers, and a gay red and white skull-cap (standard wear for the village boys). His baby brother Shahvahram had a new jacket, and some of his sisters were wholly transformed, the smallest, Mandana, being enchanted by her new skirt, which she kept smoothing in solemn delight. Among the preparations for the new year had been the dying of quantities of hard-boiled eggs in bright colours (green, red, and yellow) and elaborate patterns, and these were piled in bowls, looking very pretty and awaiting distribution in the days to come.

Meantime two places were carefully prepared for welcoming the new year. One was *šīv-e vījū*, 'under the hanging larder'. The *vijū* is a square of wood hung by ropes at its four corners from the hole in the domed roof of a store-room, on which food can be kept safe from ants, mice, or thieving cats.[7] For the festival everything black (such as smoke-darkened pots and pans) was taken out of this room, which was scrupulously dusted and swept. Then a number of

---

[6] The seasons in Gujarat being quite different, the Parsis abandoned the secular spring No Ruz, which was, however, reintroduced among them under Irani influence in the late nineteenth century and named by them the 'No Ruz-e Jamshedi'. It is still ignored by some of the orthodox there. The adjective 'Jamshedi' derives from the legends associated in old books with the feast, according to which it was founded by Jamshed. Such legends seemed to have no living association with either the religious or the secular No Ruz among the Yazdis, and one would hear them only from those well versed in the *Shahname* or the *Rivayats*.   [7] See Sorushian, *Farhang*, 178.

things were set out, in rigidly prescribed order, on the earthen floor directly below the *viju*. A mirror was lent against the wall, and a lamp lit before it. To the right of the lamp was placed a green-wrapped sugar-cone, to its left a pitcher full of curds. In front of the lamp was a vase holding sprays of evergreen (cypress or pine); to its right a bowl of water containing a pomegranate stuck full of silver coins, and dried marjoram leaves sprinkled on its surface, to its left a pitcher of *ōwpāra* (water in which segments of dried fruit —apricot, plum, and the like—had been steeped for three days). In front of the vase was a glass filled with *pālūda*, a sweet drink, white in colour,[8] with to its right a new earthenware pitcher with pure water, its mouth closed by a green-painted egg, to its left a little woven basket full of fresh greenstuff, such as coriander, parsley, or lettuce. Finally, in front of all, there was a platter bearing *čangāl*, or *komāč-e Nō Rūz*, a sweet dish made only for this festival.[9] The predominant colours were thus white and green, which seemed to symbolize the colours of spring,[10] as the sweetness of the dishes symbolized its delights. The tall sugar-cone was put in position last of all, just before the announcement of the new year; and it was believed that, as that announcement was made, the *viju* itself would turn in a full circle overhead. This belief stemmed, presumably, from the ancient tradition that history began with the first No Ruz, when the sun (which had previously stood still at noon) started to revolve, and thus set in motion the cycle of the seasons, with birth and death.

[8] This drink, common in Iran, is made by squeezing starch jelly through a strainer to form thin fibres; and it was prepared as a treat in the Belivani household on festive days in summer.

[9] For *čangāl* fresh stoned dates were steeped in a little hot water, and then mixed with rose-water, sugar-candy water, and a paste made from sesame seeds. Hot fresh bread was kneaded until soft, and wrapped round the moist mixture; and the whole was put on a plate, dried rose-petals and cinnamon were scattered over it, and it was pressed under another plate while it cooled.

[10] That there is a long tradition in associating such things with No Ruz is suggested by a passage in the *Kitāba-'l maḥāsin wa-l aẓdād*, ed. Van Vloten, Leiden, 1898 (repr. 1966), 362, transl. R. Ehrlich, 'The celebrations and gifts of the Persian New Year . . .', *Dr. Modi Memorial Volume*, Bombay, 1930, 99: 'New clothes were worn, and food was of the new season . . . Among other things which it was thought propitious to begin this day with, was a mouthful of pure fresh milk and fresh cheese', also 'white sugar with fresh Indian nuts pared'. There is no custom among the Zoroastrians of setting out seven things whose names begin with the letter 's', as the Moslems of Iran do, though the number seven is highly significant for them in connection with the religious feast (see below, pp. 215, 230-1).

There was none there to see this happen, however, for all the family were then gathered in the main room of the house. Here a second place had been made ready to welcome the new year. A table was set out with a silver standing mirror, a small portrait (brought from Bombay) of Zoroaster, a *Khorda Avesta* in a green silk covering, and two silver vases with sprays of pine and the purple-flowering Judas tree. In front was a small radio set. The children of D. Khodadad and Paridun Rashidi had drifted in early in the afternoon, and their mothers and fathers followed, so that all three families were assembled. As sunset approached, Agha Rustam said the košti-prayers. Then the new year was proclaimed over the radio, and he went round the whole family, sprinkling everyone with rose-water and wishing each a happy new year. Sweets were distributed, and the evening passed convivially, with fish for supper, a rare treat on the plain of Yazd.

The next day (21 March) would by traditional Zoroastrian usage have been the true beginning of the new year. It broke grey and windy, with rain-clouds louring and dust blowing along under the foot-hills. Maintaining the last vestige of his father's attempt to introduce the reformed calendar, Agha Rustam sent his daughters Piruza and Pourandukht up on to the roof to light a fire before sunrise—a ritual that belonged to the religious No Ruz. On 31 July there would not be a single Zoroastrian roof without its glowing fire, but on that chill March morning theirs was the only one, lit with difficulty between gusts of wind, while a few heavy raindrops fell—though in compensation a pair of swallows, the first of the year, flew overhead twittering. After the small fire had burnt itself out, it was comforting to go down to breakfast with the family on bowls of steaming *harīsa*, a pottage made of pounded wheat, maize and a little meat, a dish which was regularly cooked for festive mornings.

Thereafter the day was full of comings and goings, as the first No Ruz visits were paid. Three different groups of visitors came then and throughout the first week of the festival (which for the Zoroastrians lasted a full twenty-one days, an auspicious three times seven). First, there were those—mostly Moslems—who had worked for the family in any way during the year, such as baker, miller, quilt-maker, pedlars of firewood and garden-produce, the village shopkeepers. They were given new-year greetings, with two to four painted eggs, a handful of *ājīl* (dried sunflower and melon seeds, with pistachio nuts), and sometimes some money. Then there were Zoro-astrian children, up to the age of twelve or so. Those from sub-stantial families went only to the houses of relatives and close friends, but poorer children made their rounds more widely, to receive in their turn painted eggs, *ajil*, and some little presents—a coin or two, pencils, writing books, and the like, as well as the painted eggs, which they played with rather as English children do with conkers, holding them in their hands and striking them together to break the shells. Finally, there came friends, relatives, and acquaintances to pay formal calls and to exchange greetings and token gifts—often in Sharifabad sprays of cypress or pine, or pomegranates, stored through the winter in underground cellars. (These particular gifts belonged also in their symbolism to the religious No Ruz, for they represent endless life, and should bring to mind the immortality that is to come.) Leading men such as Agha Rustam stayed at home for the first days of the festival to receive visits, which they repaid later. The visitors were mostly men, with a few women of the ex-tended family, and they were formally received with rose-water and sweetmeats, as well as the exchange of gifts. Some stayed only a few minutes, others (especially those who had returned to the village for the holiday) settled for a comfortable talk until new arrivals displaced them.

  D. Khodadad joined the family for a midday meal of chicken broth with bread and curds, and Agha Rustam, with Piruza and myself, went back with him afterwards for the *purse* of his late brother, D. Gushtasp, who had died that autumn. It was the custom at every feast throughout the first year after a death to hold a brief ceremony in the home for *šad-ravani*, to comfort the departed soul by drawing it into the festivities; and this custom was observed at the secular No Ruz as at the holy feasts. At the Dastur's house a white cloth was spread in the *pesgam-e mas*, and on it were laid sprays of evergreen, pomegranates, and painted eggs. (Different things would be put out for a *purse* at different festivals, according to the season. At Tiragan and the religious No Ruz, for instance, an abundance of fresh fruits were available. The only foodstuff that was forbidden at a *purse* was 'nuql', white sweetmeats, which were avoided altogether by the immediate family during the first year after death.) It was usual to place a photograph of the dead person, if one were available, in the *pesgam-e mas*; and the family would seat themselves in the lesser *pesgam* opposite, and talk of the departed, and his doings and virtues. Meanwhile anyone in the village who wished would come, bringing some small gift from the fruits and herbs of the season, and place this on the cloth take and up something from there, thus acting, as it were, as the guest of the invisible soul. (By a similar gracious custom, whenever *yad-bud* was sent to a family from a service for the dead, some small gift was always put in the bowl when it was returned.) Then, after exchanging some words with the family, the visitor would take his leave, saying as he did so, *Khodā be-āmurzadeš*, 'May God have mercy on him!'.

Agha Rustam himself soon withdrew from this No Ruz *purse* to receive more guests at his own house; but Piruza and I lingered to listen to D. Khodadad speaking of his brother. He had been the older by twenty-five years, though born of the same mother, and had been a very hard-working, conscientious priest of the old school, belonging to the generation who still themselves wove the košti, taught, and performed all manner of rituals. He had served for some years as atašband in the Dadyseth Agiary in Bombay; and then, suddenly feeling a longing for his homeland, had set out and walked back to Yazd, earning his living in Pauline fashion along the way by plaiting rope and cord. He settled in his father's house in the village of Cham, became hušt-mobed there, and taught daily in the village school. Eventually, as an old man, he became mentally confused, and Paridun Rashidi went to Cham, set him on a donkey, and brought him to Sharifabad, where he had lived his last years with his brother, devoting himself to the recital of Avesta.

In the evening of the first day of the festival there was a big family gathering at the Belivani house, with fourteen children and their elders. In traditional Persian fashion the merry-making came first, and the meal (a delicious meat-stew, with trays piled high with rice and freshly baked bread) was eaten late in the evening, in appreciative semi-silence, and the party then soon broke up. No one had worked in the village on that first day, No Ruz itself, except at essential tasks such as irrigating growing crops and feeding stock; but spring brought urgent work, and already on the second day cotton-sowing was in progress again, and thereafter the seasonal farm-work went on in the intervals of merry-making. The morning of the second day still saw many visitors coming to Agha Rustam's house; but in the afternoon he and several members of his family set off for the mountain-shrine of Pir-e Hrišt, for his great-uncle

Turk Jamshidi, with his wife Sarvar, were offering a sacrifice there, and had invited their relatives to join them. Shahnaz, Agha Rustam's eldest daughter, walked the whole way in fulfilment of a vow, but her sister Piruza rode on the high-peaked saddle of the family cow (peaked because the Yazdi cows are a hump-backed breed), with bedding and utensils hung all around her, and the others took turns on donkey-back, while Shehriar the Dastur's son and I cycled, and Agha Rustam himself went on his moped. The whole party spent that night at the shrine, and the sacrifice was offered soon after sunrise the next day. There were other groups at the Pir, from Sharifabad, Mazraʿ Kalantar, and further away, and many gahambar-e toji were celebrated there, whereby piety and pleasure were blended (for though the spring No Ruz was a secular festival, Sharifabadi celebrations tended naturally to take religious forms).

That night a big double wedding took place in Sharifabad. The spring No Ruz is by tradition an auspicious time for betrothals and marriages,[11] and this tradition had been reinforced latterly by practical considerations, since so many of the young men worked away from the village, but could return there for the national holiday. Betrothals were held to be as binding as marriages, since a Zoroastrian's word is his bond, and to revoke it was regarded as shameful, and so they took place with almost as much ceremony as the marriage itself, and with many guests invited as witnesses.[12] There were three weddings and a betrothal in Sharifabad during the No

---

[11] See 'On the Zoroastrian calendar', 534 and n. 85.

[12] Formerly betrothals often took place at a very early age, and this was still occasionally the case in the 1960s. The youngest which I encountered was that of Shirin-e Jehangir, who had been betrothed at ten to a boy of seventeen, to make a double match, her eighteen-year-old brother becoming engaged at the same time to the sister of her fiancé. Seven years later, in 1964, neither pair was yet married, and only the other girl still wanted to fulfil their betrothal vows, the other three heartily wishing not to; but the pressure of the community on them was great. In a relatively large number of cases after an early betrothal the youth would depart—for Bombay or Tehran, Europe, or America—and the girl would wait, three, four, seven years, sometimes receiving few or no letters, to have him eventually return, by then a stranger, to marry her. (Occasionally, of course, he did not come back, and she remained virtually a widow without ever being married.) A number of the village marriages continued rather on this pattern, with the wives staying at home and tending the family fields with help from neighbours, while the husband worked away, and returned only at intervals. This was partly due to economic pressure (since the cost of living was high in Tehran), partly to love of an ancestral home, and a wish not to sever attachment to it.

Ruz holiday that year.[13] By custom both ceremonies were solemnized at midnight at the bride's home.[14] Formerly many rites were performed before this, and three days of feasting and rejoicing (*sūr kartwun*) took place thereafter;[15] but all this had come to be much curtailed, and ceremony and festivities were largely crammed into one joyful occasion. The guests usually assembled about half-past eight or nine,[16] presents were exchanged between the two families, and various folk-customs were enacted, before the actual ceremony was performed by the priest at midnight. Before he recited the words of the ancient service, he, the groom, and the father of the bride all 'made new the košti'; but thereafter the groom untied his košti again, for during the ceremony there must be no knot or closed pin on his or the bride's persons, otherwise their affairs would become knotted and confused. During the service a brother or close kinsman of the groom held over his head a small tray on which was the untied košti, together with needle, thread, scissors, a raw egg, a pomegranate or apple, dried marjoram, and white sweetmeats, all covered by a green kerchief. (After the ceremony he would go out into the courtyard and throw the egg up on to the roof.) In front of the groom was a big tray holding *lurk*, with myrtle and cypress twigs, and the two fathers clasped their right hands over this during the service. When it was over, the *lurk* was distributed to the assembled company, with sherbet. The priest then departed, leaving it to the dahmobed to conduct the subsequent rites. A brazier full of glowing fire was put on a tall stool in the middle of the courtyard, and the dahmobed took the left hand of the groom in his own left hand, and the groom the bride's; and thus he led them very slowly round the fire, withershins, singing the many verses of a bridal song, while the encircling company looked on with murmurous approval, and marked its end with a tumultuous *Hāvorū, hāvorū, hāvorū, ay šō-boš.*[17] Thereafter merry-making became

[13] The betrothal was of Erdeshir Qudusi's second daughter. Her fiancé had been several years in Tehran, and had sought her hand before leaving the village; but etiquette had required him to wait until her elder sister had married and left home.

[14] Traditionally Parsi marriages 'are generally performed in the evening, just a little after sunset' (Modi, *CC*, 20).

[15] It is hoped to describe elsewhere an old traditional wedding, for which the multifarious details were furnished me by Khanom Humayun Kayanian (wife of Arbab Jamshid Soroushian), and by Tahmina Khanom.

[16] At each of these No Ruz weddings there was a great gathering of relatives and friends, but what was essential (it was said) was that at least seven persons should be present to act as witnesses.

[17] This shout was raised by the Yazdi Zoroastrians on all occasions of rejoicing, (see further below, p. 234 n. 30).

general again, with the usual robust jokes proper to such occasions, and always an obscene dance, performed with varying degrees of gusto or grace by one of the young men of the village.

A wedding party would break up in the small hours of the morning; and early the next day D. Khodadad would go with the groom, the dahmobed and a group of male relatives and friends to the bank of a stream. They took with them a bowl of milk, with rose-petals and herbs in it, for the libation to water, and a tuft of couch-grass (mōwr), dug up by the roots and washed. This was dipped into the milk, and the Dastur then performed the rite of āb-zōhr, with recital of Avesta. The grass was then dipped in the stream, and carried by the groom to his bride. He put it into her hand, and thereafter it was planted again, to grow and symbolize their marriage, which was to be as firm-rooted and flourishing as this useful and almost indestructible grass.

Many of the hardy wedding guests were also likely to be up early on the morning after the festivities, and at work in the fields. As the sun shone more warmly, the fodder-crop, lucerne, began to grow fast, and girls would go out to cut it with sickles, often taking with them the family cow or calf to graze on the new grass along the banks of the irrigation ditches. These were dotted with bright yellow hawkweed, and there were blue and white butterflies already on the wing. Every day more swallows were to be seen, some darting up and down the village lanes near their nesting sites, others in flocks flying steadily overhead on their way further north. Once a score or so of Alpine swifts broke their journey to hawk for insects over the fields, and for two or three days in succession a superb falcon appeared there, striking terror among the resident wagtails and crested larks. The winter wheat was growing tall and the trees along the field paths were breaking into leaf. Occasionally there were showers of rain, and then for a while the air was deliciously fresh and cool, and the mountains beyond the desert took on beautiful deep colours; but usually it was already hot at noon, and the children paddled joyfully in the streams. Sometimes this was only as a break from their regular task of weeding the crops, but sometimes during the No Ruz holiday groups of women and children went out to the fields simply to enjoy themselves. Such outings usually took the form of an 'aš-e khairat'. A family, that is, would take it on themselves to cook and distribute a charity pottage in the open, and would invite relatives and friends to share it. One afternoon when Piruza and Pouran and I were going to the fields rathei late with Agha Rustam, to plant melons, we met such a party returning, colourful in their gay red and green clothes. The smallest children were on donkeys, or being carried pick-a-back, the others straggled along, happily tired from hours of paddling, chasing insects, and picking flowers in the warm sunshine. One of the women carried a big empty cauldron, another a full basin of pottage to share among their menfolk.

On the thirteenth day of No Ruz it is the universal custom in Iran to pass as many hours as possible out of doors. In Sharifabad the Belivani family spent a happy day in a walled garden, playing traditional games, and eating a picnic meal with relishes of freshly picked lettuce and parsley, and tiny green unripe apples (for the apple blossom was already over and the fruit setting). Agha Rustam chose rather to visit Hasanabad, and Erdeshir Qudusi and I cycled after him to that fertile village. In its gardens, under elm and ash trees in new leaf, there were thickets of roses in flower, some clear pink like the English wild rose, others yellow, and in one place a bush of the 'two-faced rose', its petals flame-red inside but yellow-backed. There were whitethroats singing and swallows skimming over green wheat, so that in some ways it seemed more like England in May than a Yazdi village, until one noticed a hoopoe perched on a wall or a string of camels padding past.

Meanwhile, by the traditional calendar we were well into Azar Mah, the month of Fire, whose first day coincided with the seventh day of the spring No Ruz. Since this was one of the two 'beloved' months of the Zoroastrians, in which the merit of each good work was reckoned as tenfold, many pious acts were performed during the latter part of the spring festival. These included several celebrations of the rites of 'exalting the fire' and making the libation to water.[18] The fourteenth to seventeenth days of No Ruz were, moreover, those of the official pilgrimage to the Pir-e Hrišt,[19] and they included one very holy day, Ruz Azar of Mah Azar, the name-day feast of the yazad of Fire. Twenty-four sheep were offered up that day at the mountain shrine, and there was much prayer and rejoicing there. Times of pilgrimage were opportunities for the devout to say all the five daily prayers; but although the spring equinox was past, the return of Rapithwin could not be acknowledged before the celebration of

[18] For both these rites see the following chapter.
[19] See below, pp. 243–8.

the religious No Ruz at the end of July, and so the prayers of the third watch were still devoted to Mihr.

The twenty-first and last day of the No Ruz festival (9 April) was signalized by small evening gatherings; and as a stranger I received yet more presents from my most kind hosts—a sugar-cone, pistachio nuts, a green silk kerchief, and from Piruza a cloth beautifully embroidered with the winged symbol from Persepolis, which the Parsis have established as the Zoroastrian emblem. And so a period of happiness and delight came to a close, spindle and loom were busy again in the houses, the children returned reluctantly to the village schools, and field-work was carried on even more strenuously.

Yet it was not very long before there was another break in the daily routine, this time for a religious occasion; for 22 April co-incided with Aštad Ruz of Azar Mah, and that for the Yazdi Zoro-astrians was the feast of Sada, which marked the hundredth day before the religious No Ruz on the first day of Farvardin. Sada has a more complex history than any other Zoroastrian feast, except No Ruz itself, for two different days were observed for its celebration in different parts of ancient Iran.[20] The other day, which was the one kept by the Kermani Zoroastrians, was Aban Ruz of Vahman Mah, which was the hundredth day after the gahambar of Ayathrima, held to be the beginning of winter. By either tradition Sada was properly a midwinter feast,[21] celebrated with a huge fire to drive back demon-created darkness and cold, but the reform of the third century A.D. set both days wandering with the 365-day year, and the resulting confusion led to their being first duplicated, like all the other feasts, and then extended into six-day festivals. The Sharifabadis came (for reasons that will be clear later) to know Sada as Hīromba, and in 1964 they celebrated it in late April for three days only, begin-ning on Ruz Aštad. They were then alone in all Iran in keeping the feast on the traditional Yazdi date, for the reformers had adopted the Kermani one for their calendar, and during the brief period when this calendar was generally observed in Yazd the confusion there became so great that it ended in the celebration of Sada being abandoned except in Sharifabad and Mazraᶜ Kalantar.[22] Mazraᶜ

---

[20] See 'Rapithwin, Nō Rūz . . .', 212–14; 'The two dates of the feast of Sada', *passim.*

[21] Thus by the fixed calendar Aštad Ruz of Azar Mah coincided in 1964 with 11 December, Aban Ruz of Vahman Mah with 24 January.

[22] The observance had been artificially revived in the city of Yazd when I was there, but on the Kermani date, and without, it seemed, much popular support.

maintained the feast, but on the Kermani date as calculated by the reformed calendar. This was the only holy day which the villagers there kept according to this calendar; and their reason for doing so was that if they gathered wood for the fire on a fixed date in January they knew it would be dry, without sap, whereas wood gathered in April would be green and moist, and so it would be a sin to put it on the fire. The Sharifabadis admitted the soundness of this reasoning, felt themselves to be in a dilemma, but followed their consistent practice of holding to the ways of their forefathers.

The chief preparation for Sada was in fact the gathering of wood, which was a scarce commodity on the Yazdi plain. So every year on the day before the festival the young men and older boys of Sharifa-bad (the latter firmly abandoning school) went up to the mountain shrine of Pir-e Hrišt to collect γīδal (camel's thorn). A boy had usually to be ten or eleven before his parents allowed him to become one of the wačayun-γīδalī, the 'camel's thorn-boys'; and this was a noteworthy step for him on the way to manhood, the first time, probably, that he had spent a night away from his family. The year before, Agha Rustam's son Gushtasp had gone for the first time, and afterwards his parents had followed tradition by giving a party for him, where everyone toasted him in sherbet and wished him long life. So in 1964 both he and his fifteen-year-old cousin Shehriar, D. Khodadad's son, were of the party, and his elder sisters went too, to help with the cooking. On Ard Ruz, the eve of the festival, a strong wind was blowing, bringing clouds and a threat of storm, and Shehriar and I, on bicycles, were driven before it across the desert with unusually little effort. The others were mostly on donkey-back, with Piruza perched high above the rest on her cow.[23] One of the salars was there, walking by his small son, who was mounted on a donkey with two long shovels lashed along its flanks, and a bigger boy led a sacrificial ram.

All of us had reached the pavilions at the foot of the shrine by late afternoon. As it grew dark the men and boys gathered in a big pavilion, and seating themselves in a horseshoe in one of its *pesgams* began to sing songs. The women gradually drifted into the

[23] This animal had so much to do because the Belivanis had a cross-grained donkey (belonging to a friend) in their stables which resolutely refused to exert itself, and so the cow, a rather wild-eyed, hasty creature, did more than her fair share. She had some odd traits, and disconcerted us by munching in a sinister manner sheep-bones which she found on the ground at Hrišt—presumably to remedy some deficiency in her diet.

opposite *pesgam* and arranged themselves in another horseshoe, as audience. The whole company was served tea with grave courtesy by the son of the shrine's guardian, a youth of sixteen or so; and as the merriment grew, mime and dancing followed the chorus songs. The wind had by now blown away the clouds, and the moon shone down on the open *pesgams*, with flickering lamp-light showing from the shrine on the hill above. Eventually supper was eaten—a picnic meal, for everyone had brought his own (bread, hard-boiled eggs, white cheese, mint, radishes, and the like), and so to as much sleep as the donkeys would allow. The Belivani cow was snug in the stable behind the pavilions, but the hardier donkeys were tethered in the open, and, excited by each other's company, kept up a constant braying, and several times one managed to pull up its peg and start a fight. (They were all jacks, as the Sharifabadis never owned jennies.) Then someone, roused by the racket, would rush out into the moonlight to identify the culprit, and would raise a shout for its owner to come to settle the brawl, after which peace would settle again for a while.

At first light, about five o'clock, the boys were up and streaming away in twos and threes across the little mountain-locked plain. Six central points were established where ropes and sticks were dropped on the ground, and the boys worked around them in teams. In each team one of the bigger youths prized the low bushes—a prickly round tangle of thorns, dead leaves, and new growth—out of the ground with a long-handled spade, and the boys picked them up by the roots and carried them to the nearest collecting point. The wind was still tearing over the ground, and this made the work more difficult, for it sometimes carried off whole bushes; and there were fewer boys than in former years (only about twenty-five), so they had a struggle to gather enough. At each of the collecting points two men and one of the bigger boys worked the prickly bushes into great bales, with the help of the sticks, and roped them neatly together. When finished, these bales were about seven feet high, and far too heavy for a man to move; and at each collecting point two of them were made and were lashed together at the top, so that they stood leaning inwards against each other, tent-fashion. After some three hours, six such great triangular shapes dotted the plain, and the weary workers headed back to the pavilions, where men had already arrived with six more donkeys to carry the bales to the village in the afternoon (for even in late April no one exerted himself under the midday sun if he could avoid it). One of the men who had been making the bales was the dahmobed Erdeshir Khosrowi, and he said to me, factually, that the tradition was doomed, since the young men of the village were scattering all over Iran. When his generation died, the old ways would die with them.

Meanwhile the present scene was all bustle and cheerfulness. The ram that had been brought along the day before had been sacrificed just after sunrise, while the boys were at work. This was through a *khairāt*, a benevolence on the part of Kay Khosrow-e Dinyar, who lived in Tehran but came each year by bus especially for this observance. His womenfolk did the cooking, and the boys helped with water-carrying, sang more songs, and were happy. Breakfast was ready by about half-past nine, and they sat down to it with sharp appetites. There were fried *sirog*, and quantities of good meat-broth, and everyone supplied his own bread. Then the boys rested, or played about, while the women cleared up and cooked again; and at midday there was another meal of rice and meat, with radishes, and after that three of the men provided sherbet for the boys and all who had come to help. Then a communal gahambar-e toji was celebrated at the shrine, and, the heat of the day being past, all set off back to the village. The fierce wind was now head-on, and as Shehriar and I fought against it on our bicycles we came abreast of one of the pairs of great bales just as a donkey was being led under it. The little animal vanished beneath its load, and from the side only four small hoofs remained visible, though as we looked back we saw its head emerging from the mass of brushwood. There was a man at each side to prevent the load tipping, but even so it was clearly going to be a hard struggle to get it back in the teeth of the wind.

In Sharifabad itself there had been varied activity throughout the day. In the morning three cauldrons of pottage, an aš-e khairat by three individuals, had been cooked in the open space outside the shrine of Mihr Ized, where the Hiromba fire itself would later be lit. Big bowls of pottage were carried to the schools, to be eaten appreciatively by the children there. After a morning of not very concentrated work the schools closed, and the small boys set out, in three or four groups, to go from house to house collecting wood. At each door they chanted the following verse as loudly as they could:

Šāx-ē šāx-ē (h)armanī!	'A branch, a branch . . . !
Har kas šāx-ē be-dehad,	Whoever gives a branch,

odā murād-eš be-dehad!	May God grant his wish!
Har kas šāx-ē na-dehad,	Whoever does not give a branch,
Khodā murād-eš na-dehad!	May God not grant his wish!'

Every household produced something, from a broken spade-handle or spinning wheel to logs from their own wood-store; and that year the wild wind had torn branches off trees, and these were added, their leaves already withered by the sun. The boys brought their spoil to the shrine of Mihr Ized, and there men heaped it in a big circle to form a base for the brushwood to come from the mountains.

An hour or so before sunset people began to gather round the shrine, on the flat roofs, packed round the open space, and along the lanes leading to it. There were many Moslems among them, for the Sada fire is a glorious spectacle. Formerly, Agha Rustam said, the Moslems had been silent, appreciative witnesses, but now their growing numbers had emboldened the hooligans among them, who took pleasure in mocking and in disrupting the proceedings, so that the rites proper to the fire-ceremony were now performed after it, in the seclusion of the fire temple.[24] Eyes kept turning to the one lane which had been kept clear, that led towards Hrišt, but it was nearly dark before a shout went up, and to cheering and clapping the first towering load of brushwood appeared. It moved slowly forward, under the illuminated archway near the shrine, and into the midst of the throng. Four men were waiting by the wood-pile, with long-handled spades. They cut the ropes binding the two bales together and these fell apart, revealing the little donkey, which just stood, too tired even to shake itself, till its master led it away. Then the ropes holding each bale together were cut, and the camel's thorn, full of desert dust, was knocked apart and spread over the pile of wood. After a longish wait a second load arrived, and then a third. Moslem boys on one roof, growing impatient, began to chant obscenities, and one of the Ardekan policemen who were present went up and cleared them off. A lovely moon rose, and by its light the last three loads came wearily in together. They were piled on to what had now become a huge dark pyramid, and, the due religious rites being postponed, one of the four men put a torch to the pile without more ado. The wood caught instantly, and the flames

[24] Similarly at Kerman, Arbab Jamshid Sorushian told me, the Sada fire had formerly been lit by a stream outside the walled garden of the Pir-e Mihr Ized; but rowdyism among the ever-growing throngs of Moslems had forced the Zoroastrians to withdraw inside the garden itself, where they could light the fire and say their prayers in peace.

went rushing up in a huge beacon, hot and bright and fierce, and the fire burnt splendidly for a long time, turning night to day, and lighting up the faces of the throng.

A *qanat* stream flowed under the place where the fire was lit, and the choice of this place—above water, and near a shrine to Mihr—was traditional;[25] for the great fire was originally meant, like winter fires lit by peoples the world over, to help revive the declining sun, and so bring back the warmth and light of summer. It was also designed to drive off the demons of frost and cold, who turned water to stone, and thus could kill the roots of plants beneath the earth. So for these reasons the fire was lit over water and by the shrine of Mihr, who was lord both of fire and the sun. For Zoroastrians, the festival was also a defiance of Ahriman, who ruled in darkness and was master of death, and this was expressed especially in the religious rites of Sada.

On that April night the Zoroastrians remained watching the great fire until it sank into a heap of glowing embers, and then withdrew in a body to the Ataš Varahram. The temple was filled to overflowing, and there was so much talk and excitement in the closely packed congregation that not a word could be heard of the Afrinagan-e Do Dahman being celebrated by D. Khodadad, though the atašband, standing close beside him, gave the usual signs for the responses. As the service finished, a wave of excitement rippled through the people, with murmurs of *Hiromba!*, and the *wacayun-yiδali* got up and pushed and struggled themselves into two opposing lines, stretching in two curves from the fire-altar in the outer hall to the *pesgam-e mas*, their arms over each other's shoulders, in order of height, the bigger boys nearer the *pesgam*. Properly, these two lines should have been drawn up earlier on each side of the unlit Sada fire. Between them stood one of the dahmobeds, another boy beside him; and he now began a long, impressive recital of the names of the great ones of the faith, from Kay Vištasp onward, down through ancient times (as recited, for instance, in the Afrin-e Rapithwin), coming then to the notables of Sharifabad and of Yazd in living tradition, and ending with the name of one dead person from every household in the village (either a leading family figure, or one recently dead). These last names were taken in geographical order, up and down the lanes. After each name, the dahmobed called out *Khodā āmurzad-eš!* 'God have mercy on him!'. The boy standing

25 See 'Rapithwin, Nō Rūz . . .', 214 and n. 90.

by him swung up either his right arm or his left, and the line of boys to right or left gave a great shout of *Hīrombō*!, going down together at the same time in a bow like a breaking wave. At the next name the shout and bow were made by the opposite line, and so it continued for name after name, for nearly half an hour. By the end the boys were visibly tiring, but they kept up the ritual gallantly, shouting *Hirombo*! at full pitch to the very last name, high young voices blending with deep ones, and each side competing with the other in volume. The culmination of the muster-roll was naturally deeply moving for the villagers, as they listened to so many familiar names of their own well-known dead.

No one in the village could explain the meaning of the word *Hirombo* which had given its name to their festival; but the ceremony, performed of old around the unlit fire, seems meant to affirm the triumph and immortality of the souls of the good over the forces of evil and annihilation, just as the flames of the fire were about to affirm the power of light and warmth over the blackness and cold of winter night; and in performing the ceremony one hundred days before No Ruz, the worshippers were helping to strengthen Rapith-win, and were creating briefly, in midwinter, the warmth and beauty which would return with spring.

Formerly, when the Hiromba ceremony was performed in the open, the Dastur then recited the *Ataš Niyayeš*, and the fire was lit; but in the temple, when the ritual was over, the *lurk* of the gahambar was distributed and the congregation then dispersed, the boys to sleep the sleep of glorious weariness. Men went to the remains of the great fire and drew the ashes together, to keep the centre burning through the night; and the next morning Parvin Rashidi, Paridun's elder daughter, was knocking at the Belivani door at first light. Piruza and I hurried out to join her, Piruza carrying a small empty brazier, and Parichihr, Turk Jamshidi's daughter, came to join her cousins from another side. The lanes were chill and empty, but many of the Zoroastrian women had already sprinkled and swept the area outside their doors, and swallows were beginning to twitter overhead. We reached the Hiromba fire to find its embers still glowing red. Three or four girls were before us, each armed with a long metal *bara* or a pair of tongs, and they were beginning to fill their own small braziers with these embers—a tricky task for those with sandalled feet, for a wide area round about was still covered with hot grey ash. Gradually a circle formed, mostly of girls, but with a young boy from a daughterless house, and one old woman, Banu, sister-in-law of the atasband, who alone said the košti-prayers, facing east. Parizad, the Dastur's daughter, came with a big silvery *afrinagan*, and Shahnaz, Piruza's eldest sister, was there from their grandparents' house. When almost all the embers had been taken, she and another girl began to rake the ashes together, but just then two old women arrived, one with a white-painted clay brazier, kept from the All Souls' festival of the previous year, and Shahnaz helped them to find some glowing bits. Finally all that was left was a soft grey heap of ash, the Hiromba fire being thus reduced to nothingness before the greater fire, the sun, rose to shine upon it.

Piruza, like the others, then carried her brazier carefully home, and fed the embers with twigs and charcoal, until she had a glowing fire. No one could explain the ritual in so many words, but presumably it was to spread the blessing of the winter-defying Sada fire to every house in the village. Then she joined her cousins again and all the others who were carrying their braziers back to the fire-temple. The sun was now up, and the lanes were full of light and bird-calls. Some of the girls had tucked roses under their head-veils, and they made a pretty sight as they hastened along, their eyes on the bright fires which they were carrying. The atašband, who had passed us in the grey dawn, was now seated in the hall of the fire-temple, near the entrance, with a big round metal tray before him, already full of glowing fire. He had a *bara* in his right hand, and with this he took some fire from each brazier as it was brought and added it to that on the tray. The girls then took their braziers over to the door of the fire-sanctuary and sat there quietly for a while, reciting Avesta. After this they emptied their braziers in the corner to which consecrated fire was usually brought,[26] and left the temple.

The extension of their festivals in Sasanian times forced the Zoroastrians either to protract or to repeat observances, and in Sharifabad the impressive Hiromba ceremony had come to be performed three times. So on the second night of the festival, about two hours after sunset, there was again a packed congregation at the fire-temple. Three gahambars were solemnized, one after the other, but once again the words were inaudible through the general hubbub. Yet even the noisiest youth stood up and 'made new the košti' before each separate service. This time it was the blind Palamarz Rashidi,

---

[26] See above, p. 73.

clad in white, who called the muster-roll, and the boys once more did their part with zest. Three lots of *lurk* were then distributed, and it was nearly eleven o'clock of a moonlit night before the congregation dispersed. The boys, refreshed by the *lurk*, then gathered themselves into three groups, two led by the dahmobeds, and the third by Palamarz, and proceeded to visit every house in the village. At each house, standing in the lane outside, the leader recited the names of everyone, man, woman, and child, known to have died there. After each name he called *Khoda amurzad-eš*, and the boys shouted in unison *Hirombo!*, each making the ritual bow separately this time, with right arm upraised and swung down on the shout, for emphasis. It was Palamarz's group which came to the Belivani house, where twenty-four names were recited, beginning with that of Agha Rustam's great-grandfather, Khodarahm-e Gushtasp, who had built it. After the last name there was a general *Khoda amurzadi* for the ancestors of the family, and a blessing was invoked on its living members, and their crops and cattle. Then Agha Rustam went to the door, and a plateful of roasted melon-seeds, dried peas, and the like, was handed round, and the boys, munching busily, went on to the next house. The ritual, bringing the living and dead thus together, with the thrilling shout of *Hirombo* echoing along the moonlit lanes, was very moving, and I persuaded Piruza and Pouran to go with me across the roofs to hear it at house after house. It was well after midnight before the blessing on the last family had been recited, and Gushtasp came wearily but happily home, to drop instantly asleep.

The next day was an ordinary school-day for all the boys, but early in the evening Gushtasp was a guest at a party given for a boy who had joined the *wačayun-yīδali* for the first time that year. There were sherbet and sweets for all his fellows, to soothe their much-taxed throats, and they drank long life to their new companion. Then they went round the whole village again in the same way as the night before, repeating the Hiromba blessing on the living and the dead at every home.

The following day, Ruz Manraspand (25 April), was the last of the festival. Soon after sunset the boys made the round of the village for the third time, and then went to the place of the Sada fire. Here many of the villagers were already gathered, and the great recital of the names of the illustrious dead was also made for the third time, with the boys once more drawn up in two opposing lines. Their

VIIa (*above*). *Sedra-pušun* at the boys' school (see p. 238). (The boy on the right of the photograph is Rashid, Paridun's elder son.)

VIIb (*right*). *Sedra-pušun* in the Dastur's house by D. Khodadad for his niece Pourandukht, Agha Rustam's third daughter (see p. 240).

VIIIa. A sacrificial procession up the stairway to Pir-e Hrišt during the spring pilgrimage (see p. 245). (The player of the *surna* is Rustam Shehriari.)

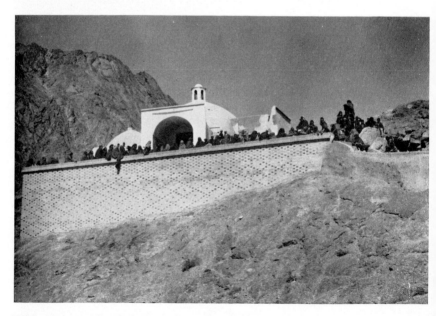

VIIIb. Women gathered on the terrace of Pir-e Hrišt during a communal Afrinagan service within the shrine (see p. 244).

shouted *Hirombo*! echoed finely under the arch outside Mihr Ized's shrine, and all the while a tiny curly-headed boy in a bright blue jacket stood stock-still between the lines, gazing in wide-eyed wonder at each as they made their bow in turn. Just before the final *Khoda amurzadeš* his father, Erej Nekdini, strode swiftly over, seized him and bore him to safety as on the last, loudest *Hirombo*! the two lines rushed at each other and grappled joyfully. The dahmobed then distributed great handfuls of dried melon-seeds and peas to all the company, and he and most of the elders departed, leaving the others to merry-making by moon- and lamp-light. Rustam Shehriari played the *surnā*, which produces wild, stirring music not unlike the bagpipes, and there was other music, singing and dancing until past one in the morning, when the gathering broke up, and the festivities of Hiromba were over.

Unlike the spring No Ruz, Sada is a deeply religious festival, of which Biruni wrote, about A.D. 1000:

People used to make great fires . . . and were deeply engaged in the worship and praise of God; also they used to assemble for eating and merriment. They maintained that this was done for the purpose of banishing the cold and dryness that arises in winter-time, and that the spreading of the warmth would keep off the attacks of all which is obnoxious to the plants in the world. In all this, their proceeding was that of a man who marches out to fight his enemy with a large army.[27]

In Sharifabad the energy and zest of the *wačayun-γiδali*, together with the splendour of the great fire, and the corporate activity of the whole village, preserved the ancient spirit of the festival admirably.[28] Thereafter it must have been the duty of priests in days of old to count the hundred days that were to pass until No Ruz, the greatest single festival of the Zoroastrian year, for which Sada was the harbinger.

[27] Sachau, ed., *Chronology*, 222. Biruni calls the feast simply *Ādur-jašan*, the 'Fire-Feast', but the date which he gives for it, 1 Shahrevar, was 100 days before the 'Greater No Ruz' when this was celebrated on 6 Adur, after the second Sasanian reform. See in detail 'The two dates of the feast of Sada'.

[28] Although the Sharifabadi observances embodied the spirit of the communal festival so well, it is likely that the institution of the *wačayun-γiδali*, and the Hiromba ritual, were special to the village, for they were unknown at neighbouring Mazraʿ Kalantar.

8

SOME RITES OF EXPIATION OR COMFORT FOR THE LIVING AND THE DEAD

THE words of their ancient holy texts were a source of immense comfort and strength to the Zoroastrians, who believed unquestion- ingly that these had all been directly revealed by God to their prophet. They had faith that by uttering verses from them they could procure divine aid and blessings, and it was usual to say a prayer before embarking on any enterprise, whether this was sowing the new season's crops or setting off on a bus journey to Yazd. (The Ahunvar was most often recited.) Moreover, the power of the words, they held, could be increased by appropriate actions, and there were accordingly a number of individual rites which were regularly performed to obtain grace or help in this life, or to benefit the departed.

One of the most impressive of these rites, with a history going back at least to Parthian times,[1] was that of 'exalting the fire', *ātaš buzorg kardan*, in Dari *taš mas kartwun*. In the past at least four priests took part in this, and sometimes eight or more; and Arbab Jamshid Sorushian recalled how beautiful the ceremony had seemed to him, solemnly enacted by white-clad mobeds in the hall of the Ataš Bahram of Yazd (it had never been performed during his own lifetime in Kerman). In Sharifabad the rite was necessarily reduced to a greater simplicity, but all its elements were faithfully preserved. Essentially, it is an ancient ritual performed to redeem such fire as has suffered contamination in this world, by purifying it and joining it to the purest fire of all, that which burns in a fire-temple. Since the theologians taught that all fires were essentially one, part of the life-force, as it were, of the world, to rescue even one small sullied flame was to contribute to the great struggle against the pollution of the good creation of Ohrmazd. Hence the rite of 'exalting the fire' was highly meritorious and was often performed in the Yazdi

---

[1] Cf. Vd. 8.81 ff. (on which see 'On the sacred fires of the Zoroastrians', 65–6).

area. Sometimes a whole village would unite to have it done on behalf of their dead (to compensate for any transgressions by them against fire while they lived). More usually it was performed at the behest of individuals, occasionally for their own welfare, but much more frequently for their dead. This was especially done during the first year after a death.

As we have seen, the Yazdis usually chose to have this and other rites performed in one of the two 'tenfold' or 'beloved' months, Azar or Urdibehišt, and it was enacted accordingly several times in Sharifabad during the No Ruz holidays of 1964, since these co-incided in part with Azar Mah in the traditional calendar. The first time that I witnessed it was when it was carried out for Rustam-e Hormezdyar, who had died some six months earlier. Three days before the public ceremony was due, Rustam-e Rashid, the atašband, took the big silvery *afrinagan* of the fire-temple and a kerchief full of sweetmeats and *lurk*, and, forming *paivand* with another man, went with him to Ardekan to collect embers from nine fires belonging to Moslem traders, which necessarily suffered pollution. They visited a coppersmith, blacksmith, and locksmith, a baker, con-fectioner, and a man who made sugar-loaves, a dyer, a turner, and a bath-attendant. To each they gave a handful of *lurk* and sweets, and received from each in return embers from his fire. (The transaction was too regularly carried out to evoke surprise or comment, even in unfriendly Ardekan.) They then carried the *afrinagan* to the Dastur's home, and for three days his wife fed the fire with charcoal, and for three nights D. Khodadad solemnized a Vendidad over it, and for three mornings a Yasna (although, single handed and hard-pressed as he was, he had of necessity to omit considerable portions of these long services). On the second day Rustam brought another *afrinagan* full of embers for a second performance of the rite; but this was kept apart and tended separately by Piruza Khanom, until the prayers over the first were finished, so that there should be no confusion between the two observances.

On the third morning, having finished the Yasna (dedicated to Sroš), D. Khodadad carried the *afrinagan* to the fire-temple, where the public ceremony was performed in the late afternoon, before a fairly large congregation. The door of the fire-sanctuary was open, and within the sanctuary itself D. Khodadad had set out nine square bricks a few inches apart, in a curved line leading from the threshold to the foot of the fire-altar, and on each was a neat bundle of clean corn-stalks, stripped of the outer sheath.[2] The *afrinagan* with the now consecrated fire was just outside the door. D. Khodadad said the košti-prayers, and then summoned the dahmobed, who came to stand beside him and announced to the congregation, 'The fire belongs to Rustam-e Hormezdyar, may God have mercy on him!' All the men and youths rose and said their košti-prayers while the Dastur recited the *Khoršed-Mihr Niyayeš*. He then lowered his mouth-veil, and made *paivand* by means of a košti with the dahmobed, before lighting two straws at the fire in the *afrinagan*. Then, reciting the *Ataš Niyayeš*, he lifted the bundle of corn-stalks from the first brick, and kindled it from these two burning straws (which he then pushed back into the *afrinagan*). Then he lifted the second bundle and lit it from the first, which he put back, still blazing, on its brick, and so on, steadily, all along the line, until the ninth bundle was alight. Then he dropped the košti (the ninefold filtering, as it were, of the already consecrated fire being thus complete), and placed the ninth bundle of corn-stalks, flaring brightly, on a big bundle of kindling wood at the foot of the fire-altar; and when this was well alight, he lifted it and placed it carefully on the sacred fire itself. The fire-altar was invisible to most of the congregation,[3] but at this point the flames from the burning wood leapt high and illuminated the whole sanctuary, so that the doorway became filled with brightness. The Dastur gathered the flickering remains of all the corn-bundles on to the ninth brick, so that they made a separate little fire, which quickly burnt out, at the foot of the altar; and then, standing facing the sacred fire, he recited the *Ardvahišt Yašt*. Then he came to the sanctuary-door, took up the *afrinagan*, and carried it to the sacred fire. With the metal *bara* he smoothed the ash at the very edge of the fire-bowl, and covering the *bara* with ash from the *afrinagan* three times, put this ash at three places round the rim of the bowl, so that ash rested on ash, in a form of *paivand*. Then he carefully set down the *afrinagan* on the ground so that its rim touched the stone at the base of the fire-altar.[4]

[2] They were prepared for the rite, that is, just as wood was prepared for the sacred fire by stripping off its bark.

[3] The word 'fire-altar' has been used here for clarity's sake; but in fact by 1964 the sacred fire was burning in a Parsi-type metal container shaped like the little *afrinagan* (see above, pp. 78–9).

[4] Another time when I was present he put ash in four places round the bowl. When I questioned him about this, he said that the amount of ash thus used was ritually unimportant, and that the vital *paivand* was that of the *afrinagan* with the stone.

All this while the members of the congregation had themselves been reciting Avesta in a steady continuous murmur, essentially the familiar *Khoršed-Mihr* and *Ataš Niyayeš*, amplified by the *Ardvahišt Yašt* or other prayers. Many recited by heart, but most of the younger people on entering took a *Khorda Avesta* (in Persian script) from a bookcase, and read some prayers from this. When D. Khodadad came out of the fire-sanctuary he went into the main *pesgam* to solemnize a gahambar-service, while the atašband closed the sanctuary door. After the service, *lurk* was distributed in the usual way. (When the ceremony of 'exalting the fire' was performed in Yazd, some of the wealthier families also gave money to the poor, but this was not part of village usage.)

The next performance of the rite that April was for one Ferangis, also six months dead, but the third was asked for by the khadem of Banu-Pars for his mother, who had died some fifteen years earlier, and the fourth was for Rustam-e Khodabakhsh, dead twenty-four years. His widow, who was present at the service with her daughter and granddaughter, had had the rite performed for him once previously. There was an especially large congregation that afternoon, since it was a Friday, the national day of rest. When the service was over and the others were leaving, the widow warmly pressed Piruza Belivani and me to stay behind with the family and eat the 'Avesta-food' (*čom-e Avestāī*), that is, the *varderin* and what had been cooked to make *boy-o-brang*. (The *varderin* included some of the first mulberries of the year, and there were pink rose-petals scattered over it.) The fifth *ataš buzorg kardan* of the month was again for a villager who had died within the year. In May the rite was asked for in Mazraᶜ, and then Rustam the atašband collected the embers of nine fires as usual in Ardekan, using a small *afrinagan*; and after the three days' consecration of the fire, D. Khodadad put this small vessel in one of the panniers on his bicycle, and a quantity of charcoal in the other, and cycled across the desert, pausing to tend the fire on the way.[5] It took about two hours, once he had reached Mazraᶜ, to gather the congregation there, and during this time he prayed by the fire and cherished it. On the rare occasions when a Hasanabadi family wanted the rite to be performed,

---

[5] I was at first surprised when he told me that he would also use dried camel-dung, if he came across it, to maintain the fire; but since the camel is a creature of Vahman its products are 'clean', and the sun beating down on desert sand dries the dung swiftly and completely.

they used to come to Sharifabad, having no fire-temple of their own.

The rite of *āb-zōhr* the 'libation to water' (called in Dari *ōw-zūr*, or, with metathesis, *ōw-rūz*) was also much performed, like that of *ataš buzorg kardan*, in the two 'beloved' months, for similar reasons; and, since it was less costly, there were few families in Sharifabad which did not have it celebrated at least twice a year. The libation itself (the *zohr*) was provided by the laity in the following way: a bowl, usually one inscribed and kept for ritual use, was filled with milk directly from the cow, a handful of oleaster fruits was added, and rose-petals or marjoram leaves were sprinkled on the surface, and then the bowl was taken to the Dastur.[6] The first time that I saw him make the libation was on an April day in Mazraᶜ Kalantar, at the little stream which flowed at carefully regulated intervals through the main lane of that drought-stricken village. The *zohr* had been brought to him in a handsome copper-plated bowl, with a deep copper-plated spoon, both inscribed, and there were yellow rose-petals floating on the milk. He seated himself cross-legged on the bank of the lower pool, bowl in his left hand, spoon in his right, and dipped out three spoonfuls, one after the other, and poured them into the water. Then he began to recite the *Ābān Niyāyeš* and, miraculously it seemed, the still water instantly started to flow (although it must have been simply that, by a happy chance, it was at just that moment that Isfandiar, who controlled the water, pulled up the big stone stopper in the upper pool). Having finished the *Aban Niyayeš*, he went on quietly reciting other familiar texts (precisely which, he said, was immaterial, though naturally there must be no invocation of fire in the presence of water, any more than of water in the presence of fire); and at intervals, while he recited, he poured single spoonfuls of the *zohr* into the water. The family for whom he was performing the rite sat, with some others, on the bank above him, watching; and around him the ordinary life of the village went on. Two men were slowly roping up an immense bundle of raw cotton, and beside them the camel which was to carry it was lying munching straw, its halter-bells jingling as it ate; a black calf, roving about, tried from time to time to snatch a mouthful of the

---

[6] On the essential identity of this libation with that made at the end of the yasna service see '*Ātaš-zōhr* and *Āb-zōhr*', 111–18. The villagers tried whenever possible to have rose-petals among the ingredients, fresh in the spring month of Azar, dried during Urdibehišt (which by the traditional calendar corresponded to August/September).

cotton, and was shouted at lustily by the men when it did so. A patient white dog lay watching the Dastur and twitching off flies, and two women were washing clothes downstream. The recital took about half an hour; and finally the Dastur poured what remained of the libation directly from the bowl, in three pourings, into the water. He then immersed bowl and spoon in the stream, scoured both thoroughly with sand from the bank, and rinsed them again so that every drop of the consecrated liquid was carried away by the running water.

In Sharifabad D. Khodadad regularly made the offering, not in still privacy at the stream running beneath the Dastur's House, but at the communal watering-place where all the women went to wash dishes, steep straw, water their animals, and exchange the daily news; but he sat, naturally, at the point where the stream emerged from its underground channel, so that all this activity went on below him. In Hasanabad each house had its own water-supply; and there I watched him later that month in the garden of Shirinzaban, performing the rite for her late husband in solitude, she being busy preparing a meal for him indoors. The silvery libation-bowl was inscribed with her husband's name, and he carried it to a stream that flowed through the garden, and seated himself by a big rose-bush in flower.[7] The stream ran there through a bricked channel, so he brought wood-ash from the hearth-fire for scouring the bowl and spoon at the end of the rite.

It was when the villagers wanted the rite performed for the dead that they entrusted it to the Dastur, so that it should be ritually correct and fully effective; but during the 'beloved' months, girls used to do it more simply for the living members of the family, carrying the libation to every stream in the village, and pouring a little of it into each while reciting some piece of familiar Avestan. The rite was naturally obligatory for anyone who had actually polluted water; and Agha Rustam recalled two instances when Sharifabadi Moslems asked the Dastur to perform it for them after death, at the time when their bodies would be washed in running water— to Zoroastrians the grossest pollution of that pure creation.[8]

---

[7] See Pl. IIIa.

[8] These Moslems were presumably *jadid*, recent converts, and not fully *seft*, convinced. Another Moslem practice which deeply troubled the *jadid* was burial (see Jackson, *Persia Past and Present*, 396–7); and by the track leading to Cham, off the Yazd-Taft road, there was a roofed but open structure beside an ordinary Moslem graveyard where (I was told) by a curious compromise some *jadid* families placed their dead, neither buried nor exposed.

A rite on behalf of the dead which seemed to have no element of atonement in it, but was simply to offer comfort, was the Yašt-e daur-e dakhma, also called Yašt-e bar-e dāzgāh 'The act of worship at the dakhma' (termed alternatively the *dādgāh/dāzgāh*, because it was the 'appointed place' for the dead). This was performed at will by individual families, or groups of families, often during the first month after a death, or during the 'beloved' months of the first year. It was solemnized, ideally, throughout the hours of darkness, and probably evolved as an elaboration of the practice of keeping a fire or lamp always burning outside a dakhma, in order to comfort the souls whose bodies had been carried there;[9] and this in turn was almost certainly a prolongation of a usage whereby fire was lit outside the tower during the three nights after a death, when the soul was held to linger upon earth. When there was a larger Zoroastrian population, funeral must have followed close on funeral, and so it would have been natural to institute an ever-burning fire to meet this need. This development must have taken place well before the ninth century, since the custom is common to the Iranis and Parsis.

In 1964 Sharifabad had two funerary towers standing on rising ground in the desert just to the south of the village. One had been built in 1863 with the energetic help of the Parsi agent, Manekji Limji Hataria, whose memory was still green in Sharifabad.[10] This replaced an old earth-walled one on the northern side of the village, which was afterwards razed by Moslems. The American traveller Williams Jackson, passing that way in 1903, heard tell both of this old earthen tower and of Manekji's dakhma;[11] but he did not see either, because then the Yazd–Isfahan road passed along the other side of the plain, and the places chosen by the Sharifabadis for their funerary towers were utterly lonely and remote. Manekji's tower, a wide low one, without outside steps, continued in use for a hundred years, which, according to tradition, is as long as is proper, for otherwise the pollution in that one place will become too great.

[9] See below, p. 195. This usage is referred to in the *Rivayats*, but there is no mention there of the rite of Yašt-e daur-e dakhma, which appears to be a relatively recent development (i.e. since the seventeenth century). There is no similar observance among the Parsis.

[10] Hajji Khodabakhsh was proud of the fact that Manekji had stayed under his great-grandfather's roof while overseeing the building of this dakhma.

[11] See his *Persia Past and Present*, 403–4. He also heard tell then of other disused dakhmas in that region whose sites were marked by 'mounds of earth which are still pointed out by aged Parsis of Sharifabad'.

So, under the inspiration largely of Agha Rustam, and with contributions of money from individual Sharifabadis and the village
Anjoman, and some help also from the Parsis, a new dakhma was
built beside Manekji's and was brought into use in 1963. The village
was proud of the fact that this was erected with the full elaborate
rites prescribed in the *Rivayats*.[12] A number of Yazdi priests colla-
borated, and there was a large attendance of Zoroastrians from far
and near for the final consecration. It seems fitting that it should
be Sharifabad, that bastion of the old faith, which had the piety and
communal spirit to build, with great labour and devotion, what
circumstances suggest will be the last dakhma ever to be raised
within Iran.

Manekji's dakhma was then enclosed by a circular blank wall to
discourage Moslem violation. The new tower was higher, and set on
a round stone base with steeply sloping sides, designed to prevent a
recent method of climbing in (practised during the last years of the
old dakhma), which was to drive a lorry close up to the wall and
scramble in from its roof. There were solid steps leading up to the
door, which was a massive metal one with double locks, imported
from Bombay. For a whole year this had resisted persistent attempts
by hooligans to break it down, but twice while I was in the village
their efforts jammed the locks. In the first case a child's body had to
be lowered over the wall into the old dakhma, in the second one the
salars managed to get the door open, with the help of an Ardekani
locksmith, just in time to carry the bier inside before dark. Within,
the tower was designed according to the evolved Parsi plan,[13]
and its central well went down to some six feet below the level of the
surrounding desert, being filled at the bottom first with fine and then
with coarse sand. Without, the dakhma was whitewashed, so that it
stood out, proud and stark, against the brown of the desert; and
since the Yazd–Isfahan highway now runs along the northern side
of the plain, the tower was conspicuous to travellers, and even the
kindly Maybod bus-conductor used to point it out to strangers as a
sight of morbid interest. The Anjoman of Yazd, less sturdy of spirit
than the Sharifabadis, offered the latter enough sand-brown paint

---

[12] See *Riv.*, Unvala, i. 99–100; Dhabhar, 102–3; and in even more detail
Modi, *CC*, 231–8.
[13] On the evolution of the Parsi dakhmas see 'An old village *dakhma* of Iran',
3–5. To judge from the size of the enclosing wall, Manekji's dakhma at Sharifabad
was much like the one which he saw erected at Qanat-ghesan near Kerman, see
art. cit. 7–8.

to camouflage it, but the villagers replied, politely but firmly, that they liked it white and saw no reason to disguise it. To them the rite of exposure was not only simple and practical; they preferred to think of the body swiftly reduced to bare bones, which then lay in sunlight and moonlight, and were blown upon by winds, rather than being put to putrefy in a coffin or directly in the ground, Moslem-fashion, thus being thrust into darkness and corrupting the good earth.

The doors of both dakhmas, in orthodox fashion, faced east, where the sun rises to draw the soul up to heaven; and about thirty paces in front of each was a *sangōk*, or offertory table. This was a low platform made of stones, with a recess, open on the side further from the dakhma, in which fire could be kindled.[14] There was a hole on the other side, about a foot above ground, so that the light of the fire could reach the tower. One of the tracks from Sharifabad to Mazraꜥ led past the dakhmas, and whenever I went that way with D. Khodadad he used to put some small offering, of fruit or herbs, on each of the *sangoks*, and say his košti-prayers—an act of family piety, for his father and uncle had been carried to the old dakhma, his brother to the new one. On the further side of the *sangoks* was a low complex of buildings, which included a fine open *pesgam* facing the towers, the *ganza-taš* or room for the ever-burning fire, kitchens, and a yard for donkeys. (In the following pages, for clarity's sake, this range of buildings will be referred to as the dadgah, to distinguish it from the dakhma itself.) The *ganza-taš* was small and inconspicuous, with a tiny dome, and it was entered by a padlocked metal door no bigger than that of a safe. The fire was cared for by Paridun Rashidi, the dakhmabān (Dari dāmavun) or guardian of the dakhma. He was a tall man, and he had to drop flat and twist through this door head-first, returning feet first. Formerly the fire burnt in a mud-walled enclosure in a corner of the little room, but now it was set in a stone basin on a mud-brick pillar. This too was in a corner, but nevertheless hooligans would try to get at it, prodding about with a long pole through the small roof-hole, knocking over anything stored in the room and breaking the glass which used to be set in the two tiny openings in the wall facing the dakhma. Paridun visited the dadgah every evening, just before sunset, to tend the fire

[14] The *sangok* in front of Manekji's dakhma was rectangular (about 7 × 4 feet) and made of largish stones surfaced with smooth clay. The one before the new dakhma was round (about 7 feet in diameter), of smaller stones.

(in the same manner that the sacred fire was tended in the temple), and to light an oil-lamp, which stayed alight for several hours; and during the three days after a funeral he remained there all night, to keep the fire burning brightly and the lamp lit through the hours of darkness.

It was the custom in Sharifabad that once every seven years notice was given to all the people in the parish, and the families of those who had died within that period (and others if they wished) gathered at the dadgah soon after sunrise on the appointed day. The Dastur recited the *Ahunavad Gah*, seated in the main *pesgam*, with the salars sitting on the other side, but not directly opposite him (so as not to approach their impurity too closely to his purity). Then they made *paivand*, took the *baj* of Sroš, went to the dakhma and entered it each carrying a *blisk*—a long-handled metal implement like a *bara*. With the *blisk*s they gathered together the sun-bleached bones and pushed them gently into the central well (the *srāda*), where they would crumble in time to dust. They sprinkled *pajow* over them and over the stone floor of the dakhma, and withdrew, leaving all in order for another seven years. The Dastur continued to recite Avesta while they accomplished this task, seated before a fire near the *sangok*, and fixing his eyes alternately on it and on the door of the dakhma; and the women in the meantime made *boy-o-brang*. The whole ritual took about two hours; and again that same day the Dastur returned to recite Avesta for about two hours around sunset —the time when the fravašis chiefly visit the earth.

The Yašt-e daur-e dakhma, as solemnized in Sharifabad, seemed to have developed through a blend of this septennial observance with the regular one of keeping fire burning brightly to solace and help the newly dead. A group of Sharifabadi families joined together to have the ceremony performed late in April in 1964,[15] and about an hour before sunset on the appointed day I cycled out with D. Khodadad to the dakhma. On the way we passed three men on foot, carrying acetylene lamps, and a colourful group of women were

[15] This was after Hiromba, and the 'beloved' month of Azar had already given way to Dai Mah according to the traditional calendar; but it had been impossible to get additional priests to come out earlier from Yazd, so busy were they there with pious observances of the 'tenfold month' for their own parishioners. However, by one of those inconsistencies available to them, the Sharifabadis made the best of things by choosing for their rite Vahman Ruz of Dai Mah, which corresponded to Azar Ruz of Urdibehišt Mah according to the reformed calendar—a day which is especially holy, since it brings together the two guardians of fire. Urdibehišt Mah is, moreover, the other 'beloved' month of the year.

already busy at the dadgah. Two of the Yazdi priests—D. Gushtasp-e Adargushnasp and D. Sorush, the hušt-mobed of Taft—were there already, having come by bus and walked across the short stretch of desert from the highway. They were dressed like ordinary towns-men, in dark-coloured clothes and trilby hats, for no priest in Yazd or Kerman was willing to court trouble by going about in white; but they changed at the dadgah into more appropriate garments. Paridun was busy bringing water from the nearest tank, but after three or four journeys he sprang on his big donkey and galloped off bareback to meet his wife Murvarid and Sarvar, who were coming burdened with utensils and food. In the end twenty-four Sharifabadis were gathered at the dadgah—twelve men and twelve women, but for once no small boys, since this rite was restricted to adults (un-less, exceptionally, a girl came to represent her family when no one else could so so). Five families, recently bereaved, had given money for the ceremony, and the others, less directly concerned, contributed food and fuel.

While the light lasted, there was tea and talk. Paridun had placed fire in both the *sangoks*, carrying out embers from the dadgah kitchen, and offerings were already scattered over both—fruits, herbs, and rose-petals. As the sun began to sink, one of the women sprinkled white lime over the *pesgam* floor and on the sand in front of it, in welcome to the spirits; and a big *afrinagan* full of glowing fire was set on the ground about half-way between the *pesgam* and the *sangoks*. D. Khodadad produced a brown woody piece of *buδ-e nakoš*[16] and placed it, with camphor, on this fire; and then he and all the other men gathered outside the *ganza-taš*, facing the sun as it went down behind the old dakhma, and said their košti-prayers, with the *Khorshed-Mihr Niyayeš*. Then after a pause, when the sun had vanished, they said the prayers of the first night-watch, with *Sroš Yašt sar-e šab*, and a *patēt* or confession on behalf of the departed. The darkness quickly deepened, but an acetylene lamp had been put near the *afrinagan*, and its strong light just reached the two dakhmas. It showed too that by an odd trick of a shifting breeze the smoke and incense from the *afrinagan* was being wafted steadily now towards one dakhma, now towards the other, as if being deli-berately bestowed by the Wind Yazad upon them both impartially.

The three priests meanwhile had seated themselves cross-legged in a row on a carpet in the *pesgam*, with food offerings before them

[16] See above, p. 149.

to be blessed. By D. Khodadad's right knee was a small square of white cotton and on it were five small stones, carefully washed, one for each of the five souls for whom, specifically, the rite was to be performed, and whose names would be uttered repeatedly during the course of the night. At first each of the priests recited what Avesta he pleased, for about an hour and a half (during which time Agha Rustam arrived, on his moped). Then there was a pause for supper, the priests changing back into their travelling clothes to eat. It was a *ruz-e na-bur* by the traditional calendar, when no meat could be eaten,[17] so the food was *sirog*, fresh bread, and vegetable dishes. The men ate in a second *pesgam*, the women in the kitchen or in the open, on the still warm sands. Then began the most serious, concentrated part of the night's observances. Paridun lit a fire on the sand close to the *afrinagan*, and this was kept burning through the rest of the night (some biggish logs of wood being used, brought like everything else on donkey-back). The three priests, meanwhile, left the *baj* of their silent meal, and 'made new the košti'. They then donned their white clothes again, and, having taken their places once more, began reciting the *Ahunavad Gah*. Following the usual Zoroastrian custom, though they began together and would end together, they did not recite in unison, so that unless one concentrated on one voice it was impossible to follow the words; but the effect produced by the three voices, different in pitch and tone, blending together, was dignified and impressive. The blind Palamarz was one of those present, and he also recited, sitting in a corner opposite the priests. (His young and much-loved wife had died that winter in childbirth, and her soul was one of the five for whom the ceremony was being performed.) Some of the other men slept; but the women were busy cooking *sir-o-sedow* in a big pan over the fire in the open, so that the *boy-o-brang* would carry, with the light of the fire, to the dakhmas. (Each had brought her own small contribution of pure oil, vinegar, and other ingredients.) When the pungent brew was sizzling hot, it was poured into a copper bowl and carried before the priests to become consecrated; and from time to time during the recitation D. Khodadad cut up some of the *varderin* on the carpet to release its fragrance also.

The moon rose through some small clouds, the light wind went on blowing the smoke towards the dakhmas, and the night grew colder. Manekji's dakhma, behind its enclosing wall, was dark and

---

[17] Cf. above, p. 89 n. 47.

low, but the new white one caught the moonlight and stood out dramatically against the dunes and dark hollows of the desert. The sonorous Avestan continued until eleven o'clock, and then there was a two-hour pause, to allow for the changing of the watch at midnight, when the world passed under the protection of Sroš. The women served tea, and D. Sorush borrowed from Sarvar her husband's camelteer's coat of thick felt,[18] and warm in it went to sleep, while the other two priests talked a little with us, and dozed, and woke again. At one o'clock they began to recite once more, this time each the Avesta of his choice, and Agha Rustam recited with them for over an hour. Most of the rest of the company slept from time to time, but there were always two or three women by the fire, tending it, or cooking food which they then brought to the *pesgam*.

The moon shone very brightly during the latter part of the night, and then yielded to a lovely dawn, apricot for a brief few minutes and then pale yellow behind the mountains. The men all gathered in the main *pesgam*, where the tired priests were still reciting, the women having prepared *sir-o-sedow* afresh. Suddenly, tiny in the distance, two lonely white figures appeared on the track leading from the village, and came steadily on, shoulder to shoulder. They were the salars, coming to complete the rite. While they were approaching, a woman carried a big glass bottle, full of the sir-o-sedow that had been consecrated by the night's prayers, to three paces beyond the *sangok* of the new dakhma, and set it on the ground. Then she returned and took the five stones in their white cloth, which D. Khodadad had knotted with seven knots (for the seven great Amahraspands), and put that too beside the bottle. When the salars finally drew near, they swung off the track and went to the new dakhma without approaching the *pesgam* or in any way acknowledging those gathered there. The sun had not yet risen, and they sat on the dakhma steps, facing east, and waited motionless for it to appear. They showed strikingly white even against the white tower, for not only were all their garments white, but they wore white headgear and white gloves as well, all of coarse homespun cotton. As soon as the sun's rays touched the dakhma they rose and said their košti-prayers. Then, as the sunlight reached the steps, they came down together and advanced to fetch the glass bottle and the cloth with the stones. On reaching them they made *paivand* with a košti, picked

---

[18] For a photograph of her brother-in-law Jehangir wearing this heavy coat, with closed sleeves for additional warmth, see 'Some aspects of farming', Pl. XI.5.

them up, returned to unlock the iron door, and disappeared into the dakhma. There, so Piruza the Dastur's wife told me, they would sprinkle the *sir-o-sedow* first in one semicircle, sun-wise, from the door, and then, returning on their tracks, in another semicircle, withershins. Never must they make a complete, unbroken circle of the tower. Then they would untie the seven-knotted cloth, and scatter the consecrated stones on the thus purified surface of the tower. These actions took some ten minutes, during which time the priests once more recited *patets*, and the laity thought of their own dead, and prayed aloud for their salvation, and for all souls. Then the salars emerged, silent as before (for they were with *baj*), broke the empty bottle on the dakhma steps, left the cloth there, and relocked the heavy door. Then, still without look or gesture for the company, they returned side by side as they had come, their retreating figures visible all the way to the edge of the fields, white against the grey-brown desert. As we watched them go, one elderly man broke down and wept for his wife, who had died that spring, leaving him desolate and alone.

Comfort came with the warmth of sunshine and food. First tea was drunk, and then the men ate breakfast in the *pesgam* and the women round the fire—a meal like the supper of the night before, of consecrated dishes. Big portions of everything, with great piles of bread and *sirog*, were put aside for the salars, to be taken to their houses. The two Yazdi priests then left, striking across the desert to the highway, and most of the men set off for the village and their day's work, leaving Paridun and two others with the women, to sort and clean and sweep, and load everything on the donkeys. While they worked, a pied wagtail came dipping out of the desert, and alighted confidingly among the offerings on the old *sangok*.

D. Khodadad lingered a little, to rest, and then we set off together to cycle back to the village. On the way he spoke about the rite, which he thought had been improperly modified by the women through the use of *sir-o-sedow*. Properly, he maintained, it was purifying *pajow* which should be taken with the stones into the dakhma, and nothing else. He added that sometimes when a villager died in Bombay, or was buried in the Zoroastrian cemetery in Tehran, an absolutely 'pure' sheet of white cotton, like a shroud, was put for him in the tower during the performance of this rite, to give his soul a physical link with the place where the bones of his forefathers lay, and where rites would be carried out for it down the years.

The rite of Yašt-e daur-e dakhma was performed in the 1960s in all the older Zoroastrian villages. In Qasimabad, for instance, which carried its dead to the dakhma of Yazd, high on a hill, the villagers gathered in their own pavilion at the hill's foot, and kept a fire burning through the night between it and the dakhma, while priests recited Avesta; but no one approached the dakhma, nor were salars employed to enter it. Despite the greater complexities of the Sharifabadi version of the rite, the essentials there too seemed to be the light of the fire reaching the dakhma throughout the hours of darkness, and the recitation of holy words; and it is easy to see how these basic observances could have evolved into the present rite under the influence of usages at the septennial cleansing of the dakhma. The Sharifabadi rituals were well-established, however. Formerly, Agha Rustam said, when there were many priests, sometimes six would be asked to come, and they would pray alternately in groups of three; and if the family means sufficed, the rite would be repeated on a second, and if possible a third night during the month after death. When this was in winter (when the cold in the desert is piercing), priests and the laity would return to the village during the two hours' pause around midnight, instead of resting then at the dadgah.

The next time that I went to the dakhma for a religious rite was in June, for the communal service called by the villagers the 'Dadgah-e Tir-Mah' (by the Tehranis the 'Purse-ye Tir Mah'), which seemed to be a more recent elaboration of an old observance. Comparison with Parsi usage suggests that the Zoroastrians early evolved the practice of going once a year to their dakhmas and there holding services for the dead. The Parsis did this on Farvardin Ruz of Farvardin Mah, the name-day feast of the fravašis,[19] and there is evidence to suggest that this was the old usage, at least in the eastern parts of Iran.[20] The Iranis perhaps did it at one time on Farvardin Ruz of Spendarmad Mah, the last (instead of the first) month of the Zoroastrian calendar, a day known to them as Forudōg, the 'Little fravaši'

---

[19] See Seervai and Patel, 'Gujarāt Pārsis', 216.

[20] This evidence lies in the fact that the Parsis went again to the dakhmas on Ruz Farvardin of Azar Mah, a usage which evidently developed during the period when the religious No Ruz was in Azar Mah, i.e. between c. A.D. 507 and 1006 (see 'On the calendar . . .', 528–35). So in eastern Iran at least (whose usages the Parsis seem in general to follow) this communal rite belonged, it seems, to Farvardin Ruz of the first month of the religious year (originally Farvardin Mah itself).

festival.[21] If this were so, then they later transferred the usage to the religious No Ruz, 1 Farvardin. This perhaps came about because that day, although traditionally so great, in fact lacked observances, having lost its secular ones to the spring feast, and its religious ones to the 'Greater No Ruz', on 6 Farvardin;[22] and there were, moreover, special reasons for associating it with the fravašis.[23]

So the Iranis went to the dakhma on Ruz Hormazd of Mah Farvardin; and probably some time after A.D. 1006 they established a second day for this observance, namely Ruz Hormazd of the preceding month, Mah Ispandarmad. This was the first day of the festival known to them as Jašn-e Sven or Sven-e mas, that is, the five-day feast of Spendarmad, yazad of the earth. Hers was the farmers' festival, and greatly beloved in the rural Zoroastrian communities; and it became extended, at the calendar-change of A.D. 1006, to a ten-day festival, for the same reasons that Farvardigan or All Souls had been so extended at the third-century reform.[24] So, just as Farvardigan became divided into two pentads, Panji-mas and Panji-kasog,[25] so too there came to be a Sven-e mas and Sven-e kasog; and perhaps it was partly because of this parallelism that the custom developed of going to the dakhmas at this earlier festival also. There may too have been a contributory reason in Spendarmad's association with the earth, for the Yazdis held that the 'Dadgah-e Sven' was for those who had died violent and sudden deaths and had not been carried to the dakhmas—for all those, they said, who had been slaughtered in the Arab invasion, or who had died in cruel persecutions since, or had perished as wayfarers, or been lost in the desert. Their bodies would have lain on or in the good earth, so there was especial need for rites on their behalf in the month devoted to Spendarmad, the earth's guardian.

By the 1960s these memorial rites had come to overshadow the distinctive observances of the feast as a farmers' festival, the ancient Jašn-e barzīgarān. By the traditional calendar the Jašn-e Sven had come to fall late in June, and so (with the early Yazdi ripening of crops) it could be celebrated as a harvest festival. In the reformed calendar it had been restored to what was evidently its rightful place

---

[21] See further below, pp. 230 ff.

[22] Now called Havzorū, see below, p. 229. On the shifting of the dakhma observance from 1 Farvardin by the reformists, see p. 227 n. 19.

[23] For the prolongation of the All Souls' Feast until Ruz Aban of Mah Farvardin see below, p. 235.

[24] See 'On the calendar . . .', 535–6.   [25] See below, pp. 212–13 ff.

at the beginning of February, when the worst of winter was over, the sheep were lambing, and the trees coming into leaf, so those who used this calendar kept it as a celebration of the beginning of the farming year. Those elderly people who remembered celebrating it in their youth spoke of it as a very happy festival, but by then lasting effectively only a single day, 'Ruz Sfandarmaz of Sven Mah', that is, the fifth and last day of Sven-e mas, and the name-day feast of the yazad. That was kept as a general holiday by the villagers, and variously celebrated. I could find no clear memories of it in Sharifabad itself, but old people in the Yazdi villages spoke of each household cooking mutton broth, or wheat pottage, and carrying the cauldrons to the fire-temple, and there, after a brief service, eating all together, in merry mood; and in Kerman a century earlier this had been the day for *kharafstar-kušī*, when the Zoroastrians went out into field and plain, and slew venomous insects, snakes, scorpions, and the like, which crawled or crept on the good earth, and harmed men, animals, and crops.[26]

This latter observance would clearly have been easier to carry out at a June than a February feast; and probably it was the confusions attendant on the introduction of the reformed calendar which led to the final fading away of the farmers' festival, which then yielded wholly to the funerary observance. Yet even the Yazdis, after reverting to the traditional calendar, continued to keep the 'Dadgah-e Sven' according to the reformed one, with unhappy consequences that in 1964 it coincided with the fifth and greatest day of Mihragan by the old reckoning. So villages such as Sharifabad and Mazraᶜ, which still kept Mihr's feast with full rites, went to the dakhmas instead on the day before that festival began.

Since all things in Zoroastrianism should be done in threes, if possible, the reformers instituted a third annual visit to the dakhmas on Ruz Hormazd of Mah Tir, and this, being a new observance, was also kept everywhere according to the reformed calendar, in mid-June. Nevertheless, it in its turn succeeded in absorbing or

[26] Information verbally from Arbab Jamshid Sorushian, see Boyce, *History*, i. 299 n. 26. In his *Farhang*, 104, Arbab Jamshid identifies Sven-e mas with the Dadgah-e Sven (on Ruz Hormazd), and describes Sven-e kasog as having been in the past a feast for women (cf. Biruni, *Chronology*, ed. Sachau, 229). Spendarmad, guardian of mother earth, and herself the only female yazad among the great Amahraspands, is traditionally the guardian also of women, but none of the Yazdis whom I questioned knew of any particular association of the Jašn-e Sven with women, and by them as by the Parsis (see, e.g., Modi, *CC*, 435) it was kept simply as a farming festival.

putting an end to most of the charming observances with which the ancient festival of Tiragan used to be celebrated later that month (on Ruz Tir, the thirteenth). Presumably these observances, like those of the farmers' festival, would soon have faded away in any case under the pressures of modern living, which make it easier to maintain instead the repetitive rites of remembrance; but undoubtedly these developments of the twentieth century have helped to reduce the diversity and delights of the old devotional year.

Since the practice of going to the dakhma on the first day of Farvardin was long established, Sharifabad and its two neighbours had a firm pattern of observance for this, which they merely extended to the two other days. For over a hundred years all three villages had carried their dead to the same place, which though within sight from the edge of the Sharifabadi fields, was a three-hour ride on donkey-back from Mazraʿ, and almost as far from Hasanabad. Moreover, during all that period 1 Farvardin had fallen in late summer, a time of blazing heat. So the customs of all three visits to the dakhma were based on the facts of relative distances and remorseless sunshine. There was no shade near the dakhma, except for what little was cast by the buildings there, and no water near at hand (for the Iranis strictly followed the prescriptions of the Vendidad, that the dead should be exposed in barren places, far from fertile earth, water, or growing things). So it was prudent for the villagers not to go there all at once. Accordingly, those from Mazraʿ and Hasanabad set out soon after dawn and travelled in the cool of the day, reaching the dakhma before the sun was high. In Sharifabad, however, the only persons who left so early were Paridun Rashidi and his three helpers. For days before, Paridun's wife Murvarid had been busy taking out of store and washing all the jars and pitchers, pans and other vessels which belonged to the dadgah, mostly through pious bequests (for nothing could be kept there, because of pilferers); and Paridun himself had swept the *pesgams* and kitchens of the dadgah free from their accumulation of wind-blown sand. After sunrise on Ruz Hormazd he loaded up his donkey, tied a big tin water-urn on his own back, and set off for the dakhma. His helpers soon arrived one after another at his door, and loaded up in their turn. Bahram-e Škundari also had a donkey, a wise little animal which, as soon as the last pitchers were tied on its back, turned briskly round and set off for the dakhma ahead of its master. Rustam-e Tehrani, one of Paridun's brothers, had a thickset black cow, which took a slightly lighter burden, and a brother-in-law, Jamshid Khosrowi, followed with a third donkey. They would be busy most of the day carrying water—drinking-water from a tank near the edge of the fields, and water for other purposes from a *qanat*-stream of slightly brackish water nearer the dakhma.

Meanwhile the other Sharifabadis went to the Dastur early in the morning with the names of their dead whom they wished to be remembered, either individually at separate gahambar-services, or in the list of names that would be recited at the final gahambar for all souls (*hamō urun*). D. Khodadad, having gathered these names together, left for the dakhma soon after nine, where he found those from Mazra' and Hasanabad already well advanced in their preparations for him to celebrate their services. In the meantime the Sharifabadis made all the preparations which they could at their own homes. These were for the food to be blessed at the services and eaten thereafter in assembly. Women from seven related families met at the Belivani house that morning for this purpose. Each brought a contribution of flour, a little rice, eggs, tomatoes, potatoes, and onions, and 'pure' sesame-seed oil, as well as some firewood. The flour was sieved on to a big cloth, the eggs went into a little basket, and the potatoes and onions were peeled and wrapped in damp cloths inside pots and pans. Then, soon after midday, half the flour was mixed into a dough (but without leaven, which would be added later), and this dough too was put into a big pan. The rest of the flour would be given to the dakhmaban and his helpers, in recognition of their labours. All the rest of what had been brought was then loaded on the Belivani cow and the three or four of the women set off for the dakhma, braving the blazing heat of early afternoon, since the way was short.

On 1 Farvardin I was allowed to share in these preparations at home; but for the earlier 'Dadgah-e Tir Mah' I set out about seven o'clock to walk with Gushtasp and his aunt Murvarid to the dakhma, where Murvarid, as the dakhmaban's wife, had much to do. The June sunshine was already hot, but was tempered by a north wind, and it was pleasant to go on foot through the fields, where patches of lucerne were in lovely blue flower between stretches of ripening wheat, and the green cotton-bushes were just breaking here and there into primrose-yellow blossom. Moslem women hailed Murvarid repeatedly to ask where we were going (knowing full well the answer), and Murvarid parried their questions ingeniously. Then abruptly, without wall or ditch, we passed into the desert—at first patches of white salt and then shingle—and were soon joined by Paridun's helpers coming from the water-tank, with two donkeys and the distinctly wayward cow. At the dadgah a jeep, which had already done the journey from Mazraᶜ, was just unloading a group of Hasanabadis—mostly old men at that stage, and women of all ages—and the scene was animated. The bustle had attracted a solitary Egyptian vulture, which circled for a while overhead,[27] but otherwise the desert around was empty of any sign of life.

A woman whose husband had died that spring was busy tending fires in the two *sangoks*, and everyone as he or she arrived went to them, put incense on the fires, and laid offerings on the stones—in that month of June mostly cucumbers and early apples. These, having been offered, were taken up again soon after, to refresh some toiler, or to slake the thirst of the ubiquitous small boys. D. Khodadad arrived about half-past nine, took his place in a side-*pesgam*, where there was some breeze and coolness, and began to solemnize the first of thirteen separate *gahambars*. The women meantime were busy cooking the food to be blessed. The kitchens soon became hot and smoky, and from them they had to come out into the burning sunshine in order to carry the food to where the Dastur sat. While this work was going on, an impudent Moslem camelteer, returning from carrying salt to Ardekan, brought his beast right up to the dadgah buildings and made it kneel, bubbling loudly, on the sand. He was quickly surrounded by a group of wrathful Zoroastrians, some of whom were for beating him soundly for his unmannerly intrusion; but gentler counsels prevailed, that 'whether he were good or bad' it was better to give him a handful of *lurk* (for which he had come) and let him go in peace, rather than to bring rancour into a holy occasion.

Just before noon D. Khodadad celebrated a final communal

---

[27] I occasionally saw an Egyptian vulture—a relatively elegant black and white bird—when cycling to Mazraᶜ with D. Khodadad; and once when I visited the dakhmas of Yazd a pair of common vultures circled high overhead. D. Khodadad told me that when he was young there were many vultures in the region, of different kinds, and some (presumably lammergeyers) so huge that they stood taller than a man, and were very terrifying. Already by the 1960s, however, the number of animals kept locally had shrunk drastically, with lorry, jeep, and bicycle replacing camel and donkey, and the vultures had almost all vanished with them. Their work at the dakhmas was performed accordingly mostly by the black crows of the desert—handsome birds whose glossy plumage shone in the sun—and by the hoodie crows which hung around the villages.

gahambar for 'all souls' on behalf of Mazra‛ and Hasanabad. The hot, tired women emerged from the kitchens, and a midday meal of consecrated food was eaten wherever there was shade—in the *pesgams*, or close under the walls. Then everyone rested or slept through the noonday heat. One group of women, sitting in a side-*pesgam*, amused themselves by playing a form of *moradūla*, a diversion that belonged properly to Tiragan, and which was being enjoyed that morning in more traditional fashion by girls at home in the villages. *Moradula* means simply 'bead-pot'; and the evening before in Sharifabad a group of girls had gone together to fill a big pot (*dūla*) at sunset with pure running water. This pot had been kept covered from the light of the sky; and each girl had put a token into it—a bead, or ring, or bracelet. A *Khorda Avesta* was then put over the mouth of the pot, and this was carried to a place where it 'could not see the sky'—that year an earthen oven in the orchard of the Ziyafat family. The next day the girls met there under a sweet pomegranate tree, and one who was the first-born daughter in her family fetched the pot, covering it with a corner of her head-veil. The others sat in a circle, and she, having sung a song, drew out a token, and before its owner could reclaim it, she too had to sing something, and so it went on round the circle until the last ornament had its owner again.[28]

The use of water in this game of forfeits linked it with Tiragan, the rain-festival; and there was another pretty Yazdi custom, whereby in every house where a *purse* was held on Ruz Tir there would be a big bundle of plaited silken threads of the seven colours of the rainbow. Every woman or child who came to the house was given one of the plaits to bind round the wrist; and they would wear these gay bracelets for ten days, until Ruz Bād, devoted to the yazad of wind; and then they would either throw them into running water, or go to some high place and toss them into the air for the wind to carry away, after which they would sprinkle one another with rose-water and make merry. But in the 1960s it was only old people who could remember such customs, with which they had once

---

[28] In Yazd and its villages this game was known instead as *čokadūla* 'fate-pot'. There it was insisted that the girl who drew out the forfeits should be young— say nine or ten years old—rather than a first-born daughter; and Sarvar told me that in Aliabad a variety of things, other than an Avesta, were put on top of the pot, including a fan, a handful of the short corn-stalks used in lighting fires, a short-handled broom, a cucumber quartered in vinegar, and a mirror, all to be covered by a green cloth.

celebrated what was known locally either as the Jašn-e Tīr-o-Teštar, or the Jašn-e Tīr-o-Bāz ('Feast of Tir and the Wind').[29] In Sharifabad and Mazraᶜ the custom of the rainbow-bands does not seem to have been known, but there the youngsters still splashed one another with water on Tir's proper day, even if they had come, by the confusion of customs, to play *moradula* on the first of his month.

It was hard to think of a rain-festival, though, in the arid heat at the dakhma. The relative quiet of the sun-scorched noontime pause was broken into by the arrival of the first Sharifabadis, and soon the *pesgams* were full of men and boys, and new groups of women were at work in the kitchens, while outside the handles of metal vessels grew too hot to touch with the bare hand, and the water-carriers toiled endlessly to and fro. D. Khodadad took up his priestly duties again, and celebrated fourteen gahambars in succession, with only one or two distributions of *lurk* reaching the women in the kitchens. (Only at the Dadgah-e Tir-Mah was it permitted to use fruit, that is, cucumbers and apples, in the *lurk*, which was therefore pleasantly cooling.) As well as cooking all the usual foods for *boy-o-brang*, the women made *gondolī* for the evening meal—a bright yellow mixture of chopped meat, rice, saffron, and herbs, folded in dough and cooked in broth, like dumplings; and they also prepared fried dishes, with meat, rice, and onions.

About five o'clock the heat began to relent, and half an hour later the jeep ventured back to fetch some of the Hasanabadis, and some Mazraᶜ Kalantaris began to load up their donkeys and depart. The last gahambar for 'all souls' was celebrated for the Sharifabadis, and then the men and boys gathered together in family groups, and settled down in a huge horseshoe on the sands to the east of the dadgah, each group taking up a fixed traditional place, with a strip of sand separating one from the next.[30] All around and in the middle of the horseshoe there were tethered donkeys and stacks of bicycles. The women streamed out of the kitchens bearing panfuls of food for their families, and filled their plates, while Rustam-

[29] Among those who spoke of it was D. Rustam Khodabakhshi of Yazd, who said he could remember as a small boy going to such a *purse* on Ruz Tir simply to get the silk band. D. Khodadad too remembered as a child the pleasure of wearing the seven-coloured bracelet, and what great store was laid then by old men and women on this observance.

[30] See Pl. IIIb, and cf. Seervai and Patel, 'Gujarāt Pārsis', 216: 'On All Souls Day Parsis go to the Towers of Silence, offer prayers for dead relations and friends and in the large yard round the Towers different families . . . spread carpets and hold private *jasans*.'

e Tehrani went round with a big pitcher of water to slake thirsts (instead of the wine of older days). Having supplied the men's needs, the women retired either to the kitchens or to the sands just outside, and ate there themselves. The meal was enjoyed in the usual brisk, silent fashion, and soon the big assembly broke up, and a long line began to form along the track back to the village, first boys and youths on bicycles, and then donkey-parties and those on foot, a colourful chain stretching across the desert in the fading evening light. Piruza and Pouran insisted, half in jest, on my mounting the Belivani cow, while they walked on either side; and leaving Paridun, Murvarid, and their helpers to the task of clearing up, we joined the end of the procession. The ride on the stiff peaked saddle was surprisingly smooth and comfortable, but neither then or on any other occasion could I discover the mystery of guiding the animal, which was controlled simply by a rope tied to one side of her nosering. The villagers themselves managed this with an incommunicable skill, even when their bovine mounts were wilful, or skittish on frosty winter mornings.

In general rites for the departed were filled wholly with devotion and care; but there was one small observance whose intention was propitiatory, and which had a touch of ancient fear of the dead. This was called *sāma-āsa*, from *sahm-e āste* 'dread for the bones',[31] and it was regularly performed by a woman who married a widower, or a man who married a widow, in order to assuage the possible resentment of the dead partner. Thus Turk Jamshidi had been married three times, first to his cousin Piruza, who became ill and could bear him no children. Then at Piruza's own wish and during her lifetime he married her younger sister Daulat, by whom he had three children. (Such second marriages, if the first were childless, were permitted in both branches of the Zoroastrian community, until the Parsis adopted the English marriage-laws in the second half of the nineteenth century.) When Piruza died, Daulat, taking her place, as it were, as Turk's only wife, had *sama-asa* performed. Then Daulat died, and Turk married Sarvar from Aliabad, a lovely young chestnut-haired bride, who had the rite performed in her turn for Daulat, with considerable care. It was carried out by four priests

---

[31] This rite is mentioned by Jackson (*Persia Past and Present*, 396), who refers there also to one called Yašt-e bīn-e Spendārmiz, intended to expiate any sins committed against Spendarmad, yazad of earth; but he gives no details about its performance.

in the city of Yazd. Her part in it, she told me, was to make a ritual ablution, put on fresh clothes, and be present at the ceremony. The priests took their places in the four corners of a *pesgam*, and performed the Yašt-e čōr-sīja, the 'service of the four corners', reciting the Vendidad from midnight until dawn, with invocation of the dead woman's soul. One of the priests had *paivand* with a garment that had belonged to Daulat, and Sarvar herself lay down beside another of them, made *paivand* with him by a košti, and slept peacefully. There were seven things on the *pesgam* to be blessed in the service—pure water (with a little milk in it), loaf sugar, granulated sugar, white sweetmeats, and three different kinds of borage (called *gō-zabun* or 'cow's tongue' from the shape and feel of its rough leaves). At dawn, when the Vendidad was concluded, Sarvar was given some of the consecrated water to drink, and more to carry home with the six other things. There she made ablution with water into which she poured this consecrated water, standing in a basin so that no drop of it should touch the earth, and pouring it over herself so that it reached every bone in her own body. Thereafter she ate the consecrated sweet things, and drank an infusion of the three kinds of borage.

This rite, which was performed in Yazd during the April that I was there, could also be solemnized by a single priest. D. Khodadad did it thus for his own parishioners, reading, however, only a part of the Vendidad for two or three hours between midnight and dawn. Sometimes too it was asked for by someone for himself if he were sick, to drive away the aches which had come for some other cause into his bones.[32] Thus in Urdibehišt Mah in 1964 D. Khodadad did it for an ailing woman. She was present throughout, just as Sarvar had been; but it could also, it was held, be done for an absent person. Then, after the ceremony, a garment which had been blessed at it would be sent to him to wear, together with the consecrated water, and the sweetmeats and borage to be consumed.

In this form the rite was similar in intention to the simpler *tandorostī*, the rite for 'health of the body', which could be performed at any hour, the priest being free to recite what Avestan he thought appropriate (which often included the *Bahram Yašt*). For the rite

---

[32] A description of the rite performed for this purpose very elaborately in earlier times, with 'two, three, four, or even forty mobeds, praying together' was given by Khudayar D. Sheriyar, *Sir J. J. Madressa Jubilee Vol.*, ed. Modi, 299–301.

to be effective, it was held, there had, however, to be *paivand* between priest and patient. Thus one hot July evening D. Khodadad came to the Belivani household to perform it for his little niece Mandana, who had been ailing for some days. (He came late, because he had already performed a *si-šuy* and an *ataš buzorg kardan* that day.) The child was laid on a folded shawl, and the Dastur sat beside her, so that the shawl formed *paivand* between them. Tahmina Khanom put before him a plate with barley-grains and dried marjoram leaves, and another with the three kinds of borage, together with sweet-meats, cinnamon, and the herb called *siyāvašan*. Further, two lumps of alum were tucked into the child's clothing. Fire had of course to be present, but the evening was so warm that at first the brazier was put at the other side of the *pesgam*, and only gradually brought nearer. The Dastur recited for about forty minutes, at intervals sprinkling the barley and marjoram leaves over the child and across the floor; and towards the end he took the lumps of alum and laid them on the fire, turning them with a metal pin. When the rite was over, Tahmina Khanom studied these lumps for an omen, but Agha Rustam refused to look, saying that the Avestan was powerful, but searching for signs was mere superstition.[33]

There remains a rite which was occasionally performed by a living person for his own welfare, not in this life but hereafter, namely *zande-ravānī*.[34] This consisted of having the whole of the first-year ceremonies for the dead performed for oneself while alive, which, D. Khodadad said, was 'like a light cast before one on a dark road, instead of behind one'. The observance took its name from the fact that throughout the texts which were recited the words *be-rasād ašō zande ravān . . .* , 'may it [i.e. the merit] reach the righteous living soul', were substituted for the usual prayer for the dead. The ordinary rites for the dead were fully performed, with at least one sedra being consecrated, and at least one blood sacrifice being made; but they could be fitted into a month, or spread out in the usual way through the year. In either case, the observances could be private, with only the close family present, or carried out exactly like funerary ones, with many guests. The more elaborately it was done, thought D. Khodadad, the more merit was acquired for the

[33] The alum, softened in the fire, was held to take some shape that would in-dicate the cause of the illness, 'whether man, animal, spirit or other thing' (see Khudayar D. Sheriyar, art. cit. 300).

[34] A good deal is written about this rite in the *Rivayats*, see Dhabhar, 657, s.v. '*zinda ravan* ceremony', for references.

hereafter. When all the observances had been completed, a 'gaham-bar-e cakhra' might be founded, to be celebrated annually for the rest of the person's life. Agha Rustam's father Noshiravan had had the rite performed for himself in middle age, the observances taking a full year, and had then established a gahambar-observance at the second festival (Maidyōšem), which he himself celebrated for the remaining thirty years of his life, and which his son maintained after him. Occasionally in the 1960s elderly people had *zande-ravani* performed if they thought there might be no one to carry out the due funerary ceremonies when they were dead. Thus in 1963 D. Khodadad celebrated it for a pious old woman, Mah-Khorshed, formerly of Jaʿfarabad, who was then living alone in Hasanabad. She had been twice *no-šwe*, once in Yazd and once in Sharifabad, and thought much about the life to come. She was not well off, so in her case the observances were kept very simple and private, and were completed within a month, leaving her with a sustaining sense of safety and tranquillity.

9

THE FESTIVALS OF ALL SOULS
AND THE RELIGIOUS NEW YEAR

UNTIL the beginning of the Sasanian era the ancient festival of All Souls, Hamaspathmaedaya, was evidently celebrated on the last night of the twelfth month, directly after the day's celebration of the sixth gahambar. The spirits of the dead were entertained as honoured guests in their old homes throughout the hours of darkness, and were then bidden a formal, ritual farewell at the dawn of the new year. This pattern of observance, going back in all probability to at least Indo-Iranian times, was broken by the third-century reform, whereby five extra days were introduced after the twelfth month, Spendarmad, to create a 365-day calendar.[1] Since the fravašis, welcomed back to earth on 30 Spendarmad, could not, according to ancient custom, depart before the dawn of 1 Farvardin, New Year's day, this measure created deep bewilderment and distress; and its working was interpreted to mean that these invisible guests must now be ministered to for the five 'Gatha' days as well. Moreover, in the first year of the reform the bulk of the population evidently ignored these newly introduced (or, as they called them, 'stolen') days, and made their own private calculations as usual, reckoning, that is, the first 'Gatha' day as 1 Farvardin. The result was that by the end of that year they were already five days behind the new official calendar when the 'Gatha' days were reached. Since, clearly, they were not allowed to celebrate No Ruz till the king permitted, they were forced to entertain the fravašis for a night and the ten days which then elapsed between their 30 Spendarmad and the official 1 Farvardin. Thereafter the worst of the confusion was over and a single calendar was observed, with everyone, perforce, recognizing the same day as 1 Farvardin, and acknowledging the existence, however suspect in origin, of the five new days; but plainly the reform, though it had thus, through the power of the throne, become fact, was neither widely understood nor willingly

[1] See above, pp. 31–2, 164–5.

accepted, the people at large being filled with anxiety lest they were being forced to fail in their proper duties to the divine beings. So, in order to avoid being coerced into any negligence, they not only kept double feast-days thereafter (according, as they understood it, to both the old and new calendars), but also maintained the ten-day festival of the fravašis which had come into being at the end of that first year. These ten days were called *Rōzān Fravardīgān* 'the fravaši days';[2] and in time they came to be regarded as the true All Souls' festival (since the night of 30 Spendarmad, being no longer at the year's end, gradually lost its significance); and so this festival grew to be known simply, by abbreviation, as Fravardigan (popularly Frōrdīgān), and the ancient name Hamaspathmaedaya was used only for the sixth gahambar. Through the duplication of feasts this gahambar was celebrated twice, first on its old day of 30 Spendarmad, and then again on the fifth 'Gatha' day. With the joining together of the two celebrations it became a six-day feast, kept up during the four intervening 'Gatha' days as well; and finally it was reduced to a five-day observance, to coincide exactly with the 'Gatha' days themselves.

This last development kept Farvardigan divided into two clearly distinct pentads. These the Iranis knew as Panjī-kasōg, the 'Lesser Pentad', which lasted from 26 to 30 Spendarmad, and which had come into being through the confusions of the first year of the calendar reform; and Panjī-mas, the 'Greater Pentad', which embraced the 'Gatha' days, and was an inevitable result of that reform. With colloquial casualness, however, they referred to the whole festival as Panji, the name Fravardigan having dropped entirely out of popular use.[3] Similarly, the ancient name Hamaspathmaedaya was no longer familiar to the laity, who referred to the sixth gahambar simply as the 'gahambar-e Panjivak'.

Gradually, down the generations, special beliefs had come to attach to the two pentads. Thus in Sharifabad it was said that Panji-kasog belonged to the souls of children and of those who had died without sin, who were allowed to spend a longer time with their kindred on earth,[4] whereas Panji-mas was truly for all souls, even

---

[2] 'Fravard' is the Middle Persian equivalent of Avestan 'fravaši'.

[3] Among the Parsis the old Sasanian term has been replaced by a Gujarati one, 'Muktād', which is also used for the whole ten-day festival.

[4] This seemed more reasonable than the belief which I heard from Golchihr-e Manuchihr, daughter of the dahmobed of Cham, who said that the souls of sinners were released at 'Forudōg' and remained free from then until the last day

for those then suffering in hell. They were released from there only for this one festival in the year, whereas the fravašis of the righteous could come whenever they were invoked, to any religious service or to any gathering.

Ten days make a long time through which to maintain observances which originally belonged to a single night, and no doubt during the 1600 or so years since the festival was first extended its celebration has varied a little according to the leisure and piety of those concerned. The priests naturally evolved religious services appropriate to each of the ten days,[5] and the laity were expected to devote the time as far as possible to prayer and acts of charity, as pious old people still do among both the Iranis and Parsis. Moreover, there are still some Parsi families who make their preparations for the

of Panji-mas. 'Forudog' or the 'Little fravaši-festival' was celebrated on Ruz Farvardin (the nineteenth of Spendarmad Mah, eleven days, that is, before the beginning of Panji-kasog). In the 1960s it was no longer fully maintained anywhere, but it had been celebrated within living memory in Yazd and the villages nearby, and its special rite was still observed here and there by mothers who had lost young children. By this, three stones, carefully washed, were put into the embers of the hearth-fire, and when they were glowing hot they were brought on a *bara* to the priest, who had come to the house; and he, while reciting Avesta, would drop them one by one into a bowl of milk, which sent up steam as he did so. The household meantime made the usual *boy-o-brang*. Khanom Simindukht, the mother of Arbab Faridun Kayanian, who was my chief informant about this observance, said that in the past many babies died while still at the breast, and this rite (she thought) was meant especially to comfort their souls. Forudog was in general regarded as being for the souls of children, which were thus cherished before the general festival of the dead began. It was not kept in Sharifabad or Mazrar Kalantar.

[5] With so few priests, these could not be maintained in the 1960s, and even the Parsis were then no longer able to observe them everywhere, because of the pressure to perform the many family rites. The old Bhagaria rituals (which in most cases coincided with the Irani ones) have, however, been listed by Modi (*CC*, 450). Reduced to essentials, these, to be performed by two fully qualified priests at a fire-temple, are as follows: on each day of Panji-kasog the priests celebrated two Yasnas, usually devoted first to Sroš and then to Ardāfravaš ('All Souls'). On the first night they solemnized a Vendidad devoted to Ardafravaš. On the fourth day, Ruz Mahraspand (which is held to be the day on which Zoroaster converted Vištasp), the second Yasna was devoted to Mīnō Mahraspand, as was a Vendidad solemnized that night. During the first four days of Panji-mas the two daily Yasnas were devoted first to Sroš and then to the genius of whichever Gatha the day was named for; and on the fifth day a Visperad was celebrated in honour of the sixth gahambar. A Vendidad was solemnized on the night of the first day, in honour of all the Gathas, and of the third day, in honour of the gahambars. On the fifth night two Baj (i.e. Yašt-e dron) services were performed after midnight, devoted to the Gathas and Sroš. Baj-services were also regularly performed, with various dedications similar to the Yasnas, during the daylight hours on each of the ten days.

festival on 25 Spendarmad, the eve of Panji-kasog, so that all is in readiness for the first holy day.[6] Life on the Yazdi plain was too hard, however, for such prolonged observances, and in practice the villagers there, although regarding Panji-kasog as holy, spent its five days mostly in preparing (during the intervals of necessary work) for the greater festival to come.

There was a pattern for these preparations, although it was not rigid. Thus it was usually on the first day of Panji-kasog, Ruz Aštad of Isfand (Spendarmad) Mah, that boys fetched clay to model figurines for the gahambar-e Panjivak.[7] The figurines were actually shaped on the following day, Ruz Asman, when the worked clay had hardened sufficiently; and on that day in the Belivani household Pouran stitched tiny panniers of homespun cotton to put on the little clay camel, and also some small cotton bags. These, with two little wooden boxes, were carefully washed in running water, and filled with clean earth; and then seeds of seven kinds were sown in each, and they were watered with pure water and put in a corner of the courtyard, under a dampened cloth, for the seeds to sprout by 1 Farvardin. For this, the seeds had to be sown by the third day of Panji-kasog at the latest. This observance, which is an old one, celebrates both aspects of the religious No Ruz, since the fact that there are seven seeds is a reminder that this is the seventh feast of the creation, while their sprouting into new growth symbolizes its other aspect as a feast of the resurrection and of eternal life to come. The little rite was thus highly significant, and its importance is shown by the fact that some old houses had fixed clay containers for it, something like flower-boxes, set in the angles of the courtyard walls (high enough to be out of the reach of children and hens), and occasionally there were four bigger containers on the roof above for the same purpose.[8]

On this third day Pouran and her sister Bibi Gol swept the whole roof of the house from end to end before sunrise, sending down a shower of fine dust into the courtyard, and thereafter all the rooms were thoroughly dusted and swept. On the fourth day their mother took a little woven basket, lined it with white cotton, moistened this, and sowed herbs in it. Piruza meantime washed melon-seeds at the stream, salted them, and left them to dry in the sun. It was not till the fifth day, however, Ruz Anērān, which was both the

---

[6] See, e.g., Modi, CC, 449.
[7] See above, p. 49, and Pl. IVa.   [8] See 'Zoroastrian Houses', 135.

eve of Panji-mas and, by the ancient 360-day calendar, New Year's Eve, that preparations reached a crescendo. On that day, very early, Gushtasp took the family cow and filled both its panniers with fine clay. This he mixed with chopped straw and clean water, and then (having washed thoroughly himself) trod it all happily into a smooth mass, ending up with his legs and arms and clothes and even hair gloriously covered with mud. He then went off to wash in a stream (itself a pleasure in the summer heat), while his sisters Piruza and Pouran, having bathed at home, went, fasting, to the Dastur's house to drink *nirang*—a general practice during the Panji festival, especially for women, to cleanse away the impurities of the past year.[9] Being thus in a state of physical and ritual purity, they set about preparing the *ganza-pāk*, the 'holy room', for the coming of all souls.[10] This room opened off the *pesgam-e mas*, and it was used for setting out the ritual offerings of Panji, rather than the open *pesgam* itself, because these offerings would be made on each of the five days, during which time Moslem tradesmen and visitors (not to speak of cats) might come and go. In the *ganza-pak* were kept, along the walls, great red-brown jars of unfired clay for storing flour, and smaller greyish-white ones from the kilns of Maybod, which held rock-salt; and all were sunk several inches into the floor, because of its annual resurfacing at Panji. The old floor was swept with care, and then Piruza, kept supplied by Pouran, carefully covered it, thinly and smoothly, with Gushtasp's mixture of clay and straw, to make it fresh and new for the spirit-guests. Then while the clay was drying, the family sheep were all washed in the little pool in the courtyard, and this was then emptied, scrubbed, and refilled. (Such a pool was a unique luxury in Sharifabad, and their sister Shahnaz had to wash their grandmother's one ewe at the communal stream, along with the household pots and pans, from where the affronted animal hurried home in damp dignity, not waiting to be led.) So by the evening of the last day of Panji-kasog the whole house, with everything in it, was as clean as possible, and all was in readiness to celebrate the five great holy days which were to come.

Even of these five days, it was the last three which were regarded as the holiest, and the first two still had a feeling of preparation

---

[9] The Parsis also drank *nirang* and underwent ritual purification during Panji (see Modi, *CC*, 93 and 96).

[10] The Parsis too set aside a special place for this festival (see Modi, *CC*, 443).

about them. On the first day Agha Rustam rose before dawn and went in his turn to the Dastur's house to drink *nirang*. Thereafter Tahmina Khanom whitewashed the little clay figures, and she and her daughters spread out a white cloth on the clean new floor of the *ganza-pak*, and arranged all the proper objects beside it: a mirror leaning against the wall, a low brazier full of fire (which was replenished morning and evening from the ever-burning kitchen fire), a lamp which was kept lit day and night, and the charming group of little white figures, the camel with its head to one side, as if craning to see itself in the mirror. The nightingale had a fragrant gourd, striped red and orange, in the hollow of its back, and grapes between its cane legs. Thereafter *boy-o-brang* was made each morning and evening, to delight the spirits. Frankincense and marjoram leaves were regularly burnt on the fire, and that first morning wheat-grains were roasted and set, piping-hot, in a little copper bowl on the three-legged clay stool. Piruza roasted her melon-seeds too, and brought a bowlful of them. There were plenty over (for the Sharifabadis always shared what they offered their spirit-guests), and the children munched them freely through the morning. Indeed, nearly all the children and young people of the village were going about with pockets full of seeds, roasted for the Panji offerings. Meanwhile, in the courtyard of the Belivani house Tahmina Khanom prepared a *kūza-tara-tījog*, or 'spice-jar'—a little green pitcher of unfired clay, which she filled with pure water and swathed in a bit of white cotton. Over this she put a wadding of cotton-wool, held in place by cotton thread; and then she scattered seeds of pepper and other spices, steeped and smelling pleasantly pungent, over the wet surface, and covered the pot with a damp cloth, so that they should germinate and be green for Havzoru.[11]

The village generally was in a bustle, with relatives arriving from Tehran, and preparations being made in various houses for the first of the many gahambars that were endowed for Panji. Gushtasp departed at about ten o'clock to take part in these, and returned much later, eyes shining and a napkin full of consecrated bread, meat, and *lurk*, which he shared among his appreciative younger sisters. On that and every other day of Panji-mas invitations came to the family, often three or four at once, to share the *čom-e nīmrūy* or midday meal at houses which were celebrating gahambars. Agha Rustam would divide his family up, to show courtesy by accepting

[11] See Pl. IVb.

as much of this hospitality as possible, and on this first day he and
Piruza and I ate at the house of Turk Jamshidi, and stayed for the
celebration there of two gahambars. Afterwards Piruza and I went
with Khorshedchihr, Turk's granddaughter, first to make the
offering to the waters and then to give the *čom-e šwa*. It being only
the beginning of the festival, we readily found a hungry animal at
the end of the lane, and while it ate we looked out over the fields,
beautiful under a dappled evening sky. The corn was mostly reaped
and the pale stubble had been swept bare with Yazdi thoroughness.
Here and there brown stretches of newly turned earth showed between green bands of lucerne and cotton, and some of the crops
were bordered with tall sunflowers, bright even in the fading light.
There were no Zoroastrians working in the fields on that first day of
Panji-mas, but Paridun Rashidi passed on his bicycle on his way to
tend the dakhma fire—a task that could never be neglected, whatever the day. It was growing dark when we returned home, and the
evening *boy-o-brang* had been made, and the door of the *ganza-pak*
was closed. The light of the lamp, burning within for the spirit-guests,
showed through the crack, and it shone steadily throughout that
and every other night of Panji-mas, visible from the place where
Piruza, Pouran, and I slept on the roof.

On the second 'Gatha' day Pouran sprinkled white all over the
house-roof in sign of welcome to the fravašis, and noted approvingly
that the 'seven seeds' had sprouted in all their pots, bags, and boxes.
After the making of the morning *boy-o-brang* we visited the house of
her uncle Paridun next door. He and his family had been hard at
work during Panji-kasog, pressing sesame-seeds to provide 'pure'
oil for gahambar-cooking in all three villages of the parish;[12]
and they had only just covered the floor of their *ganza-pak* with
fresh clay, so that it was still cool and damp, with a very pretty
set of white figurines set out beside it. Parvin, their elder daughter,
was roasting wheat for *boy-o-brang*, and the tired cow was patiently
going round and round the press, Paridun having started again
early after working late the night before. (Since pressing oil for
ritual use was highly meritorious, it was permissible to do it even on
a holy day.) We were hospitably entertained by Murvarid Khanom
with melons, and roasted sesame-seeds mixed with sugar, which we

---

[12] For the very first time Paridun had used an oil-fired stove to roast the seeds
instead of the traditional wood-fired one, and he was delighted by how much it
eased the work.

ate by the spoonful. Meantime the first gahambars were being recited in the village. They finished soon after noon, for D. Khodadad had to to go to Mazraᶜ to solemnize a *siroza*, one of the observances which a priest would never willingly neglect, however pressing his other duties. Some laymen had meant to accompany him, but the weather turned unfriendly, with a hot, dust-laden wind blowing from the north, and in the end he pedalled away on his own, a slight, valiant figure.

The next morning all was activity soon after sunrise in the Belivani household, for elaborate *boy-o-brang* had to be made on each of the last three days of Panji; and this had, as always, to be offered either early in the morning, before the first gahambar began, in order to please the spirits in their own homes before they gathered at the religious service, or in the evening, when the last gahambar was over. So Pouran was quickly at work, pounding roasted wheat-grains and dried dates together in the big stone mortar to make halva, and the younger ones gathered round her for shares of the sweet mixture. Her mother in the meantime pounded up spices in a smaller mortar, filling the air with sharp, hot smells; and Piruza, being *no-šwe*, cooked *sirog* and eggs and finally *sir-o-sedow*, which gave off its familiar agreeable tang. Everything, as soon as it was ready, was carried swiftly to the *ganza-pak*.

That day all the girls of the family went to the house of their maternal grandparents, Mundagar and Sultan Abadian, for a gahambar. Mundagar was a fine big man, handsome even in old age, but crippled.[13] We found him already seated, cross-legged and immobile, in the *pesgam-e mas*, ready for the religious ceremony. His mind was affected by time, but nevertheless he greeted me with all the instinctive courtesy of the Sharifabadi towards a stranger; but soon after, apprehending that the Dastur had passed his house over, he filled the little courtyard with a great shout of rage. There were sixteen gahambars to be solemnized that day, which was one of the most beloved in all the year, and though the Dastur might start wherever he pleased, from there on he should take every house in strict order (unless one family were not ready in their preparations and asked to be passed by). Soon after, however, the usual irruption of small boys into the courtyard heralded the coming of priest and elders, and the gahambar was duly celebrated, to Mundagar's deep content. D. Khodadad too was satisfied, with the sense of

---

[13] It was he who had founded the Pir-e Mundagar (see above, p. 88).

a hard day's work well done, but at the same time he was feeling a need for sympathy. He had duly solemnized the *siroza* and a *sal* at Mazraᶜ the previous day, and had risen early there that morning, to celebrate the Dron-e gahambar at the fire-temple. Then he had set out at seven o'clock, and had had to trudge almost the whole way back across the desert, pushing his bicycle, because of the fierce head-wind. By eight o'clock the July sun was blazing down, and the journey had taken three hours instead of the usual one; and then he had had the many gahambars to celebrate in Sharifabad. Mundagar's was in fact the last, and we returned with the Dastur to his own house, to see his *ganza-pak* and Panji figurines. Instead of resting there, he began at once to recite the evening prayers, since the sun was nearly setting. Thereafter he went to the empty 'Dastur's House' to recite the *Sroš Yašt sar-e šab* there. His wife had swept the place with special care, and throughout Panji she kept a lamp burning there, and made *boy-o-brang* there too for the ancestors; and in every empty Zoroastrian house in the village kinsfolk or friends performed similar rites for its fravašis.

The next morning Piruza rose at three to help her aunt Murvarid cut a patch of lucerne before sunrise. This essential fodder-crop was cut by sickle every twenty-four days or so, and it could not be left longer or the leaves would wilt under the blazing sun. So such work had to be done on even the holiest days, but it was then dealt with very early, so that it did not interfere with the rites and pleasures of the festival. That fourth day was the one on which the most *boy-o-brang* was made in the Belivani household, and so there was great activity in the kitchen, enormously enjoyed by the children, both for the sense of excitement and for all the delicious tastings and mouthfuls that came their way. The cooking began soon after six in the morning. By that time of year the last of the rendered fat from the Mihr Ized sheep had been used up in ritual cooking, and so the 'pure' dishes for the fravašis were cooked in sesame-seed oil, bought from Paridun Rashidi, and additional quantities for the family were cooked in shop-bought vegetable oil. As well as all the usual ritual dishes, Tahmina Khanom made several that day which were proper only to Panji. There was *halvā-ye san*, for which steeped and roasted wheat-grains (*san*) were pounded up with dried stoned dates and fresh dates with their stones in, and mixed with 'pure' water into a creamy fawn-coloured paste. This was then fried to a golden-brown, and the portion for the *ganza-pak* was turned on to a plated copper dish, and prettily decorated with peeled almonds. *Halvā-ye konjed* was made from sesame-seeds (*konjed*) and fresh dates, both lightly browned in sesame-seed oil and beaten together with a copper spoon in a copper bowl. Some of the stiff sweet mixture was then shaped into the torsos of little men with their arms held out at right angles, and these were ranged round the edge of a copper dish, as if holding hands, with a little sugar-cone in the middle of it. From the rest of the mixture were made fat little men with legs as well as arms (like the gingerbread men of English cookery), animals, stars, and the like. Then there was *halvā-ye šekār*, which was prepared for other festivals as well as Panji. This was like *halvā-ye san*, but had pounded pistachio nuts among its ingredients. Among the savoury dishes was *nān-e āganja*, 'filled bread', cooked only for Panji, and needing a good deal of skill in its preparation. For it meat and onions were pounded together and browned in a frying pan, with salt and spices. This mixture was then spread thinly on a round of dough, another round was put on top and the edges of the two were pressed firmly together (in the manner of a Cornish pasty). The whole was then clapped against the hot side of an earthen oven, and at this moment the skill of the cook was tested, for only if the preparation had been just right would the pasty stay in place and cook properly. An easier savoury dish was *nān-e pīnā*. For this onions were browned with spices and salt, and then a dollop of dough was dropped on top of them in the frying-pan, and they were worked into it. The dough was then taken out of the pan, a pleasant bright yellow, and baked in the usual way, producing a very appetising smell. Since such smells were at their strongest when the food was just ready, Pouran was standing by, and as soon as her mother had finished a dish she would seize it, using the ends of her head-veil if the copper plate were hot, and carry it at a run to the *ganza-pak*, where the white cloth gradually became covered with the varied foods. A great effort was made at Panji to provide many dishes, since all the departed were present then as guests, who in life would have enjoyed some this, some that; but by an act of delicacy poppy-seeds (often otherwise used in decorating festive dishes) were not added to Panji cooking, for among the invisible guests were perhaps sinners, who might include among their ranks opium-addicts, and it would be heartless to remind these of the cause of their damnation.[14]

[14] It was noticeable that the only sins which were ever referred to by Zoro-

With all this cooking, and hearth-fire and oven-fire both burning brightly, the kitchen grew very hot and full of smoke. The sun was blazing relentlessly down by eight o'clock, Tahmina Khanom shed her flowing head-veil, and Gushtasp earned his share of the sweet dishes by bringing the cooks glasses of water every quarter of an hour or so. All was accomplished, however, by ten o'clock, when the first gahambar was due to begin. Even Gushtasp was too happily full, however, to attend it, and he, like the rest of the family, succumbed, what with heat and tiredness, to some well-earned sleep. Later in the morning there came four invitations to gahambar meals, and the family scattered in accepting them, leaving Tahmina Khanom and the infant Shahvahram to enjoy a rare peace and silence.

The fifth day of Panji-mas was the most strenuous of all for the Belivanis, since in addition to the rituals of the day itself they had an endowed gahambar-e lurki to hold in their own home (though even so Piruza and Pouran were out in the fields before sunrise to cut a patch of lucerne). The evening before, Tahmina Khanom had sent Azarmindukht with a copper bowl full of wheat to a neighbour who had a cow in milk; and early in the morning the neighbour's small daughter brought the bowl back one-third full of milk—all that could be spared, since so many wanted milk for ritual cooking on the last day of the festival, especially all those who, like Tahmina, had lost small children, for it was proper then to cook *nān-e šekārī* for them (a sweetened bread, for which the dough is mixed with milk, not water). *Varderin* for the Dron-e gahambar (melons, cucumbers, and grapes) was sent early to the Dastur, and Tahmina went herself to a Zoroastrian house where each year, on the last day of Panji, two sheep were sacrificed, and the 'pure' meat and fat sold for ritual cooking. While she was away, a Moslem brought a camel laden with two bales of brushwood to the bottom of the lane. Agha Rustam bought one, Paridun the other, and Paridun rolled each in turn up the lane and into the houses, while his wife

astrians were opium-addiction and suicide—sins against oneself rather than against others. The standard of sexual morality among them was very high, and theft, murder, and arson seemed unknown, the community being in such respects sinned against rather than sinning. Opium poppies had been grown by the Sharifabadis before the crop was forbidden under the Pahlavi dynasty, but Agha Rustam said that he had never himself known an addict in the village. A little was enjoyed as an annual pleasure at the time of harvesting, as winegrowers enjoy their wine, and the dried seeds were sprinkled on festival days on the harsh, heavy rye-bread, which was the staple of village diet until the late nineteenth century.

Murvarid carried out the big *afrinagan* used in dakhma-rituals, full of embers from her hearth-fire, and scattered rue on it to sanctify the bringing of firewood.

When Tahmina Khanom returned, she and her elder daughters became busy with the special cooking of the fifth day. The *nan-e šekari* was baked both in ordinary little rounds, and also in shapes— a shuttle, a ladder, a star, a fat little man, a hanging larder. (The villagers, as we have seen,[15] regarded this practice as providing playthings for the child-fravašis, but it seems probable that this was a reinterpretation of an old observance which belonged originally, like the clay figurines, to the sixth gahambar.) Tahmina Khanom also cooked *komačōg* that day—little balls of saffron-flavoured dough fried to a golden-brown, and decorated with strips of dough criss-crossed over them (like hot-cross buns) and studded with dates.

Once the cooking for *boy-o-brang* was finished, Pouran took a little glass filled with *lurk* to another neighbour, and returned with it half-full of milk for the gahambar-service. The family could itself provide home-made vinegar (to represent the wine), and Pouran and Bibi Gol carefully washed more fruits (bought from a Moslem trader) to be blessed. All was set out in readiness by eleven o'clock, with one of the big pots of 'seven seeds', now freshly green, beside the carpet on which were the things to be consecrated. The courtyard was cleared of the water-vessels and everything else, and newly swept. The Dastur had started his celebration of gahambars at the other end of the village, however, and it was half-past four before he and the dahmobed arrived with the rest of the congregation. The women of the house instantly sped into the kitchen, leaving Agha Rustam to receive his guests, and began the ritual cooking. Piruza and her aunt Murvarid (also a *no-šwe*) shared this work, with the others helping. The recital of the gahambar was over by a quarter-past five, and since it was the last of the day, Piruza and I went with the Dastur to his house, and watched her aunt Piruza make the evening *boy-o-brang* there. She had herself lost a seven-year-old son,[16] and so like Tahmina Khanom she made

15 Above, p. 51.
16 By all accounts her son Tehmurasp had been a dear little boy, handsome and eager; but he died suddenly (perhaps, it was thought, from a rupture) carrying wood for the Hiromba fire. D. Khodadad had known much sorrow, for his first wife had died, and also the son Rashid whom she bore him, in his twentieth year. Rashid had felt the call to the priesthood, and was on the point of departing to India to be made mobed when he died suddenly.

nan-e šekari among all the other dishes. We returned in time for Piruza, as *no-šwe*, to give the *čom-e šwa* from the gahambar before sunset. We duly found two dogs, one of them 'four-eyed', who made a gallant effort to accept the offering, but they were plainly suffering from Panji repletion, and could not swallow it all.

Meantime preparations were under way for the end of Panji-mas and a welcome to the new year. Piruza, as the eldest daughter at home, made a *kōpī*. Her sister Shahnaz had brought from their grandfather's orchard-garden a bunch of anice, which the villagers called 'shāhvasrām'. They used its seeds in sherbet, and sowed it regularly in their gardens 'when the mulberries were ripe', to be ready for Panji. Piruza's bunch was between flowering and setting its seeds. She took its stems and thrust them into a fair-sized lump of moist clay, which she then moulded to have a flat base and rounded top, and left to dry. Meantime, Gushtasp had begun to carry the whitened clay figures up on to the roof while it was still light. The house next door was occupied by Moslems, and their son, a little older than Gushtasp, was on its roof and on seeing him began to practice the *āzān* very loudly. Gushtasp took this as provocation and dealt with it promptly by a well-aimed stone. The Moslem boy fled weeping to his father, who hastened round to complain to Agha Rustam, who beat Gushtasp, and for a while the happy harmony of the household was broken. This state of affairs could not be allowed to last, however, on this holiest of days, to distress the fravašis; and before the sun sank, cheerfulness had been restored. The Moslems having retired to sleep when it grew dark, Gushtasp was able to carry out in peace his task of taking all the figures up on to the roof and arranging them in a quaint row overlooking the courtyard. The pots of 'seven seeds' were set beside them, together with Piruza's *kopi*, which had had a green silk kerchief tied over the anice stems. A big bundle of brushwood was also carried up, and a storm-lamp was lit and set to burn on the place where the Panji fire would be kindled. There were other lamps already burning on Zoroastrian roofs round about, steadfast yellow flecks under the starry sky. After a quiet family meal of consecrated food from the gahambar (pottage and bread with *sir-o-sedow*), Agha Rustam withdrew to read Avesta in the now almost empty *ganza-pak*, and the rest of the household went to sleep with the sound of the holy words coming softly to their ears.

It was not a long sleep, however, for Tahmina Khanom roused us all at half-past three. The moon was shining, and there was as yet no sign of dawn. She had already lit a fire on the roof where the lamp had been, and on a few other roofs flames were leaping up, and women, ever the first to rise, were tending them. Within a few minutes a fine but challenging *azan* was being broadcast as usual from the minaret of the Husayniya,[17] and more and more little twinkling fires leapt into life beside the lamps on the Zoroastrian roofs. Agha Rustam came up and said the košti-prayers, facing the fire; and then he seated himself before it and began reciting the appropriate Avesta: the prayers of the second night-watch, the Avestā-ye Rūz-e Vahištōišt (i.e. of the fifth 'Gatha' day), and the Afrinagan-e Dahman. Gushtasp meantime tended the fire and put *buδ-e nakoš* on the flames—for this demon-daunting plant belonged to the ceremony. Father and son thus played the parts of celebrant and server (*zōt* and *rāspī*), which in the past would have been performed (at least in such a leading family) by priests. D. Khodadad was himself praying before his own roof-fire, his white-clad figure showing clearly against the wind-tower. Paridun was by the fire on his roof beside us, and his elder son Rashid had carried the big dakhma-*afrinagan* to the roof of an empty Zoroastrian house opposite, where they had also put a lamp to burn through the night, a *kopi*, and some of their clay figures. While the men prayed, the women were busy, Martha-like, cooking a farewell meal for the fravašis, the hot dishes, together with some that had been placed in the *ganza-pak* overnight, being brought up and ranged on a sort of shelf that ran along the side of the barrel-roof where the fire was lit.

Soon after the *azan* ceased (it lasted some twenty minutes), the east began to grow light, and the shape of Hrišt appeared, and then slowly the other mountains to the south of it, and last of all the noble mass of Pir-e Sabz. Agha Rustam had finished the Avestan service and sat quietly looking eastward, waiting for the sun to rise and mark the departure of the fravašis, to whom he had thus bidden farewell. The roof-fire was allowed to sink as the fravašis withdrew, and just before the sun appeared Gushtasp gathered its last embers into a whitened clay pan, a *kuwa*, to be taken later to the fire-temple. Dark-clad Moslems began to emerge from their sheets (having one and all, it seemed, peacefully disregarded the *azan*), and the Zoroastrian men stood up singly and 'made new the košti' once more, this

---

[17] Unfortunately electricity enabled this to be very loud and (to Zoroastrian ears) aggressive at such close quarters.

time with the prayers of Havan Gah, the first watch of the new day. One elderly woman did the same, but otherwise the women were already busy at their various tasks. As soon as the sun was clear of the mountain-tops, a girl on each roof took a big bowl of pure water, with marjoram leaves scattered over it, which had been standing by the fire, and sprinkled the water with a ladle over all the roof. (Parvin, Paridun's elder daughter, had both their own house-roof to sprinkle thus, and that of the empty house opposite.) Perhaps this act was in origin the last rite in a loving ceremony of farewell to the dead, which had also an ancient element of exorcism in it; or perhaps it was a first libation to the sun, rising to bring in the new year.

The family then drank tea together on the roof, rejoicing in the early morning sunshine and freshness. Formerly it was the custom to breakfast up there, families and neighbours joining together, and all, men and women, drinking wine, with many toasts. With Moslem households now interspersed among Zoroastrian ones, however, breakfast was eaten in seclusion below. So down we went, and Paridun and his family joined us, bringing consecrated food with them from their own Panji cooking, and Tahmina Khanom provided all with bowls of hot *harisa*, just as at the spring No Ruz.[18] It was a leisurely, happy meal; but long before their elders had finished eating and talking, Gushtasp and his cousin Jehangir, Paridun's second son, had taken their *kuwas* full of glowing embers from the roof-fires, and set off for the fire-temple. After they had deposited the embers there (just as their sisters had done after the Hiromba fire), they and other boys forgathered on a piece of empty ground beside the temple, and bashed their *kuwas* against each other, to see which would break last. Gushtasp triumphed that year, and returned merrily. His sisters meantime had gone up to the roof again to fetch the clay figures (which had gazed down on us, white against the blue sky, while we breakfasted below). Piruza took the green kerchief off the *kopi* and tied it briefly on her own pretty head— a traditional custom; and Parvin appeared on the next roof, a *kopi* in either hand (held by the anice stems), and challenged Pouran to a duel. Pouran, ever active, seized Piruza's *kopi*, climbed nimbly over, and flung herself on her cousin, and amid laughter broke both her *kopis* with it, one after another. Down in the lane I saw two little girls meet and clash their *kopis* earnestly till one broke; and

[18] See above, p. 169.

others gathered in a group, as the boys had done with their *kuwas*, and went on till the last survivor. This was an annual custom. (Subsequently Piruza's unbroken *kopi* remained till Havzoru on the Belivani roof; and on the eve of that festival the house-sparrows descended on it in a twittering group and in seconds cleared the anice of all its sun-ripened seeds.)

After breakfast a number of visitors came to see Agha Rustam, as at the spring No Ruz (for though Panji did not coincide with any national holiday, some of the Tehranis managed to take their annual leave then). But although this was 1 Farvardin, the traditional New Year's Day in Iran since time immemorial, no one in the village referred to it as No Ruz, or thought of it as such. To the Parsis, 1 Farvardin is 'Naoroj', regardless of the time of year when it comes; but the Iranis, keeping that name for the secular spring festival, had come to know the summer one simply as the day of the 'Dadgah-e Panji'—the third annual occasion for a communal observance at the dakhma.[19] The day was thus annexed, as it were, to Panji, despite the fact that the fravašis had been bidden farewell (an illogicality that arose from the confusion attendant on the third-century calendar reform). So not long after the family breakfast Paridun, as guardian of the dakhma, set off for there laden himself and leading his laden donkey, to be followed by his usual helpers. As at the Dadgah-e Tir-Mah,[20] the women of seven families gathered at the Belivani home in the morning to make all the preparations there that they could; and in the early afternoon everything was loaded on the Belivani cow and a little group set bravely off under the remorseless sun—Piruza the Dastur's wife, her great-aunt Daulat, the sister of Turk Jamshidi, and her niece Piruza. I followed only later, when the heat was relenting a little, with Erdeshir Qudusi

[19] See above, p. 201. Those who followed the reformed calendar could not keep this observance on 1 Farvardin, since this was for them identical with the spring No Ruz with its many rites; and they had accordingly transferred it to Khvar Ruz (the eleventh) of Dai Mah, which is the day recorded in Pahlavi books as that of the death of Zoroaster (see further 'On the calendar . . .', 530–1). There seems to be no genuine tradition of the observance of this day among the Iranis before the twentieth-century calendar reform. Thereafter a 'gahambar-e lurki' in the fire-temple was instituted in Yazd and its neighbouring villages on that day, the one in Yazd itself being paid for by the Parsis. In Sharifabad Noshiravan established a similar gahambar when he tried to introduce the reformed calendar there, and this was maintained by his son, Agha Rustam. Speeches were made in both Sharifabad and Yazd on the occasion—a wholly untraditional activity in conjunction with a religious service.

[20] Cf. above, p. 204.

and a Tehrani visitor, on bicycles. Even on that last day of July
there was greenness still to enjoy in the fields, with the cotton
bushes and small patches of dye-madder and unreaped lucerne;
and the Tehrani was all the more dismayed at the contrast when we
reached the bare burning desert. From the edge of the fields we
could see the animation at the dadgah. There were Sharifabadi
men ahead of us on the track, but already a jeep had arrived to take
Hasanabadis away, and a contingent from Mazra‘ were preparing
to depart on donkey and bicycle. Murvarid was standing wearily
by the two big urns, dispensing water, and women were coming
up to her with bowls of flour in recompense for her husband's
labours. Fires were burning in both *sangoks*, which were covered
with offerings, including little cotton bags sown with wheat or barley
(one light green, the other dark). The Dastur's wife had already put
hers and her sister-in-law Tahmina's on the *sangok* by the old dakhma,
since their children had been carried there. Those who had not lost
children kept these little bags, as well as the boxes and other containers of seeds, in their houses until Havzoru, 'so that the fravašis'
horses could graze on them'—though the original purpose, Agha
Rustam pointed out, was simply to make their homes as fresh and
pleasant as possible for the spirits to visit, and these folk-beliefs
had grown up afterwards. (The Parsis, more fortunately placed,
use flowers instead.)

Then, despite the many rites already performed at Panji, gahambars for the dead were celebrated again at the dakhma, ending as
usual with a communal observance for all souls. The Sharifabadis'
services ended soon after six o'clock, and the evening meal was
eaten once more in a great horseshoe on the desert shingle. The two
salars were both present, but they ate separately in one of the
pesgams, each using his own cloth and glass.[21] Again the gathering
broke up as soon as the meal was over, the boys dashing off on their
bicycles, followed by family parties with donkeys and on foot. There
was a low band of white dust hanging like mist at the edge of the
fields, and the head of the procession was vanishing into it as the
tail was still forming at the dadgah. Erdeshir Qudusi and I lingered
to share their meal of consecrated food with Paridun and his weary
helpers, and then cycled back ahead of them through the dusk.

The next day D. Khodadad departed to spend three days at
Mazra‘ Kalantar and Hasanabad, reciting the 'Avesta-ye Panji'

[21] Cf. above, p. 46 and n. 17.

(that is, an Afrinagan-service with appropriate dedication) for every family which wished it. Later he would do the same in Sharifabad in any house where a 'gahambar-e čakhra' had not been celebrated during the 'Gatha' days. This rite was valid for the first ten days of Farvardin Mah. In the times of many priests, the rites of Rapithwin (who had returned above earth at noon on 1 Farvardin) would have been performed at the fire-temple on the third day of the month, Ruz Urdibehišt, but these were now perforce neglected.[22] For the rest of the village, life now returned to normal, except for careful watering of the pots of greenery. The Belivanis had sown one box with seeds of the castor plant, which is a slow grower, to be at their freshest in time for Havzoru; and on 1 Farvardin Murvarid sowed more herbs in a little basket to be ready too for that great day. But on 2 Farvardin the spinning-wheels were turning again in the houses, and out in the fields teams of men were at work digging up stubble or threshing the corn, the rhythmic thumping of their club-like flails carrying far through the dusty air. During the following days five of Agha Rustam's fields were winnowed and threshed, and the grain and straw were put into store-rooms at the back of the house.

Yet despite all this mundane activity, thoughts were gilded by expectation of Havzoru to come, on 6 Farvardin, for this was the most beloved single festival of the year. Once, as the written tradition tells us, this day was known as the 'Greater No Ruz'; but just as the 'Lesser No Ruz' of 1 Farvardin had lost its old name for the Iranis, so too had this second celebration, which was known to them prosaically as Havzoru (Persian 'Hivdah Ruz'),[23] that is, the 'Seventeenth day'. In the ancient 360-day calendar, as we have seen, No Ruz was celebrated immediately after 30 Spendarmad; but in the first year of the Sasanian reform the people at large found that, having come to the day which they reckoned to be Hamaspathmaedaya, that is, 30 Spendarmad, this was only 25 Spendarmad by the official calendar; and so they then had to count to the seventeenth day (30 Spendarmad, the ten days of Farvardigan, and the first five days of Farvardin Mah) before they could celebrate No Ruz on what they firmly believed to be its rightful date.[24] That is to say, they reckoned that sixteen days had to be devoted to the

---

[22] See above, p. 50; and for the rites themselves see 'Rapithwin . . .', 209–11.

[23] The pronunciation varied slightly from village to village in the Yazdi region, and in Kerman the form was 'Arvedārū' (see Sorushian, *Farhang*, 5).

[24] For more detailed discussion, with a table of these complex developments, see 'On the calendar . . .', 513–22.

fravašis, and that the seventeenth was the true No Ruz. Naturally before written calendars were available (which for the laity was not until the 1940s), such methods of reckoning the relative dates of observances were essential; and so the 'Greater No Ruz' came to be known simply by this practical designation. The Parsis called it equally prosaically after the name of the day on which it falls, that is, Khordād, qualifying this by the word *sāl* 'year', that is 'Khordad of the (New) Year'. All the great legends that attached to New Year's Day—that it had seen the birth of the prophet himself, and every epic achievement of old—were associated since Sasanian times with this feast, 6 Farvardin, and not with 1 Farvardin (as must have been the case before the third-century calendar reform).[25]

In some ways, inevitably, the observances of the eve of Havzoru repeated those of the eve of both the secular spring No Ruz and the 'Dadgah-e Panji' since in origin these were all three one feast. So there was again sweeping and tidying, and in the late afternoon the *pesgam-e mas* was set out with the pots of greenery, a brazier, and a bright mirror. A lamp was lit there at dusk, and the air became full of the sharp tang of *sir-o-sedow* as the Zoroastrian houses began to make *boy-o-brang*. These observances repeated those of the fifth 'Gatha' day, for the ancient pattern was that the feast of All Souls preceded No Ruz, as night the day. So the lamp burnt through all the night, but there was no re-enactment of the farewell to the fravašis at the next dawn.[26]

The custom of donning new clothes to welcome the new year was maintained at this religious festival also. Thus Agha Rustam's fifth daughter, Azarmindukht, who was living at Turk Jamshidi's and helping there, had come home the evening before dressed from head to foot in new clothes, and in the morning several of her sisters wore something new and pretty. Everyone, said D. Khodadad, should put on that day seven new things, and men and women alike should drink seven sips of wine—for (though he did not add the explanation) this was the seventh feast of obligation, in honour

---

[25] See, e.g., Sorushian, *Farhang*, 5, s.v. 'Arvedārū'; Modi, *CC*, 431, s.v. 'Khordād Sāl' (both treatments being based on the literary tradition).

[26] In Taft the custom was that in the evening before Havzoru the villagers would gather at the fire-temple, and the priest would solemnize an Afrinagan-service in honour of all souls. The Parsis of Navsari called 5 Farvardin *valāva-nī rāt* 'eve of farewell', sc. to the fravašis, and solemnized the same ceremonies then as on the evening of the fifth 'Gatha' day (see 'On the calendar . . .', 521).

of the seventh creation, fire, and the number seven should run through all its observances.[27]

Everyone was up at dawn of the great day, and exchanging the greeting of the festival: *jašn-e Havzorū-t mobārak*! We breakfasted once more on *harisa*, and soon afterwards Sarvar, Turk's wife, came to offer her greetings, with sprays of greenery, and rose-water was sprinkled and sweetmeats handed round. At half-past seven Piruza and I went by invitation to the Dastur's House, where D. Khodadad was already preparing to perform the Visperad, washing all the Yasna utensils in the running water of the stream. The Visperad is held to be a service evolved especially to celebrate the seven obligatory feasts, but as a busy parish priest D. Khodadad managed to solemnize it only once a year, on this the last of them, when it was the centre of the village's observances. Lacking any fellow priest to act as server, and having to adapt to the villagers' own established customs, he celebrated the long service as an 'outer' rather than an 'inner' ceremony; but he did not omit one syllable of the liturgy or any of the fundamental ritual, finding a spiritual satisfaction in performing the ancient act of worship as perfectly as he could, in lonely faithfulness.

Instead, therefore, of seating himself within ritually drawn furrows in a place apart, he spread a pure white cloth in an inner corner of the smaller *pesgam*, where none would approach him closely, and sitting there, white-clad, and wearing the mouth-veil (*padān*) he began, at about eight o'clock, the preliminary service to consecrate the vessels and offerings of the Visperad. As well as all the things obligatory for the service itself, laid out before him, there was to one side a glass flagon full of pure water, to be consecrated, and a silver vase with myrtle-sprays.[28] D. Khodadad concentrated utterly on the words and rituals, and seemed wholly oblivious of the activities in the rest of the narrow house.

Paridun had arrived earlier from the Dastur's own home with a big cloth over his shoulder full of flour, and had set about mixing it into dough in two huge basins; and from eight o'clock the women of the village began to arrive, at first in ones and twos, and then in little groups. Each carried a small copper bowl full of *varderin*. There was a melon, a cucumber, and an egg in every bowl, with a variety, at choice, of grapes, apples, small, prettily striped gourds, green pomegranates, tomatoes, dried dates, and the like. In the end

---

[27] Cf. above, pp. 49–50.   [28] See Pl. Va.

there were 115 such bowls, covering the whole floor of the smaller *pesgam* around the Dastur's cloth, and every ledge and sill. After each woman had put down her *varderin*, she went to D. Khodadad's daughter Parizad and gave her a list of all those over the age of nine who were living in her house. Only one man, recently a widower, appeared carrying his own bowl, and he, having put it down and handed over his list, absent-mindedly uttered the familiar words *Khodā be-āmurzad-ešān* 'May God have mercy on them!', only to be heartily laughed at by the surrounding women. He acknowledged his error and retreated grinning, since what he should have said was *Zande bāšand!* 'May they live!'; for Havzoru, the 'Greater No Ruz', feast of the resurrection, was the one festival of the whole devotional year which was celebrated entirely on behalf of the living.

For an hour and a half the women came and went. Many carried sprays of myrtle or mint, which they exchanged with the festival greetings; and there was plenty of talk and laughter, while small children ran about among their mothers' skirts. The lists of names, when they had all been collected, were placed near D. Khodadad. Paridun meantime was snatching a little sleep after the dough-mixing, but he was ruthlessly shaken awake again at about ten o'clock to begin the baking. He and his two helpers armed themselves, despite the August heat, with the heavy clothing needed for working at an open oven, and set about their task. Women, meanwhile, carefully boiled and peeled the 115 eggs, and at eleven o'clock the two dahmobeds arrived. By that time, the Dastur was deep into the solemnization of the Visperad itself, but it was nearly noon before he had made the ritual *čašni* or partaking of the first preparation of the *parahōm*, and summoned them with a gesture to begin their work. They first 'made new the košti', facing the fire in the vessel before the Dastur, and then began cutting up the now consecrated *varderin*. All the fruits were halved, and one-half of each melon and cucumber was put back in the family bowls, still on the *pesgam*. These bowls had already been colourful, with the gleaming melon-skins, dark green and light green, striped and plain; but now there was a glorious display of red-fleshed melons with black seeds, white or creamy ones with golden seeds, and pale translucent cucumbers. The other halves of the cucumbers and some of the melons were put in to big basins to be carried later to the fire-temple; and the rest of the fruit was shared at once among the helpers, and any others who came. An eager group of small boys were fetched in from the lane and ranged along a courtyard wall, where they sat and ate melon-slices. Old Hajji Khodabakhsh turned up too, in his bright new clothes from *no-šwa*, and accounted for a whole melon, and Agha Rustam arrived later to share a more formal communion meal.

Meanwhile the big new rounds of freshly baked bread had been halved, and two halves were put on each of the family bowls, *sir-o-sedow* was sprinkled over one, turning it a bright yellow, and half an egg was set on the other. All the while D. Khodadad continued steadily to recite the Visperad liturgy. Since he now celebrated this immensely long service only once a year, he had open beside him on a wooden stand a big Avesta, to prompt his memory for those portions of the service which are additional to the ordinary Yasna liturgy. He was still reciting, swiftly but clearly, when at about half-past one the women began to return. A big brown cotton sheet had been spread in the courtyard, and on to this each poured a small amount of wheat, till slowly a golden pyramid of grain was formed. Part of this wheat was to replace the flour which the Dastur had himself provided for the bread to be blessed, part was to recompense him for the services which he would solemnize that day. Each woman then went to Parizad, and received from her a spoonful of consecrated water infused with some of the second preparation of *parahom* made ready by D. Khodadad during the service. The women had not tasted food for several hours in readiness for this rite. The consecrated liquid was given them from a deep copper spoon, and it was poured from above, so that the spoon did not touch their lips.[29] Nearly every woman in the village came at Havzoru to receive the *parahom*, and several took some away in a little copper bowl, or a deep spoon, for their husbands. Either before or after this, each woman found her family bowl, covered it with the cloth which had held the wheat, and carried it away for the consecrated varderin to be shared by all her family at their festive midday meal.

The Dastur, as well as solemnizing the Visperad, had to celebrate a Dron service and an Afrinagan in honour of Rapithwin, who returns above earth at No Ruz; and also to pray by name for the well-being of every single person on the lists which had been put before him. So he did not finish until half-past three, by which time he had been reciting with barely a pause for six hours in the August heat. He then left the *pesgam*, bearing a silver pot full of the second

[29] See Pl. VIa.

preparation of *parahom*, and carried this down the steps to the stream to make the libation to water, which concludes every Yasna and Visperad service. After this he broke his fast, modestly, with consecrated food—a *sirog*, half an egg, and half a melon; and rested a little before going to the Ataš Varahram to hold a service for the men of the village. Paridun had already taken round the *varderin* for this—two big basins of cucumbers, cut into neat chunks, with a few pieces of melon to give colour (but only a few, since melon-seeds are difficult to dispose of in a place of worship), and a smaller bowl with bread broken into pieces, chopped hard-boiled egg, and smaller fruits such as grapes. The fire-temple was packed with men and boys, who even overflowed into the outer *pesgam* where the women usually sat, the only women present being Piruza the ataš-band's wife, there to cook the *sir-o-sedow* and *sirog* for *boy-o-brang*, another woman to keep her company, and myself. The Dastur celebrated an ordinary gahambar service, and then two men carried round the bowls of *varderin* while Erdeshir the dahmobed combined their contents to make *čašni* for each person present. The men produced big folding knives to cut up the *varderin*, while boys ate the melons off the rinds. After this communion meal, *lurk* was distributed, and then the temple, as usual, emptied rapidly.[30]

These, together with family gatherings and rejoicings, were the celebrations of Havzoru, the feast of a single day. It was a day for consecration and a sense of renewal, and it was both beloved by the community, and regarded by them as the high and solemn point of the religious year. In this, as in so much else, the Sharifabadis undoubtedly preserved ancient orthodoxy, according to which this seventh feast both crowned the old year and brought in the new one in a spirit of joy and hope. So while at Panji it was proper to make

[30] At Yazd and most—perhaps all—of the villages apart from Sharifabad and its two neighbours, it was the custom to make a public appeal at this service for yearly contributions to the communal funds (for the upkeep of the fire-temple, the purchase of wood and oil, etc.). As each man came up and gave a sum of money, the congregation would raise a lusty long-drawn shout of 'Hāvorū, hāvorū, hāvorū, ay šō-boš!'—a shout which had come to be generally used, in Sharifabad also, in the sense of 'Hurray!' (cf. above, p. 173). The word *šo-boš* is a reduction of Persian *šād bāš* 'be happy!', and the usage provided an alternate name for Havzoru, namely *Jašn-e šō-boš* (see Sorushian, *Farhang*, 54). The custom was unknown in Sharifabad and Mazraʿ, where such public displays of generosity were frowned on by the villagers as unbecoming. Gifts to the community should be made, they held, privately and unostentatiously. In places which had the *šoboš* ceremony, sherbet was often given by pious individuals, and drunk merrily at the gatherings.

confession and drink *nirang*, in order to cleanse away the sins and impurities of the past twelve months, at Havzoru it was fitting to partake of the *parahom*, a source of spiritual refreshment and energy, so as to quicken one's spirit and gain zest and strength for the endeavours of the year to come.

After Havzoru the 'seven seeds' in pots and boxes were no longer watered, and wilted at once in the dry heat, their essence having been enjoyed (so the simpler people said) by the spirit-steeds. The great festival-season of Panji and the religious New Year was over, and yet it was still thought valid and effective to perform any of the appropriate rites which had been neglected up till Aban Ruz, the fourth day after Havzoru.[31] Thus, for example, the Belivanis had been unable to make the ritual *boy-o-brang* on the eve of Havzoru, because they had no 'pure' oil left, and Paridun had sold the last drop. So they postponed this until Aban Ruz, when D. Khodadad came to the house and recited an Afrinagan in honour of all souls. There is no appropriate tradition attached to Aban Ruz to account for its being the last day for such observances, and the explanation seems to be simply that it is the twenty-first day from the eve of Panji-kasog (25 Spendarmad), which was popularly regarded at one time as being the true New Year's Eve. No Ruz was traditionally a three-week festival, lasting, that is, the auspicious number of three times seven days; and so it seems, the religious New Year festival was regarded, like the secular spring one,[32] as lasting this length of time, although it began now on 25 Spendarmad instead of 1 Farvardin. As a result Havzoru, a feast of the living, is embedded in a twenty-day festival devoted to the dead. All such confusions and duplications arose from the third-century calendar reform, which the Sasanian kings had had the power to enforce, but not the means to explain adequately to the devout. When one considers how doggedly their subjects resisted, as far as they could, the changes which their absolute rulers then sought to impose on them, there is no reason to wonder at the Yazdis' rejection of the twentieth-century calendar reform, which too was a measure that outraged those feelings of loyalty and devotion whose strength has enabled Zoroastrians to remain true to the faith of their forefathers throughout millennia.

[31] For the special Kermani observances on Aban Ruz of Farvardin Mah see Sorushian, *Farhang*, 54, s.v. '*jašn-e ṣaddar*'.
[32] See above, p. 176.

10

INITIATIONS AND PILGRIMAGES

ACCORDING to the Avesta, initiation into the Zoroastrian community, with full responsibility for one's own religious and moral life, should take place at fifteen years of age (which in ancient Iran was regarded as the time of maturity).[1] Among the Parsis this had been reduced to seven or eight, much as the age of confirmation has been reduced in some Christian communities, but the Irani villagers usually initiated their children at between twelve and fifteen years. In the old illiterate days a boy would prepare for the rite by going to the family priest to be taught by word of mouth the essential prayers —the Ahunvar and Ašəm vohu, the košti-prayers and the Sroš Baj. By the 1960s, with schools in every village and so few priests, it was the school-teachers who made sure that the boys learnt these prayers from the *Khorda Avesta* (of which copies, printed in Bombay or Tehran, were readily to be had); and since it was they who had the trouble, it was usually they too who performed the simple ceremony, and received gifts in recompense from the family.

While the boy struggled to memorize the incomprehensible Avestan words, his mother would stitch him a sedra, the sacred shirt made from homespun undyed cotton, with the little pouch at the neck to be filled symbolically with good deeds, and a košti would be bought for him. Until the early decades of the twentieth century it was the priests themselves, in their purity, who wove the sacred cord, with its seventy-two threads, on a simple wooden frame. D. Khodadad still had a man-sized frame in his empty house in Yazd, and a woman from Mazra' told me that she well remembered as a child seeing his uncle, D. Bahram, sitting in the courtyard of his Sharifabadi home and weaving the cords. The last košti woven by D. Khodadad himself, with continual recital of Avesta, was a specially thick strong one which was kept for funeral purposes.[2] The wool for this (from a lamb or yearling sheep) was spun for him on a distaff

---

[1] See Yt. 8.13–14.
[2] i.e. for tying the shrouded corpse to the bier.

by Jehangir Jamshidi, since a spinning-wheel produced too fine a thread; and even for regular wear, D. Khodadad maintained, the košti should be sturdy, a real cord which a man could use for practical purposes if sudden need arose. (He cited in this connection the epic tale of Hom, who used his košti to bind Afrasiyab.) The urban Parsis have gradually, however, evolved a cord of exquisite fineness, spun by women of priestly families, which is suitable for wearing over their fine muslin sedras; and during this century the Iranis have slowly been following suit. But since the 1920s the work has become entrusted by them to lay women. In that decade a group of half a dozen priests instructed the women of Aliabad in the art (that village suffering then from drought and poverty); and as the dwindling band of priests had perforce to abandon the work under pressure of their other duties, this small village came to supply koštis for all Irani Zoroastrians. Then as Aliabadi women married into other places, they took their skill with them. Thus Sarvar from Aliabad, Turk Jamshidi's wife, wove koštis in Sharifabad, and had taught her step-daughter Parichihr how to do so; and while I was in the village Piruza Belivani was struggling to acquire the skill— though her uncle Paridun and a number of the other men still wore the thick, sturdy koštis woven for them by D. Khodadad, which naturally had a much longer life than the fashionably fine ones. (It was held to be improper, indeed useless, to pray with a košti in which a single thread was broken.)

The women undertook their task with high seriousness, and strove to maintain a strict standard of purity in weaving the košti. It was unthinkable, of course, that any woman should touch wool or frame while bi-namaz,[3] nor could the work be done during the hours of darkness. The first košti which a girl wove by herself had to be given to a shrine. She would hang it on the wall, and whoever wished would take it and leave the money there. Some bestowed their first ten or more koštis in this way, and Piruza had vowed to give fourteen—one to each of the seven shrines of Sharifabad, one

---

[3] The period of bi-namazi was regarded as lasting seven days, but the regulations were relaxed a little after the third day (see above, p. 103); and Sarvar told me that once, when she had an urgent order for a košti, feeling herself to be clean on the sixth day, she made ablution, and wove one. But all that night she was tormented by bad dreams, in which she was alone among hostile, mocking Moslems, while Zoroastrians passed by without greeting her or going to her help. After that experience she never wove a košti again until the full seven days were over. For a photograph of her at work see Pl. VIb.

to each of the six great communal Pirs, and one to the Ataš Bahram
of Yazd.

The first time that I myself witnessed an initiation ceremony
(called in Dari *sedra-pušun* 'putting on the sacred shirt') was in May,
on the auspicious day of Ruz Dai-be-Din of Mah Dai by the traditional calendar, which is one of the name-day feasts of Ohrmazd
himself. One of the three boys concerned was Rashid, Paridun
Rashidi's elder son. He went to school in the ordinary way that
morning, and at about half-past ten the womenfolk of his family
set off after him, gathering relatives and friends along the way, and
meeting near the school the women of the other two families.
(*Sedra-pušun* among the laity was very much a women's affair, the
men being at work in the fields.) The mother of each boy carried a
large round tray, on which were the new sedra and košti, a set of
clean clothes, and a big new handkerchief, all covered by a green
cloth. Others in the group bore a lamp, greenery in a silver pot,
rose-water, and sweetmeats. At the school the boys were in the
playground. They had just been drawing water from the well, and
the leather bucket lay wet and gleaming in the sunshine. We all
went into the school hall, and the boys stood in orderly lines round
the walls, while the women sat on benches put for them near the
door. The three candidates took the trays and, leaving the koštis
behind, departed to make ablution and put on their sedras and clean
clothes. Rashid returned wearing a beautiful old wool-embroidered
cap, bright green, which his father had worn at his *sedra-pušun*.
The other two had the usual red-and-white striped caps, and all
three looked shiningly clean in their new clothes. The headmaster
called for the threefold cheer for them—*Havoru, Havoru, Havoru, ay
šo-boš!*[4]—and then they went to him and the two assistant masters,
who heard them recite the appropriate prayers before they helped
them tie the košti in the proper manner.[5]

Each boy as he finished put on his new jacket, glowing with
pride and relief at having remembered the texts, and tied the knots
correctly; and then the scene became very animated. One of their
schoolfellows went round gleefully sprinkling everyone with rose-
water, while another followed with a mirror which he held before

---

[4] See above, p. 234 n. 30.

[5] See Pl. VIIa. These lay instructors did not, however, imitate the priests in
the manner in which they helped the candidates, for the priests (Parsi and Irani
alike) always stand behind the child and guide his hands with theirs (cf. Pl.
VIIb).

each in turn. Then the eldest woman in each family group put sweets between the lips of the teachers and into their hands, and distributed sweets to all the boys. Other women followed them, including old Shirin-e Set Hakemi, bent double as always, and carefully bestowing her small bounty from a little box. The delight of the boys was pleasant to see, and one chubby little three-year-old, the son of Erej Nekdini, stuffed his small pockets full as well as his mouth. Two of the families also distributed sherbet, and each of the teachers was given a small tray with a green-wrapped sugar-cone in the centre, a ring of white sweetmeats round it, and a handful of *lurk* and fruits. One family also gave the headmaster an apple with three or four silver coins pressed into it. Then after more cheering the boys filed off into the class-rooms, and Piruza the wife of the atašband took the *afrinagan* in which fire had been burning throughout the ceremony, and set off for the fire-temple. The three boys followed her, each carrying one of the silver pots full of greenery, which they laid on the pillar-altar in the hall there. Piruza kindled fire on this pillar, and the boys, facing it, each 'made new the košti' again, with grave concentration and only a little fumbling over the knots, while they recited the prayers in their high unbroken voices. This completed the initiation ceremony, and they were then carried off by their families to celebrations at their own homes. A few days later Sarvar's son Rustam was initiated, with another schoolfellow, and on that occasion Piruza and I joined the family party afterwards. Rustam was placed in the seat of honour on a carpet in the *pesgam-e mas*, and his mother and aunts (come that morning from Hasanabad) gave him presents and sprays of cypress, and kissed him heartily. (After each kiss Rustam rubbed his cheek as vigorously and churlishly as any English schoolboy.) Then there was a cheerful midday meal, the aunts went off to visit Sharifabadi friends, and Rustam slipped away to enjoy his half-holiday with the other boy.

In the past, poverty and harassment brought it about that *sedra-pušun* among the laity was often by necessity even simpler, the boy merely going alone to the priest, košti in hand, when he was ready; but the priests always invested it with greater solemnity for their own children. So when a few years earlier D. Khodadad's son Shehriar was initiated, his father asked three of his fellow priests to come from Yazd for the occasion. That morning Shehriar went through a full threefold cleansing, with *pajow*, sand, and water, drinking after it an infusion of crushed pomegranate twigs and leaves. About a quarter of an hour later he drank *nirang*, and the priests recited a confessional on his behalf. Then they celebrated an Afrinagan for the soul of his dead brother Rashid, whose *pol-guzār* Shehriar was, and another for Shehriar's own well-being, and then D. Khodadad performed his son's *sedra-pušun*.

Essentially a girl's initiation was exactly the same as a boy's, but less notice was taken of it in a family, and it made less outward difference to her thereafter, since women did not usually tie the sacred cord at public gatherings, whereas a boy's initiation set him proudly among the men at all assemblies. Sometimes, therefore, a girl's initiation was still left till she was nearly fifteen, and she herself felt that she wished to undergo the ceremony. Thus it was that Pourandukht decided to prepare herself for *sedra-pušun* in the summer of 1964, two or three years after she had left the little village school; and almost at the last moment her cousin Parvin (Rashid's elder sister) decided to join her. They taught themselves the prayers from the *Khorda Avesta*, with some help from their uncle, D. Khodadad; and it was decided that the ceremony should take place in the Dastur's House late in July, on the tenth morning of a *no-šwa* there. The two girls made their ablution at home, and arrived looking very pretty in their new clothes, with traditional green head-veils, in time to drink *nirang* with those just finishing their retreat. Then came their families bearing the usual lamps and gifts. A thick cloth was spread on the floor of a *pesgam*, and a pure white cloth was laid over that. Two trays, bearing the sugar-cones, rose-water, and other things, were set on either side of the cloth, and the Dastur performed the initiations one after the other.[6] Agha Rustam was present, and when the ceremony was over his wife and sister offered rose-water and sweetmeats to everyone, and gave the green-wrapped sugar-cones to the Dastur. Then after breakfasting with the *no-šwe*'s, the two girls carried their pots of greenery to the fire-temple in company with them, and there made their offerings and said their first independent košti-prayers, as the boys had done. *Sedra-pušun* was also performed by women-teachers at the village girls' school, exactly as at the boys' one.

It was usually some years before he put on the košti that a boy had that other initiation which he valued, as a youngster, almost as highly, when he became one of the 'camel's thorn boys', and was allowed to sleep the night in the mountains, at the shrine of Hrist.

[6] See Pl. VIIb.

This shrine has figured often in the preceding pages, since it was so close to Sharifabad, and had so great a place in the religious life of the village; but it is in fact only one of five great sanctuaries in the mountains which fringe the Yazdi plain. These sanctuaries were very dear to the Zoroastrians, so much so that one explanation which they gave for their seemingly miraculous survival as a community was that they had been spared 'for the sake of those in the hills', that is, so that they might continue to worship at these remote places, and to maintain the rites which were proper to them. The five sanctuaries, and one other in the plain near the city of Yazd, were in communal trust. Each village looked after the shrines in its own fields and lanes, but all joined together to care for these six. To visit any of them on any occasion was an act of much merit, but the merit was greatest when one joined in the yearly pilgrimage at the time appointed. Each pilgrimage (generally referred to by the Moslem term *hajj*) lasted officially for five days, like each of the major festivals; and just before it the guardian of the shrine would visit Yazd and all the Zoroastrian villages in turn, and collect contributions for maintaining the sanctuary during the year to come. Money was given, and oil for the sanctuary lamps, and individual gifts were also made by the many pilgrims.

Collectively these shrines were called the great Pirs, and they had a dominant place in the thoughts and affections of the plain-dwelling Zoroastrians. Visiting them was an undertaking of spiritual significance, as well as one of incidental pleasure and delights; and traditionally a pilgrim waited to be 'called' by the holy ones. He attended, that is, for some prompting, through a dream or portent, to tell him that he should go. Thus D. Khodadad told me that fifteen years once passed between one pilgrimage which he made to the Pir-e Nareke and the next. Sometimes a special reason would lie behind the prompting which took a worshipper to a shrine. He might have cause, that is, to make an act of thanksgiving, or to fulfil a vow. Sometimes too a wedding was arranged to take place just before the *hajj*, and the whole bridal party went on pilgrimage together, so that the marriage should begin auspiciously. Conversely, no one went to one of the great Pirs during the first year after a death in the family, when sorrow still clung to him.

The mountain shrines consisted essentially of sacred rocks in high and lonely places, and in going up to them each year the Yazdis appeared to be maintaining an age-old observance which existed long before the establishment of sacred fires, being inherited by Zoroastrianism from pagan times. In the early days of the faith, it seems, there were two main acts of worship required of the individual, namely praying daily in the presence of hearth-fire or the sun, and joining in seasonal ascents into the mountains, where sacrifice would be offered to the divine beings. This latter observance was recorded of the Persians by Herodotus in the fifth century B.C., when he wrote:[7] 'It is not their custom to make and set up statues and temples and altars . . . but . . . they offer sacrifices on the highest peaks of the mountains.' There is no trace of any ancient edifices at the Yazdi mountain shrines, and the Islamic period was probably well advanced before each sacred rock was covered by a small domed mud-brick building, which gave it the conventional appearance of a humble Moslem *imām-zāde*, or tomb of a local saint. The Zoroastrians probably first created such buildings in order to gain some recognition of their holy places, and naturally by now no tradition survives of a time when the sacred rocks were open to the sky. The original shrine-buildings were very modest ones, tiny and dark, with thick walls, and either a very low door, or a very narrow one, impassable for the fat. The pilgrims, it seems, slept either in rough shelters nearby, or on the open mountainside, among their tethered donkeys. Then, as conditions became less harsh for the Zoroastrians, more solid mud-brick buildings were put up to shelter man and beast; and later still, as the community flourished, the tiny mud-brick shrines were replaced by larger, more dignified edifices in baked brick and stone, which still looked agreeably modest and unassertive in the vastness of their mountain settings. Further, pious individuals, or villages acting collectively, built pleasant pavilions where pilgrims could stay, sheltered from heat and cold, and these now cluster round the shrines. They again are unostentatious, and in no way isolate pilgrims from the immensity of the mountains, and the sense of awe which this induces.

During the centuries of oppression—as probably in the remoter past also—the mountain shrines were left in solitude between times of pilgrimage, for there were only the sacred rocks there and the humble little buildings over them, nothing that could be stolen or harmed. But when the dignified new shrines were erected it became usual to appoint a guardian or 'khadem' to live there all the year round, keeping a lamp lit in the sanctuary by night, and caring for

[7] *History*, i. 131.

the buildings and for the vessels which were given to the Pir as charitable bequests. This post tended (like most others) to become hereditary, and several families in the region accordingly took the surname of Khadem or Khademi. Up till the 1920s the office could be dangerous as well as lonely, and about a hundred years ago a guardian of Pir-e Sabz was tortured and burnt to death by robbers who thought that he held the secret of hidden treasure; and on other occasions a khadem only saved his life by flight when bandits approached.[8]

The first of the annual pilgrimages, beginning seventeen days after the spring No Ruz, was to Pir-e Hrišt, the mountain shrine nearest to Sharifabad. Even travelling by traditional means, that is, on foot or donkey-back, the Sharifabadis could reach there in about three hours. The sacrificial animal (a sheep or goat) often rode most of the way, lying comfortably across a saddle. The track from the village went first by fields and orchards, and then out into rough shingle desert. There was a water-tank along the desert-stretch, built not long previously to help pilgrims; and after that the track began to climb a little, and at last wound round the foot of a hill, the Kuh-e Surkh,[9] and suddenly the Pir was visible. The shrine was on the crest of a ridge which thrust up from the shingle of a little plain set in an oval of mountains—a sheltered natural arena where once a vast congregation could have gathered on all sides of the sacred rock. The mountain of Hrišt towered up beyond the hill of the shrine, and was a landmark from afar, but the sanctuary at its foot was wholly secluded, and could only be seen after one had entered its arena. Once there, one could oneself see nothing but the shrine, mountains, and the sky.

The sacred rock was a slightly sloping, fissured slab at the highest point of the hill's crest, an admirable natural altar. The little mud-brick

---

[8] Thus when at the turn of the century a notorious robber, Husayn Kaši, led his band to Pir-e Sabz one year to lie in wait for the pilgrims, the two khadems heard their horses' hooves (Zoroastrians were not allowed to ride horses) and fled to a cave higher up the mountain. Rumour of danger reached the villages, and Sharifabad sent one Sorush to scout ahead. When he did not return, the pilgrimage was abandoned. The disgruntled thieves left in the end with the shrine-vessels and Sorush, whom they had captured; but they had not gone far before a quarrel broke out among them, there was a fight, and a number were killed. The survivors attributed the misfortune to having stolen consecrated vessels, so they abandoned these to Sorush and rode away. He buried the vessels in the desert and walked home, and eventually they were all recovered.

[9] See above, p. 159.

chapel first made to enclose it had been rebuilt some twenty years earlier, in baked brick. Because of the position it could not be enlarged, but an outer room was added, along the ridge of the hill, and a terrace was created below it on which worshippers could gather.[10] A wide brick stairway was made leading up to this terrace, replacing rough steps cut in the rock, and at the foot of the sacred hill there was a cluster of pavilions and two tanks for storing rainwater—for Hrišt was the only one of the great Pirs which had no natural spring, and of old pilgrims had to bring all the water they needed on camel-back.

The rites of pilgrimage remained unchanged, regardless of any embellishments of the holy place; and they appeared to be very ancient. An essential part of the *hajj* was the offering of blood sacrifice. The old orthodox Zoroastrian teaching in this respect is that in the present imperfect world, corrupted as it is by Ahriman, men must kill in order to live themselves; but they must limit the wrong which they thus do to animals by slaying them as mercifully as possible, and always consecrating them first—that is, offering them sacrificially to the divine beings—since by this means only the body is killed, and the creature's spirit is released to live on and nourish the species. To eat meat other than from a sacrifice—thereby destroying the creature's spirit—was held to be a grievous sin down to very recent times. In case this practice seems to set Zoroastrianism apart among the great living religions, one should perhaps remind oneself that Islam too practices blood sacrifice, and even in slaughterhouses Moslem butchers are required to dedicate the animals to Allah before they are slain. Blood sacrifice is by no means incompatible with a highly ethical faith, and by Zoroastrian doctrine represents indeed a respect for the animal kingdom.[11]

[10] See Pl. VIIIb. For a ground-plan of the enlarged shrine see G. Gropp, 'Die rezenten Feuertempel der Zarathustrier (II)', *AMI*, N.F. IV, 1971, 283.

[11] The Yazdis used the Moslem word, *qurbān*, 'sacrifice', for the blood offering, and the simpler people felt no qualms at all about the rite, which to them was a fit and natural expression of devotion; but since the beginning of the century the leaders of their community have been aware of ever-mounting pressures, first from Bombay and then from Tehran, to end the observance. Feeling against it among the Parsis has been intensified by the influences of Hinduism and theosophy, which have led relatively large numbers of them to the mistaken belief that vegetarianism forms part of Zoroastrian orthopraxy. These Parsis accordingly attack blood sacrifice both as cruel and as of Moslem origin. Under this assault the Yazdis were insisting in the 1960s on the charitable aspects of the rite, which (as they truly said) was a *khairat*, and benefited the poor and deserving.

The sheep and goats which the Sharifabadis brought to Pir-e Hrišt were in general used to living among people, and accepted all the ritual placidly. They were carefully fed and watered, and usually spent the night comfortably in the corner of a pavilion. Sacrifice was generally offered soon after sunrise, and always before noon, since it had to be made during the first watch of the day, which was under the protection of Mihr. It was usual to adorn the sacrificial beast with coloured ribands or a kerchief (preferably green) tied round its horns or neck. A procession formed, led by musicians. Usually it was tambourines and drums which were played, but sometimes also the *surna*, with its wild stirring music, fit for a mountain setting. After the musicians came the sacrificial beast, either led or carried shoulder-high up the stairway, followed by a throng of worshippers, who shouted and clapped their hands.[12] The old custom was that the animal was led or carried several times withershins around the sacred rock itself, but with the extended buildings this was no longer possible, and instead it was taken round the pillar-altar in the outer room. Those who followed often scattered dried marjoram over both animal and sacrificer, so that man and beast emerged from the shrine sprinkled with little pale-green leaves. Then the animal was brought down the stairway again to a place apart, was consecrated with recital of Avestan, and swiftly slain.[13] Formerly this was done by a priest, but by the 1960s the task was of necessity assigned to a respected layman. Hens also were often sacrificed at Pir-e Hrišt, and they likewise were carried round the pillar-altar in the outer shrine-room.[14] It was usual for an animal to be dedicated to the shrine long before it was brought there for sacrifice,[15] and this was sometimes done with hens also. Thus at the Panji gahambar in the house of Tahmina Khanom's parents there were three half-grown chicks running about, and one with curly feathers had already been dedicated to Pir-e Hrišt four or five years later.

[12] See Pl. VIIIa.

[13] For the Avesta and ritual see '*Ātaš-zōhr* . . .', 109. The contrite kiss on the animal's cheek was a fixed part of the ritual; and once, before the sheep were taken down the stairway, one for some reason turned back into the shrine, and a man pushed it gently down the steps again and kissed its cheek as he did so.

[14] Before the brick terrace was built, in the 1940s, it was the custom to cut the birds' throats outside the shrine itself, and to toss the fluttering bodies down the steep rocks, to be gathered up below. This rite had almost been put an end to, and I saw only one youth perform it on his own.

[15] See 'Mihragān . . .', 108.

The flesh of the sacrificial animal could not be roasted at a mountain shrine, but was seethed (just as Herodotus described) in a cauldron. The custom of Hrišt for the Sharifabadis was that only a quarter of the meat need be consumed convivially at the shrine. Another quarter must be given to the poor, and to the servants of the community, but the remainder could be taken home for household use, though the devout sometimes gave it all away in an act of supererogation. Naturally a ritual share must be given to a dog, and often Sharifabadis brought dogs along with them, though the guardian of the shrine kept a fine animal of his own. The ceremonial dish of *sirog* was regularly cooked and taken up to the inner shrine-room, to make *boy-o-brang* by the sacred rock itself, and such offerings were part of the perquisites of the khadem.

Sacrifice is essentially an act of giving, an offering to the divine beings which is shared with one's fellows; and the other rites of pilgrimage were variations on ways of giving, both of worship and material offerings. Pilgrims from Sharifabad usually reached the shrine in the afternoon, and as soon as they had unloaded and watered their animals, and settled into one of the pavilions, they climbed up the sacred hill. Containers of water were kept on the terrace, so that all could make the ritual ablutions before they entered the outer shrine-room and said the košti-prayers. Then in a state of purity and grace they passed on into the inner room and the presence of the sacred rock. This room would have been wholly dark but for a lamp set in a niche above the rock, and the many candles which pilgrims lit and put beside it.[16] Some also burnt frankincense and scattered dried marjoram and rue. There was an almost continuous murmur of Avestan there during pilgrimage time, for then both men and women tried to say the five sets of daily prayers, and the devout recited other Avestan texts too, and also *monājāt*—prayers composed in Persian.

As well as praying in the shrine-room, pilgrims also obeyed the Zoroastrian instinct to worship in the open, especially towards sunset, standing on the ridge of the sacred hill; and sometimes as they did so they cast a handful of grain on the dome of the shrine—an act which they explained as an offering to the Pir which also

[16] Formerly the candles were put directly on the rock itself. But after a legend was evolved for the shrine (see below, p. 267), a pious person dreamt that the heat of the candles distressed the princess to whom it was held to be devoted, and thereafter the rock was enclosed with a broad metal surround, on which the candles were placed.

fed the wild birds. (Neat little grey-brown birds, like rock-pipits, came about the shrine, and occasionally a dove.) Women often performed the rite of Nakhod-e mošgel-gošay in the shrine-porch, and younger people used to sing and dance in the shrine itself, especially in the evenings, in the same joyous fashion as at the village sanctuaries.

Since Hrišt is so close to Sharifabad, the villagers often went there at other times as well as during the *hajj*—indeed it was the only mountain shrine whose pavilions had winter quarters, that is, side-rooms with doors which could be shut against the cold. There was a regular rite to ensure one's speedy return, which was to build a little pillar of stones, when one left, on the side of the Kuh-e Surkh, or to add stones to one of the small cairns there. (Erdeshir Qudusi always made what he called a 'soul-house', *khāne-ye ravān*, with three stones to each of its walls, and a big one for the roof.)[17] One especially popular time to visit Hrišt was in the autumn, to give thanks for the harvest which had been gathered in, and by offering sacrifice to help ensure good crops in the coming year; but individuals went then according to the pattern of their own farm-work, and not in a concerted body as at the spring pilgrimage.[18] Since the shrine was so near, many of the villagers still travelled there on donkey-back, rather than by lorry or jeep, and the tethered animals made the nights noisy with their braying. Even without this disturbance, not much sleep was possible during the *hajj* itself. There was a great holiday feeling then in the air, and a sense that time was wasted spent in sleeping which could better be devoted to prayer or jollity, with all the opportunities which the occasion offered for meeting relatives and friends from other villages. In earlier times there was a great deal of music-making, with stringed instruments and all kinds of pipes and flutes, as well as tambourine and drum; but by 1964 the transistor radio was beginning to encroach on this. Singing and story-telling still went on, however, and the men spent much time playing cards, and occasionally the old Persian game of *nard*, often sitting up far into the night, while the women, who still had work to do, snatched some sleep. In warm weather many chose to sleep on the roofs of the pavilions, and among the joys of pilgrimage

[17] Cf. the funerary usage, above, p. 152.

[18] Thus a man often went with his family when he had hung up his plough for the year; but a favoured day was Ruz Mihr of Aban Mah in the traditional calendar, which in 1964 coincided with 12 November. This day was presumably preferred because Mihr Ized was lord of the harvest (see 'Mihragān . . .', 113–14).

were the cool mountain air, the starry skies, and the sense of space
and emptiness compared with the close crowding of their village
homes.

By day men and youngsters sometimes enjoyed the unfamiliar
setting more actively, making expeditions during the long empty
hours of late morning or afternoon into the mountains round about.
Thus one day Agha Rustam led a little group of us—Shahnaz,
Piruza, Gushtasp, myself, and half a dozen eager small boys—up
into the Sangāb-e Rustam, a cleft cut through the rocks by storm-
waters. There had been good rain and snow that winter, and there
was still a little stream running down the cleft, with spring flowers—
yellow and purple and white—along its course, and mint and
marjoram to give out their fragrance as we brushed their leaves.
There were no fish in the pools, which dried out completely in
summer, but an elegant yellow wagtail flitted ahead of us from stone
to stone. The air was cool and clear, and Gushtasp, shouting with
joy, raised a splendid echo from the mountains above.

Such pleasures were more varied and extensive at the higher,
remoter shrines. One of these was, like Hrišt, under the care of
the Sharifabadi Anjoman, namely Pir-e Bānū-Pārs, the 'Shrine of the
Lady of Pars'. This, perhaps once the greatest of the Yazdi Pirs,
was in the mountains at the north-western end of the plain, and its
hajj had come to be early in July. The old donkey-track to it struck
off the highway to Isfahan a few miles north of Sharifabad, climbed
over a low mountain ridge and dropped down into a dry river-bed,
strewn with huge boulders. This led up into the higher mountains
and eventually to the shrine itself. The journey from Sharifabad
to the shrine used to take just over twenty-four hours; and the
custom was for the main body of pilgrims from Yazd and the
southern villages, led by their priests, to arrive at Sharifabad
the day before the *hajj*, and to sleep there in houses and orchards.
Then the whole band would set off together about three hours before
dawn, and arrive at the shrine just before dawn on the following
day, having spent the midday heat resting in the shade of wild almond
and fig trees on the hillsides. In the past it was prudent to travel
thus in large groups, to reduce the danger of molestation; and pilgrimages were in general a great means of fostering solidarity among
the Zoroastrians, with news being exchanged between villages,
marriages arranged, and friendships kept in good repair. In the
dangerous years the pilgrims were mostly men, with a sprinkling

of boys and redoubtable matrons; but sometimes a father would take a favourite small daughter with him, for whom the experience would be an especial wonder and delight. Dogs sensibly joined the cortège in numbers, to enjoy the ritual offerings, and they helped to guard it against thieves and wild beasts; but even so a middle-aged woman told me how her father had been in a pilgrim band which was set on by armed robbers on the way to Banu-Pars and stripped of everything—donkeys, bedding, food, and most of their own clothing.

All this had become a matter of recollection only. The ways had been made safe under the Pahlavi dynasty, and modern pilgrims to the shrine boarded lorries or ramshackle buses in their own villages, which travelled further north up the highway, entered the dry river-bed where it opens on to the plain, and somehow managed to clatter and lurch their way up to the shrine. In doing so they trundled pilgrims past the 'Stone of the Curse' (*Sang-e la'nat*), a big free-standing boulder which formerly everyone struck and abused in passing. For there was a legend attached to the shrine of Banu-Pars.[19] This runs as follows: when the last Sasanian king of Persia, Yaz-degird III, was fleeing with his family from the invading Arabs, his daughter, Banu-Pars, came alone to the head of the Yazdi plain. Here, faint with thirst, she begged for a drink from a peasant. He milked his cow for her, but just as the bowl was full the animal kicked it from his hands, and, the pursuit drawing near, she had to go on with parched throat. She turned into the mountains (the old pilgrim-track is said to follow her steps) and stumbled up the dry river-bed. She begged the 'Stone of the Curse' to open and take her in, but it remained unmoved. She went on further and further into the mountains, and at last, despairing, cried out to Ohrmazd for help, and he opened the rock before her and she hastened in, never to be seen again; but a piece of her dress was caught, it is said, by the closing stone, and old people declared that their grandparents spoke of having seen the fragment of cloth, before the piety of pilgrims wore it away.

This legend closely resembles one attached to the Moslem shrine of Bībī Shahrbānū, the 'Lady of the Land', set high on a hillside overlooking the old city of Ray, to the south of Tehran. Only there the Sasanian princess is said to have been married to Husayn, son

[19] On this legend and its evolution, see in more detail 'Bībī Shahrbānū and the Lady of Pārs'.

of ʿAli, and to have been taken living into the rock to save her from
ʿUmmayyad troops, pursuing her after Husayn's death at the battle
of Karbala. It has been shown that this shrine at Ray was probably
dedicated originally to Anāhīd, the Zoroastrian yazad known to her
devotees as 'the Lady', whose ancient sanctuary was thus consecrated
anew for Moslem worshippers, who continue to pray and sacrifice
there to this day. The strong probability—one can almost say
certainty—is that the 'Lady' of the Pir-e Banu-Pars was also Anahid,
and that in course of time the Yazdi Zoroastrians adapted the
legend shaped for her northern sanctuary to their own holy place.[20]
It was a legend which must have held a powerful attraction for them,
since it linked their beloved shrine with the last Zoroastrian king
of Persia, who, they believed, traced his descent back to Vištasp, the
first ruler on earth to have adopted the faith of their prophet. So,
they thought, he had divine grace with him; and the tale of his
daughter's sufferings, lonely and exhausted by the pursuit of a pitiless
foe, embodied both the community's sorrow for the fate of their
kings, and their own sadness as a persecuted minority, with centuries-
old memories of massacre, rape, and forced conversion. Moreover,
according to the legend Ohrmazd intervened in his mercy to save
the princess in the very sight of the heathen Arabs. There was thus
faith and hope in the legend also. So although as they approached
the shrine pilgrims thought of the fugitive princess, and expressed
their pity and grief for her, yet once they reached it they were
able to rejoice in her escape and be merry again, as Zoroastrians
should be.

Anahid is a yazad of the waters, and she could have had no
more magnificent natural sanctuary than at Banu-Pars. Here the
sacred rock is part of an outcrop of stone which forms a platform
a few feet above a wide river-bed. Two other river-courses join this
one just below the shrine, and though now there is ordinarily only

[20] G. Gropp, 'Die Derbent-Inschriften und das Adur Gušnasp', *Monumentum
H.S. Nyberg*, i, Leiden, 1975, 321, has challenged this, on the grounds that none
of the Zoroastrians whom he questioned knew of an association between the
shrine and Anahid. It is likely, however, that the legend associating the sanctuary
with the fictive Sasanian princess was shaped already by the tenth century A.D.,
a matter of almost 1,000 years ago. The legend was clearly carefully fostered and
ardently believed, so it is hardly reasonable to look for memories of an older
dedication some thirty-three generations later. The continual popularity in the
Yazdi region of the traditional girl's name Āb-Nahīd (Dari Ōw-Nair), 'Anahid
of the Waters', is, however, a stubborn witness to the existence there once of the
yazad's cult.

a trickle of water in them, still at times of rain and storm a fierce flood, flowing off the high mountains to the south, rushes through the three channels and joins yet a fourth which comes in lower down. A great mountain ridge then blocks their path, and the combined torrent is forced to swing north and churn round this barrier and out on to the plain—thus cutting the river-bed which pilgrims travel up in dry July. Those who have seen the rivers in spate earlier in the year say that both sight and sound are tremendous; and even in the driest summers there is always water at the shrine itself, for there is an unfailing spring just above the sacred rock, which bubbles up to fill a little pool there. The mountain-ridge which deflects the main torrent lower down shuts off the whole area from the distant plain, and on the hillsides around the sacred rock a great congregation could once have gathered, as at Hrišt; but here they would have gazed down at ceremonies conducted by the waters, instead of upwards at hill and sky.

I first visited Banu-Pars in company with Agha Rustam and a few of his family and friends during the spring holiday of 1964. The guardian of the shrine, Bahram Khademi (who was headmaster of the Sharifabadi boys' school), came with us, and so did D. Hormezdyar, a priest who was troubled a little in his mind, and did no regular priestly work, but spent most of the year wandering on foot between the villages and mountain shrines. By a happy mischance our jeep foundered in the river-bed, not far from the 'Stone of the Curse', and we had to finish our journey on foot, walking up through the thickets of wild almonds, which were in full flower, scenting the air. As we climbed past a flock of foraging goats we came to little terraced cornfields, stone-walled, and showing bright green against the bare hillsides. Then tiny orchards appeared, of apricot and pomegranate and apple trees in bloom, their walls topped with dried thorn-bushes to discourage jackals; and above them on the hillside to the left was the hamlet of Zardju, some twenty houses huddled protectively together. Its inhabitants, a goodlooking, kindly people, lived (as one of them put it) 'hidden from God', in poverty and isolation; and in their need they had gradually appropriated a handful of tiny fields, the Mazraᶜ-e Pir, which had once belonged to the shrine. Despite this, they and the Zoroastrians were on good terms, and they welcomed the summer *hajj*, when they were able to sell a few things to the pilgrims. Bahram Khademi's mother-in-law lived in Zardju, as his representative, for a month at a time (alternately with another elderly woman from Sharifabad), so that she could care for the sanctuary and light its lamp towards sunset each day. (Once it grew dark, she preferred to be back in the hamlet with the warmth of human companionship, for the mountain solitude could seem very menacing.)

The shrine itself was on the right bank, a little higher up than Zardju. The tiny old building, cramped and dark, had not been rebuilt until 1962 (for it was a difficult and costly business to bring men and materials up there for the work). Kai Khosrow-e Yadgar of Sharifabad[21] told me that he had made his first pilgrimage to Banu-Pars as a boy in 1914, on the eve of departing for Bombay, and well remembered creeping through a dark passage to the dark little shrine-room, where there was just space for two or three worshippers and a small pillar-altar beside the sacred rock. Since there was more level ground here than at Hrišt, the new shrine was larger, but still modestly proportioned, consisting of a round, domed sanctuary and a rectangular outer hall. A flat table-altar had been set over the sacred rock, but this was raised on three legs, so that pilgrims could still stoop to touch the rock itself and lay their offerings directly on it, if they wished. Every pilgrim brings some offering, large or small, to a mountain Pir, as to a village shrine; and that spring some had plucked sprays of white almond-blossom to place on the rock, together with cypress-twigs brought from the plain; and as they did this they greeted the Pīr devoutly and turned to encourage one another with the salutation 'May your pilgrimage be accepted!'

Men and women alike said the košti-prayers, and other Avestan. Then some walked over to Zardju to greet the villagers, and were in time to see the goats, reunited with their gambolling kids, being penned for the night; and returned as a full moon began to rise, to drink tea, and pray again, and sing in the shrine-room. The evening meal was a merry one, with wine and drinking of toasts, and we all went contentedly to our beds. There were seven pavilions around the sanctuary, but they were meant only for summer use and had no doors; so the men slept in the khadem's quarters and the rest of us in the hall of the shrine itself, while outside the moonlight poured down and the silence was unbroken.

Later that year, in July, Agha Rustam took us again to the

---

[21] See above, p. 126, and Pl. Ia.

shrine for the summer *hajj*, going a day early since it was the Moslem 'feast of the sacrifice' and a national holiday. The heat was then fierce in the plain, and the car-engine boiled twice before we even left the highway, so that it was evening before we crept up the formidable river-bed. The almond trees now bore ripe nuts on their upper branches (lower down they had been stripped by the goats), and the tiny cornfields were reaped and showed bare stubble. We were the first at the shrine, where we settled into the Sharifabadi pavilion, and many insects hastened to join us at our lamp-lit evening meal. There was a friendly glow of oven-fires from Zardju, and later the villagers held a *rōza-khānī* to celebrate their own festival, so many prayers went up from the mountainside that night. Another little group of Sharifabadis arrived in the small hours, having walked from the highway; and soon after sunrise the villagers, looking out from their hillside, raised a shout of welcome to a battered bus which crawled valiantly up to the shrine and disgorged an astonishing number of pilgrims—from Aliabad and Narseabad, Nusratabad and Moriabad—who scattered themselves about the other pavilions. One of these belonged to the priests, who had built it for their own use; but for the first time ever (it was said) no priests came on the *hajj* that year from Yazd, and only the roving D. Hormezdyar was there to perform their rites for the pilgrims. Nor were there as many of the laity as in previous years, although in the evening of that first day the local jeep arrived packed with pilgrims from Sharifabad and Mazraᶜ Kalantar, and hastened away at once to fetch more, so that our pavilion became full, and the whole place grew animated, with greetings and comings and goings between the shrine and pavilions. Prayer and singing and dancing went on far into the night, and the sounds came pleasantly to us as we lay on the roof under the glorious stars, with nightjars churring as they hawked to and fro for the insects attracted by the lamps.

In the early morning the villagers from Zardju added to the usual pilgrim bustle by coming to sell what little they had—tiny roasted almonds, little baskets woven from almond shoots, firewood, dried herbs, a handful of eggs, some goats' meat. (At that time of year they had almost no milk from their goats, and lived themselves largely on thin corn-gruel.) One man from Moriabad bought a live goat, and this was offered at the Pir with full ceremony. Formerly the custom was to sacrifice bulls and cows at Banu-Pars, a great offering for impoverished villagers; and it was held that this was done in retribution for the act of the animal which kicked over the milk before the princess could drink it. The cow, was, however, of old the due sacrifice to 'Anahid of the waters', and so, it seems, the ancient offering was maintained down the centuries at this her former shrine, the legend being adapted to accommodate the ritual. The practice naturally shocked the Parsis when they encountered it in the nineteenth century, for they had learnt a Hindu abhorrence for killing cows; and their agent, Manekji Limji Hataria, persuaded the Yazdis to abandon it. He made no objection, however, to their substituting the usual offerings of sheep and goats, which continued here as at the other shrines.

The next day more pilgrims came by car from Ahrestan and Moriabad, so that there were about a hundred met together in all—not many, but enough to make the seven pavilions cheerfully full. The women's work kept them for hours in the hot kitchens, but for others Banu-Pars offered shade and beauty on every side—so much so that one Tehrani girl (there for the first time with village relatives) declared that she wished she could remain for ever. Round the shrine itself there were big old mulberry trees, and the almonds gave patches of shade everywhere. Until some fifty years earlier there had also been a noble plane tree growing by the pool above the rock, which was much loved and venerated; but a *sayyid* from Aghda, a notably *na-najib* town nearby, maliciously had it cut down. (He died before the Zoroastrians could take legal action against him, which they regarded as divine retribution.) So the pool itself was no longer shaded, but was nevertheless much resorted to for its prettiness and the pleasant sound of running water. From the rocky slopes above the shrine one could see jagged peaks and torn river-channels with their huge boulders; and there was the lovely Tutgin valley to explore on the further side of Zardju. Here between almond thickets and wild fig trees one would come on tiny fields walled in with careful labour. Little breezes blew constantly down it, and the air was sweet with the scent of herbs.

In earlier days bold spirits sometimes pressed on to the head of this valley and over the mountains for some ten or twelve miles, until (if they had followed the right track) they came to the Shekaft-e Yazdān, the 'Cleft of God'. This was entered by a hole high up in a mountainside—itself a steep and frightening climb, D. Khodadad told us. The hole was hardly bigger than a door, but opened into an immense cavern; and at the further end of this was a low passage-way, out of which a wind always rushed, extinguishing lamps and candles. This passage, he said, was believed to lead down to the cavern where the heroes of the faith lie asleep, waiting for the last battle to be fought at the end of time; and so to go to the cave and pray was a highly meritorious act, and caused all one's sins to be forgiven (a statement which Agha Rustam promptly and vigorously challenged as flat superstition).

The battered Aliabadi bus arrived again in the late afternoon of the fourth day, to take its passengers to spend a night at Pir-e Hrišt before they returned home. Somehow they were all loaded in once more, together with a goat and a hen that had been bought to offer at Hrišt. (As the hen's legs were tied together, Banu-Pars's name was invoked over her.) While we were waving them off, Pouran nearly trod on a dust-coloured snake, which the men then pursued and killed. Earlier Shehriar, D. Khodadad's son, had slain a big, crab-like tarantula that emerged from the stone wall by the pool, but in general the insect life, however aggressive, was simply endured.

When the Dastur dasturan lived at Turkabad, at the northern end of the plain, Banu-Pars was probably resorted to more than any other of the great Pirs. It is certainly the only one to be mentioned in the old letters which the Irani priests wrote to their co-religionists in India.[22] After the removal of the priests to Yazd, however, it became relatively remote for them, though the fact that they built their own pavilion there shows how firmly it remained in their affections. By the 1960s, however, for a variety of reasons, the most popular pilgrimage of all had come to be to Pir-e Sabz, a dramatically beautiful sanctuary on the other, north-eastern side of the plain, about half-way between Sharifabad and the city. Here the sacred rock is high up on the steep face of a great square-shouldered lime-stone mountain, beside a pool of water. This pool is fed by a spring that flows, seemingly miraculously, out of the bare cliff above. The course of the trickling water is green with maidenhair fern, which the Zoroastrians call *parr-e syāvušān*, and there are fat black fishes in the little pool. This shrine too may well have been dedicated of old to 'Anahid of the Waters', and in time a legend came to be attached to it also, which was that another daughter of Yazdegird, called Hayat Banu, the 'Lady of Life' (perhaps a cult name of the yazad, Arab-icized) was taken here living into the rock, like her sister Banu-Pars.

[22] See *Riv.*, Unvala, ii. 159.3; Dhabhar, 593.

The maidenhair fern is said to be her hair, and a huge old plane tree which shades the sacred rock is held to have grown from a stick on which she leant, and which she thrust into the ground before vanishing. This tree was believed to catch fire and renew itself, phoenix-like, every thousand years, and its great hollow trunk (which two men could hardly span with outstretched arms) was undoubtedly blackened and burnt. Beside it new stems had sprung up, and with them the tree, still vigorous, formed a lovely curtain of dappled green over the shrine, its long trailing branches hanging down the mountainside to far below its own bole.

There was another beloved tree by the pool, a giant willow which age had bent right over so that trunk and branches spread across the water and down the rocks beyond. When pavilions were being built below the pool, one man decided to remove this willow, and cut away a section of the trunk, some six feet long, from its roots to where it rested on the further edge of the pool; but as he hewed the sap ran out as red as blood, and he stopped his work, and a few months later was dead. No one else dared lay hand to what remained of the tree, and when spring came it brought a seeming miracle, for the huge upper trunk with its many branches, though severed from its roots, put out fresh leaves, and years later it was still beautifully alive, spreading a curtain of interlacing branches under the higher canopy of the plane. The reason must be that the severed section was kept moist by the continual splash of the waterfall, and the tree lived from this moisture; but it is small wonder that it was regarded with awe and reverence, as having been saved by the Pir. There were other trees around the pool which were also venerated: a big myrtle, which grew from the rock-face above, and a younger willow, to whose branches pilgrims tied ribands after making vows, or to ensure a return to the shrine. (At Banu-Pars the ribands were tied to the tall legs of the table-altar over the sacred rock.) There was also a wild fig at the pool, grafted to bear fine fruit, and a rose-bush and sweet pomegranates. The third great tree of Pir-e Sabz grew on the edge of one of the terraces. This was a tall slender cypress, some hundred and twenty years old, which raised a noble spear of green against the red-grey rocks behind it.

The sanctuary thus fully merited its name of the 'Green Shrine'; and its canopy of shade was a special source of wonder and delight in that bare mountain setting, where in summer the limestone rocks baked till they were too hot to touch. Its *hajj* was in June, when the sun was at its height; and Agha Rustam had us at the mountain foot soon after dawn on Zamyad Ruz of Tir Mah, the first day of the pilgrimage. There were many others already at the shrine, and the hubbub of voices came faintly down to us on the valley floor. We paused in traditional fashion to eat something before beginning the climb; and as we sat looking up at the honey-comb of terraces and little buildings (for there were seventeen pavilions at this beloved shrine, clinging like some Tibetan monas-tery to the rock-face), Agha Rustam was led to reminisce about old times—that is, up to some thirty years earlier, when motor vehicles were still unknown to Yazd. Then it was a full twenty-four hour journey to the shrine for the most southerly villages, and even the Sharifabadis used to travel all through the night. They sent an advance party the night before with donkeys laden with food and bedding; and some of this party would return with the donkeys, and the main band of pilgrims would set off in the cool of the even-ing, heading straight across the desert. If the night were dark, the leader of the caravan sometimes played the *surna*, to keep them together, and occasionally lit a flare-fire along the way. They halted at a water-tank made by one Shehriar, a distant kinsman of Agha Rustam's, and then pressed on to reach the mountain just before dawn. Some would bring with them white cocks, a living offering which was made only at Pir-e Sabz (together with the usual sacrifice of sheep and goats). Orthodox Zoroastrians would never kill a cock of any colour, since he is the bird of Sroš, who crows to put an end to demon-haunted night and to bring in God's new day; and white being the Zoroastrian colour, a white cock was especially holy, and the Yazdi custom was to bring such birds (which are not unduly common) to this mountain shrine. There they were kept in a shed near the upper pavilion, and the dawn was full of their crowing. (In Kerman the custom was to take them to the shrine of Shah Varahram Ized, within the city.)

At the shrine the Sharifabadis met pilgrim bands from the other villages, all arriving in orderly fashion on the first day of the *hajj*. They occupied their own pavilions, and to these they would invite one another in turn in the cool of early evening. Guests were received with formality at a cloth laden with fruit and nuts, wine was offered, and toasts were drunk to benefactors, living and dead. As the party grew livelier, men sang in turns, or played instruments, or told stories. (Women, though present, took no active part.) As the

evening wore on, the cloth would be removed, and there would be
dancing and mime. Supper was eaten about midnight, and most
people went to their beds at one or two in the morning. Not everyone
chose to be so convivial, however. One man from Moriabad, for
instance, slept early and rose when the last revellers were in bed;
and then for two or three hours he would softly play a *kamunče*, a
one-stringed fiddle, in the star-lit darkness, with the trickling of
water for accompaniment. Agha Rustam said that he used to lie
awake listening to him with delight, until the white cocks began to
crow, and it was time for everyone to rouse themselves to say the
dawn prayers. After the noonday prayers it was the custom to take
a long siesta in the summer heat, and so the days passed in an orderly
mixture of piety and pleasure. There were then (Agha Rustam
remarked a shade wistfully) no young children at the *hajj* to care for
and be noisy. However, the donkeys were almost as restless, and
with some thousand of them tethered up and down the mountainside
and in the stables the braying and fighting were impressive.

On that day in 1964 there were instead a few buses and lorries
at the mountain-foot, quiet at least in repose, and some Moslem
porters from Ardekan, come to earn a little money by carrying
heavy loads up to the shrine. There were one or two *jadids* among
them from Mazraᶜ (who had once been *seft*, I was told, but had
repented), and a respectable-looking elderly man who approached
Agha Rustam and greeted him courteously, inquiring after his
health. It was only later that Agha Rustam told us that this was
Sayyid Gulab, who lived in a village nearby, and who as a young
man had shot the guardian of the shrine and made off with the
sanctuary vessels to sell in Yazd. On the way he was stopped by
gendarmes, who seeing the words *pir* and *vaq f* on his booty arrested
him. The vessels were returned to the shrine, the wounded khadem,
one Dadiset from Mazraᶜ, spent a month in hospital, and Sayyid
Gulab four years in jail. Dadiset himself had died, a centenarian,
only a little previously. His other claim to fame was that once during
Panji he had climbed the Pir-e Sabz mountain, and had found it
nobly flat-topped, a towering giant among the surrounding peaks.

We meantime had only the short, stiff ascent before us to the
shrine itself, and it was not long before we reached the fringes of
pilgrim activity. A camel had been hauled up before us to that
height, and sat by the path sardonically chewing its cud and causing
alarm to townspeople. For this, unlike the gathering at Banu-Pars,

was a mixed, indeed a cosmopolitan throng, with Zoroastrians from Kerman, Tehran, Abadan, and other Iranian cities, and even one or two Parsis, mingling with the local pilgrims. This diversity caused some shocks to the village girls, who encountered for the first time women who went bare-headed and in short, sleeveless dresses. The boys too had their surprises, and Gushtasp, who had run lightly on ahead, came flying back, wide-eyed, to say that there were *bamerds* (Moslems) asleep in the Sharifabadi pavilion. When we reached there, however, they proved to be young men from the Tehrani 'Sāzmān-e Farōhar' (a Zoroastrian society), one of whom was dressed from head to foot in black, thus causing Gushtasp's consternation. The reason why Pir-e Sabz attracted so many seemed to be partly its striking beauty (more immediately impressive than that of the other shrines), partly ease of access; for its mountain rises sharply from the valley floor not far from the main highway to Yazd, and the journey there was by more or less level ways, so that vehicles could be driven with little hazard to the mountain's foot. The pavilions accordingly were packed, and though this was a source of joy to the pilgrims, as contributing to a worthy act of veneration, there were inevitably minor discomforts, such as queues at the baths (made in the old donkey stables), where travellers sought to make ablution before approaching the Pir, and others at the communal ovens and cooking places.

Six priests had come to the shrine that year from Yazd, and they occupied their own pavilion, which was just above the Sharifabadi one. They, like the solitary fiddler of old, took no part in the convivial side of the pilgrimage, but ate their meals separately and in silence, and rose long before dawn to recite Avesta, the steady murmur of their prayers drifting down the mountainside to us through the sound of falling water. When the white cocks began to crow, many of the laity rose and contributed their prayers also, standing on the terraces and facing the brightening sky in the east. By day the priests sat for hours on the low terrace outside the shrine itself, above the pool, and there pilgrims sought them out to recite Avestan for them. Often they wanted special prayers against sickness or misfortune, and while these were being said priest and sufferer would make *paivand* with a košti. One text much recited then was the *Bahram Yašt*, potent to bring aid against all evils.

The sanctuary itself is the smallest of the mountain Pirs, and is always dark and cool, for the sacred rock is in a recess beside the pool. The round sanctuary, whose small dome almost touches the overhang (blackened by the smoke of centuries) has been rebuilt in brick and lined throughout with tiles, but it could not be enlarged except by a rectangular porch, reached by three high steps. During the *hajj* animation in and around it went in waves. Sometimes the Pir itself was crowded as well as the terrace outside, and the whole place was full of noise—not only from talk and prayer, but also from flute and drum and the clapping of hands, as a procession came surging up the stairway to the shrine bearing a sacrificial animal, and sometimes meeting another such procession coming joyfully down. Because of the steepness of the hillside the animals were always carried shoulder-high, and I watched one enterprising creature get hold of a mouthful of a woman's head-veil and nibble it vigorously as it was borne along. Then gradually the milling throng would melt away to the separate pavilions, to eat or sleep, or perhaps hold some ceremony there, and for a while the hubbub died down again almost into silence and mountain peace.

Although Pir-e Sabz was much more thronged than Banu-Pars, the crowd of pilgrims was more or less penned into the tiny oasis of the sanctuary itself, with its cluster of pavilions. There was only one expedition to be made, and that was by a rough track across the mountain face to a narrow, steep-sided valley, poetically named the *Bāgh-e Golzār* 'Garden of Flowers'. In the spring a stream ran down it and there were indeed flowers, but at the time of the *hajj* there was only a small reed-fringed pool left at the head of the valley, overhung by a willow and with leeches in it. The *haoma* plant (an ephedra) grew thickly round about, kept low by browsing sheep and goats, and in June the berries were showing red (rather like yew-berries) on the dark-green bushes. The bushes themselves were so plentiful that they were dried and used for burning, so that the Sharifabadi children hailed the plant as *hīδma-e hūm* ('*haoma*-firewood'), only the priests making use of it for ritual purposes. Rue and marjoram were also plentiful in the little valley, and were gathered by the villagers for use throughout the year.

Not many pilgrims cared for the hot, rough walk across to the valley, however, most preferring to enjoy the multifarious activities at the shrine itself. Apart from all the usual rites of pilgrimage, there were two bridal parties there that year, and they distributed sherbet and sweets, and exchanged presents between the families, these being carried head-high from one pavilion to the other in gay procession, with music and cheering. There was also a *sedra-pušun* for a girl of about ten from the village of Khorramshah. This took place on a terrace beneath the branches of the ancient willow, with nothing beyond but blue sky and the peaks of distant mountains. The girl, like the priest, was all in white, for Parsi influence in this respect had made itself felt in Yazd and the suburban villages. The simple ceremony attracted the lively interest of a number of Tehranis, some of whom did not wear the košti, and had never seen an investiture. Others, who did, sometimes wore the sacred cord in modified style. Thus one matron with a commanding air had hers slung like a baldric from one shoulder, over her short dress; and indeed some such modification becomes necessary with European clothes, for neither men nor women can untie and retie the košti with modesty and ease while wearing such garments. The local Zoroastrians seemed courteously tolerant of all such variations of practice, the only matters on which they insisted being that shoes must be left at the door of the sanctuary, and heads covered; and in 1963 a Yazdi established a benefaction whereby a constant supply of clean white kerchiefs was kept in the porch of the Pir, to be used by the bare-headed.

Another modern touch at the pilgrimage was that there were often Moslems about the terraces, from rifle-bearing gendarmes (sent, it seemed, for the Zoroastrians' own protection) to porters bowed under heavy loads, and vendors of firewood and even of food—sour milk distributed from black leather bags, and joints of goat's meat; for the Tehranis, disapproving of sacrifice as a part of worship, preferred to buy unconsecrated meat from Moslem butchers, who set up their stalls and slaughtering-places half-way up the mountainside. This trade in necessities was, however, the only commercial element even at Pir-e Sabz, the Zoroastrian shrines remaining blessedly free of the tawdry exploitation which mars the holy places of numerically greater faiths.

The offering of sacrifice was most frequent on the last two days of the *hajj*; but before then there was a good deal of coming and going by car, and one group of Tehranis was swept off in a 'pilgrim bus' which, having brought them to Pir-e Sabz for three days, then took them on to other mountain shrines within the week. The Sharifabadis, however, stayed for the full period of the *hajj*, and on the afternoon of the last day celebrated a communal gahambar on the terrace beside their pavilion, hanging, it seemed, in sheer space. This was their invariable practice, at Pir-e Sabz as at Hrišt. In the old days they would then have departed together that night on donkey-back, arriving home by the next dawn; and there is a little hollow to the south of Mazraᶜ which its villagers call the Tal-e sopra-kašun, the 'Cloth-spreading valley', for there the returning pilgrims used to stop to share a last meal at day-break, before separating to go about their ordinary affairs.

In those times of donkey-travel the Sharifabadis and their neighbours had to journey two days to make their pilgrimage to the southernmost shrines. One of these, Nāreke, is at the foot of a mountain of that name which towers over the broad, flat-floored valley of Gaigun. This runs from north-west to south-east in the mountains at the lower end of the Yazdi plain. For the Zoroastrian villagers to the south of Yazd it was a twelve-mile journey to the shrine. They used to ride their donkeys along the highway to Kerman, and then strike up the barren valley from its lower end, having a long, rough plod up it, but passing two tiny villages where they could get water. The Sharifabadis approached by the more dramatic route down the Pass of Gaigun at the valley's head. All who had once ridden this way had vivid memories of it, for the pass is so steep that even a pack-donkey had been known to lose its footing and roll abruptly to the bottom. The Sharifabadis reached the pass on the second day of their journey. The first they spent riding down the south-westerly side of the Yazdi plain, through a chain of fertile villages whose green fields and trees they much enjoyed; and by evening they reached the upland village of Taft, on the Yazd–Shiraz road. Here they would spend a blissfully cool night in the orchards of co-religionists, who plied them with delicious wine and fruits to supplement their traveller's fare of hard-bake and goat's cheese. There is a string of Zoroastrian villages between Taft and Yazd, and pilgrims would come up from there too, and a merry cavalcade would set off at dawn for the formidable pass. In 1964 the Taftis themselves still rode that way on donkey-back to Nareke, just as the Sharifabadis still rode to Hrišt; but by then the northern villagers used to go to Yazd by bus, spend the night at the Zoroastrian rest-house there (built in the 1930s), and travel on the next day up the easier valley route.

From the Pass of Gaigun the old track winds down the valley, across some deep, rocky channels and under a towering wall of mountains; and suddenly there is the Pir, a tiny domed sanctuary at the foot of Mount Nareke, which rises as an almost sheer cliff above slopes of scree and fallen rock. At the base of the cliff, still high above the valley floor, there is a deep cleft, shaded by wild fig and pistachio trees; and here a spring of sweet water wells out and sends a stream down the hillside, its course marked by a tangle of water-mint and other plants. As it drops down the hillside it nourishes some fine plane and walnut trees, and fills a stone-lined pool; and eventually it reaches the shrine itself at the mountain foot, and, flowing past it, waters a little patch of fields and a tall cypress tree. There are almost as many pavilions here as at Pir-e Sabz, and it too has a 'Pavilion of the Priests'; but in Nareke the pavilions (all built this century) climb up the slope above the Pir, clustering especially around the tree-shaded pool, and they can therefore be seen far out across the valley. The shrine itself is hidden by a long low hill of grey-white detritus, sharp-capped and bare of vegetation, which runs parallel with the mountain-wall and makes a secret, sheltered place for the sanctuary. Here many could once have gathered, looking down on the sacred place, which in this respect resembles Banu-Pars.

In the case of Nareke it is difficult to see now why the shrine stands exactly where it does, for if there is living rock there (as seems likely) it has long since been covered by the loose scree which lies everywhere at the mountain's foot. The first mud-brick shrine-building is still standing, with a deep shelf for offerings in the wall nearest to the mountain and sacred spring; but early this century a bigger outer hall was added on to it, and in front of that a building was set which is like a little two-*pesgam* house, with courtyard and kitchen for ritual cooking. Later a house for the khadem was built against the east side of the sanctuary, so that, with a small garden and yard, there came to be a square group of buildings forming the shrine complex. In 1950 the shrine itself and the adjoining hall were lined throughout with tiles, and both rooms were fitted with strong metal doors, for the Pir is in a lonely place. Its khadem in 1964 was Bakhtiyar Jarrah of Kuče Buyuk, but he delegated his daily duties to two villagers from the village of Saniabad, which lies on the valley floor, a tiny patch of green, not far from the foot of Nareke. (Beyond it, another such patch, was Tejeng, once famous for its glass-making.[23]) Both villagers were of course Moslems; but one, Ramazan Ali, a simple soul, was convinced that the Pir-e Nareke had saved

[23] See above, p. 124.

his wife's life when the doctor had despaired of her, and so he tended the sanctuary lamp with grateful devotion. His fellow, Murtaza, was an intelligent man, better versed than many pilgrims in the shrine's history. One or other fetched the oil for the lamp each month from Bakhtiyar.

In 1964 the *hajj* of Nareke was in mid August, so that it was the last of the annual pilgrimages according to the reformed calendar, but fell just after the religious No Ruz (Havzoru) by the traditional one. So for those who reckoned by the latter its *hajj* was the only one at which the noonday prayers were addressed to 'Rapatven', who was held to return above earth on New Year's Day.[24] Although the pilgrimage took place only ten days after Havzoru, nevertheless in 1964 it 'called' many pilgrims, and here too the priests were well-represented, white-clad in their separate pavilion, and solemnizing many rites. (Blind Palamarz from Sharifabad was also there, and was accepted into their company.) Because it was not so easily reached as Pir-e Sabz, Nareke probably preserved better the atmosphere of the old pilgrimages, with their sense of close-knit community, and their ordered pattern of devotion and delight. The devotional atmosphere was well created on the first evening, when the shrine was full of the sonorous murmur of Avestan, uttered by priests and laity, men and women. A gleaming *afrinagan* holding fire was set on the pillar-altar, and sent out the odour of incense, while reflecting the light of many candles around the altar's rim; and other candles shone through the lattice-opening in the inner sanctuary wall. In one part of the room D. Sorush of Taft and Palamarz were reciting *tan-dorosti* for two women, seated in traditional manner cross-legged upon the floor rather than on the tiled bench that ran round the walls; and on these walls, hung there especially for the *hajj*, were (as was customary) not only bright mirrors, but also photographs of notable Zoroastrians of earlier generations, who seemed to gaze down benevolently on their faithful successors. Once outside the shrine again, we found that a bright lamp had been set on its small dome, which shone throughout the night all during the *hajj*.

If all was piety at the shrine, in the pavilions the atmosphere was one of gaiety and laughter. There was one big pavilion which had been built by a man from Narseabad for the use both of his own village and of the northern ones, and the Sharifabadis found themselves sharing it that year with a betrothal party, nearly fifty strong,

[24] See above, p. 50.

from Narseabad. The largest group was from the groom's family, he (a young man of about twenty-five) being supported by many kinsmen and friends. His young fiancée, a fourteen-year-old first cousin, was from the village of Nusratabad. There was much dancing and singing in the pavilion, and morning and evening the bride's mother used to carry an *afrinagan* with incense round it, to bless all there. (As she approached, Tahmina Khanom would cover the infant Shahvahram with her head-veil, for he had a slight fever, and it was thought that incense, otherwise so beneficial, harmed the sick.) On the third day the bride's family sacrificed a goat (bought from a Moslem shepherd, who had led his flock to the shrine for the *hajj*), the bride herself preparing the meat carefully; and on the next day the groom's family did the same. On both occasions some of the meat was brought as *khairat* to the Sharifabadis, and Tahmina Khanom, having accepted it, returned the dish filled with sweets and nuts, as was proper. A man and several youngsters from Sani-abad came to the pavilion to beg for (and receive) a share of the 'charity meat'.

Many other sacrifices were offered during the *hajj*, and the flock of goats, folded at night in the little yard by the shrine, dwindled steadily away. At Nareke the joyful processions wound downward to the sanctuary from the pavilions, along the course of the little stream, and there was altogether more space and ease than on the precipitous slope of Pir-e Sabz. The pleasure of rambling about around the shrine existed here, even if less freely than at Banu-Pars. Whereas the wild almond was characteristic of the latter sanctuary, Nareke's tree was the wild pistachio, with its pretty grey-green leaves, the nuts showing a bright reddish-brown among them in August. There were wild figs too, whose tiny fruits were just ripe, to the delight of the boys, who went scrambling about the scree-slopes after them. Gushtasp, while doing so, came (to their mutual shock) on a huge dragon-like lizard sunning itself, and brought back a porcupine quill which he had found. The stone-lined pool among the pavilions attracted animal as well as human life, with frogs which croaked by night, and by day flights of tortoiseshell butterflies and a pair of martins. Traditionally, Zoroastrians for some reason regarded the frog as the most Ahrimanic of creatures, which it was highly meritorious to kill, so I watched anxiously one day when Gushtasp caught one; but he simply, boy-like, put it carefully in his pocket and carried it away to release in the stream higher up. (In the same way, the old hostility to corn-stealing ants had been abandoned in Sharifabad. The Moslem villagers there looked for the nests, destroyed the ants, and took the corn back again; but the Zoroastrians said tolerantly that they could spare the relatively small amounts which the hard-working little creatures garnered. Perhaps their own sufferings had forged a wider kindliness in them towards all forms of life which did not appear deliberately hostile or dangerous.)

On the last night of the *hajj*, the Taftis rose, according to custom, by starlight, loaded their donkeys, and set off at dawn. Formerly most of the other pilgrims would have gone with them, back up the Pass of Gaigun, to spend another night in the pleasant orchards of Taft. Then many of them—including often the Sharifabadis— would travel together down the road to Yazd, to spend the following night at Cham. Erdeshir Qudusi told me that sometimes they were so bemused when they set off at dawn, by drowsiness and the night's revels, that they slept in the saddle and left it to their wise donkeys to find the way for them. Cham is an old Zoroastrian village, whose fire-temple is built against the trunk of a magnificent cedar, the Sarv-e Cham, which is loved and venerated by all the Yazdi Zoroastrians.[25] So to rest here was both pleasant and an act of devotion, and many prayers were said and candles lit under the tree's spreading branches. D. Khodadad's father, who owned fields in the village, had built a rest-house for pilgrims, and some used to sleep there, and others in hospitable houses or gardens.

The next day saw the Yazdis and those from the southern villages at their own homes; but the Sharifabadis often went on through the city to pay their devotions to Seti Pir. This is the only one of the great Pirs which is down in the plain, just to the east of Yazd. The area where it stands is called Jangal or the 'Forest', and probably once tamarisk and other trees grew thickly there; but all trace of them has disappeared, thanks to charcoal-burners, goats, and drought, and the shrine now rises like a little fort out of desert sands, which the wind blows in scalloped ridges against its walls. Inside these walls there is a range of buildings, which include rest-rooms for pilgrims, kitchens, and stabling. Beyond these one passes along a dark stone-floored passage, worn smooth by many feet, to the

---

[25] In the 1920s the great tree was attacked by a swarm of locusts and stripped bare of foliage. It was some time before it recovered, and one of its branches never revived, but remained brown against the green.

sanctuary itself. The passage slopes downward, for again the holy place is a living rock, which is now far below the level of the shifting sands. The shrine-room has two side-chapels, which has led to the popular etymologizing of the name as the 'Three Saints' (*Se-tā Pīr*). The main room is rectangular, long and narrow, and has at the further, eastern end a broad bench-altar for candles and offerings, over which there is a sort of wide chimney-opening, allowing a glimpse of the sky. This room has a tiled floor, but on entering either of the two dark little side-chapels one steps down on to the solid rock. At the western end of the passage leading to the sanctuary there is a sacred well.[26]

What is evidently a late legend attaches to Seti Pir. It is said that this shrine marks the place where Yazdegird's queen, the mother of the princesses Banu-Pars and Hayat-Banu, herself fleeing from the Arabs, sank exhausted and was taken living into the rock, together with her two attendants. This miracle was revealed in a dream to a Zoroastrian of Yazd, perhaps as late as the nineteenth century; and subsequently others received similar revelations through dreams about the other three shrines which lacked a legend. So Hrišt is now held to be where a married princess vanished, with her child in her arms. Nareke is believed to belong to another wedded princess, and Narestan, in the mountains beyond Seti Pir, is regarded as the shrine of a young prince; but not every Zoroastrian is conversant with these extensions of the legend of Banu-Pars, which was evidently itself first evolved in Islamic times. It is only since the coming of Islam that it has seemed proper in Iran to link holy places with persons, rather than with divine beings, and the Zoroastrians were evidently only gradually influenced by the dominant religion in this respect, the process being finally completed by the spread of literacy. A *ziyārat-nāme*, or account of the legend of the shrine, was then duly composed for each place. A framed copy was kept at each sanctuary, and during the *hajj* pilgrims often read the stories aloud to one another.

The *ziyarat-name* of Seti Pir relates a curious tradition about the revelation of the shrine's legend. It is said that this Yazdi Zoroastrian made the perilous pilgrimage to the great Moslem shrine of Imam Reza at Meshed (a beloved shrine for Zoroastrians too, because according to the legend of Bibi Shahrbanu the later Shiʻi *imams* had Sasanian blood in their veins). He was recognized there as

---

[26] For a ground-plan of the shrine see G. Gropp, *AMI*, N.F. iv, 1971, 280.

a non-Moslem and was imprisoned, to be put to death the next day; but as he slept three persons, clad in green and white, appeared to him, told him the story of Seti Pir, and bade him have no fear, but to prepare to make this story known to others. And the next morning, miraculously, he awoke, not in the cell, but safely back in Yazd. Whatever the explanation of the miracle, the story up to then is wholly credible. Thus Agha Rustam's great-uncle Khodabakhsh also made the pilgrimage to Meshed, but was likewise identified as an unbeliever, and was so savagely assaulted that he died of his wounds.

Seti Pir was thus regarded as the mother of the five great Pirs; and through the year the shrine was in fact visited chiefly by women. Its general *hajj*, when the fort-like building was packed with people, coincided with the first day of the *hajj* of Pir-e Sabz, so that Zoroastrians from Yazd and the suburban villages would visit Seti Pir in the early morning, and travel on together in late afternoon to the greater shrine. At other times the sanctuary was often locked and empty, but any Zoroastrians who wanted to visit it could get the keys in Yazd or Moriabad, close by.

In the past the Sharifabadis themselves, having visited Seti Pir, sometimes went on to pay their devotions to the Pir-e Narestan, before starting on their slow thirty-mile journey homeward—although the *hajj* of Narestan was properly in June, soon after that of Pir-e Sabz. In the 1960s Narestan, though very lovely, was somewhat neglected in comparison with the other great shrines. The sanctuary is set in the Kharuna mountains to the east of Yazd, a bare harsh range which supports no villages; and, though it is only some six miles from Yazd, these miles had become difficult ones, and were forbidding to motor vehicles. The first stretch was across treacherous sand desert, where sometimes the track, rough at the best of times, disappeared under shifting dunes. Then it climbed painfully up a valley with a dry river-bed, crossing it from side to side. At the head of this valley the track stopped, and only a donkey-path went on through a narrow winding gorge, so overhung by rocks that even in June there were still some small pools of water there. Then suddenly the green spire of a cypress showed ahead, and a bend in the defile brought one out into what seemed like a demi-paradise—an enchanting bowl-shaped valley, ringed by formidable mountain peaks, but itself green and welcoming. There was a pretty patchwork of tiny fields, a scattering of pomegranate and mulberry trees, and near the cypress a thicket of roses, still flowering at that height in June. At the head of the valley (which was just fertile enough to support a single family) there were graceful aspen trees, and a group of young pines had been planted below the sanctuary, though these were flagging because of drought.

The sacred place itself consisted of a shallow cave, about twenty feet high at the entrance, but with sharply sloping roof, so that it ran back only about nine feet into the mountain. At the back there was a fissure from which water flowed out across a flat rock at the cave-mouth, to fill a pool below. This pool was overhung by three myrtles, their branches so entwined that they looked like one tree; and in June they, like the roses, were in full bloom, their white, scented flowers loud with bees. Once many people, spread out below, could have witnessed rites performed at the sacred rock above the pool, until the usual mud-brick shrine was built over it. In 1941 this was incorporated in a bigger building, which was unusually long and tall, because of the shape of the site. This building wholly screened the cave-mouth from distant view, but one could pass round it to the cave itself, where a little platform had been built on which pilgrims could lay their offerings of candles, incense, *sirog*, or the like. The shrine-buildings contained the usual pillar-altar, and also enclosed the trunks of the three myrtles, whose branches passed out into the sunlight through a brick lattice-work on that side; and anyone wishing to circumambulate the pillar-altar had to stoop under the arching trunk of the biggest tree. The stems of the myrtles inside the shrine, like the willow at Pir-e Sabz, were adorned with strips of cloth and ribands, tied round them by devotees.

Narestan was the most enclosed and solitary of all the sanctuaries, and its pilgrimage had special rigours in modern times. Since there were no friendly villagers nearby with things to sell, and no wandering shepherds with their flocks, the pilgrims had to bring everything they needed with them and carry it all through the rocky defile and up the little valley. This had been less of a hardship in the days of donkey-travel than now, when vehicles had to be abandoned in the dry river-bed. Further, at the turn of the century the shrine-fields were seized by an unscrupulous *sayyid*, who harassed the Zoroastrians greatly; and the Moslem family which worked them for his descendants had little regard for the shrine. Yet despite these disadvantages. Narestan continued to call the faithful, and half a dozen pavilions had been erected there, two fairly recently, at the head of the valley near the shrine. Naturally it was Zoroastrians from Moriabad and the other villages to the south-east of Yazd, and Yazdis themselves, who visited this sanctuary most often; and when they had performed the rites of pilgrimage, they could sit in these pavilions, looking out over the green valley and frowning peaks, and sleep to the sounds of wind soughing through the little pines, and the rustle of aspen leaves. Among the huge tumbled rocks at the head of the valley was a little cave devoted to Mihr Ized, and at the time of the *hajj* pilgrims, especially women, would climb up to this, and light candles there and pray.

It was perhaps at the mountain shrines that one was made most sharply aware of the ancientness of Zoroastrianism, and the closeness of the links between its worship and the physical world, Ohrmazd being venerated here with archaic rites in the temple of his own creation. The gulf was also demonstrated (especially at Pir-e Sabz) between traditional Zoroastrianism and the religion which the urban reformists were striving to evolve. Some of the young people who came from Tehran were deeply serious in their attachment to their ancestral faith, but they shrank from the blood sacrifices, the singing and dancing in the shrines, and the general robustness of the old and to them alien ways. They were in search, not only of a devotional experience, but also of some philosophy or mysticism, and found little sustenance in the traditional beliefs and usages; and these, it was plain, could not survive unmodified much longer even in the rural communities, where modernizing influences were pressing in ever more urgently. The Sharifabadis and their neighbours on the Yazdi plain have been the staunchest upholders of the ways of their forefathers, despite both oppression and persuasion; and through their steadfastness they have preserved much of the ancient practices and beliefs of Zoroastrianism, before this venerable faith has everywhere to come to closer terms with the contemporary world.

BIBLIOGRAPHY

I. BOOKS

Note: abbreviated book-titles are set in square brackets at the end of the appropriate entries.

ANKLESARIA, T. D. (ed.), *The Datistan-i Dinik*, Pt. I, Bombay, n.d.

BAILEY, H. W., *Zoroastrian problems in the ninth-century books* (Ratanbai Katrak lectures), O.U.P., Oxford, 1943.

BIANCHI, U., *Zamān ī Ōhrmazd, storia e scienza delle religioni*, Torino, 1958.

BOYCE, Mary, *A History of Zoroastrianism* (*Handbuch der Orientalistik*, ed. B. Spuler, i. 8.1.2), vol. i: *The Early Period*, E. J. Brill, Leiden, 1975. (Three more volumes in preparation.)

BRIGGS, H. G., *The Parsis or Modern Zerdusthians*, Andrew Dunlop, Bombay, 1852.

BROWNE, E. G., *A Year amongst the Persians, 1887–1888*, 2nd edn., C.U.P., Cambridge, 1926.

CHARDIN, Chevalier, *Voyages en Perse et autres lieux de l'Orient*, vol. 2, 2nd edn., Amsterdam, 1735.

DHABHAR, B. N., *The Persian Rivayats of Hormazyar Framarz and others, their version with introduction and notes*, K. R. Cama Oriental Institute, Bombay, 1932. [*Riv.*]

—— *Saddar Naṣr and Saddar Bundehesh, Persian texts relating to Zoroastrianism*, published by the Trustees of the Parsee Punchayet Funds and Properties, Bombay, 1909.

DONALDSON, Bess A., *The Wild Rue, a study of Muhammadan magic and folklore in Iran*, Luzac and Co., London, 1938.

DROUVILLE, Gaspard, *Voyage en Perse fait en 1812 et 1813*, 3rd edn., Paris, 1828.

DUBOIS, J. A., *Hindu Manners, Customs and Ceremonies*, ed. and transl. into English by H. K. Beauchamp, 3rd edn., O.U.P., Oxford, 1906.

GONDA, J., *Die Religionen Indiens I, Veda und älterer Hinduismus, Die Religionen der Menschheit* 11, Kohlhammer, Stuttgart, 1960.

HODIVALA, Shahpurshah H., *Studies in Parsi History*, Bombay, 1920.

JACKSON, A. V. Williams, *Persia past and present, a book of travel and research*, Macmillan & Co., New York, 1909.

KHODADADIAN, Ardeshir, 'Die Bestattungssitten und Bestattungsriten bei der heutigen Parsen', unpublished thesis, Freie Universität, Berlin, 1975.

KOTWAL, Firoze M. P., *The Supplementary Texts to the Šāyest nē-šāyest*, ed. and transl. with notes, *Det Kongelige Danske Videnskabernes Selskab, Historisk-filosofiske Meddelelser* 44, 2, Copenhagen, 1969 [*Šnš.*]

MALCOLM, Napier, *Five Years in a Persian Town*, John Murray, London, 1905.

MODI, Jivanji J., *The Religious Ceremonies and Customs of the Parsees*, 2nd edn., Bombay, 1937. [*CC*]

—— *The Persian Farziāt-Nāmeh and Kholāseh-i Dīn of Dastur Dārāb Pahlan, text and version with notes*, Bombay, 1924.

—— (ed.) *Sir Jamsetjee Jejeebhoy Madressa Jubilee Volume, Papers on Iranian Subjects*, Fort Printing Press, Bombay, 1914.

PELLAT, Charles (ed.), Mas'ūdī, *Les Prairies d'Or*, translated into French by Barbier de Meynard and Pavet de Courteille, revised and corrected, vol. 2, Societé Asiatique, *Collection d'Ouvrages Orientaux*, Paris, 1965.

SACHAU, E. (ed.), *Chronologie orientalischer Völker von Al Bērūnī*, Deutsche Morgenländische Gesellschaft, Leipzig, 1923; (transl.) *The Chronology of Ancient Nations*, Oriental Translation Fund of Great Britain and Ireland, London, 1879.

SCHIPPMANN, Klaus, *Die iranischen Feuerheiligtümer*, De Gruyter, Berlin-New York, 1971.

SCHWARZ, Paul, *Iran im Mittelalter nach den arabischen Geographen*, vol. 1, Leipziger Habilitationsschrift, 1896.

SEERVAI, Kh. N., and PATEL, B. B., 'Gujarāt Pārsis from their earliest settlement to the present time (A.D. 1898)', *Gazetteer of the Bombay Presidency*, vol. ix, Part 2, Bombay, 1899.

SORUSHIAN, Jamshid S., *Farhang-e Behdinan*, ed. Manochehr Sotoodeh, Tehran, 1956.

TAVADIA, Jehangir C., *Šāyast nē-šāyast*, text with German translation and notes, Hamburg, 1930. [*Šnš.*]

TAVERNIER, J. B., *Six voyages en Turquie, en Perse et aux Indes*, vol. iv, Paris, 1676; Eng. transl., London, 1684.

UNVALA, Manockji R. (ed.), *Dārāb Hormazyār's Rivāyat*, 2 vols., British India Press, Bombay 1922. [*Riv.*]

II. ARTICLES BY THE PRESENT WRITER, IN ALPHABETIC ORDER (cited in footnotes without author's name, and by title only). An initial definite article is sometimes disregarded, as in the footnotes.

'An old village *dakhma* of Iran', *Mémorial J. de Menasce*, ed. Ph. Gignoux and A. Tafazzoli, Louvain, 1974, 3–9.
'*Ātaš-zōhr* and *Āb-zōhr*', *JRAS* (1966), 100–18.
'Bībī Shahrbānū and the Lady of Pārs', *BSOAS*, xxx. 1 (1967), 30–44.
'The fire-temples of Kerman', *Acta Orientalia*, xxx (1966), 51–72.
'Haoma, priest of the sacrifice', *W. B. Henning Memorial Volume*, ed. M. Boyce and I. Gershevitch, London, 1970, 62–80.
'Iconoclasm among the Zoroastrians', *Christianity, Judaism and other Greco-Roman cults, Studies presented to Morton Smith*, ed. J. Neusner, vol. 4, Leiden, 1975, 93–111.

'Manekji Limji Hataria in Iran', *K. R. Cama Oriental Institute Golden Jubilee Volume*, ed. N. D. Minochehr-Homji and M. F. Kanga, Bombay, 1969, 19–31.

'Mihragān among the Irani Zoroastrians', *Mithraic Studies*, ed. J. R. Hinnells, vol. I, Manchester, 1975, 106–18.

'On Mithra, lord of fire', *Monumentum H. S. Nyberg*, vol. i, *Acta Iranica*, Leiden, 1975, 69–76.

'On Mithra's part in Zoroastrianism', *BSOAS*, XXXII. i (1969), 10–34.

'On the calendar of Zoroastrian feasts', *BSOAS*, XXXIII. 3 (1970), 513–39.

'On the sacred fires of the Zoroastrians', *BSOAS*, XXXI. i (1968), 52–68.

'On the Zoroastrian temple-cult of fire', *JAOS*, xc. 3 (1975), 454–65.

'The pious foundations of the Zoroastrians', *BSOAS*, xxxi 2 (1968), 270–89.

'Rapithwin, Nō Rūz and the feast of Sade', *Pratidānam, Studies presented to F. B. J. Kuiper*, ed. J. C. Heesterman *et al.*, The Hague, 1969, 201–15.

'Some aspects of farming in a Zoroastrian village of Yazd', *Persica*, iv (1969), 121–40.

'Toleranz und Intoleranz im Zoroastrismus', *Saeculum*, xxi. 4 (1970), 325–43.

'The two dates of the feast of Sada', *Farhang-e Iran-Zamin*, xxi. 1–4 (1976), 25–40.

'Zoroaster the priest', *BSOAS*, XXXIII. i (1970), 22–38.

'Zoroastrian *bāj* and *drōn* II', *BSOAS*, xxxiv. 2 (1971), 298–315 (with Firoze Kotwal).

'The Zoroastrian houses of Yazd', *Iran and Islam: in memory of V. Minorsky*, ed. C. E. Bosworth, Edinburgh, 1971, 125–47.

'The Zoroastrian villages of the Jūpār range', *Festschrift für W. Eilers*, ed. G. Wiessner, Wiesbaden, 1967, 148–56.

GENERAL INDEX

Note: in the alphabetic order no distinction is made between č and ch, š and sh, ə and e. The Greek letters δ and γ are set after d and g respectively, and Arabic ʿain is ignored, as are differences in vowel-lengths.

INDEX OF PERSONAL NAMES

(Note: in general, for the villagers, these are listed under given names, since these were the most commonly used; but certain family groups have been brought together under surnames, with cross-references under the given ones. The *izafe* of relationship (see preface, p. ix) is ignored in the alphabetic arrangement.)